The Eighteen-Day Running Mate

The Eighteen-Day Running Mate

McGovern, Eagleton, and a Campaign in Crisis

Joshua M. Glasser

Yale UNIVERSITY PRESS

New Haven and London

Yale University Press books may be purchased in
quantity for educational, business, or promotional
use. For information, please e-mail sales.press@yale
.edu (U.S. office) or sales@yaleup.co.uk (U.K. office).

Set in Linotype Palatino type by Duke & Company,
Devon, Pennsylvania.

Printed in the United States of America.

Library of Congress Cataloging-in-Publication Data

Glasser, Joshua M., 1987—
The eighteen-day running mate :
McGovern, Eagleton, and a campaign in crisis /
Joshua M. Glasser.
     pages   cm
Includes bibliographical references and index.
ISBN 978-0-300-17629-2 (alk. paper)
1. Presidents—United States—Election—1972.
2. McGovern, George S. (George Stanley), 1922–.
3. Eagleton, Thomas F., 1929–2007. 4. United States—
Politics and government—1969–1974. I. Title.
E859.G55 2012
973.924—dc23
2012002582

A catalogue record for this book is available from
the British Library.

This paper meets the requirements of ANSI/NISO
Z39.48-1992 (Permanence of Paper).

10 9 8 7 6 5 4 3 2 1

To my family

The first principle of contract negotiations is don't remind them of what you did in the past—tell them what you're going to do in the future.
—Stan Musial, St. Louis Cardinals

The stigmatized individual tends to hold the same beliefs about identity that we do; this is a pivotal fact. His deepest feelings about what he is may be his sense of being a "normal person," a human being like anyone else, a person, therefore, who deserves a fair chance and a fair break.
—Erving Goffman, *Stigma: Notes on the Management of Spoiled Identity*

Contents

The Eighteen-Day Running Mate

The Conundrum

Around 11 P.M. on Sunday night, July 30, 1972, George McGovern sat opposite Thomas Eagleton in the library of a campaign donor's suburban Washington mansion. McGovern was the Democratic Party's nominee for president, and Eagleton was his running mate. The fifty-year-old McGovern's graying hair had receded to expose a vast forehead cut by deep lines. Thick eyebrows and a protruding chin defined a warm, familiar face. Eagleton was forty-two, and, at the Democratic National Convention in Miami Beach three weeks earlier, a Tom Eagleton vice presidency had seemed to make sense.

Described by the media as a "casting director's ideal for a running mate," Eagleton offered a political profile that balanced McGovern's weaknesses. An urban Catholic with Kennedy good looks and support from his state's establishment politicians, Eagleton was known as a phenomenal campaigner, and his "gregarious good nature" had earned him the respect of old-school labor leaders and new-style liberals alike. The Brooks Brothers–clad junior senator from Missouri reminded some of the actor Jack Lemmon. However, Eagleton's social grace and ease sometimes ceded to abrupt gestures,

shaky hands, and profuse perspiration. He ripped through two packs
of unfiltered Pall Mall cigarettes each day, often taking just three
or four puffs before stubbing one out, only to find himself lighting another within minutes. One reporter described this practice
as Eagleton's way of cutting back on smoking after trying to quit.
Others dismissed this theory as nonsense. "Absolutely not," said one
longtime staffer. "It was just a nervous habit." Another reporter suggested that Eagleton at times seemed "as tightly wound as a spring."
But Eagleton had never lost an election, and the politicos and press
alike considered him "one of the brightest and most ambitious young
stars of the Senate."[1]

Yet in the seventeen days since Eagleton joined the ticket, the
tone of the media's coverage had changed. A string of anonymous
calls and the investigative legwork of two journalists had finally
compelled Eagleton to reveal on day twelve the secret he had long
concealed. He had been hospitalized for "nervous exhaustion and fatigue" three times over the previous decade and treated with electroshock therapy twice. Though the running mate insisted that he was
a cured man, capable of weathering the strain of the campaign trail
and the duties of the vice presidency, Eagleton's revelation provided
reason for serious concern. McGovern, in turn, initially guaranteed
that there was no one sounder in mind, body, and spirit to serve
as his running mate. The next day he stressed that he continued to
stand by Eagleton "1,000 percent."

But escalating pressure from his staff, supporters, and reporters soon prompted McGovern to reconsider his stance. Now, approaching midnight on Sunday, July 30, it seemed almost certain
that McGovern would ask Eagleton to leave the ticket the following
evening at a meeting being touted by the news media as a "showdown" between the two candidates. But first, McGovern wanted
to speak with Eagleton in private, sheltered from the scrutiny that
promised to surround their much-publicized one-on-one.

At around 9:45 P.M., McGovern and Eagleton dodged the press
corps encamped at each of their suburban Washington homes and
headed to their secret meeting point, the residence of the campaign
finance chairman Henry Kimelman on California Street, a way lined

with grand foreign embassies. McGovern lived in a Japanese-inspired home on a quiet, leafy street in northwest DC, near American University. Eagleton resided in a classic four-bedroom white colonial, just beyond the Washington border, in Chevy Chase, Maryland.

Eagleton arrived at Kimelman's home first, and McGovern followed soon after. The two candidates were then left alone to talk in the library. When it seemed their conversation had reached an impasse, McGovern spoke up. "Tom," he said. "Tell me what you feel in your heart."

"George," Eagleton replied, "I'll give you a double answer. In my heart, conscience, and soul I want to remain on the ticket. When you picked me [at the Democratic convention] in Miami I was an absolute zero. I didn't add a damn thing to the ticket, and I didn't subtract a damn thing. . . . But, George, since all of this has happened I believe I'm a plus."

Judging from his reception at public appearances, Eagleton believed that the grace under pressure he had demonstrated over the previous week had won the ticket support, especially from an element of the electorate previously disillusioned with McGovern's candidacy—the white, Democratic labor establishment.

"Sure, I'll cost you some votes amongst the worry-warts," Eagleton continued. "But, George, I'll get you more votes amongst people who respect a fighter. George, I'm fighting for my political life."

Was Eagleton simply fighting for his own political life, or would keeping him on the ticket prove politically advantageous for both men, McGovern must have wondered.

"Tom," McGovern finally whispered. "You're one hell of a guy. Let's go home and sleep on it."

When the two candidates emerged from the library to join their aides, Eagleton noticed Gary Hart, McGovern's campaign manager, "quiet and observing." It was no secret that Hart wanted Eagleton off the ticket.

As the vice presidential candidate and his staffers rode back to Eagleton's house, the senator recapped his conversation with McGovern for his aides. "You know," he said, "deep down in his personal heart, the man wants to keep me. He likes me. He respects me,"

Eagleton explained. "[McGovern is] in a struggle between his heart and his staff."

"Chief," Doug Bennet, Eagleton's top aide, piped up. "If that is the contest, you lose."[2]

The Eagleton question—whether to keep him or drop him—inspires no easy answer. On the one hand, punishing someone for seeking help when needed—help that, according to Eagleton, enabled him to overcome his depression and succeed in public life—seems unjust, if not cruel. The likable and earnest Eagleton had proven he could endure an arduous Senate campaign and shine in Congress, unhindered by relapse. As he phrased it, he could "cut the mustard." On the other hand, with its suggestions of the electric chair, shock therapy has conjured images of a searing, last-ditch treatment used to sedate the insane. If Eagleton required shock therapy, it seemed, he must have suffered from more than mere "nervous exhaustion and fatigue." Many Americans—inside and outside the campaign—thought he should have come clean to McGovern up front.

The McGovern decision makers found themselves in a novel and bewildering predicament, asked to examine their feelings toward a stigmatized minority to which the nation had rarely given serious consideration, especially in a political context. Most Americans felt uncomfortable deeming Eagleton's history of mental illness disqualifying in and of itself, as doing so appeared to contradict their sense of progress and decency. However, discriminating against the mentally ill differed from discriminating against racial minorities and women because mental illness can affect job performance. Besides, psychiatry circa 1972 could not alleviate public doubts about Eagleton's fitness to withstand the stress of the vice presidency and, if necessary, the presidency—especially in the Cold War era.

The Eagleton affair mesmerized America not simply because it included the usual ingredients of political theater, like ambition and idealism, backstabbing and selflessness, triumph and despair. It captivated the nation because it also posed a fascinating, seemingly unanswerable moral and scientific question. The Eagleton case asked George McGovern, a man widely reputed for his decency, to make a choice that few knew how to decide themselves. There seemed no right answer, and, even today, the politically prudent and personally decent are not so clear.

My curiosity about Thomas Eagleton, George McGovern, and their eighteen-day alliance on the 1972 Democratic presidential ticket began in March 2007, shortly after Eagleton's death, when I came across his *New York Times* obituary. The story gripped me. I had only a cursory notion of shock therapy and found the concept frightening. I was also unsure of why Eagleton had failed to disclose his treatment before his selection and wondered how the news had broken. McGovern's oscillation from "1,000 percent" support of his running mate to calling for his withdrawal perplexed me, and I was intrigued by McGovern's eventual admission of remorse. Eagleton's obituary reported that McGovernites long blamed the candidate's first vice presidential pick for the magnitude of McGovern's loss, but that Eagleton dismissed his role as merely "one rock in a landslide."[3]

My ongoing interest in the moral, political, and historical questions at the heart of this story led me on a nearly two-and-a-half-year investigation into this unusual episode in American history. I read the newspaper coverage and reviewed contemporaneous broadcast reports. I visited the personal papers of the key players—McGovern, Eagleton, and their top aides—and explored the wealth of behind-the-scenes notes and memos that provide an unvarnished look at a presidential campaign at its most exuberant as well as its most desperate. I spoke with McGovern, his strategists, and people who lived, worked, and traveled with Eagleton. I met the journalists who covered the candidates and the reporters who drove their fate. The Nixon Tapes let me eavesdrop on the strategizing at the White House.

In exploring McGovern's confrontation with a crisis unlike any other in election history, I tried to immerse myself in the web of influences that guided McGovern's ethically fraught decision-making process. The behind-the-scenes drama of the Eagleton affair is riveting by itself, but it becomes even more fascinating when situated in its time and place, with respect and empathy for the key players— their grand aspirations and intensely human flaws.

As Haynes Johnson of the *Washington Post* once wrote, the

Eagleton affair is "worthy of a major novelist's talents." I cannot claim to have a fiction writer's gifts, but as a journalist with a passion for history, I attempt to capture the intense human and political drama that defines this story, set against the backdrop of a frenzied and transformational year in the nation's history.

The Candidate

On September 1, 1970, when the Senate rejected the McGovern-Hatfield Amendment that would have set an end date for the Vietnam War, George Stanley McGovern could not contain his frustration. "Every senator in this chamber is partly responsible for sending fifty thousand young Americans to an early grave," he told the floor in a well-publicized remark. "This chamber reeks with blood."

George McGovern had built his presidential bid on early and fervent opposition to the Vietnam War, as well as on the candor evident in his disgust at the Senate's McGovern-Hatfield vote. But in the heat of the primary season, Democratic rival Hubert Humphrey had been quoting passages from Robert Sam Anson's authorized precampaign biography suggesting the South Dakotan had, in fact, equivocated on the war.[1]

So on Saturday, July 8, 1972, on the plane to the 1972 Democratic convention in Miami Beach, McGovern wandered down the aisle and leaned over Anson's seat. "There was never a moment when I didn't think [the war] was terrible and immoral," McGovern said. "But I had to work on Johnson, and you can't do that unless you are credible."

Young George McGovern poses aboard a training aircraft. "It galls the hell out of me that every time Pete McCloskey says something about the war, it's 'war hero Pete McCloskey.' Why don't they ever write about 'bomber pilot McGovern?'" McGovern later commented. (AP/ Wide World Photos)

"You treat Vietnam as if it's a principle," McGovern told Anson. "You have to remember, I am a politician."[2]

Born July 19, 1922, McGovern was raised in small-town Mitchell, South Dakota. Located about seventy miles west of Sioux Falls, Mitchell boasted "The World's Only Corn Palace" and approximately fifteen thousand people, mostly farmers and Protestants. The only Democrat who ever mustered the townspeople's approval was Franklin Delano Roosevelt. The son of a Wesleyan Methodist preacher, George grew up in a house where prayers and Bible readings followed breakfast each morning, and religious schooling and worship consumed Sundays. Though George's father, the Reverend Joseph McGovern, had played professional baseball before becoming a minister, he taught his sons that prostitution and gambling ravaged professional athletics and dissuaded them from participating in sport. He directed his sons' attention toward their studies instead. Wesleyanism's lessons shaped George's life, persuading McGovern to look beyond himself and serve the common good.[3]

When McGovern's mother, Frances, asked him what he hoped to be when he grew up, the twelve-year-old George could not say for certain. However, as his younger sister, Mildred, remembered, he did know that he wanted "to learn as much as he possibly could about as many things as he could, and that he wanted to get into some type of service where he could do the most possible good for the largest number of people." Mildred thought that one day her older brother would become president of the United States.[4]

Though timid as a young boy in the Depression- and dust-storm-spoiled prairie, in high school McGovern found his niche on the debate team, and the pale, simply dressed George grew into a champ. McGovern's knack for identifying inconsistencies in his opponents' reasoning and for backing up his own arguments with impeccable logic compensated for what he lacked in bravado. Furthermore, his desire to excel drove him to undertake the preparation that success required, spending hours after school each day researching various cases, documenting his facts on three-by-five and then four-by-five note cards. High school debate showed McGovern how history intersects with the present and that what seemed radical could be possible. Furthermore, it exposed George to life beyond Mitchell and to the "delicious sensuality of winning," as Anson described it. Debate "really changed my life," McGovern would reflect years later. The qualities of George McGovern the high school debater were the qualities that would push him to become George McGovern the United States senator. McGovern's 1940 high school yearbook noted, "For a debater, he's a nice kid." This evaluation foreshadowed the reputation he would hold as a politician: for a senator, he was a nice man.[5]

For college, McGovern settled on Dakota Wesleyan University, a small liberal arts school with about five hundred students. Its location in Mitchell meant McGovern did not have to pay room and board. Eleanor Stegeberg and her twin sister Ila also entered DWU that year. They were the daughters of the Democratic chairman of nearby Woonsocket County and made up the only team on the South

Dakota high school debate circuit to have beaten McGovern and his partner. Ila was already romantically entangled, and she established the connection between George and Eleanor at a roller-skating party their freshman year, as George was too shy to do so himself. When a friend dating Ila asked George whether he and Eleanor wanted to join them for an excursion to the Mitchell Hill School play, McGovern jumped. Within two years, Eleanor became his wife, and later—though hardly five feet tall and less than one hundred pounds—she was to prove "a tireless, smooth-talking, rarely ruffled campaigner," as the press described her. Eleanor offered McGovern steadfast companionship and uncompromising loyalty, supporting her husband's efforts no matter how much they compromised her stability—emotional or otherwise.[6]

On December 7, 1941, news of Pearl Harbor called McGovern to duty. "We were confronted with totalitarian powers bent upon the destruction of freedom," McGovern recalled years later. "And that was all I needed to know." Along with ten DWU classmates, he enlisted in the Army Air Corps, and his intellect and steady temperament propelled him to the top of his training class soon after he started training in the winter of 1943. But McGovern longed for Eleanor, and he decided to marry her shortly after enlisting. He described his rationale for an early marriage in a letter to a boyhood friend: "We've simply got an old fashioned love affair on our hands, and it's pretty hard to stop love even for war." As McGovern hopscotched to various training camps across the United States, Eleanor moved alongside him.[7]

In 1944, at age twenty-two, McGovern was deployed to Europe. From his base in southern Italy, McGovern captained his B-24 Liberator named for Eleanor, *The Dakota Queen,* on thirty-five strategic bombings of Axis supply lines and weapons factories in northern Italy, southern Germany, Austria, and Yugoslavia, bearing responsibility for the eight other men in his crew. The B-24 was a notoriously unforgiving vessel, concurrently delicate and robust, but affording pilots little room for error; McGovern and his peers witnessed many of their colleagues crash to their deaths in training and saw even more die in war. The linchpin in American's strategic bombing of

Axis territories, the B-24 could pack a heavy load, but it lacked power steering, windshield wipers, and bathrooms, and required pilots to wear oxygen masks to withstand its poor insulation. Though flying scared McGovern, he confronted his task with characteristic equilibrium. As one member of his crew recalled, "If he ever panicked, I never knew about it. Whatever happened, that sort of nasal twang of his came over the radio as clear and flat as it was on the ground." The army awarded McGovern a Distinguished Flying Cross for averting disaster on one particularly treacherous landing, citing his "intrepid spirit, outstanding ability, and devotion to duty."[8]

After the war, McGovern returned to Dakota Wesleyan to finish his bachelor's degree in history. Eleanor had given birth to their first child, and he remained active in speech and debate, taking home first place in the South Dakota Peace Oratory Contest for his oration "From Cave to Cave." In it, McGovern meditated on his nascent personal philosophy, something he called "the applied idealism of Christianity." He lamented America's errant values, warning, "We place such a high value on our daintily pampered appetites and pleasures that we sometimes lose sight of people dying of starvation the world over."[9]

Upon graduation from Dakota Wesleyan in 1946, the twenty-four-year-old returned to religion and studied in the Methodist ministry, at Garrett Theological Seminary in Evanston, Illinois. But McGovern grew disillusioned with the clergy as he watched ministers compete for posts at the wealthiest congregations. He turned to academia and sought a Ph.D. in history at Northwestern University, right across the street from Garrett. McGovern envisioned the academy as a better venue than the church for reaching a wide audience. At Northwestern, he studied under Arthur S. Link, the celebrated Woodrow Wilson scholar. In his dissertation McGovern explored the efforts of Colorado coal workers to unionize that resulted in the April 20, 1914, massacre at Ludlow. He painted the miners' struggle as a "revolt against capitalism" that provoked "unrestrained class warfare," sympathizing with the workers' cause but rebuking their leadership. In a January 1950 letter of recommendation, Professor Richard W. Leopold ranked McGovern's work among the best he had encountered in his career, at both Harvard and Northwestern. He praised McGovern's "imaginative, orderly, and inquisitive" mind, and wrote, "I can think of no one who could fit better into any situation and win the admiration of a greater number of people."[10]

After McGovern received his doctorate and returned to Dakota Wesleyan to teach, another friend and professor of his from Northwestern asked him, "George, what makes you tick?" Channeling the teachings of his father and the lessons of the Bible, McGovern quoted the Gospel of Matthew: "Whosoever shall save his life shall lose it, and whosoever shall lose his life for my sake shall find it," McGovern replied. The young professor's response not only conveyed the Christian altruism that charged McGovern's politics, but also captured the moralism that would saturate his rhetoric through his public life. McGovern's father had instilled in him a sense of duty, of exceptionalism, of responsibility for leadership. As his older sister Olive described the McGovern children's upbringing, "Everything that other Christians did, we had to do double," and Joseph McGovern envisioned his son as God's messenger. Though George would eventually stop practicing religion, he forever grounded his politics in that "applied idealism of Christianity," as he termed it. Issues reducible to moral terms—such as ending war and fighting poverty—animated him, and his stump speeches would come to approximate sermons.[11]

It did not take long for McGovern to grow restless at Dakota Wesleyan. He realized that his temperament, his relentless curiosity and impatience to make an immediate difference, made him unsuited for academia. In an application for a professorship at the University of Denver, McGovern admitted, "I should perhaps confess that I am troubled with both a sensitive social conscience and a rather wide range of interests," finding himself "devoting a considerable amount of time to the study of contemporary social and international problems," and not a narrow academic specialty like universities desired. By 1953 McGovern quit teaching to become executive secretary of the downtrodden South Dakota Democratic Party, settling for a $6,500 yearly salary despite a mortgage to pay and a wife and four children to clothe and feed. McGovern said he wanted to make history, not merely teach it, and he knew the steps he needed to take.[12]

The South Dakota Democratic Party did not constitute much of a platform. Republicans captured 90 percent of state elections between 1889 and 1967. Still, McGovern did not lack for faith, idealism, and a sense of practicality. He saw that if he ever sought elected office he would need an organization behind him, taking it upon himself to build the requisite infrastructure. As one Democratic official noted, George McGovern was not so much rebuilding the Democratic Party in South Dakota as establishing the George McGovern Party. By 1956, after installing party chairmen in every county, McGovern deemed himself ready to run for Congress, targeting Harold Lovre of the First Congressional District, who was armed with four terms in the House and a track record of staggering margins of victory. But McGovern recognized and capitalized on two fundamental traits of the region's voters. First, South Dakotans demanded staunch anticommunist and pro-agriculture stances. The three pillars of the state's economy were corn, wheat, and cattle. Second, he understood that South Dakotans valued a sense of personal connection with their public officials, the perception at least of compassion for their conditions. In other words, the voters seemed to care more about the man than about his politics. As candidate, McGovern resolved to project the impression of principle, rootedness, and neighborly interest. Though naturally uncomfortable with the superficiality of the campaign handshake, McGovern eventually conceded that there was no better way of establishing that personal connection with voters. While Eleanor minded the campaign office with only one other volunteer, McGovern traversed the thirty-eight thousand square miles of South Dakota territory east of the Missouri River that composed the district, shaking hands with as many people as he could, at as many picnics and church dinners as possible. George Cunningham, the former president of the fledgling South Dakota Young Democrats who had recently finished army service, accompanied McGovern on his travels, and they sold campaign buttons at each stop to finance their journey to the next town on their itinerary. As McGovern gained traction, Lovre's campaign began to insinuate that the Democratic candidate sympathized with the communists. But McGovern fought back, reminding the voters of his service to the nation during World War II while Lovre had stayed home. McGovern won that fall—by twelve thousand votes—becoming the first Democrat sent to Congress from South Dakota in twenty years.[13]

Four years later, McGovern was ready to move on, eyeing the Senate seat held by Karl Mundt. But Mundt's willingness to play dirty combined with John F. Kennedy's place atop the 1960 Democratic ticket hampered McGovern's chances. Virulent anti-Catholicism predominated in the state, and Mundt suggested that McGovern, who was a Protestant, nonetheless belonged to that year's "Catholic plot" to seize the White House. In antilabor South Dakota, Mundt also alleged that McGovern had received $454,000 in union contributions, when, in fact, the total stood at just $8,000. This time, the smears proved too much for McGovern; he finished fifteen thousand votes behind Mundt, but received thirty-five thousand more votes than Kennedy in South Dakota, a testament to McGovern's own promise.[14]

After the election, word got back to McGovern that Kennedy was considering appointing him agriculture secretary, and McGovern wanted the post badly. He even called Arthur Schlesinger Jr., urging the Kennedy confidant to make his case to the president-elect despite never having met Schlesinger. But in the end, Kennedy felt he owed the cabinet slot to veteran Minnesota governor Orville Freeman, naming McGovern coordinator of the Food for Peace program instead. McGovern had been one of the House's most vocal advocates for overhauling the Food for Peace program, which was struggling to distribute America's surplus foodstuffs to the world's poor. The Food for Peace job promised McGovern access to the president while satisfying a crucial need of his home-state constituency—the elimination of surplus grain and beef would make prices more favorable to South Dakota's farmers—but McGovern would not accept the appointment before guaranteeing that the post came with the optics of prestige. He asked to be called "program director" instead of "coordinator" and to be granted the title of "Special Assistant to the President for Food for Peace," which would also elevate the perception of the job's importance. McGovern got his wish, and as director of Food for Peace, he resuscitated the program. Yet McGovern still imagined himself elsewhere.[15]

In late June 1961, while preparing for a trip to South America as Food for Peace director, McGovern contracted hepatitis from an infected vaccination needle, condemning him to sixty days at Georgetown University Hospital. While bedridden, McGovern read Theodore H. White's best-selling *Making of the President 1960,* and the narrative reawoke his craving for electoral politics—his longing for the "opportunity to lead and to affect the course of events . . . for the better," as McGovern recalled of his sensation reading White's book. He scribbled a note to himself: "Make a pact with self on 1962 Campaign—the highest and most [educational], inspiring, friendly, and [Christian] I can make it with complete [Christian] resign, in a happy warrior spirit as to the outcome. No tears or joy—win or lose and no concern over outcome—except high-mindedness and inspire as many S. Dakotans as possible." There was never any doubt McGovern would try again for the Senate.[16]

When he returned to South Dakota to campaign for his 1962 bid, McGovern found an electorate convinced that he had become an outsider—no longer a native, but a firmly established member of the East Coast elite. Some suspected that, this time, the Kennedys planned to "take over" South Dakota, with McGovern as their Trojan Horse. But McGovern enjoyed the good fortune of GOP bad luck. In late June the incumbent senator, Francis Case, died of a heart attack, forcing the state's Republican central committee to choose a replacement candidate. After several contentious rounds of balloting, the party nominated Lieutenant Governor Joe Bottum, perhaps the least formidable of the options. Rumors implicated Bottum, his wife, or both of alcoholism, leading to Bottum's televised and teary-eyed denial of the allegations. Meanwhile, McGovern stuck to the handshaking campaign that had first sent him to Washington six years earlier, barnstorming the state until early October, when, after addressing the Sioux Falls Corn Picking Contest, he felt faint. Cunningham and a few other campaign staffers laid the candidate down in the back of a Ford station wagon and shuttled him to a hospital in Sioux City, Iowa, opting for the privacy of the neighboring state,

just in case McGovern had a relapse of hepatitis. He did. Cunningham, however, told the news media that McGovern was combatting
a "mild kidney infection." Eleanor stepped in for her husband on the
campaign trail and kept McGovern's chances alive.[17]

For her performance that October—and her dependability
throughout McGovern's political life—Anson and other McGovern
observers have given Eleanor credit for her husband's success. By
1972 she had become a fierce advocate for early childhood education,
not to mention for her husband. She cycled through her isometrics
and circulatory exercise routine every morning to stay fit, and a
steady supply of fruits, nuts, honey bars, vitamins, and other health
foods helped her maintain her energy through the campaign grind.
Between regular visits to the beauty parlor, she trimmed and set her
cropped and frosted hair by herself.[18]

Round two of hepatitis sidelined McGovern for two weeks that
October 1962. In addition to Eleanor, McGovern could thank Charles
Guggenheim for keeping him a viable candidate. The filmmaker
crafted a superb documentary, *A Dakota Story*, that showcased the
most appealing aspects of the man from Mitchell: his small-town,
faith-based family values; his wartime heroism; his intellect; his devotion to public service; his compassion; his patriotism; his unpre-
tentious, down-home decency. McGovern won his Senate seat by a
scant hundred votes on first tally, and by 597 after a recount. This
tenuous victory would shape the senator that George McGovern was
to become, at first obliging him to check his more liberal inclinations
and calibrate his focus to the needs of his constituency of 666,507
people in a state with 4,543,000 cattle and 4,218,000 chickens. Mc-
Govern opted for spots on the agriculture and interior committees,
sentencing himself against his natural disposition to engagement
in the drudgery of farm price support and water project authoriza-
tion legislation and to taking a longer route to committee seniority.
McGovern's attention to South Dakotans would compromise his
standing with organized labor, the core of the Democratic Party, in
particular. Yet McGovern recognized that he was a South Dakotan
before all else, and it was the folks back home who had sent him to
Washington. South Dakota was a right-to-work state, and he knew

its voters considered keeping it that way a top priority. McGovern also returned to South Dakota frequently, always mindful of the need to nurture his relationship with his constituents. As one former aide explained, "A guy may not like the way you voted, but when you write his kid saying you were darn glad she was the high school valedictorian, he'll be your friend for life." McGovern never ran as "George McGovern, Democrat for Senate." Rather, he branded himself the "Courageous Prairie Statesman." That, South Dakotans could respect.[19]

McGovern's improved status in the heartland on key agriculture and labor issues afforded him increasing latitude to speak his conscience on other matters. As a representative of a state with only 1,627 black residents, for example, McGovern attacked "white racism" because it was the right thing to do, not because it was the politic thing. He also questioned America's strategy in Vietnam long before others discerned a problem, admonishing the Senate in September 1963, "America will exert a far greater impact for peace and freedom in Asia and elsewhere if we rely less on armaments and more on the economic, political, and moral sources of our strength." Even back in South Dakota, McGovern proved unafraid to propound his antiwar creed, telling a Methodist convention in Aberdeen in fall 1967, "To remain silent in the face of policies we believe to be wrong is not patriotism; it is moral cowardice—a form of treason to one's conscience and to the nation." He explained, "I want to be reelected . . . but I do not want reelection so badly that I will ever sacrifice my convictions to achieve it," speaking so strongly that voters would feel betrayed if they ever suspected this was not always the case.[20]

To most observers, the respect for others that marked McGovern's politics also seemed to permeate his everyday actions. He packed his own luggage instead of delegating responsibility to his aides; whenever he received food ahead of his staff, he insisted on waiting for everyone else before eating. And the press took note. But McGovern's decency also included an aversion to confrontation that led to confusion and inefficiency. He would often assign multiple staffers with writing the same speech and then cull elements from each so as not to offend anyone. His reluctance to fire mediocre employees weakened his staff, but McGovern justified it by saying he valued loyalty above competence. When he did fire an employee, McGovern used the "sideways method," hiring someone to assume a similar role and hoping the law of natural selection would prevail, the message making itself clear.[21]

However, McGovern's gentility coexisted with an aggression often concealed from public view. After delaying a commercial airliner, for example, McGovern paced down its aisle apologizing to passengers for the wait. But when an old woman returned the gesture with insults, McGovern leaned in close and called her "a horse's ass," maintaining his composure all the while. He savored his rebuttal, the *Washington Post* described, "like a fighter remembering a great punch."[22]

In late summer 1967 the Democratic political operative Allard Lowenstein approached George Stanley McGovern, the freshman senator from South Dakota, and suggested that he challenge the Democratic incumbent, Lyndon Johnson, for the presidential nomination. Senator Robert F. Kennedy of New York had recommended that Lowenstein speak to McGovern, and, despite Lowenstein's initial doubts about the relatively unknown senator from the middle of nowhere, McGovern seemed "almost too good to be true." The centrist midwestern senator was both a war veteran and a vocal opponent of America's involvement in Vietnam. But after summoning his staff's counsel, McGovern resisted jumping into the 1968 race. He faced reelection to the Senate that year, and his aides feared that seeking the presidency would mean relinquishing his seat. McGovern advised Lowenstein to ask Senator Eugene McCarthy of Minnesota instead, and McCarthy agreed to run. Kennedy soon followed, frustrated that McCarthy had become the figurehead of "New Politics"—the spokesman for the "campus, ghetto, and suburb" alliance that was attempting to challenge the entrenched powers of the Democratic Party.[23]

Within the year, McGovern and Lowenstein met again. It was June 8, 1968. They shared a car back from Robert Kennedy's funeral at Arlington National Cemetery. Kennedy had been assassinated three days earlier while campaigning for the presidency in California. "You know, Al," McGovern told Lowenstein as they rode through Washington, "if I had taken your advice back in August, I don't think we would have been here today." If McGovern had represented the party's antiwar wing that year, and not the quixotic McCarthy, Kennedy would never have run, and the chance of his assassination would have been significantly diminished. In all the years that Eleanor had known George, she first saw her husband cry in the days following Kennedy's death.[24]

Uneasy about both Humphrey and McCarthy, Kennedy's former aides asked McGovern to assume the mantle of their hero's cause. Yet McGovern's staff still feared that a presidential bid would distract him from his Senate race that fall, and McGovern also initially resisted out of concern for his family. His nineteen-year-old daughter, Terry, had distanced herself from her parents during her teenage years, and in late July, while she was canvassing for her dad's Senate campaign in Rapid City, South Dakota, a motel housekeeper found marijuana among her luggage. Terry avoided jail time on a technicality, but McGovern still felt at least partly responsible for Terry's troubles. He took his family on vacation to South Dakota's Black Hills to spend the time with them that his political career rarely afforded. But the McGovern family holiday represented a gesture more than a realignment of the senator's personal priorities. "If the country is so mixed up that even our daughter is playing with drugs, maybe I ought to [run for president]," McGovern told Eleanor.[25]

On Saturday, August 10, 1968—sixteen days before the Democratic National Convention in Chicago—McGovern announced his candidacy. "I believe deeply in the twin goals for which Robert Kennedy gave his life—an end to the war in Vietnam and a passionate commitment to heal the divisions in our own society," he told the crowd gathered in the Senate Caucus Room, the same room Kennedy had used to launch his own campaign just five months earlier. "If I have any special asset for national leadership, it is, I believe, a sense of history." Nevertheless, McGovern's bid came too late. Eighteen days after announcing his candidacy, he lost the Democratic nomination to Vice President Hubert Humphrey, who had been Mc-

Govern's neighbor when he first moved to Chevy Chase as a young congressman. Though Humphrey and McGovern had developed a close friendship—with the Washington veteran advising the newcomer on negotiating the halls of the Capitol—"personal affection has nothing to do with political conviction," McGovern explained.[26]

As the 1968 Democratic National Convention was wrapping up in Chicago, Teddy White of the *Making of the President* books reinforced McGovern's guilt at not entering the race earlier. Suspecting that McGovern could have won had he only gotten in when Lowenstein first approached him, White asked, "How does it feel to be the guy that booted away the presidency of the United States?"[27]

The Democrats emerged from their 1968 convention in Chicago battered by the belligerent antiwar and equal rights protests that filled the city's streets, as exclusion of blacks and other minorities continued to taint that year's nominating process. As riots filled Chicago's streets, the convention narrowly passed the Minority Report of the Rules Committee, moving to guarantee that all Democrats—blacks, women, and youth included—were to receive a "full and timely opportunity to participate" in their states' processes to select delegates to all future conventions.[28]

In February 1969 Senator Fred Harris of Oklahoma, the newly appointed chairman of the Democratic National Committee, selected McGovern to head the party's Reform Commission. In McGovern, Harris saw a leader capable of placating the party's disparate elements. McGovern had been a New Politics candidate sympathetic to the agenda of Chicago's protesters, but had also abandoned any sense of disappointment following his defeat and proceeded to campaign for Humphrey through November 1968. McGovern committed himself to the greater goals of party unity and sending a Democrat to the White House. He had proven he was a Democrat, not an ideologue.[29]

The Reform Commission's mantra, "Reform or Die," captured the urgency of revising the party rules. McGovern feared that without reform the party's disenchanted elements would resort to third- or fourth-party politics, thereby incapacitating the Democratic Party for the foreseeable future. "We have seen the end of the loyal, faithful, and innocent electorate," McGovern proclaimed. The party could no longer count on keeping its frustrated factions committed Democrats. Yet intent on placating the New Left, the Reform Commission—formally titled the Commission on Party Structure and Delegate Selection—failed to hedge against the possibility that its mandates would alienate the essential party regulars.[30]

In 1968 the New Left presidential candidates had not received convention delegate representation that matched their success in the primaries. In some instances, states had selected their delegates up to two years before the convention, eliminating the electorate's role in the selection process. Backdoor delegate selection by the party bosses seemed to diminish the chance that a leftist candidate could ever obtain the Democratic nomination, so the Commission's *Mandate for Reform* recommended that state parties overcome their histories of discrimination by taking "affirmative steps" to ensure that the composition of each convention delegation reasonably reflected the proportion of racial minorities, women, and youth in their state's population at large. While the commission added a footnote specifying that this provision did not translate into the institution of quotas, many interpreted this regulation as just that—quotas that were antagonistic and even discriminatory toward the white, male, labor establishment that had heretofore ruled the party.[31]

While Kennedy campaign veteran and commission member Fred Dutton anticipated that such reforms would attract vast and underrepresented segments of the population to the Democratic Party, instead they alienated many white, working-class voters who had long formed the party's bedrock. Suddenly, the Democratic Party appeared to stand for blacks, women, and youth, and no longer for the white, ethnic workingman. As the reforms' public face, McGovern evolved from party unifier to polarizer.[32]

Though McGovern was spurned by the labor establishment, his work on the Reform Commission and his continued, outspoken opposition to the Vietnam War made him a favorite son of the New Left. It did not matter that he lacked charisma. McGovern was kind, humble, and decent. His politics, principles, and personality seemed interchangeable: he was moral through and through.

Yet in truth, success in politics demands placing the interests of one's profession before the purity of one's principles. As McGovern framed it, it requires compromising on details—resisting impulse, and favoring tact. While it seems that a combination of idealism and vanity drives most men to seek public office, McGovern let his supporters forget, as he did not, that success in American politics requires a modicum of Old Politics—privileging ambition over ideals, whatever the sacrifice might entail.

On July 18, 1969, at approximately 11:15 P.M., Massachusetts Senator Edward Kennedy flipped his Oldsmobile off Dike Bridge on Chappaquiddick Island, just east of Martha's Vineyard. The brother of Robert Kennedy and former President John F. Kennedy was driving home twenty-eight-year-old Mary Jo Kopechne after a night of partying in honor of the "Boiler Room Girls," the six women staffers on Robert's 1968 campaign. Kennedy escaped, but Kopechne, one of the six "girls," did not. And Kennedy neglected to call for help until the following morning, after the police had discovered Kopechne's corpse, and after Kennedy had placed five long-distance phone calls to friends and family. The incident raised questions about Kennedy's integrity, judgment, and decency. It appeared to shatter his presidential aspirations.[33]

Before the full story had surfaced from Chappaquiddick, Senate Majority Leader Mike Mansfield issued a statement supporting Kennedy, and McGovern wanted to do the same. He ran the idea by Kennedy's top aides. "You can do that, George, if you want to," one Kennedy staffer told him, "but you ought to know that when the facts come out, you may have to retract it." McGovern sent Kennedy a private telegram instead.[34]

Amid the fallout from Chappaquiddick, McGovern asked his friends their thoughts about his seeking the presidency. "If you run, George," Senator Abraham Ribicoff of Connecticut warned him, "you have to be willing to give up your life, your fortune, your family, even some of your ideals." But McGovern yearned for another run. Here was McGovern's second chance for a place in history, and, this time, he would not let it get away.[35]

The Campaign

early a year after Chappaquiddick, on Sunday, June 14, 1970, Dartmouth College awarded McGovern an honorary degree. Ever since Chicago, McGovern had been tantalized by the idea of running, and the senator had just hired thirty-four-year-old Denver lawyer Gary Hart to help organize a presidential bid. They intended to use McGovern's visit to the New Hampshire campus as an excuse to scout out the political climate of the early primary state.[1]

Hart was born Gary Hartpence, the son of Nazarene evangelicals from Kansas. His father sold farm equipment, and his mother taught Sunday school. Like McGovern, Hart grew up forbidden from movies, dancing, drinking, and sex. "Gary was always worried that at the end of his life he might not have made a contribution," a high school friend said of Hart in a comment that seems just as applicable to McGovern. "There was a fire burning inside him." Though the son of a conservative state, Hart spent summers on the railways working alongside blacks and Hispanics, an experience that instilled in him an empathy for the impoverished that nudged him toward the Democratic Party. After graduation from Bethany Nazarene College in Oklahoma, Hart enrolled in Yale Divinity School. But like

23

McGovern campaign manager Gary Hart, left, and political director Frank Mankiewicz (AP/ Wide World Photos)

McGovern, he had a change of heart, questioning his desire to enter the ministry. He switched to Yale Law School and moved to Colorado after graduation. He practiced law and, in 1968, helped organize Bobby Kennedy's campaign in the Rocky Mountain states.

When McGovern visited Denver to speak at the Colorado Democratic Party's Jefferson-Jackson Day festivities in March 1970, his office asked Hart to chaperone the visit. McGovern immediately took a liking to the tall, handsome, and soft-spoken young man with piercing blue eyes. Myra MacPherson of the *Washington Post* described Hart's comportment as a "'yep,' 'nope' and 'pardon me ma'am?'" cowboy demeanor. McGovern found Hart warm, easy-going, and capable. He always set his watch fifteen minutes ahead of time to stay punctual and productive, and he opted for toothpicks over cigarettes. He always kept a file on hand to camouflage his bitten fingernails. Politically, he was a pragmatist, not a purist. And he never considered himself above ringing doorbells or calling voters. Hart still had not given up his Denver law practice by that weekend at Dartmouth, June 1970, but he had already started planning McGovern's operations in the western states. When he took the job, Hart mistakenly presumed that McGovern had a more robust campaign organization back east.[2]

On Friday night of Dartmouth commencement weekend, McGovern and Hart met with local Democratic leaders at the home of a former congressional candidate. Though Senator Edmund Muskie of Maine was widely considered a leading national contender and held a built-in advantage in New Hampshire as a native of the neighboring state, none of those present that evening was ready to place his money on a Muskie victory. "You know," McGovern whispered to Hart, "this state reminds me a lot of South Dakota. A lot of small towns, and the people are pretty conservative, but they will vote for a man who says what he believes and who personally goes out and asks for their vote."[3]

Graduation Sunday was clear but blisteringly hot, and McGovern received his honorary doctor of laws degree from Dartmouth with the citation, "Your destiny is not to teach history but to shape it." The Dartmouth president's remarks could not have spoken any better to McGovern's conception of his destiny, and they appeared to goad him to action.[4]

Flying home that afternoon, looking down on the rolling New Hampshire landscape through the plane's window, McGovern turned to Hart. "I think we ought to run in New Hampshire," he said.[5]

The next month, McGovern convened a group of advisers at Cedar Point Farm, his summer home near St. Michael's, Maryland, about eighty miles outside Washington. Rick Stearns, a twenty-seven-year-old Rhodes Scholar originally from Fresno, California, was among those in attendance. He had written his Oxford thesis on the constitutional underpinnings of the Democratic National Convention, inspired to pursue the subject by his confusion at the outcome of the 1968 nominating contest. As a McCarthy organizer while an undergraduate at Stanford, he could not comprehend how, in a democracy, Humphrey could have won the party's nomination despite having entered only one primary. Eli Segal, one of the young and influential staffers on the Reform Commission, had invited Stearns to draft reports for the group during Stearns's Oxford summer reading period, and—with his graduate degree now complete—the McGovern campaign promised to provide the preppy, dark-haired Stearns the opportunity to test his theories in the laboratory of the real world. George Cunningham, Gary Hart, City University of New York professor Richard Wade, and Pat Donovan, McGovern's longtime secretary, rounded out the group.[6]

By the time of the Cedar Point meeting, it was inevitable that McGovern would run. The essential questions on Hart's agenda were timing and organization. McGovern wanted to let the public know his intention to get in the race as soon as possible and said he imagined other candidates would jump in before the end of the year, especially New York City mayor John Lindsay, who McGovern suspected would switch his affiliation from Republican to Democrat. Lindsay was planning to campaign for several Democrats nationwide, and if those candidates prevailed, the results would confirm Lindsay's kingmaking bona fides and cement his status as "the white hope of the more rational and humane elements of the party," as McGovern framed it. McGovern also considered Senator Harold Hughes of Iowa a contender. And with the Democratic National Committee's finances in shambles and the party devoid of a "titular head" as the elder Adlai Stevenson had been, McGovern was convinced that support would gravitate toward the first man to enter the race.

In addition to the conflict of interest attendant in McGovern's chairing the Reform Commission while seeking the presidency, Hart raised another concern: as soon as McGovern announced his candidacy, every columnist would examine his merit, questioning his seriousness, support, and—most significant—organization. Everything hinged on whether McGovern could establish an effective operation, and McGovern could not announce his run until he could prove he had done so. Members of the Cedar Point group agreed that they should exploit McGovern's upcoming appearances throughout the country to generate a nexus of support, test potential staffers in various roles, familiarize themselves with the particularities of each state, and secure the organizational underpinnings of what would eventually become the McGovern campaign.

The conversation soon turned to how to position the candidate with respect to the field, and here, McGovern was unflinching. Aside from Lindsay and Hughes, McGovern expected challenges from Muskie, Humphrey, Senator Henry "Scoop" Jackson of Washington, and Senator Birch Bayh of Indiana. McGovern stood to the left of all of the likely contenders, and he considered this differential a distinct advantage, especially given his ardent and widely known commitment to the Democratic Party. "[It's] conceivable that while I might be the most left-leaning candidate, I am also the most reconciling candidate," McGovern assessed. After all, he could "present liberal values in a conservative, restrained way," as McGovern later told Teddy White. He also believed that, as a tenacious antiwar liberal, he would preempt or foreclose any third- or fourth-party candidacy, if conservative Democratic Governor George Wallace of Alabama ultimately decided to contend as an independent. Advisers such as the documentary filmmaker Charles Guggenheim recommended that McGovern bend his candidacy distinctly to the concerns of the Middle American, the "forgotten man," the people "outside the glandular and issue-oriented constituencies of the American seaboard." But to adapt was not McGovern's style. The experience of 1968 had taught McGovern to privilege his instinct over his advisers'. His gut told him to stay true to himself and the purity of his ideals as he sought the nomination for the presidency.[7]

Considering himself his best coach, McGovern habitually scratched instructions to himself on any paper with room for ink. "I want [the campaign] to be as honest, as straightforward . . . and as enlightening as we can make it. . . . And if the Fates shine on us, we might even make it to the White House," McGovern wrote in one such example. "We're going to demonstrate faith in the nation and in the decency and common sense of the American people." Yet at times, McGovern's self-confidence could come across as self-righteousness. "We're going to have a good time because we will be doing God's work," McGovern concluded.[8]

Though McGovern dismissed suggestions that he lacked charisma, he still understood the need to appear presidential and to pace himself in order to withstand the vicissitudes of an inevitably treacherous run. As campaigning in the fall of 1970 had served as a dry run of sorts for 1972, McGovern documented its lessons: "(1) Don't schedule extended trips without weekend breaks or mid-week breaks at home. (2) Plan rest periods or a day of rec. before I speak—especially after long flights. Fla., Calif., etc. should always have a day in the sun. (3) Don't do frantic type campaigning." McGovern reminded himself to do his calisthenics routine each morning and evening, just as Eleanor did hers. And he made time for a swim at the gym almost daily. Despite the ardors of the campaign trail, he also hoped to become a good tennis player.[9]

McGovern officially announced his candidacy on January 18, 1971, from a Sioux Falls, South Dakota, television studio. His address reinforced the principles upon which the country was founded—"life, liberty, and the pursuit of happiness"—and he suggested that America needed restoring, not remaking. McGovern mourned the citizens' loss of faith in their government, their loss of trust. "The most painful new phrase in the American political vocabulary is 'credibility gap'—the gap between rhetoric and reality," he explained. "The kind of campaign I intend to run will rest on candor and reason. . . . I make one pledge above all others—to seek and speak the truth with all the resources of mind and spirit I command." For a year, at least, it seemed that McGovern would live up to his campaign promise and match his reality to his rhetoric. Though he mustered only 6 percent in the December 1971 Gallup and Harris polls of the Democratic candidates, McGovern withstood the pressure to conform, remaining virtuous even when his candidacy looked hopeless. His early opposition to the war imbued him with self-confidence, and he trumpeted his proposal to cut the nation's defense budget by $30 billion, equating the Vietnam War with barbarism. McGovern also sought to close an additional $30 billion in tax loopholes that favored the rich and was eager to introduce higher income taxes for citizens earning more than $12,000. He proposed a welfare program that would furnish all indigent citizens with $1,000 grants. In nearly every speech, McGovern bemoaned "the curse of racism," and he supported busing as an unfortunate but necessary means of obtaining racial integration and equality of educational opportunity for all citizens.[10]

Through relentless, grassroots organizing, McGovern built a committed base, primarily among the antiwar youth who could never warm to Hubert Humphrey or Edmund Muskie because of their earlier endorsements of America's intervention in Vietnam. McGovern's direct-mail solicitations netted small-scale donations that, in sum, bankrolled the campaign with more cash than any other candidate received. Though he languished at first, McGovern was pursuing the same strategy as General Kutuzov in Tolstoy's *War and Peace*. As Gary Hart explained, like Kutuzov facing Napoleon's invasion of Russia, McGovern resisted the pressure to counterattack and remained patient. "There is nothing stronger than those two: patience and time, they will do it all," says Kutuzov, and his motto, "patience and time," became the campaign's modus operandi. As his rivals divided the center, McGovern transcended the fray, extracting enough votes to put him in contention and eventually make him the party's front-runner.[11]

In the post-Chappaquiddick void of Democratic leadership, Humphrey's 1968 vice presidential pick, Senator Edmund S. Muskie of Maine, had been chosen to deliver the Democratic Party's response to President Nixon's address to the nation on the night before the 1970 midterms. Speaking from the kitchen of his quaint and all-American summer home in Cape Elizabeth, Maine, Muskie told the country, "In voting for the Democratic Party tomorrow, you cast your vote for trust, not just in leaders or policies, but trusting your fellow citizens, in the ancient tradition of the home for freedom and, most of all, for trust in yourself." Muskie aced it. He was "Lincolnesque," according to the press, and the performance buoyed the Democrats the next day, establishing the Mainer as the man to beat in 1972. Endorsements ensued, bestowing upon Muskie an aura of invincibility as he clutched the blessing of the Democratic establishment.[12]

But as Muskie became a candidate, there was little daring or exciting about his campaign. His stances represented a sloppy amalgam of Democratic Party positions because his aides thought sticking to generalities would enable him to sustain the wide support he had already amassed and allow it to snowball into a bandwagon psychology that would carry him through the nomination. Their plan appeared to be working, but syndicated columnists Tom Braden and Frank Mankiewicz believed it would be a mistake to take Muskie's nomination as a given and write off McGovern's run as fruitless. In a January 1971 column, they explained, "The reason lies in an observation arrived at independently by two senators, one of them himself mentioned as a presidential candidate. It is that McGovern really is what Muskie only seems to be. The point of that remark is that McGovern is in fact strong, decent, profound, and conciliatory," while Muskie was just a pretender.[13]

In July 1971 Frank Mankiewicz agreed to join the McGovern campaign, bringing experience and credibility to an operation packed with novices—a link between the party's new and old, and a wellspring of experience. He had rebuffed McGovern's original plea for him to join by insisting he had already done the campaign thing with Bobby Kennedy. But McGovern countered, "You've only done half of it. Now is the time to finish it."[14]

Political ideology aside, Mankiewicz and McGovern were not a likely pairing. The son of screenwriter and director Herman Mankiewicz, of *Citizen Kane* and *Duck Soup* fame, as well as the nephew of Joseph Mankiewicz—another celebrated Hollywood writer-director and producer, perhaps best known for *All about Eve*—Frank grew up in the glamour of Hollywood. His parents hobnobbed with the likes of Ben Hecht, Dorothy Parker, the Marx Brothers, Orson Welles, and William Randolph Hearst. It was as far removed from the Mitchell, South Dakota, of George McGovern's youth as you could get. But Frank's father, a hard-drinking native New Yorker, taught Frank to resent Hollywood, constantly reminding his son of all its superficialities and telling him it was not the real world. Dinnertime conversation in the Mankiewiczes' Jewish home revolved around politics and current events, never the movies. After finishing college at UCLA, where he edited the student newspaper, and law school at Berkeley, Mankiewicz gave up his career as a Beverly Hills lawyer to enroll in journalism school at Columbia. From there, he variously served as a newspaper reporter, a Peace Corps director in Peru, Robert Kennedy's press secretary, and an evening news anchor for the local CBS affiliate in Washington, DC. Most prominently, as Bobby Kennedy's press secretary, he was saddled with the burden of telling the nation that, indeed, another Kennedy brother had been killed. After the tragedy, Mankiewicz joined the forces behind McGovern's eleventh-hour presidential bid of 1968 and reportedly told McGovern that he could win only by inciting Humphrey to commit a horrific gaffe, preferably inducing him to repudiate Johnson's Vietnam policy and thereby compelling President Johnson to "pull the rug out from under Hubert" at the convention. Alternately described as "Machiavellian . . . cool, pragmatic, brilliant, arrogant, vain, charming, testy, condescending, aloof, petty," Mankiewicz earned the reputation of being a "cold-blooded" political operator, as well as "a one-man smoke-filled room." Even his wife once admitted to harboring mixed feelings about Frank. "When I met him I didn't like him," Holly Mankiewicz once told a reporter. "I admired him but I thought he was Mr. Know It All. I knew he was very, very smart, but I didn't think he knew much about humility."[15]

Mankiewicz could be uncommonly warm and devastatingly funny. For instance, he called Humphrey "the used car you wouldn't buy from Nixon." One reporter said of Mankiewicz, "You can see the one-liners forming, as the eyes start to laugh before his face does." A stocky man with a slight comb-over, Mankiewicz rarely was without a menthol cigarette, and he was almost always tethered to the telephone. Dick Dougherty, who became McGovern's press secretary, noted that Mankiewicz's head seemed to cock rightward from years of tilting it to hold the phone in place. A voracious reader particularly fond of Joyce and Orwell, Mankiewicz possessed a photographic memory and a passion for baseball. "All my fantasies used to revolve around being a baseball player—the ones that didn't involve girls," he told a reporter, flaunting the trademark concoction of humor and honesty that made him—as his wife said—never boring.[16]

Mankiewicz's sharp critiques challenged McGovern to become a more dynamic, media-savvy candidate. "At the beginning and end of the speech, and particularly, when you enter the hall, I think you should, painful as it might be, wave to the audience. Give them that standard one-arm semaphore from time to time, or even a peace 'V' at the end," Mankiewicz instructed McGovern in one memo. As "political director," he also coached McGovern to give punchier, less professorial answers during the question-and-answer sessions that were the hallmark of McGovern's campaign events. As 1971 wound down, Mankiewicz wrote McGovern: "Be confident—appear to be enjoying the campaign more, and start being tougher and more acerbic about your opponents. Joy and Toughness—the theme for the Holiday Season."[17]

The introduction of such a spirited personality to the campaign unsettled the order of things in the McGovern high command. Within a month of joining the campaign, Mankiewicz was hatching a plan with Ted Van Dyk, his fellow Washington veteran, to oust Hart as campaign manager. Like others in McGovern's orbit, Van Dyk flowed between law as a profession and—when the opportunity presented itself—politics as a passion. In 1968 he had enjoyed a close relationship with Hubert Humphrey and wide respect within his organization, serving as the candidate's chief wordsmith and leading tactician. Dougherty said Van Dyk looked like a "scholarly accountant." In private, Mankiewicz and Van Dyk warned McGovern that he needed experienced leadership at the helm, someone who could tighten the reins on the decentralized campaign, pull the organization's finances together, someone more respected and capable of demanding action than Hart. Word got back to Hart that Mankiewicz had pressed the candidate to rethink Hart's authority, and Hart convinced McGovern that handing Mankiewicz control would damage morale, his personality destined to clash with the field organizers. Hart argued that the campaign needed balance, and McGovern agreed, telling him to "work it out" with Mankiewicz. In the end, though Hart and Mankiewicz did "work it out," aversion to conflict resulted in an "honest" campaign defined by a climate of suspicion. Hart oversaw the vast network of field leaders and the overall organizational infrastructure of the campaign; he had the confidence and loyalty of the antiwar youth that gave the campaign its soul. Mankiewicz, meanwhile, assumed the role of public face, political mastermind, media fixer, chief networker, and schmoozer extraordinaire, acting as liaison with the party regulars.[18]

Gary Hart had the habit of diagraming the McGovern camp's vision of the Democratic Party on napkins or any scrap of paper he could get his hands on. He illustrated for reporters a vast left wing of the party and a smaller right wing sandwiching an even more slender center. As McGovern cemented his hold on the left, trumpeting his longtime opposition to the Vietnam War and ardent support of civil liberties for women and minorities, his lieutenants were able to build a network of committed, if sometimes overideological, volunteers nationwide. McGovern's antiwar stance—not his charisma—won him fervent support among the constituency with the most time to volunteer and the most to lose in Vietnam: America's youth. Eighteen-year-olds could vote in the presidential election for the first time in 1972.[19]

Partrick Caddell, a twenty-one-year-old Harvard senior and polling whiz employed by the campaign, discerned McGovern's position to tap into the mood of the nation, or at least a particularly large segment of the American population—the alienated, blue-collar voter who feared a disintegrating America, engulfed in war and battered by inflation. "They are the voters who will disagree with a candidate's position on an issue, but will vote for him because of his concern or character," Caddell wrote McGovern in a December 1971 memo. "They are generally decent, concerned, and fairly open-minded," Caddell said of this constituency. "Unlike those who tend to be well-educated and opinionated, these alienated voters are generally persuadable and malleable," he explained. Caddell cited a recent Harris survey that highlighted the people's sharply declining confidence in the leadership of America's institutions, especially the executive branch, which suggested to him a political climate ripe for upset as it seemed the electorate sought new blood in office. Hubert Humphrey, whose entrance in the race was imminent, was a worn-out old face. And whatever footing Muskie seemed to hold amounted to little more than superficial traction; he was the wide second choice but rare favorite of Democratic voters as his campaign on "trust" failed to offer more than slogans. Caddell believed McGovern's "ruthless honesty" and underdog status furnished him with built-in appeal. "The secret does not really lie in being a charismatic, glamour candidate, but rather in responding directly to the concerns of the voters," he wrote.[20]

By studying the electorate with academic rigor, the McGovern strategists tailored their candidate's events to meet the particular needs of the 1972 primary voter. "Wherever McGovern goes, the emphasis ought to be on dialogue. McGovern listening to ordinary people as well as explaining his ideas," Caddell advised. "He must identify with them and their problems. He especially must *listen*. . . . When these voters feel that no one really cares or gives a damn about them, they must be convinced that McGovern is different." In essence, Caddell recommended the type of handshaking campaign to which McGovern owed his career.[21]

As 1972 dawned and the primaries neared, the Democratic establishment statesmen and officials overlooked early warnings about Muskie's failure to connect with the voters and dutifully handed him their endorsements. They heightened the perception of Muskie as heir apparent but lulled the Mainer's campaign into complacency by giving him little motivation to innovate. The Muskie organization ignored the new nominating rules, relying on the playbook that had delivered presidential aspirants the nomination in previous contests: television advertising and the endorsements of party leaders. Meanwhile, with Rick Stearns and other reformers as the architects of its strategy, the McGovern campaign concentrated on tapping into the reservoir of delegates in the caucus states and not simply the higher-profile primaries, enlisting hordes of young and dedicated volunteers to call voters, ring doorbells, galvanize supporters, and deliver impressive turnouts. The absence of endorsements reinforced the image of McGovern as "above or apart from politics," as Gary Hart put it, matching the mood of the electorate. And Muskie's high polling numbers compelled Humphrey to enter the race during the primaries, scrapping his initial plan to emerge after the bitter primary fights as the clean, unifying leader. Humphrey's presence after New Hampshire would add another competitor at the center-right of the Democratic Party's range of political beliefs, leaving McGovern free to dominate the left.[22]

Controversy also imperiled the Muskie bandwagon. Ten black picketers congregated outside Muskie's hotel in Tampa to remind America that back in September "Endorsement Ed" had said a Democratic nominee could never win with a black running mate. Similarly, despite Muskie never having indicated otherwise, an ad in the February 8 edition of Miami Beach's Jewish newspaper asked, "Muskie, why won't you consider a Jew as a vice president?" Mysterious incidents such as these sent a shiver of discomfort down the Muskie campaign apparatus, rattling the candidate's confidence and composure. And in the *Making of the President* era, the press had begun to pay close attention to the candidate's psyche, not just his platform. Teddy White's book on the 1960 campaign had demonstrated that the inner workings of a campaign organization, the complexities of its officers, and the personal idiosyncrasies of the candidates combine for a great story.[23]

The game changer came just before the end of February, when Muskie returned to New Hampshire after a slew of events in Florida—depleted and nearly sick—only to find that the viciously conservative and influential statewide daily newspaper the *Manchester Union Leader*, had repackaged an old item from *Women's Wear Daily* and *Newsweek* under the headline "Big Daddy's Jane," alleging that Muskie's wife Jane was a secret smoker and drinker, and had a penchant for a good dirty joke or two. The *Union Leader*'s publisher, William Loeb, who was heralded by *Time* magazine as "the dominant force in New Hampshire Journalism," also crafted an editorial, "Senator Muskie Insults Franco-Americans," using a letter from a Florida voter as evidence of Muskie's prejudice against "Canucks." The fiction enraged Muskie, who called for a press conference in front of the *Union Leader*'s offices. As a blizzard descended on the city's streets, Muskie spoke to reporters from the back of a flatbed truck. "That man doesn't walk, he crawls," Muskie taunted, referring to Loeb. "By attacking me, and by attacking my wife, he's proven himself a gutless coward." Muskie paused. "It's fortunate for him he's not on this platform beside me." Perhaps Muskie released a few tears, or maybe it was just the snow accumulating on his cheeks. But what matters is what was reported, and David Broder of the *Washington Post* and Dan Rather of CBS both said that Muskie shed tears. Though other news coverage of the episode buried Muskie's emotion beyond the front page, Broder's narrative, supplemented by Rather's film, proved more compelling. "Boy! THAT's not the man I want to have with his finger on the nuclear button!" Loeb wrote of Muskie in his paper, voicing the interpretation that soon predominated.[24]

As it turns out, the Florida protests, the false scheduling, and the Canuck letter were all concoctions of Nixon aides—just a few in a slew of dirty tricks that they devised to facilitate the reelection of the president. The Nixon campaign believed Muskie posed the biggest threat to the president's chances and targeted him accordingly.[25]

When the New Hampshire vote was tallied, the count stood at 47.8 percent for Muskie, 37.6 percent for McGovern. The result was underwhelming for Muskie, commensurate with the predictions of the McGovernites, who had long considered Muskie's support "a mile wide and an inch deep." Muskie had started to slip, and his bandwagon suddenly appeared on the road to collapse. Chris Lydon of the *New York Times* described the mood in the McGovern organization immediately following New Hampshire as one of vindication rather than elation; the rest of the nation was just waking up to what the McGovern team had known all along.[26]

McGovern's long-shot status for much of the campaign had enabled him to avoid the same scrutiny the press had lavished on the leading candidates. Media executives gave McGovern limited space in their election coverage, forcing reporters assigned to his campaign to focus on McGovern's election strategy and campaign dynamics, not on his policies. After all, entertainment subsumed substance in the *Making of the President* era. When McGovern eclipsed Muskie in the polls, editors redistributed their reporters and provided McGovern more space in their publications and broadcasts. But the new arrivals on McGovern's press bus were left playing catch-up on the inner workings of the South Dakotan's campaign, without sufficient time to investigate the specifics of his policies and past performance or the nuances of his personality.[27]

Most reporters took McGovern at face value, packaging him as a bona fide "Prairie Populist"—the champion of the little guy, the son of a preacher turned pious U.S. senator, the man Robert Kennedy had deemed the Senate's most decent. "George McGovern is one of the rare good men in national politics," the *Nation* magazine concluded. "It is difficult to imagine his being vindictive or inconsiderate or indifferent to human suffering." On the stump, McGovern favored small halls that he could fill to capacity. Such intimate venues helped him create the impression of familiarity, candor, and directness. "I would never advocate a course in secret that I was ashamed to take to the American people!" McGovern often told his overflow crowds. The line never failed to incite applause. *Time* magazine editorialized that McGovern exuded a "freshness and frankness" that matched the mood of an electorate "deeply discontented with business as usual politics." A Harris poll found that five of every six Americans credited McGovern with "the courage to say what he thinks, even if unpopular." McGovern said he valued his honesty above all his other personal qualities. And his aides were quick to confirm that he did, in fact, speak the truth. McGovern "looks you in the eye. . . . He's not a politician," Mankiewicz liked to point out. "I've never known McGovern to do anything devious." George was just too decent.[28]

The press described McGovern as "unheroic" and "perhaps a touch pedestrian," and reporters loved to poke fun at his nasally, singsong delivery. McGovern, in turn, seemed to view such observations as badges of honor. Or at least he said he did. "I think people are a little suspicious of people who come on too slick, too strong," McGovern reasoned. "It's possible to dazzle a crowd if you really work at it. But that is no qualification for leadership," McGovern told Anson, his biographer. "Hitler was a master at crowds." As McGovern presented it, he was too moral, too noble for charisma, equating being inspirational with being evil. Which led to McGovern's greatest campaign liability: he bordered on self-righteous—a quality most people find unflattering, especially when exposed as hypocritical.[29]

On April 27, in the heat of the primary season, nationally syndicated columnists Rowland Evans and Robert Novak quoted an anonymous liberal senator, who years later was revealed to be Senator Eagleton—then a Muskie supporter—as saying, "The people don't know McGovern is for amnesty, abortion, and legalization of pot. . . . Once middle America—Catholic middle America in particular—finds this out, he's dead." The notion stuck, branding him the triple-A candidate: for acid, amnesty, and abortion.[30]

As the general public learned more about McGovern's positions and he was cast by the more establishment-oriented politicians as a radical, his obligatory deradicalization put McGovern in a bind: the New Left's adopted poster boy could not shed the far-left positions he had so passionately propagated without compromising the reputation for candor so ingrained in his public persona. When McGovern tried to adjust, observers would take note. Few did so in time for the convention. Richard Reeves of *New York* magazine, however, was one of the more perceptive scribes on the campaign trail. "George McGovern would rather be president than be right," Reeves wrote in early May. He perceived that McGovern's views on busing and taxes, among other issues, had begun to shift according to the audience he was addressing. The man who once proposed a $500,000 ceiling on inheritances was telling Wall Street bankers he never meant it. "The business of reaching for power does something to a man," Reeves explained. "It closes him off from other men until, day by day, he reaches the point where he instinctively calculates each new situation and each other man with the simplest question: what can this do for me?" Writing at the end of April, Chris Lydon of the *Times* also uncovered the McGovern who had long evaded public view, "The most important public discovery of the past few weeks has been of George McGovern the politician—as careful a planner as any of the Kennedys, almost as compulsive a campaigner as Hubert Humphrey; surprisingly tough, every inch a pol."[31]

In truth, McGovern was as much a realist as he was an idealist. Furthermore, he was the man who had not flinched when Senator Ribicoff warned him that seeking the presidency meant compromising his family life, his fortune, and his ideals. To McGovern, the ends justified the means. But he failed to realize that when his ambition and pragmatism clashed with his public perception and his principles, he would chip open a credibility gap to call his own.

"I honestly don't think there has been a major surprise in the last two years," Gary Hart told the *New York Times* in June 1972. Indeed, the McGovern campaign had anticipated how the primaries would unfold, shocking the chattering class and upending the status quo with each notch in McGovern's favor. As the McGovernites suspected, Muskie could never recover momentum after slipping in New Hampshire. On April 4 Wisconsin's voters handed McGovern his first clear-cut primary victory, relegating Muskie to irrelevancy and setting up a three-way race among McGovern, Humphrey, and George Wallace until May 15, when a botched assassination attempt sidelined Wallace and dismantled whatever outside chance he had at the nomination. McGovern beat Humphrey in California, 44 percent to 39, presumably handing McGovern all 271 of the state's delegates thanks to a quirk in the rules and thus assuring him the Democratic nomination. Yet to credit planning for McGovern's victory, as Hart did, ignores the role of some luck. Similarly, to blame misfortune for the ensuing challenges forgives McGovern and his campaign for allowing unsustainable practices to persist.[32]

"Yes, I will be [president]," McGovern told a reporter in May, conveying the supreme confidence that had become the norm in the McGovern operation, at least externally. "I think the conditions of the time almost demand it, if that doesn't sound too arrogant. I think my time has come, maybe that's the way to put it," he continued. "Candidates are usually elected by historical forces more than by what the candidate does. I think the historical situation today is going to propel me into the White House. I think the country is way ahead of its political leadership. People want new standards, new directions. I think 1972 could be a watershed, the beginning of a new era. I tremble for the future of this country if we don't undertake fundamental change after 1972."[33]

The Wrench

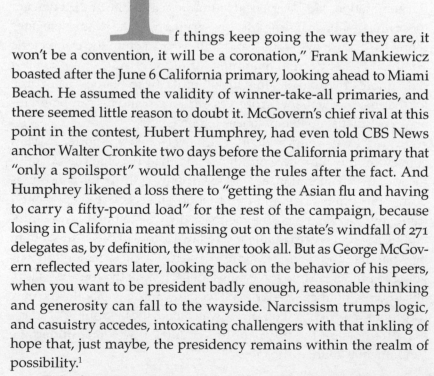

"I f things keep going the way they are, it won't be a convention, it will be a coronation," Frank Mankiewicz boasted after the June 6 California primary, looking ahead to Miami Beach. He assumed the validity of winner-take-all primaries, and there seemed little reason to doubt it. McGovern's chief rival at this point in the contest, Hubert Humphrey, had even told CBS News anchor Walter Cronkite two days before the California primary that "only a spoilsport" would challenge the rules after the fact. And Humphrey likened a loss there to "getting the Asian flu and having to carry a fifty-pound load" for the rest of the campaign, because losing in California meant missing out on the state's windfall of 271 delegates as, by definition, the winner took all. But as George McGovern reflected years later, looking back on the behavior of his peers, when you want to be president badly enough, reasonable thinking and generosity can fall to the wayside. Narcissism trumps logic, and casuistry accedes, intoxicating challengers with that inkling of hope that, just maybe, the presidency remains within the realm of possibility.[1]

To be fair, the preservation of winner-take-all primaries seemed

Senator George McGovern arrives at his campaign's Doral Hotel headquarters in Miami Beach as the threat to unseat him heats up. (AP/Wide World Photos)

to contradict the point of the reforms—of which McGovern had been an engineer—that were intended to protect minority voices and ensure that the delegate counts at the convention reflected the performance of each candidate in the primaries. But the liberal reformers allowed winner-take-all to continue that year because Fred Dutton, a former Kennedy aide and Californian on the committee, had projected that the state's winner-take-all jackpot of delegates could prove crucial to a liberal in securing the nomination in 1972. In public, Dutton and the Reform Commission justified this exception by arguing that the heightened consequence of such a contest encouraged greater participation in the electoral process. Yet the seemingly clever manipulation of the rules came back to haunt McGovern as challenges over the validity of winner-take-all in California dogged the campaign and accentuated party divisions in the run-up to the convention. It also set up the disasters to follow. In a twist of fate, the Reform Commission's compromise in principle was to contribute to the presidency's unreachability for McGovern.[2]

Two days after the California primary, McGovern pleaded with Muskie for his endorsement, promising that he would modify his platform to win the Mainer's support, a prerequisite to that elusive property called party unity before the convention. But Muskie could not bring himself to close shop and shelve his presidential ambitions, however far-fetched his shot at nomination. Muskie told McGovern he was swayed by the argument that he had no right to effectively hand over the nomination to McGovern by endorsing him; he refused to bow out.[3]

Thus, with Muskie's delegates still in play and suspecting that McGovern's spot at the top of the ticket would drag down Democratic candidates for other offices along with him, an amalgam of losing candidates for the California delegation challenged California's allotment of all 271 delegates to McGovern. They argued that the Reform Commission, in expressly prohibiting "unit rule"—whereby one unit receives undue influence—had effectively outlawed all similar systems, such as winner-take-all primaries. It did not matter whether the challengers believed in the validity of their arguments; their only concern was stopping the radical George McGovern.

On June 22 a United States District Court judge rejected the challengers' suit against California, maintaining that no one's right to a vote had been compromised in the primary. Appeals sent the case to the Supreme Court, which ruled that the Democratic Party should adjudicate intraparty squabbles internally. Then, on June 29, two weeks before the convention, the Democratic Party's Credentials Committee validated the challenge and placed 151 of California's 271 delegates in limbo, no longer committed to McGovern. The South Dakotan's victory rested in the balance.[4]

Throughout the ordeal, Humphrey swung from the brink of conciliation—meeting with McGovern to negotiate the party's platform and assuring his delegates' support of McGovern's candidacy—to utter rejection of the thought of ever giving up his fight. While Humphrey eventually vowed not to back down and leave his supporters "feeling high and dry," he did concede some empathy with McGovern's predicament. If he were in McGovern's position, he said, "I'm sure I would have been fighting for every single delegate just like Mr. McGovern, and I don't think we ought to get uptight about it." The jockeying enraged McGovern. He called the Anyone But McGovern (ABM) coalition "a negative, spiteful movement that subverts the democratic process." And he deemed the group's action "an illegitimate power play." As Norman Mailer, the prolific literary journalist, put it, "Politics, what the hell, was politics," and all the candidates knew that.[5]

Thus was the climate in which the Democratic Party began its thirty-sixth national convention. And now, McGovern—the man who once proclaimed himself to be the most reconciling candidate—was threatening to ditch the Democratic Party if the ABM coalition succeeded in usurping his California delegates. No matter how "New Politics" George McGovern was perceived to be, he would go about solidifying his nomination the old-fashioned way—by dangling favors and brokering compromises, but then executing convention floor acrobatics unlike any other in the nation's history.[6]

On the afternoon of Sunday, July 9, the day before the 1972 Democratic National Convention opened in Miami Beach, Tom Eagleton wandered from the Missouri delegation's base at the Ivanhoe Hotel down seaside Collins Avenue to Ed Muskie's campaign headquarters at the Americana.

Back in June, right before the Missouri state Democratic convention, Eagleton had rebuffed McGovern's plea for him to switch his allegiance; Eagleton belonged to Muskie's inner circle and had vowed to support the Mainer for as long as he stayed in the race. But by now, things had changed. Eagleton had come to resent the politics of desperation evident in the California Challenge and likened Muskie's tactics to "changing the rules of the game after [it] had been played," as McGovern had argued. He also had reason to suspect that his political career might transcend the Senate. After June's California primary, the *Washington Star*'s Robert Walters mentioned Eagleton as one of McGovern's vice presidential contenders, giving him "the first inkling of any sort" that he could become McGovern's running mate. In the run-up to the convention, the press continued to prophesy that if pragmatism ruled, McGovern would pick a governor or senator from a southern or a large, industrial state—most likely one of the four that Humphrey had narrowly surrendered in 1968: Illinois, Missouri, Ohio, or Wisconsin. Polls also indicated that Catholics, once reliable Democrats, were slipping away from the coalition and that, grappling with the vitriol of the party's establishment, McGovern would need a running mate who excited the labor unions as well. Furthermore, the convention's hometown *Miami Herald* reported talk of McGovern winning over the Missouri delegation by promising to put Eagleton on the ticket. Perhaps this speculation amounted to nothing more than carefully placed misinformation, but it probably had at least some influence on Eagleton's thinking.[7]

When he arrived at Muskie's suite, Eagleton warned him that even though he continued to endorse his candidacy, his conscience forbade him from supporting the Credentials Committee's ruling. He told Muskie that he believed that the committee's decision was a steal and that splitting California's delegates would fracture the Democratic Party for the indefinite future.

"Tom," Muskie answered, "Reasonable men can and do disagree on the merits of this case. . . . However, you [should] feel free to pursue your own conscience [on] this matter."[8]

For convention week, the McGovern organization descended upon Miami Beach's most expensive hotel, the Doral-on-the-Ocean, where the candidate's seventeenth-floor penthouse suite cost three hundred dollars a night and featured marble floors, crystal chandeliers, and cupid statuettes imported from a French chateau. One might call the décor "Miami Beach vulgar," as did Richard Meryman of *Life* magazine. The penthouse was adorned with muted orange wallpaper, and its second bedroom was reserved for huddles among senior staffers, so the McGovern children slept in another suite. Each of the televisions in the living room was set to a different network, and desks occupied the other side of the room. A bank of ten white telephones sent calls from the penthouse directly to the campaign's internal switchboard. Two black phones allowed calls to the world beyond. A red phone also connected this suite, or "nerve center," with the command-post trailer abutting the Convention Hall.[9]

On the Doral's sixteenth floor, the McGovernites converted the largest room into a "boiler room," whose walls were lined with desks for ten officers, each of whom was responsible for keeping tabs on approximately 300 of the 3,016 official delegates to the convention and marking updates on the status of each on index cards. This reconnaissance arrived at the boiler room through a network of 250 floor whips and an additional flank of campaign officers assigned to live with each delegation.

The Miami Beach Convention Hall was a cartoonish, white structure—a Floridian, Art Deco kitsch riff on an ancient Egyptian temple façade. It stood on Collins Avenue, the city's main thoroughfare, which was home to a wealth of Oceanside hotels of various degrees of tackiness. The Convention Hall was not a modern arena. Rather, its interior resembled a done-up warehouse or airplane hangar, replete with an expanse of red carpet blanketed with folding chairs, posts identifying the locus of each delegation, and network television booths. Placards of Democratic Party icons like Robert F. Kennedy hung from the ceiling, and everything centered on the blue, multi-tiered rostrum at the front of the auditorium, festooned with American flags jutting upward from the sides and marked with the official seal of the Democratic National Convention smack in the middle.

On the north and west sides of the Convention Hall, eighteen trailers with drab interiors sat behind a ten-foot-high, barbed-wire-topped chain-linked fence. Three of them belonged to the McGovern campaign, which set aside one for gathering with floor leaders and stealing momentary respite from the relentless noise and immediacy of the Convention Hall. Another was for the press, and the third—called the "command post"—was for Gary Hart, Frank Mankiewicz, Rick Stearns, and a team of "floor communicators." From there, the senior staffers would monitor the delegate counts and dictate instructions in real time, as the roll calls unfolded in the arena. The campaign's chief strategists could coordinate with their floor leaders from a telephone that connected directly to fifteen McGovern-only phones sprinkled throughout the convention floor.[10]

Rick Stearns had devised this network and supervised its creation on a visit to Miami back in May. In addition to connectivity,

Stearns stressed security. He diligently traced the telephone lines between the Doral and the Convention Hall in search of points of weakness and found that the city's telephone lines lay just below ground level, at easy access through open manhole covers. Stearns notified the telephone company, Southern Bell, which recommended the McGovern campaign weld the manhole covers shut. Paranoid about wiretaps and fearful of foul play even before Watergate vindicated such mistrust, Stearns did as he was told. He also arranged for an armed guard to secure the Doral's switch room, which, stocked with priceless communications equipment, was the key to the entire operation. "A guy with an axe could have demolished that communications system in thirty seconds," Stearns later recalled, suggesting just one of the nightmares that inspired these defensive measures.[11]

The Supreme Court's ruling that the Democratic Party must resolve its disputes internally somewhat ironically granted to one man extraordinary influence over what had been touted as the most open nominating process in party history. The fates of 151 California delegates fell into the lap of Democratic National Committee chairman Lawrence F. O'Brien, a bespectacled middle-aged man with an avuncular face, a college professor's wardrobe, and a widow's peak. He had developed his passion for politics by overhearing his dad, an Irish immigrant and Democratic Party organizer, plot strategies in the family's Springfield, Massachusetts, kitchen. After World War II, O'Brien achieved his first political success, helping elect his friend Foster Furcolo to Congress from Massachusetts in 1948. John F. Kennedy enlisted O'Brien in 1952 for his first Senate campaign, and Larry mobilized eighteen thousand volunteers. The campaign manual O'Brien wrote became the stuff of legend, known simply as "The O'Brien Manual." He also directed Kennedy's 1960 campaign for the presidency, and when JFK arrived at 1600 Pennsylvania Avenue, O'Brien became the administration's top lobbyist, artfully appeasing the southern opposition—Democratic and Republican alike—to usher the president's agenda through passage. O'Brien continued into the Johnson administration and became postmaster general before directing Robert Kennedy's 1968 campaign and, eventually, Hubert Humphrey's White House bid in the aftermath of the fractious Democratic National Convention in Chicago. Humphrey had begged O'Brien to "pick up the pieces" after the convention, and though Humphrey ultimately fell just short of beating Nixon, O'Brien executed his task with uncanny political instincts. Over the years, O'Brien gained a reputation for integrity among people across the ideological spectrum—an especially noteworthy accomplishment in politics, where integrity was a singular commodity.[12]

In 1972 it was O'Brien's job to pick up the pieces once again and steer the Democrats through their convention with as few wounds as possible. While it was always a given that the convention's delegates would vote to decide the various challenges, disagreement centered on the questions of who could vote and which type of majority was needed to win. O'Brien ultimately decided that delegates could not participate in the votes to determine their own fate, and he reasoned that a simple majority of all other delegates who were present at the time of a given vote would determine each issue. In accordance with the precedent of previous conventions, O'Brien also decided that the convention would vote on the challenges in the order in which they were first filed, meaning that another challenge from South Carolina would precede the big one from California. Finally, O'Brien said that he would hear an appeal only if the vote fell between the majority of those eligible to vote on any given challenge and 1,509, the absolute majority of the total number of convention delegates. O'Brien termed this range the "twilight zone" or "window."[13]

South Carolina's thirty-two-member delegation included only nine women, making it a distribution clearly disproportional to the percentage of women in the South Carolina population at large and thus seemingly in violation of the reform rules. In principle, McGovern should have backed the challenge. A professed women's rights advocate, as chairman of the Reform Commission McGovern had argued for stipulations guaranteeing women "reasonable" representation on each state delegation. But the McGovern team's procedural fears trumped conviction.[14]

Rick Stearns determined that McGovern could count on 1,451 "'til-hell-freezes-over" votes, delegates he considered in McGovern's camp no matter what. Stearns also believed that the campaign had 95 "soft" votes—delegates expected to side with McGovern on California, but who were unreliable to stick with the women on South Carolina. That meant that voting on South Carolina might fall within the "twilight zone" between 1,497 and 1,509, allowing an appeal, which in turn would leave the door open to a rules change. This scenario made a McGovern victory a little less likely. With the difference between the nomination and just a valiant try on the line, the McGovernites were not willing to risk O'Brien's reconsideration —and potential alteration—of the procedures.[15]

At 10 P.M. Sunday, the evening before the convention, Gary Hart convened all of the campaign's floor leaders, delegation leaders, and floor whips—about three hundred in total—in the Starlight East Room on the top floor of the Doral Hotel. He explained the communications infrastructure that the campaign had in place and outlined the three ways the delegates could receive instructions on how to vote on the various challenges and planks.

"Unswerving, unquestioning discipline must be maintained," Hart admonished the group. "You must not leave the floor under any circumstances unless a McGovern alternate is in your place. Tomorrow night will determine the nomination of the next president of the United States. It will be *very* close. The other side has vowed to defeat us. Your votes tomorrow will be one of the most important actions of your life."[16]

The Upstart

t 7:30 A.M. on Monday, July 10, the first day of the convention, Tom Eagleton's telephone jolted him from sleep in a sixth-floor suite at the Ivanhoe Hotel. George McGovern was on the line.

"Tom, I hope I didn't wake you," McGovern said.

"Hell no, George, I was lying here in bed waiting for my wake-up call," Eagleton quipped, blinds still shielding him from the Florida sunlight.

"Tom, I need your help on this California Challenge," McGovern continued. "I know you are still a Muskie supporter, but I appeal to you as a fair-minded individual that this California Challenge simply isn't fair or just."[1]

"George, I agree with you on the California Challenge and will vote with you," Eagleton responded. "I don't know how many Missouri delegates will follow my lead, but at least a few will."

"Will you give a speech in support of my position?" McGovern asked. "You're a great speaker and as an avowed Muskie man your speech could be effective."

"No, I can't speak on the issue on the convention floor," Eagleton

Tom Eagleton, center,
chats with donors at
a field office for his
1968 Senate campaign.
(Ruth Herbst)

submitted. "That would only . . . accentuate the difference between
me and [Missouri Governor Warren] Hearnes and would cause even
greater bitterness within the Missouri delegation."[2]

Anxious about solidifying the party's nomination, McGovern
was urging his colleagues to break promises to their friends. And
Eagleton, in turn, was reconsidering his commitment to Muskie, the
candidate he once had considered best for uniting the Democratic
Party. The conditions had changed, and Eagleton acknowledged that
party unity now meant coalescing around McGovern.[3]

Perhaps the ethics of McGovern's stance really did persuade
Eagleton to change his mind. Or maybe, as cynics would argue, it
was the press reports that listed his name among vice presidential
contenders with increasing frequency that truly did it. Or maybe it
was a bit of both. On the first morning of the convention, Eagleton
and McGovern were playing politics, a pursuit rife with changeable
rules and commutable allegiances—a pastime they both knew well.

Eagleton was born in St. Louis on September 4, 1929, to parents who
dedicated their lives to their sons' successes. His mother, Zitta, was

an "exceedingly gentle and soft-spoken woman," who, as Eagleton described, embodied the term "self-sacrificing" until her death at forty-nine, when Tom was eighteen. Eagleton's father, Mark, treasured the company of his sons, Mark Jr. and Tom, sharing with his boys his passions for the law, baseball (especially the Cardinals), and politics. The son of Irish immigrants, Mark Eagleton Sr. had no undergraduate degree but put himself through St. Louis University Law School at night and became one of the city's most successful attorneys. Known for his intellectual prowess and booming voice, he dwarfed opponents with his meticulous preparation and rhetorical finesse. In Tom's words, his father was a "ferocious competitor" and "prodigious worker," with a gift for distilling complex information into plain language to connect with his juries. Mark could also come across as abrasive. Still, his achievement in the courtroom brought material comfort to the Eagleton clan. Their property a few blocks from Tower Grove Park featured a large Tudor-style house that, by 1949, boasted the city's first residential air-conditioning system, as well as a guest cottage and separate quarters for the maid and butler.[4]

In 1937 Mark Eagleton won a seat on the St. Louis school board, and his sons began accompanying him to meetings. Though Tom was too young to comprehend all the issues, he soaked up the energy, suspense, and challenge in the room; he became hooked on politics. Mark supplemented Tom's education at the elite St. Louis Country Day School by engaging private debate coaches. "Tom received what you might term a vocational education, in that he was educated for political office," Bill Kottmeyer, the former St. Louis schools superintendent and Eagleton's debate instructor, remarked. Raised a "Bull Moose" or "liberal Republican" in the mold of Wendell Willkie, Tom accompanied his father to the 1940 Republican National Convention in Philadelphia before the family switched parties in 1944, disappointed that the GOP had passed over Willkie. But Mark also considered it his duty to expose his sons to a range of perspectives, not just his own brand of Republicanism. In 1938, for example, he took Tom to a meeting of the German Bund so his son could witness the Nazi movement firsthand and recognize that anti-Semitism and Naziism were not merely concerns of Europe, but rather plagues infesting America as well. When Winston Churchill came to Missouri, Tom listened from the audience as the once-and-future British prime minister delivered what became known as the "Iron Curtain Speech." Eagleton's Country Day School yearbook noted that Tom had "taken up where Harry Truman left off."[5]

For college, Eagleton followed his older brother Mark to Amherst, a prestigious small liberal arts college in western Massachusetts. Social life at Amherst revolved around the fraternity houses, and Tom pledged Delta Kappa Epsilon, "Deke." Every year, President Charlie Cole announced the academic ranking of the various fraternities at one of the all-college chapel meetings and, without fail, Deke finished at the bottom. But there were some conscientious students in the fraternity, and Tom, a history major, was one of them. Though he loved a good party as much as the other brothers, Eagleton also did his homework and found himself leading late-night review sessions with the other more ambitious students in the house to help the procrastinators among them catch up. Years later, Amherst history Professor Dwight Salmon described Eagleton as "an attractive boy—rather serious, quick-witted, agreeable, and lively," possessing "a nice way about him." While, like many of his classmates, Tom was clearly a boy of privilege, "he never showed it, flaunted it, or acted like that," Deke brother Ned Barry remembers. "Tom was not a humble person, but also not someone who was offensive in displaying he had more." Willie Otter, another Amherst Deke brother, recalled thinking Tom was a "born politician." Eagleton thrived on the debate team, and Barry, for instance, would go to competitions simply to marvel at Tom's gift. "I wish I could do that," he remembers thinking.[6]

Tom put his Amherst studies on hold and returned to St. Louis when his mother died in January 1948. Eagleton was close to his mother, and some believe a bout of depression ensued following Zitta's death. The loss of his mother "touched him deeply," said Ruth Herbst, later Eagleton's secretary. Eagleton took classes at Washington University while in St. Louis, then enlisted in the navy for a year before returning to western Massachusetts in the fall of 1949, a year and a half after his mother passed away. While Eagleton said the military was "not [his] cup of tea," the experience put his goals in focus. "I knew that politics was for me," Eagleton recalled of his state of mind upon returning to Amherst. "Somehow, somewhere I had to get into it, and the law seemed the best avenue." He wrote a thesis, "James A. Reed and the League of Nations," before graduating from the college *cum laude* in 1950. And, as his father had hoped, Tom proceeded to Harvard Law School after spending a summer at Oxford.[7]

Though his father appeared to have groomed Tom for politics, Mark Eagleton warned against his son making a profession out of it. "Politics is exciting and challenging, but it is no way to make a living," he explained. He viewed public service as a hobby more than as a viable career choice for his son. In the three years preceding Tom's law school graduation, Mark's bids for a Senate seat and the mayorship of St. Louis had both fallen short. In the summer of 1953, Eagleton even relinquished his coveted post on the editorial board of the *Harvard Law Review* to help his father's ill-fated campaign and spent most of the following semester in St. Louis, studying from home, though still managing to graduate on time, *cum laude*. Tom's absence from Harvard coincided with the collapse of his engagement to Mary "Peggy" Huttig, another prominent St. Louis Catholic whom he was slated to marry that November. Friends of Eagleton suggested that he called off the wedding because Peggy, a legendary partier, lacked his seriousness and direction in life.[8]

After Harvard, Eagleton returned to St. Louis to practice law alongside his father and to serve as assistant general counsel to the brewery Anheuser-Busch. But he had his sights set beyond private practice. As Eagleton later reflected, "I did not want to be compared to my father as a lawyer and to be found a second rate comparison." Though he loved and admired his dad, an element of competition marked their relationship. "It was almost as if I was fearful of being labeled as 'not as good, not as eloquent, not as successful as [my] Old Man!'" Eagleton recalled. In politics, however, Eagleton could more easily surpass his father's accomplishments. "You can't understand Tom," explained one of his aides, "unless you understand his relationship with his father."[9]

Soon after returning to St. Louis, Eagleton started dating Barbara Ann Smith, the striking blond-haired, blue-eyed daughter of Mr. and Mrs. Frank J. Smith, founder of the Smith-Sharff Paper Company. The Eagletons and Smiths both vacationed in Douglas, Michigan, a resort community on Lake Michigan popular with well-to-do St. Louisans. Years earlier, as a thirteen-year-old girl, Barbara could not help but notice Tom's older brother Mark, who zipped around the community in his flashy sports car. But the younger Eagleton, seventeen-year-old Tom, also caught Barbara's attention as one of the attractive older boys. Barbara attended the Catholic all-girls school Villa Duchesne in St. Louis alongside her twin sister Donna. "I was like many girls," Barbara recalled of her childhood, "in love with horses until I discovered boys." Her teachers remembered her as a conscientious student who thought before speaking in class and appeared to particularly enjoy discussions that connected the past to the present. For college, she spent two years at all-girls Marymount in Tarrytown, New York, but returned to St. Louis to complete her history degree at Washington University. Tom Eagleton remained in her purview, traveling in similar social circles and probably attending the same debutante balls at the University Club. As Barbara heard more about him from mutual friends who had known him during his Amherst and Harvard years, Tom distinguished himself in her mind as someone who was both fun-loving and intellectually curious. Tom and Barbara formally met when they were members of the same wedding party, and they started dating soon after. Barbara was still finishing her degree, so Tom and Barbara's own nuptials came slightly more than a year later. The day of the wedding, Tom was so visibly nervous that the priest at Our Lady of Lourdes Church, Jerome Wilkerson, had to calm him down before they could start the ceremony.[10]

Eagleton had promised Barbara that he would not enter politics, but six months later, in early 1956, he told her otherwise. Eagleton grew up across the street from Mark Sr.'s close friend George Murphy, a former chairman of the Democratic Committee of St. Louis. And as Tom prepared to launch his political career by running for the St. Louis Board of Freeholders, he sought Murphy's advice. "Don't do it, Tom," Murphy advised. "You can't come out of it . . . politically alive. If you support the 'Do Gooders' in drafting a new city charter, the politicians will hate you. If you support the politicians in drafting a new city charter, the 'Do Gooders' and the newspapers will hate you." Politics, as Eagleton learned, is about balance, testing one's ability to weigh moral impulse against pragmatism. Thus, at Murphy's suggestion, Eagleton decided to run for circuit attorney, St. Louis's equivalent of district attorney.[11]

"You're kidding," Mark said when his twenty-six-year-old son broke the news that he wanted to run. "I don't think you have a chance," he said. He advised his son to concentrate on becoming a good lawyer first. But as Eagleton recalled, "My pig-headed mind was made up!" Though initially wary of his son's plans, soon Mark was doing everything in his power to ensure Tom's success, financing the campaign, plotting its strategy, and lobbying the local political community on his behalf. With Murphy's help, the Democratic organizations of twenty-four of St. Louis's twenty-eight wards supported Eagleton's candidacy; he became the establishment candidate in the days when the endorsements of ward bosses like Turtles Reardon, Poker White, Pops Chambers, Uncle Louie Buckowitz, and Jimmy McAteer were tantamount to victory. It has been speculated, though never entirely confirmed, that Tom's father paid each ward committeeman $1,000 to mobilize support in that election. At twenty-seven, Eagleton became St. Louis's youngest circuit attorney.[12]

As the city's chief prosecutor, Eagleton championed civil liberties. He informed the police department that he would not prosecute cases founded on illegal wiretaps, unconstitutional searches and seizures, or confessions wrought by a defendant's ignorance of his rights. He drew up cards listing the rights of the accused and instructed St. Louis police officers to distribute them to suspects before questioning them—even before the Supreme Court's *Miranda* decision made it obligatory to inform suspects of their rights. Eagleton proved the strength of his convictions and the courage to stand up for his sense of justice. At a February 1958 conference of the National Association of County and Prosecuting Attorneys in Las Vegas, Eagleton was one of just two attendees to speak out against wiretapping. On May 22 that year, Eagleton testified before the U.S.

Senate's Subcommittee on Constitutional Rights, calling the practice a "threat" to constitutional rights he considered sacred.[13]

The Constitution and its protection of personal freedoms against government intrusion had fascinated Eagleton since his days at Harvard Law and his classes with Paul Freund, the distinguished constitutional law professor. As Eagleton acknowledged in his subcommittee testimony, the debate over wiretapping could not be waged "in terms of sheer practicality." But this did not stop him. He explained that even the most well-intentioned law enforcement officers were bound to overhear innocent, personal conversations. "Maybe they will be mine," Eagleton told the subcommittee. "Maybe they will be yours."[14]

At the Las Vegas conference of the nation's prosecutors that February 1958, Eagleton had lunch at the Desert Inn's coffee shop with the district attorneys of Denver and Philadelphia and another gentleman, who Eagleton did not know was an FBI inspector. In the course of the conversation, Eagleton mentioned that an FBI fingerprint examiner's testimony had blown one of his cases, recalling that the examiner's way of speaking came off as "unusual, affected, or stilted" to the blue-collar St. Louis jury, despite the scientific soundness of his explanations. The FBI inspector pushed back, and Eagleton retracted his statement, admitting that there were additional reasons that the case had been botched. But word of the young circuit attorney's criticisms of the FBI expert still made its way to the agency's director, J. Edgar Hoover, who was notoriously thin-skinned about criticism of the Bureau and prone to retribution. Hoover wrote Eagleton asking why he had not brought his concerns directly to the agency. Upon receipt of Eagleton's explanation, Hoover noted to his staff, "See that our St. Louis Office deals most circumspectly with Eagleton."[15]

As circuit attorney, Eagleton acted as the office's guiding conscience and chief administrator, leaving most of the courtroom work to the more experienced trial lawyers on his staff. Overseeing a team of forty people provided Eagleton administrative experience, and he used the post to make a name for himself as a hardworking, fair-minded, and creative official. For example, Eagleton enlisted his Aunt Hazel in an undercover investigation of a ballroom dance studio believed to be exploiting the loneliness of elderly ladies by employing debonair instructors to entice them to purchase multiple life memberships. In his first year in office, Eagleton cut the backlog of felony cases from more than seven hundred to two hundred.[16]

Ever since he had been a young boy, St. Louisans expected big things from Tom Eagleton, and as he proved himself as prosecutor, friends and colleagues prodded him about his next career move and teased him about his eventual assent to the pinnacle of power. Bob Griesedieck, for instance, an Eagleton friend and executive at the Falstaff Brewing Company in St. Louis, ended a 1959 letter to Eagleton by kidding, "Don't forget that when you become president . . . I expect . . . a very good job in government." Eagleton responded with the same levity and tacit acknowledgment of his own ambitions. "With respect to the presidency of the United States," he wrote, "whenever that high privilege falls into my hands, I shall be only too pleased to consider you as a candidate for the Secretary of the Treasury." Then, he injected his own dose of quintessentially Eagleton charm and cerebral humor, "All applicants for said position must sign an affidavit promising to refrain from taking home samples." Eagleton knew how to enchant his audience, and he collected jokes to mix in his speeches. One, "on youth," went as follows: "[It] used to be when I'd go away on a trip . . . my wife would say 'Watch out for the blondes and red heads.' Now all she says is 'Watch what you eat.'"[17]

Sure enough, as his four-year term as circuit attorney concluded in 1960, Eagleton looked to become attorney general of Missouri. During the campaign a young reporter mentioned to the *St. Louis Globe-Democrat* political director, Marsh Clark, his understanding that Eagleton would run for Senate if he prevailed in the attorney general contest. "Hell, they take the Senate for granted," Clark responded. "They're already talking about the presidency," echoing Griesedieck's speculation. Yet in truth, Tom, his family, and his supporters took nothing for granted. In 1960 Eagleton crisscrossed the state day and night, campaigning for himself, as well as for the presidential ticket of fellow Catholic John F. Kennedy at a time when anti-Catholic sentiment ruled Missouri's predominantly Baptist countryside.[18]

St. Louis Democratic Chairman Jack Dwyer and other party bosses from the big city engineered a quid pro quo with Democratic leaders in the southeastern "Bootheel" of Missouri, where cotton—and the venerable political boss J. V. Conran—reigned supreme. The St. Louis Democrats managed to broker the deal largely because Eagleton had endeared himself to Conran, the so-called Emperor of the Bootheel, on a visit to his office. Eagleton never quite understood how Conran secured the votes—and maybe he did not want to know—but he did know that the boss delivered. Conran lived up to his reputation in Eagleton's all-important Democratic primary. At that moment in American history, a little token of financial gratitude did not hurt, either. Tom's brother Mark, who became a radiologist, paid Jackson County boss Henry McKissick, for example, $8,000 to produce 8,000 votes for Eagleton in the Democratic primary. McKissick raked in 8,125 votes come election day.[19]

Over the course of his winning campaign, Tom grabbed just three or four hours of sleep most nights, and his weight dropped to 152 pounds from 178. Barbara recalled a particularly grueling night when, after driving 120 miles each way for a speech, Eagleton finally arrived home at midnight. But at 2 A.M., the phone rang. The St. Louis policeman on the line told Eagleton that he believed they had nabbed the man responsible for a string of rapes. The officer asked whether the circuit attorney would handle the questioning, so Eagleton dragged himself out of bed, deposed the suspect, and returned home by 4 in the morning. At 7 A.M. his alarm rang: he had a campaign breakfast that morning. "There was only one speed for Eagleton, and that was one hundred miles per hour," explains John Britton, a longtime Eagleton friend.[20]

When Eagleton won the race for attorney general, the *Post-Dispatch*'s editorial board wrote that Tom's victory "assured fresh leadership in the state capital" and expressed hope that the city's incoming circuit attorney's administration would be "characterized with the restraint and common sense" that had marked Eagleton's time in office.[21]

In the weeks following the election, the Eagletons visited Columbia for a University of Missouri football game. After the game, the Eagletons and another couple, the Kingslands, headed to the house of Scott O. Wright, the former Boone County prosecuting attorney and a close friend of the attorney general–elect. That evening, they "got to drinking," as Wright remembered. Their raucous good time continued until about 1 in the morning, when they headed downtown to the Tiger Hotel, where Wright had made reservations for his guests. However, when the Eagletons and Kingslands arrived, as Wright remembered it, the hotel clerk informed them that he had moved the Eagletons to another, less desirable room. Tom recalled the clerk saying he had given away the room and that there were no other vacancies in Columbia that night. Either way, the news irked Tom. "He had raised so much hell that they were going to arrest him," Wright remembered. He was called to the scene and found the hotel management had also summoned the police. Eagleton blamed his outburst on the "arrogant and abusive manner" of the hotel clerk, but it seems likely that the combination of alcohol, postcampaign fatigue—and maybe something else—played a role in the episode.[22]

On December 17, 1960, the *St. Louis Post-Dispatch* was brimming with news that John F. Kennedy's thirty-five-year-old brother Robert would become the nation's youngest U.S. attorney general. Buried on page 8A was a news item about Tom Eagleton; he was being treated for a virus at St. Louis's Barnes Hospital, the *Post-Dispatch* reported. Mark Eagleton Sr. said he expected his son to remain under hospital supervision for another ten days. "His illness was complicated by hard work in his successful campaign for the office of attorney general," the news item explained. Eagleton struggled to make the transition from the anxious bustle of the campaign to the lull of a victory complete, with the fierce urgency of competition no longer there to goad him on. As evidenced by his outbreak at the Tiger Hotel, the slightest frustration could instigate the wildest of irritations. Eagleton later described himself as moping around, "aimless," preferring to watch television than to socialize with friends. "It was the kind of situation that if you let it linger too long, it can get progressively worse and get too hard to cope with," he reflected years after. In reality, his illness was depression more than a stomach virus. Eagleton sought help and checked himself into Barnes, attempting to avert falling farther into his psychological morass. More than a decade later, Barbara wrote in *Ladies' Home Journal*, "It is easier to handle the difficulties in life if we understand that life is not all roses and sunshine. My feeling about life is that we are all here on earth for a period of trial that concerns our destiny after death," recalling the lessons of the nuns who had taught her. "In order for the Lord to make that judgment after death, you are given certain things to deal with. It's how you deal with them that determines what that ultimate destiny will be."[23]

Legend has it that Missouri governor-elect John Dalton was ready to name another attorney general in Eagleton's place if he did not show up on inauguration day. The teetotaling Dalton had spent a career working toward the attorney general post before finally reaching the governor's mansion, and he was widely believed to resent the new kid and his astronomical rise. In the end, Eagleton made it out of the hospital in time for his swearing-in, but the episode suggested the atmosphere in the state capital.[24]

When Eagleton arrived in Jefferson City as the new, thirty-one-year-old attorney general, he faced the skepticism of the capital city's regulars. Hard drinking and political gossip dominated the small-town Missouri state seat, and contention between the "wets" and the "drys," and between the city dwellers and the country folk, was pronounced. Regarded by other politicians as a "young man in a hurry" and judged with the prejudices that confronted city slickers, Catholics, and liberals alike, Eagleton was the target of whispering campaigns among the Jeff City establishment, which snubbed the man it simultaneously envied and distrusted. It did not help that Eagleton thwarted the state legislature's attempt to flout the ninety-day waiting period required before enacting pay raises in nonemergency situations. Throughout his career, Eagleton straddled the line between Old Politics and New, belonging to the St. Louis Democratic establishment but spurned by the Jefferson City Old Guard.[25]

Confirming his progressive stance on civil liberties with real action, Eagleton named George Draper the state's first black assistant attorney general. One day after work, Eagleton, Draper, and a few other assistant attorneys general settled down for dinner at a Jeff City greasy spoon around the corner from the office, but the waiter ignored the table despite knowing who the patrons were. After a while, Eagleton called him over. "I'm sorry, sir," the waiter explained. "We don't serve blacks here." Eagleton told the man that his party would not leave the restaurant until they received their meals. The waiter took their orders, and they were served.[26]

As attorney general, Eagleton built upon his reputation as an outspoken critic of wiretapping and added capital punishment to his list of targets. Longtime friend Jim Murphy described Eagleton's stance against the death penalty as "the antithesis of self-interest," but his conscience demanded that he fight capital punishment. In a pair of 1963 opinion pieces cowritten with assistant attorney general Robert D. Kingsland and published in the *Post-Dispatch*, Eagleton set forth a reasoned critique of the practice. He believed that the human impulse for revenge had driven the codification of the death penalty into the American legal system and did not consider "getting even" sufficient reason to sanction the taking of another man's life. "Our system of justice in this, the greatest free country on earth, should reflect man's nobler aspirations, not his baser human frailties," Eagleton and Kingsland wrote. They asked, "Can any of us say with complete honesty that our system of justice is so infallible or that we have reached such a point in medical and psychiatric knowledge that we can make a valid, irrevocable judgment of a fellow human being?"[27]

Roman Catholic but not devout, Eagleton still occasionally mingled his politics with his religion, which appeared to play a role in his staunchly pro-life outlook: against both capital punishment and abortion. "No man, no court, no legislature can play God. We are created in His image, instructed to do His work, but not chartered to make His decisions," Eagleton later wrote in explaining his opposition to abortion. He was "fiercely independent," according to Senate aide Gene Godley. "Tom was an interloper and an iconoclast. He didn't just come through the party system. He sort of did it his own way, and I'm sure the other side was irritated because the public loved him." Eagleton stood up for his values, no matter whether his stances were classified as typically Democratic or Republican positions.[28]

After one term as attorney general, Eagleton began to covet the part-time lieutenant governorship, envisioning it as the next step to the Senate. While he enjoyed his work in state government, Eagleton believed that as the federal government's influence continued to expand, he could effect more change from Washington than in Missouri. He surmised that the lieutenant governor's role of presiding over the Missouri state senate would offer him legislative experience, and that the post's flexibility would afford him the time to travel across the state, broadening his base and bolstering his appeal before launching a Senate bid. He bought the old Missouri political truism that, despite its lack of hard power, "lieutenant governor is the best job in the state from which to run for something else." Eagleton won handily, but the 1964 election year saddled him with double duty, as he campaigned for other Democrats in their congressional races in addition to his own contest.[29]

That December came another setback. According to his half-brother Kevin (Mark Sr.'s son with his new wife, Jane), Tom was struggling to get out of bed in the morning. The whole Eagleton clan gathered at the family compound near Tower Grove Park to plot how to proceed. Mark Sr. worried about the ramifications this depressive episode and its corresponding treatment would have on his son's career, so the family decided to have Eagleton treated out of state. A December 28 news item in the *Post-Dispatch* reported that, the day before—after losing fourteen pounds in two weeks—Eagleton had checked himself into Mayo Brothers Clinic in Rochester, Minnesota, to undergo a series of tests. The article said he was expected to remain hospitalized for another three days.[30]

When he returned from Mayo, Eagleton developed a close rapport and excellent working relationship with Governor Warren Hearnes, enabling him to become one of the most productive lieutenant governors in Missouri state history. Hearnes trusted his lieutenant to overhaul the state's dilapidated prisons and granted him oversight of the Missouri Department of Corrections and the Department of Probation and Parole. Eagleton considered it government's obligation to eradicate the root causes of crime by providing all citizens quality education and other preventatives, believing the existing system had failed in its essential task of rehabilitating criminals and stifling recidivism. When he ran for the Senate, he would refine the call for "Law and Order," stressing "Law and Order with Justice" instead.[31]

Eagleton also threw himself into the push for education reform. When he entered office, only 60 percent of Missouri public school systems offered kindergarten. Before the end of his term, it was no longer optional. Eagleton also vouched for vocational education and championed proposals to extend the inner-city school year through the traditional summer holidays to give underperforming classrooms the time to catch up to their counterparts in the suburbs. What Eagleton called "a hellish amount of work" associated with planning a 1966 statewide education conference while simultaneously campaigning for Democratic congressional candidates across the state contributed to another disabling bout of sickness, termed "gastric disturbance" in the press. As a September 21 item in the *Post-Dispatch* reported, his St. Louis law firm disclosed that Eagleton had checked into Johns Hopkins University Hospital in Baltimore for a series of tests. In truth, Eagleton had returned to the Mayo Clinic to receive treatment for depression.[32]

Eagleton had always intended the lieutenant governorship to be a transitional position, a platform for refining his brand and extending his reach while preparing to target a higher office. When a May 1967 *Life* magazine article alleged that Missouri Senator Edward Long had spoken out against wiretapping only because Teamsters leader Jimmy Hoffa's chief counsel, Morris Shenker, had paid him to, it shattered the incumbent Democrat's credibility and subjected him to a Senate Ethics Committee Investigation. Eagleton's friends advised him that the time was right to bid for the Senate, and he seized the opening. In a three-way Democratic primary that also included True Davis, the millionaire former U.S. ambassador to Switzerland and former assistant secretary of the treasury, Eagleton refrained from exploiting the charges against Long directly, but rather presented himself as a Washington outsider, "a fresh new face with fresh ideas."[33]

Upon launching his bid for Long's seat, Eagleton declared, "The very first priority for any candidate for United States senator must be to help find a peaceful and honorable solution to the Vietnam War," and his opposition to the war became the centerpiece of his campaign for the Democratic nomination. Eagleton called for a "nation-by-nation approach" to foreign policy, urging America to acknowledge its own limitations and discern the infeasibility—and, indeed, the impossibility—of remaking the world in its image.[34]

When organized labor and other traditional Eagleton patrons like August "Gussie" Busch sided with Long, Eagleton enlisted Matt Reese, a three hundred–pound freelance political consultant from West Virginia with a larger-than-life personality, who had made a name for himself pioneering grassroots tactics for the Kennedy brothers and other Democratic politicians nationwide. Reese organized a network of volunteers—mostly stay-at-home mothers and college students—to work the telephones and take the campaign for Tom Eagleton from door to door in the primary and general elections. He also employed sophisticated, scientific analysis of past Missouri voting patterns to determine whom to target, practicing the New Politics tactics that foreshadowed the McGovern campaign. It didn't hurt that Eagleton was a phenomenal campaigner, his tie loosened and his sleeves rolled up. "By the sheer force of personality and magnetism, [Tom] overcame what I call the conservative attitude [against] social and political issues that [he] espoused," explained Jim Reeves, who managed Eagleton's campaign in Pemiscot County that year. Eagleton was also helped by the remoteness of the Senate to life in Missouri; the local bosses left the state's envoys in Washington alone as long as they pulled through on the votes that mattered. In the conservative Bootheel, that meant unwavering commitment to fortifying the cotton price support system and opposition to gun control.[35]

After narrowly clinching the nomination, Tom Eagleton was pitted in the general election against Tom Curtis, a staid, old-school Republican congressman with a penchant for bow ties. Curtis was an eighteen-year Washington veteran and had a voting record to show for it, not always to his advantage—too many "no" votes, in Eagleton's opinion. In a roundup of the campaign prepared by *Time* magazine reporter Jonathan Z. Larsen for his editors back in New York, the Chicago-based correspondent presented the race between

Eagleton and Curtis as a contest between the "yin and yang of Missouri politics." As Larsen presented it, Eagleton was blessed with "Kennedyesque energy," campaign coffers now stocked with enough cash to jet around in private planes, "the kind of McLuhan charisma now considered necessary for the new politics," and a flair for the simple, penetrating—if misleading—one-liner. Eagleton flew to Washington to shoot fifty-second television spots with Teddy Kennedy, whereas Curtis was professorial in his demeanor and chose Ronald Reagan as his high-profile political godfather. Though Eagleton secured the Democratic nomination as the candidate farthest left, he successfully modified his emphasis for the general election and touted his relationship with Governor Warren Hearnes, the Old Guard conservative Democrat. "My position on the issues won't be changed," he explained as he looked toward his run against Curtis, "but my emphasis will be." Most significant, he shifted his slant on gun control, from advocating additional regulations to stressing his devotion to the rights of citizens to own and "properly" use firearms.[36]

The most revelatory information in Larsen's eight-page memo was in the third paragraph. "Tom Eagleton is also something of a character," Larsen wrote, continuing:

> Word is around St. Louis (this we cannot prove) that he has a rather serious drinking problem. He has managed to pull himself together for the primary and the main campaign, but there remains that lingering doubt in the minds of those who know him well. Perhaps as serious, he also sinks into depressed states so severe, that, according to friends, he has taken shock treatments to get himself out of them. We have not been able to confirm any of this. Most people in St. Louis are not even aware of it, and none of it has ever been printed. We put it on record only for future reference, when and if Tom Eagleton assumes a position of higher authority. We also mention it because it conveys the feeling of the man. A chain smoker who never finishes a cigarette, he goes through two packs a

day. He keeps up such a pace that, since January, he has dropped sixteen pounds, a fact which partially accounts for the pants falling around his hips.

Though Eagleton staved off another episode of depression se-rious enough to demand hospitalization, he had not emerged from the 1968 campaign without alarming the friends and staffers who shared this information with the out-of-town reporter embedded with the campaign for a few days. Larsen remembers learning about the shock therapy from a campaign adviser from outside Missouri, whose name he could no longer recall, but who presumably spoke honestly because he knew a national magazine would not break unsubstantiated, potentially career-shattering information on a state-wide race. As both an outsider and a hired hand, the aide lacked the same loyalty and protectiveness toward Eagleton that characterized the tight circle of Missourians who surrounded him throughout his career. Larsen likened the dynamic between the leaker and himself to one passenger on a cruise divulging his life story to another. Yet even without this background knowledge, to Larsen, it was clear that Eagleton had a problem. The shaking, the sweating, the rushing, the chain-smoking, the rumpled clothes. "It [all] came off as good energy to crowds," Larsen remembered, but it could be frightening up close, he said. Eagleton's rapid weight loss also struck Larsen as odd.[37]

This is not to say that the Missouri press remained oblivious to the allegations of alcoholism and speculation that Eagleton's hospi-talizations were for problems other than gastric ones. The Missouri media had a tradition of restraint that saved Eagleton from investiga-tion; they avoided scrutiny of a man's private life if it did not seem to interfere with his performance on the job. "If a man drank, ran with women, gambled, or anything else, but showed up for work and did a good job, that's what we reported," recalled Fred Lindecke, a *Post-Dispatch* political reporter. Eagleton's supposed drinking prob-lem floated through Missouri as "the biggest unconfirmed rumor I've ever heard," according to Lindecke. And, like most rumors, it appeared to have at least some basis. Tom Curtis also picked up on the various rumors as he ran against Eagleton, but refused to traffic in dirt—out of virtue, or the desire to avoid triggering a cycle of smears.[38]

As always, as he ran for the Senate, Tom benefited from the support of his wife, Barbara. As a friend observed, she could "handle anything life has to offer as long as it [included] Tom." Their son, Terry, was just eight years old and their daughter, Christin, four, but Barbara still managed to arrange all her husband's radio and television advertising spots. Throughout their marriage, Barbara shopped for all the groceries, cooked all the meals, and prepared all the parties in the Eagleton household. Her husband would "be grumpy if he weren't doing what he likes," she would tell reporters. "And I'd be unhappy with a nine-to-five lawyer."[39]

Mark Eagleton Sr., seventy-four years of age and losing his vision, remained a fixture in his son's political life. He would walk over to the campaign headquarters each morning, tireless in his insistence that Eagleton should dedicate more time to campaigning in St. Louis and scale back on his efforts outside the big city. He also worried that the campaign had tacked too far to the left. "Can't you guys do anything right?" he would occasionally bark at his son's staffers. "There were only two opinions—the wrong one and Mark Eagleton's," recalled a fellow St. Louis lawyer and friend of Tom's.[40]

Eagleton remembered December 27, 1968, the day he took the Senate's oath of office, as the "most thrilling" day of his life. He recalled the proud expressions of his friends and family members gathered in the gallery, his father's in particular. "As I looked up at my father, I wondered about the irony of life," Eagleton wrote in his unpublished memoir. "There sat Mark Eagleton, brilliant lawyer and orator, watching as Tom Eagleton became a senator. He should be taking the senatorial oath, and, in a sense, I felt I was his proxy." Reaching the Senate liberated Eagleton from the pressure he felt to impress his father. He had attained what his father had only dreamed of, and, Eagleton believed, "Vicariously, [Mark Eagleton] was becoming a U.S. Senator." Now his father would live through him, not the other way around.[41]

After twelve years of resting in no one office for more than one term, Eagleton seemed ready to make the Senate his home. "I want to be a great United States senator," he told his brother Mark after the election. "I'd like to be re-elected three terms, acquire some seniority and get some good committees, and hear James Reston or David Brinkley say someday, 'He's a pretty good senator. He works hard at it.'"[42]

The first to arrive at his Senate office each morning, Eagleton earned the reputation for being "an intelligent, conscientious, and compassionate legislator" in his first few years in Washington. Yet he understood the limits of his power as a junior senator. "I realize that no one senator alone can answer to all the great problems and dilemmas of our time," he said before arriving on Capitol Hill. "But one senator can have attitudes as to how some of these problems can be solved and can join with other senators to bring about change." He believed in the strength of his voice, hopeful his words could inspire others to join him in precipitating progress. Eagleton took to the Senate floor to critique U.S. policy on Vietnam four times in his first year in office. His most memorable exchange came August 8, 1969, when he spent four hours debating longtime Democratic senator and Armed Services Committee chairman John C. Stennis of Mississippi, among other Senate veterans, over funding for the Main Battle Tank-70. The tank's price tag had already ballooned to upward of $300 million from $80 million and was likely to climb even higher. Eagleton proposed an amendment to deny funding for the project, and—though his motion failed—his tenacity earned his colleagues' respect. Eagleton later looked back on that day as the time he came of age as a senator, and others seemed to agree. When Eagleton came across Senator Stennis in the Senate cloakroom after their faceoff, his elder greeted him with, "Hi, tank."

Within the next few years, the Missourian and the Mississippian were to team up with a bipartisan coalition of their peers to compose legislation that would more clearly delineate who, exactly, has the power to make war. The bill attempted to establish when, if at all, the president could deploy troops or authorize bombings without congressional approval, paying close attention to the constitutionally defined roles of the chief executive officer and the legislature. Senator Stennis commended his freshman colleague's "excellent work" and "fine leadership here on the floor."[43]

Domestically, Eagleton favored policies aimed at enabling the poor to help themselves and paid special attention to the needs of the cities, calling for tax-cut incentive programs to attract businesses to urban areas, as well as for investment in mass transit. He also wanted to replace the "costly and degrading welfare system" with subsidized on-the-job-training programs, believing this to be the way to build a stronger, more competitive American workforce while lifting people out of poverty. Eagleton enjoyed a near-perfect union voting record, and he considered busing obligatory to achieving desegregation, but he tempered his support where the issue proved most divisive— when it meant transporting students across non-gerrymandered district lines. Though he was a member of the District of Columbia Committee and eventually its chairman—fighting heartily for Washingtonians and their self-determination through locally elected officials or "home rule"—for Eagleton, home remained in Missouri. In 1969, his first year in office, Eagleton visited the state forty-one times, to see friends and keep in touch with his constituents. Since his 1968 election was too close for comfort, his aides liked to schedule outreach events. At one such luncheon with thirty or so conservative Kansas City bankers, Eagleton handily responded to questions, but when it was all over, he whispered to one of his aides, "Now let's go back to the kitchen and meet some Democrats."[44]

His comfort aside, Eagleton resisted classifying himself as simply a liberal or a conservative, and his friendships crossed party lines. He termed himself a "constructive" or "practical progressive" instead, pointing to his belief that pragmatism and compromise are crucial to progress. Eagleton resisted additional gun control legislation because the regulations in place, he argued, had proven unenforceable: why add more politically unpopular rules to the books? And unlike McGovern, he supported the Vietnam draft. "An all-volunteer army will be a poor boys' army," he reminded the Senate in a 1971 speech. "I believe that America is not only the land of opportunity but also the land of obligation. One of these obligations is to bear arms in a time of war—even if a foolish one." As vice chairman of the Muskie-led Senate Subcommittee on Environmental Pollution, Eagleton had seen firsthand Senator Muskie's skill as a leader and a compromiser, as he partnered with Republicans and adapted ideas he had initially resisted in order to forge timely, potent, and efficacious amendments to the Clean Air Act in 1970. Eagleton also considered party unity essential, contributing to his endorsement of Muskie for the presidency. "I thought [he] has those qualities of to-getherness, of compassion, of understanding that would have caused him to be a very acceptable candidate to the public," Eagleton said.[45]

About a year and a half into Eagleton's time in Washington, July 25, 1970, his seventy-six-year-old father Mark died of a heart attack. Tom spoke at the funeral in St. Louis a few days later, before an audience packed with members of the Missouri elite. Eagleton described his father as "the underdog's last hope," unafraid to take on corporate interests in the court of law. As a school board mem-ber, Mark Sr. had been ahead of his time, fighting for desegregation and racial equality well before the 1954 *Brown v. Board of Education* decision. "Next to his family, [my father] loved the law most," Tom Eagleton recalled at the church that day. "For it was the law through which he could translate into reality the beliefs he held so strongly."[46]

In the little down time he had in Washington, Eagleton enjoyed playing cards, especially bridge or gin rummy. He had picked up the diversion as a young lawyer through hours spent competing with Busch on long train rides from Missouri to Florida for the St. Louis Cardinals' spring training. In Eagleton's Senate office, it was not uncommon for policy discussions, political strategizing, and socializing to happen over a game of cards. Eagleton was known as a feisty, unorthodox competitor, who "didn't always play by the book." More recently, Eagleton had signed up for painting lessons. His family joked that he was trying to fashion himself after Winston Churchill—as masterful with a paintbrush as on the podium. And while Eagleton's life had changed significantly since he first sat on Stan Musial's lap as a young boy, one thing remained a constant: his zeal for Cardinals baseball. The Missouri senator considered his free pass to games among his most cherished possessions.[47]

When the Eagletons went to Washington, they settled into a four-bedroom white colonial in Chevy Chase, Maryland—the adopted hometown of several nationally prominent senators, includ-

ing Hubert Humphrey, Henry Jackson, and Eagleton's closest friends
in the Senate, Democrat Gaylord Nelson of Wisconsin and Republican Ted Stevens of Alaska, not to mention George McGovern in the
period immediately after he was elected to Congress. The Eagletons
left their yard unembellished by gardens and patios, and it became
a hangout for the neighborhood kids and the family dog, a beagle
named Pumpkin. Tom took after his father in his choice of breed and
"was absolutely wild" about Pumpkin, recalls Andrea Gibbs, Eagleton's goddaughter. Barbara volunteered in the libraries of their children's schools, Sidwell Friends for Terry, and Stone Ridge School of the
Sacred Heart for Christy. And she expanded her political education,
taking graduate-level political science courses at American University and serving on the speakers committee of the Women's National
Democratic Club of Washington. Barbara became especially friendly
with two other Senate wives, Joan Mondale and Joan Kennedy. She
stayed fit playing tennis almost every day during the summer.[48]

Tom drove himself to work each morning, and he had a habit
of picking up hitchhikers along the way, mostly students. "He really
was a classical man of the people," Senate aide Gene Godley recalled.
"Every once in a while you'd get a note in the office or a telephone
call saying, 'This guy picked me up who alleged he was Senator
Eagleton, and I just wanted to thank him for giving me a ride.'" As
a father, however, Eagleton never managed to spend as much time
with Terry and Christy as he would have liked. He dropped them
off at school on the way to work and spoke adoringly of them at the
office, but Senate work often kept him away from the dinner table.[49]

The Eagletons adjusted to life in Washington, but Tom, who
made frequent weekend trips home, kept a close circle of friends and
aides from Missouri. Some of Eagleton's Senate aides and dearest
friends had been around since his days at the circuit attorney's office.
In April 1971 Eagleton promised he would make it to Jefferson City
in time for longtime friend Bob Kingsland's surprise birthday party.
"Sorry I'm late," Eagleton said as he burst through the door forty-five
minutes after the party had begun. "I just came from Vietnam." As
was typical of such gatherings, the drinks flowed freely and Eagleton took part, though he stayed sober that Saturday night. The next

morning he held a press conference recounting his experience in Vietnam. Despite his inevitable fatigue, "his answers were precise and articulate," the *Post-Dispatch* reported. Then it was off to another engagement elsewhere in the state. The weekend represented typical Tom Eagleton: loyal, gregarious, and extraordinarily hardworking.[50]

Calvin Trillin of the *New Yorker* magazine accompanied Eagleton on one such trip home and he described how, "in small Missouri towns, Eagleton has the advantage of a friendliness and informality that make it seem natural for people who have just met him to call him by his first name," despite his status as a United States senator. He could nonchalantly stroll up to a groundbreaking ceremony for a new library in the pouring rain and deadpan that he knew only one library-groundbreaking speech, and that it took forty-five minutes to deliver.[51]

His irreverent humor made its way around Washington as well—by design or not. For example, in a crowded Capitol Hill elevator, crammed with senators and legislative assistants, Republican Senator Jesse Helms of North Carolina said aloud, to no one in particular, "I want to tell you a Polish joke, I just heard a good Polish joke," not realizing a Polish-American was in the elevator. "Careful, I'm here," Muskie piped up. "Alright then," Eagleton interrupted, "[He'll] tell it slowly."[52]

Another time, enrapt in conversation in the Senate Dining Room, Eagleton lit a cigarette, only to find his shirt aflame moments later; he was so caught up in the discussion that he had forgotten to extinguish his match. As the *Washington Post* described him, Eagleton was "a warm, casual, shirt-sleeved, laugh-at-himself senator."[53]

While the aides who had been with Eagleton since his Missouri days knew that their boss had occasionally felt less than boisterous, lapsing into spurts of depression, his hospitalizations and treatment never came up with the newcomers to the Eagleton crew, and they had little reason to suspect their boss had experienced such lows. "Tom had an ebullient, exuberant, optimistic, outgoing, friendly personality," recalled press secretary Mike Kelley, who was thirty years old in 1972 and had been with Eagleton since 1969, when the senator-elect asked the well-regarded *Kansas City Star* reporter to join him in

Washington. "That was it. There was no opposite to it. He was just a real people person," Kelley said in a recent interview. He especially admired his boss's lack of pretense. "He was just a normal, ordinary guy who just happened to be a lot smarter and more capable than most people."[54]

Gene Godley, a thirty-two-year-old redheaded Texan with a law degree from the University of Chicago, had worked for Senator Ralph Yarborough of Texas and the consultancy Booz Allen in Washington before linking up with Senator Eagleton as general counsel for the Labor and Public Welfare Committee, then following him to the District of Columbia Committee when Eagleton became chairman. Eagleton "wasn't in politics for self-aggrandizement like a lot of politicians," said Godley, who has gotten to know many over the years. "It wasn't a great need of public affirmation and acceptance. I think he was there just because he liked public service. But he also liked people." Like Kelley, Godley was unaware that his boss's past had included treatment with electroshock. He likened Eagleton's mental health history to a bout of childhood pneumonia. "I don't sit in fear that you're going to have pneumonia every day. So it certainly was not even in my frame of reference, and if it had been, it would not have mattered, because his contemporary actions were just not in any way polluted by that."[55]

The Game

Just hours before the thud of Larry O'Brien's gavel was to open the convention at 7 P.M. Monday, July 10, Ed Muskie summoned a last-minute meeting with all the candidates, including McGovern, intending to broker an agreement that he believed would unify the party. By this point, there was little chance that Muskie, Humphrey, or any of the other anti-McGovern candidates would receive the nomination; the best the Anyone But McGovern coalition could hope for was the introduction of a new candidate on whom most, including the McGovernites, could agree— Ted Kennedy, perhaps. But McGovern saw no point to meeting. "Of course there can be no compromise on California because the California delegates were elected fairly in accord with the law and the rules of the party," McGovern told the press. When McGovern refused to meet, Muskie told his supporters to vote anti-McGovern all the way.[1]

McGovern stayed away from the Convention Hall that first evening of the convention, opting to watch the proceedings in the comfort of his Doral suite. He nursed a bottle of beer and tuned his television

The 271-member California delegation, the object of much McGovern campaign consternation, celebrates the South Dakotan's nomination. The actress Shirley Mac-Laine is pictured at right. (AP/Wide World Photos)

to Walter Cronkite on CBS. Eleanor took the family to the arena to watch the events live.[2]

The McGovern team's plan was to try to win South Carolina for the women, but to abandon course if it looked as if they could not win outright. McGovern aides Gary Hart and Rick Stearns decided that they would turn the votes of McGovern delegates against the women on the South Carolina Challenge if things were not looking auspicious by the time the twelfth delegation voted. As the roll call progressed that Monday evening and the votes were not lining up for the women, Hart and Stearns resorted to their contingency plan, directing a number of McGovern delegates to vote against the women to keep the tally from falling within the "twilight zone" that would have enabled an ABM coalition appeal of the rules.[3]

In the end, the women fell short, 1,429 to 1,555. And to observers in the press and across the convention floor unable to discern the maneuvering at work, the loss seemed to mean trouble for the

McGovernites on California. But the McGovern campaign leadership upheld the charade to keep its troops in check, fearful that admitting to having sacrificed the women's cause on South Carolina would prompt retribution from the women on the vote that mattered most, California.[4]

"There must be more male chauvinists in some of those delegations than we realized," McGovern's political director Frank Mankiewicz speculated to the press after the South Carolina vote.[5]

Elsewhere on the convention floor, CBS's Mike Wallace found Gary Hart.

"Mr. Hart, isn't this a serious defeat for the McGovern forces?" he asked.[6]

Despite Hart's assurance that it was not, Wallace and Cronkite both concluded on the broadcast that Hart seemed concerned. They told viewers that the nomination was no longer so clearly McGovern's for the taking.[7]

Back at the Doral, where McGovern press secretary Dick Dougherty and other staffers were watching the proceedings with a crew of reporters, the Cronkite and Wallace analysis inspired amusement among the McGovern aides in the know. CBS's David Schoumacher was standing by, and the newscast cut to him for reaction from the Doral.

"I don't want to argue with you, Walter," Schoumacher began, with a smirk on his face, "But why are these people cheering?" Schoumacher explained how the McGovern campaign, by intentionally losing on South Carolina, had avoided the possibility that the rules would change through appeal. Chauvinistic or not, proportional representation for women on a relatively insignificant delegation was not the most important issue. A McGovern victory was.[8]

As Stearns predicted, when it came time to vote on California, the convention decided that McGovern should prevail, defeating the challenge 1,689.52 to 1,162.23.[9]

"That was the crucial vote. That wraps it up!" Eleanor McGovern affirmed for the family members and reporters joining her in her VIP box that evening.[10]

The whole McGovern team could breathe again as its supposedly motley crew of amateurs and idealists proved their mettle and showcased their wit once more, overcoming the last significant hurdle in the long quest for the nomination.

McGovern told reporters that he was "gratified but not surprised that the rule of law and the rule of fairness [had] been upheld."[11]

During the proceedings that same evening, Eagleton ran into two McGovern associates off the convention floor: Richard Hemenway of the Committee for an Effective Congress and Richard Wade, the well-connected CUNY professor who doubled as McGovern's New York campaign manager. Hemenway inquired about Eagleton's interest in the vice presidency. "I'd love it," Eagleton confessed. "At age forty-two, for an unknown senator from Missouri, it would be a great, great honor."

Though his team ruled against lobbying for his selection, Eagleton could not resist divulging his feelings. Like Hemenway, Wade shared his support, telling Eagleton that he held a spot on McGovern's list. Though rumors of alcoholism had followed Eagleton throughout his career, the McGovern associates admired the Missouri senator for what they saw: an outgoing and hardworking senator, liberal and moderate in all the right ways. They had no idea he had suffered from bouts of depression in his early career.[12]

The next morning, Tuesday, July 11, Barbara Eagleton interrupted her husband's morning shave: "How seriously do you think you are being considered for the vice presidential thing?"

"Rather seriously, I think," Tom replied.

"If you get it, won't your health history come out?"

"In all probability."

Eagleton believed that enduring his 1968 Senate campaign and his first few years in Washington without relapse had proven that he had put his history of depression behind him; it was a nonissue, he thought. Eagleton imagined that any concern, if raised in a campaign, would quickly subside as he continued to prove his fight.[13]

With speculation about Eagelton's selection intensifying, Ed Filippine, one of Eagleton's top aides, proposed to Doug Bennet, the senator's administrative assistant, that they assign someone to man the telephone in Eagleton's suite at all times: they would not want to miss the important call if and when it came. They drew up a rotation of work shifts and ensured that a staffer was always on standby.[14]

Over at the Carillon Hotel that morning, workers dismantled the sign hanging from the marquee that announced, "Welcome Home Future President Humphrey." Inside, in the Eldorado Room packed with aides, supporters, and reporters, the three-time presidential candidate and former vice president assumed the podium. Humphrey's wife, Muriel, stood by his side. One reporter noted that though Humphrey's chin trembled, he held his head high. "We bow out now with spirit of friendship, of understanding, as a good Democrat, but hopefully, as good citizens, and a good family," Humphrey said. His volunteers applauded, and some even shed tears. "My withdrawal from the presidential race is a withdrawal of candidacy only," Humphrey continued. "It is not a withdrawal of spirit or of determination to continue the battle that I've waged all my life for equal opportunity for all of our people and for social justice for this nation."[15]

The scene was similar at the Americana Hotel down Collins Avenue, where Muskie told his crowd, "In George McGovern's candidacy is an opportunity for the party to give a lasting place to the optimism, energy, and dedication of the youthful minority and the women who are our country's hope for the future. I will do everything I can to assure the success of his candidacy. . . . I congratulate him on an impressive victory against enormous odds, a victory accomplished with skill, persistence, dedication, and plain, hard work." Muskie's speech evoked the qualities that had made him the Democratic front-runner after his election-eve telecast in 1970. It remained to be seen whether party unity would ensue from the withdrawals of McGovern's rivals.[16]

The resurrection of party unity was on Scott Lilly's mind that afternoon. A former staffer of Senator Eagleton's and the current central states coordinator for McGovern, the balding thirty-something-year-old Lilly was already looking toward November, considering it crucial that McGovern visit with the establishment-oriented Missouri delegation in a display of good faith and an attempt at reconciliation for the fall. Lilly called Filippine of Eagleton's staff and urged him to persuade Eagleton to give McGovern a call, even though Missouri Governor Warren Hearnes was the only one with the authority to extend an invitation to visit with the delegation. Both Filippine and Eagleton feared that, given the escalating rumors of Eagleton's contention for the vice presidential nomination, such a call would seem like a clumsily contrived excuse to speak with the candidate. Undeterred, Lilly proposed that Eagleton call Mankiewicz instead, and Eagleton agreed. The senator touched base with the McGovern political director later that afternoon and stressed the importance of McGovern's conferring with the Missourians. Eagleton and Mankiewicz's conversation did not stray beyond the dynamics of the Missouri delegation and the necessity of McGovern paying it a visit.[17]

That evening, as the delegates hammered out the details of the party platform in the Convention Hall, Eagleton and his wife, Barbara, went to dinner at Tony Sweet's restaurant with close friends from St. Louis. About half an hour into their meal, Fred Dutton entered the restaurant with a group of Time-Life executives. Dutton was one of the few McGovern aides of the candidate's own generation. He wore glasses and bore a middle-aged paunch, and his slicked-back hair revealed a growing bald spot. Though he had drifted in and out of the McGovern organization, by the time of the convention, Dutton was viewed inside and outside the campaign as a dark horse contender for McGovern campaign kingpin—if McGovern were ever to name a solitary, incommutably chief, aide. Dutton boasted not only experience in the Kennedy and Johnson campaigns and administrations but a history with McGovern. He was part of the Kennedy core that reconvened in the South Dakotan's last-minute presidential gambit in 1968, as well as a member of the Reform Commission, where he had acted as primary culprit behind the permission of winner-take-all in California.[18]

Friendly with Dutton from the Washington social circuit, Eagleton visited his table. By coincidence or design, the vice presidential question entered the conversation.

"Tell George I'm available and can draft the quickest acceptance speech in town," Eagleton interjected, addressing Dutton and revealing the same eagerness for nomination he had shown Hemenway and Wade the night before.

"Well, it's good to know someone is interested," Dutton chuckled in response. "You are very much in contention."[19]

At the Convention Hall, Bill Dougherty, a McGovern intimate and the South Dakota lieutenant governor, stopped by the Missouri delegation with another McGovern aide. They wanted to verify that Eagleton was, indeed, Catholic.[20]

As in the sacrifice of South Carolina in the name of California, the McGovern team privileged politics over principles and employed similar maneuvers Tuesday night, encouraging its delegates to reject the most progressive planks on abortion, gay rights, and tax reform when the convention voted on the party's platform. Such compromises not only won their candidate the nomination but also ensured that the party ratified a moderate, politically feasible platform for the general election. "The reason we have to do this is that Nixon wouldn't let us get away with it if we didn't," Pierre Salinger, a McGovern adviser, told the press in attempting to justify the campaign's resort to the "sort of manipulation [that] . . . McGovern [was] supposed to be against." But in breaching the principles that his far-left base expected its candidate to uphold, McGovern disappointed his most doctrinaire—and seemingly most committed—supporters.[21]

Back in June, after McGovern had won the California primary, *New York Times* columnist James Reston mused about why many white workers and suburbanites—the people who were "supposed to be against" McGovern's policies—kept voting for him. McGovern "is a plain, simple character," Reston reasoned. For a nation tired of the "hucksters" and sick of political expediency, he suspected that this counted for something. The McGovern campaign had an innocence about it that voters seemed to find attractive. But the Democratic convention in Miami Beach tarnished this image, as McGovern's campaign took "a sharp turn at high speed" from New Politics to Old. McGovern and his staffers proved "about as amateur as the Dallas Cowboys," Reston wrote, revealing themselves to be calculating operators and schemers like the rest. William Greider of the *Washington Post* wrote that the McGovern team proved itself just as capable of wheeling and dealing as "any old pol chomping on his fat cigar."[22]

Tuesday night's cacophonous proceedings finally adjourned early Wednesday, at 6:20 A.M.[23]

George McGovern spent Wednesday, July 12, at the Doral, reviewing draft language proposed by friends and family for his acceptance speech. After a quick lunch, he continued to toil with the speech in his customary blue felt-tipped pen on a yellow legal pad without breaking until a dinner of stew and broccoli.[24]

Downstairs, protesters had been congregating in the opulent Doral lobby since about 2 P.M., rerouting pedestrian traffic in the bustling hotel. The activists ranged in age from late teens through late twenties, and most had long, shaggy hair. They belonged to the Students for a Democratic Society (SDS) and/or the Southern Christian Leadership Conference. Some were Yippies, as members of the countercultural, antiwar Youth International Party were known. Others were Zippies, the term for members of a similar group. Vietcong flags and antiwar banners dotted the crowd.

Most of the protesters had come to challenge McGovern's statement that even after the withdrawal from Vietnam, he would leave residual troops in Thailand and the Gulf of Tonkin as a means of pressing for the return of all American prisoners of war. They were joined by some gay activists calling for "justice," as well as by a contingent of blacks from the Welfare Rights Organization. About forty highway patrolmen with antiriot gear wanted to break up the mounting discord, but—with the hotel management's approval—the McGovern campaign told the police to back off, fearing a reprisal of Chicago 1968. "We Want McGovern," chanted the crowd, demanding that the candidate address them. By 6 P.M., the protest had swelled to about two hundred people, and the activists had jammed the elevator landing, forcing the Doral management to halt service.

At approximately 7:15 P.M., Mankiewicz came down from the penthouse to meet the protesters disillusioned by a candidate adapting to the mainstream. "I guess you know that there are some people in this hotel who would like to have you removed by any means," Mankiewicz told the crowd. "The people who represent Senator McGovern have been successful so far in preventing some other kind of action to get you out of here."

After a heated exchange of barbs, Marty Riefe, a Harvard woman and the SDS's Boston-area coordinator who had become the presumptive leader of the sit-in, exacted a compromise from Mankiewicz: the crowd would disperse if and only if McGovern came downstairs to witness the gathering and address their concerns in person, for all to hear.

McGovern eventually persuaded the Secret Service to let him follow through on the deal and demonstrate his commitment to openness. Already on high alert following the arrest of two blacks for weapons possession near the hotel, the Secret Service swept and cleared the second floor, and fourteen agents accompanied the candidate as he descended from the mezzanine staircase at about a quarter past 8. "Do you realize that most people here are for you?" one of the activists shouted as McGovern arrived, continuing, "We love you, but you are losing your credibility."

As the crowd settled, McGovern began to speak. "I don't have the slightest doubt [that] within ninety days of my inauguration every American troop and every American soldier will be home, and that is the pledge I make," McGovern affirmed, emphasizing his fervent commitment to leaving Vietnam. But he refused to swear off the idea that American forces could remain in the region beyond their withdrawal from Vietnam proper.

Yet the war was not the only issue animating the crowd that afternoon. Riefe quizzed McGovern on his unwillingness to sign the SDS's antiracism bill, which included a provision that would ensure life in prison for any cop who killed a black person or a member of another minority group. "Why leave out 'American'?" McGovern inquired, refusing to budge and inviting boos in the process. "I don't like the way it's stated in this bill." McGovern's stance certainly did not make McGovern a racist, yet many in the audience saw the race issue, like the war issue, in binary terms.

"I did come down because I want to manifest the possibility of communication between us," McGovern told the crowd. "Let's have an understanding. While we do disagree on some of these questions, there isn't any disagreement at all about the desperate need to improve communications in the country. We have made progress in this convention. . . . It is a more open convention, a more open party than four years ago, and if I become president of the United States . . . it will be a more open and more decent country, and I'm asking your help."

By 9:15 P.M., the protesters had disbanded, keeping their end of the compromise. McGovern's performance was pacifying, even inspiring, but the event showcased a dynamic bound to imperil the campaign in the days and months to come. When McGovern swayed from the liberal orthodoxy, he rendered himself a traitor in the eyes of many of those who had helped him capture the nomination. Furthermore, intraparty discord provoked by this perceptibly radical fringe promised to further estrange the establishment electorate, alienated by the corps of self-righteous misfits and miscreants who appeared to define the McGovern Army.

"All I can say is that we survived," McGovern told his aides as he headed back to the penthouse.[25]

That evening, Wednesday, Eleanor McGovern left George behind and headed to the Convention Hall with her five children and an assortment of extended family members. As she observed the proceedings from a box about fifty feet from the podium, she wore a long white dress and a silver bracelet designed as a symbol of her solidarity with American POWs.[26]

Back at the Doral, McGovern swapped his sport shirt and slacks for a blue seersucker suit, powder blue shirt, and dark tie, before settling in for interviews for the wall-to-wall network television coverage of the convention. Relatives, staffers, reporters, the actor Warren Beatty, and Teddy White—that icon of behind-the-scenes presidential campaign reportage—later joined McGovern to watch the broadcast in the penthouse living room. A stuffed donkey wearing a festive red hat also kept McGovern company on the sofa as the candidate's attention dipped in and out of the litany of nominating speeches, capped off by one from McGovern's close friend Senator Abraham Ribicoff of Connecticut. Ribicoff hailed McGovern as "the man for America's future" and predicted a win. He believed that McGovern had not merely read the polls but understood the nation, matching his candidacy to the country's mood.[27]

As the voting of this perpetually tardy and poorly choreographed convention finally got under way at 11:19 P.M., McGovern ditched his jacket and tie. As McGovern's tally inched toward the 1,509 votes needed for the nomination, Eleanor kept count in her notebook. When votes went to rivals like Scoop Jackson, who had refused to step aside, McGovern sneered. As the South Dakota delegation cast all its votes on his behalf, he smiled. And when former Nebraska governor Frank Morrison announced, "There's a new glow around Mount Rushmore," he let out a chuckle.[28]

"Illinois is going to put us over," aide Yancey Martin forecasted for the group in the Doral penthouse.[29]

"Come on, come on!" Eleanor whispered in the convention box as her husband homed in on victory.[30]

Illinois passed in the first round but decided to hand its 119 votes to McGovern the second time around, assuring him victory. Eleanor hugged and kissed her kids—"It's unbelievable," she gasped as she clutched one of her daughters. Reporters and cameramen descended, seeking comment from the potential first fady.[31]

Chants of "We want George" shook the arena, this time in celebration of the man, not in demand that he respond to their complaints.[32]

Back at the Doral, McGovern rose to embrace his aides and family members who had stayed behind, thanking them for their hard work in bringing about this moment. He exuded "satisfaction rather than elation," noted Lawrence Taylor of the *St. Louis Post-Dispatch*, "accomplishment rather than victory."[33]

Eleanor was less discreetly exuberant than her husband. "I thought I would know what it would feel like," she told a reporter afterward. "But I didn't expect to feel overwhelmed." As the voting climbed even higher, from 1,603.10 after Illinois, and eventually to

1,715.35 delegates for McGovern as additional delegations readjusted their votes, Eleanor rose to wave in gratitude to the crowd, which was now bellowing, "We want Eleanor." She later wondered whether her actions smacked of impropriety, but her aides assured her that the situation invited her reaction.[34]

When Eleanor returned home to the Doral from a long evening at the Convention Hall, McGovern said, "I saw you on television a lot tonight," savoring his wife's moment in the national spotlight. He was finally the Democratic presidential nominee, and it was at long last reasonable to picture him residing at 1600 Pennsylvania Avenue. As his children and their friends scurried about the Doral hallways in jeans and T-shirts, an aunt warned McGovern's seventeen-year-old daughter Mary, "You can't dress like that in the White House." "Oh, yes I can. Just wait and see," she retorted. For she knew better than most that conventional wisdom rarely applied in McGovernland.[35]

The Pipedream

As George McGovern saw it, to concentrate on selecting a vice presidential nominee before stamping out the California Challenge would have been, at best, imprudent and, at worst, arrogant—"like talking about a no-hitter in the fifth inning," as Mankiewicz later remarked. McGovern needed to secure the nomination if he ever wanted the privilege of selecting a running mate. The vice presidency had also been an afterthought at the Constitutional Convention of 1787. The framers never intended to include the role. Rather, the job arose as a solution to a problem, and not the conundrum most would guess inspired its creation. While the framers certainly grappled with how to replace the president in case of his incapacitation, there were other ready solutions to this predicament. As was suggested in an early draft from the Convention's Committee of Detail, the Senate's presiding officer could fill in as acting president until an ad hoc election determined a successor. Or the chief justice or a council of state could assume executive duties as "provisional" successor, as others later proposed. Thus, as the presidential historian Arthur Schlesinger Jr. has asserted, the framers must have established the vice presidency for other reasons.[1]

On August 6, 1787, a new drafting commission separate from the Committee of Detail created the vice presidency at a weekend meeting, just two weeks before the Constitutional Convention was to adjourn. The vice presidency "was not wanted," recounted Hugh Williamson, a delegate and new drafting committee member from North Carolina. Rather, as fierce sectionalism divided the young republic, Williamson's group resigned itself to creating the post as a way of ensuring that the citizenry elect as president a national figure of superior qualities. The new drafting commission sought to prevent the nation from choosing a man who simply responded to local issues, attitudes, and agendas, widely divergent across the new and fragile union. The framers determined that, in presidential elections, each elector should cast two votes of equal weight. The man with the highest count would win the presidency, and the next-best finisher would assume the second spot, the vice presidency. This double-vote system would stop an elector from simply voting for his local candidate and then throwing away his second vote to a seemingly unappealing, long-shot candidate to avoid giving votes to a rival. For who could guarantee that other electors would not try the same trick? If so, they risked inadvertently electing a miserable candidate who everyone always presumed would lose. Because anyone could win under this double-vote system, electors would thus be compelled to vote for the most attractive national leader. As such, Williamson called the vice presidency a "valuable mode of election," facilitating the selection of a national president of Union-wide appeal and extraordinary skill. This system required "other talents" for election. As Alexander Hamilton explained it, "a different kind of merit" was needed to win "the esteem and confidence of the whole union."[2]

While aiding the election of a national president may have been the principal reason for creating the vice presidency, it was not its only purpose. The Constitutional Convention spent more time envisioning the vice president as the Senate's presiding officer, tasked with protecting the votes of each senator. Though a nonvoting member of the Senate, the vice president would also be available to cast the deciding vote in case of gridlock. Only at the last minute did the convention determine that the vice president would succeed the president in case of the chief executive's death, impeachment conviction, or another factor that removed him from office. But it is this role of presidential replacement that has come to define the vice presidency. As Woodrow Wilson put it, the vice president's "importance consists in the fact that he may cease to be vice president."[3]

If the vice president contributes little to the functioning of government until circumstances demand he must step in as president, the office exerts considerable influence in the selection of the president, but no longer as that "valuable mode of election" in the way that Williamson originally imagined. In the 1800 election, the double-vote system led every Republican elector to vote for both Thomas Jefferson and Aaron Burr, causing each man to receive the same number of votes and thus entitling no one to the presidency because no man had the "greatest number of votes" required by the Constitution. Fear of this scenario's recurrence and the development of vote-swapping schemes led to the adoption of the Twelfth Amendment, which mandates separate voting for the presidency and vice presidency.

Senator Samuel White of Delaware anticipated the ramifications of this adjustment: "Character, talents, virtue, and merit will not be sought after, in the [vice presidential] candidate. The question will not be asked, is he capable? is he honest? But can he by his name, by his connections, by his wealth, by his local situation, by his influence, or his intrigues, best promote the election of a president?" As Senator White suspected, the Twelfth Amendment gave the vice presidency additional electoral purpose and often saddled the vice presidential decision with superficial, political calculations. Capability rarely figured into the forefront of a presidential candidate's evaluation of potential running mates. How well one could balance the ticket became the essential criterion as presidential candidates now strove to create duos that could compete on the national stage.[4]

Just as McGovern needed to concentrate on squelching the California Challenge if he wanted any chance of selecting a vice presidential running mate, he needed to choose a partner most likely to increase his chances of winning in the November election if he wanted any chance of actually being president, especially given his underdog status. Polling indicated that only Senator Ted Kennedy would boost the Democratic ticket. Kennedy had what McGovern lacked: an appeal that transcended policy, a charisma and vision that inspired voters across the ideological spectrum, as well as a last name with immense political cachet. A liberal Catholic popular with labor, Kennedy epitomized party unity. Thus McGovern fixated on persuading him to join the ticket—regardless of the moral quagmire of Chappaquiddick. His campaign ignored any concerns about Kennedy's character or ability to maintain his composure under stress. "The only question on the staff about Teddy was how many fingers they'd be willing to lose to have him," Frank Mankiewicz later recalled.[5]

As all the squabbling over the California Challenge illustrated, contention saturated the Democratic Party and distrust abounded. The line between the New Politics and the Old, between the recently enfranchised and the politically entrenched, would be hard to overcome. In redirecting its focus on generating partywide enthusiasm for the ticket, the McGovern campaign knew it needed to convince the white, ethnic, labor establishment that the candidate cared for and could respond to its concerns. If McGovern had any chance of winning, he needed the party's engine to drive him to the White House. As the authors of the influential book *The Real Majority*, Richard M. Scammon and Ben Wattenberg, described the Democratic predicament, "You can knock the 'liberal intellectuals' out of the Democratic coalition, and you've lost a front bumper; knock out the black vote, and you've lost the fenders and the back seat; but knock out labor, Middle America, or the unyoung, unpoor, unblack, and you've lost the engine and the car won't run." As the McGovern team saw it, Kennedy was akin to the gas—the juice to keep the Democratic ticket hurtling toward November. Pollsters found that support for him ran across the unions through the South, with traction among the young, old, white, and black alike. An internal campaign memo noted the results of a Harris poll: McGovern lagged 20 percentage points behind Nixon without Kennedy (55 percent to 35 percent), but with him on the ticket, was down by only seven (50–43).

Even more auspicious, the hypothetical McGovern-Kennedy ticket already led 54 percent to 40 percent in the West, a region considered a harbinger of the eventual direction of the nation at large. McGovern pollster Pat Caddell's own research found the race even closer with Kennedy in the mix: 52 percent to 38 percent without, but 47 percent to 43 percent with him.[6]

Right before the convention, McGovern's fifty-year-old press secretary, Dick Dougherty, composed a memo of talking points intended to help McGovern lure Kennedy to take a leap of faith and join the campaign, just as Dougherty himself had done. Dougherty quit his job as the *Los Angeles Times'* New York bureau chief back in November 1971, out of a midlife yearning for an "adventure." He had outsized ears for his narrow face and slight frame. He also wore thick, circular glasses. In past lives Dougherty had been deputy New York City police department commissioner and was also the author of four mildly received novels and one critically unacclaimed play. But as McGovern floundered in the polls, Dougherty's arrival, like Mankiewicz's, added heft and exposure to the campaign. As a long-time newspaperman for both the *New York Herald Tribune* and the *Los Angeles Times,* Dougherty leveraged his contacts in New York media circles to generate press for McGovern. Originally from small-town upstate New York, Dougherty saw in McGovern, "a climber of my own breed." But by the end of January 1972, he had had enough and quit full-time media consulting and press work for the campaign, drained from the "punishing schedule of trips" and frustrated by his lack of sway with the candidate. Though Dougherty found the campaign to be littered with jealousies and power-grabs, he remained a part-time adviser and eventually returned full-time in May. He sensed that the inadequacy of Kirby Jones, whom McGovern was using as press secretary, had grown more dire, and a contract to write a campaign memoir gave Dougherty extra motivation to stick with the campaign.[7]

In his talking-points memo on the vice presidency, Dougherty wrote, "A McGovern-Kennedy ticket starts out in a good position not only to seize the underdog role, but close enough to move on to victory with a vigorous campaign against Nixon," and he described a Kennedy vice presidential candidacy as "an exciting and practical opportunity to pull off one of the all-time great victories." With so much on the line, the McGovern team backed up its plea for Kennedy to join its crusade with a litany of arguments, some compelling, others desperate.

Dougherty's memo emphasized the significance of the 1972 election, arguing that a spot on the national ticket would offer Kennedy the opportunity to shape the direction of the Democratic Party and, by extension, the two-party system. The Twenty-Sixth Amendment had lowered the voting age to eighteen, adding an influx of twenty-five million first-time voters in time for the 1972 election, another sixteen million over the next four years, and an additional eighteen million in the election cycle after that. "The cumulative effect of sixty million is massive, and the patterns are being set this year," Dougherty asserted, underscoring Kennedy's potential for impact. Though McGovern had shuddered at the prospect of being vice president when he received word Humphrey was considering him at the 1968 convention, these talking points suggest that he intended to reenvision the vice presidency as a more influential post if Kennedy were in the second spot.[8]

Obsessed with getting Kennedy on board, McGovern deluded himself into thinking a Kennedy vice presidency was possible when, in reality, to borrow Hunter S. Thompson's analogy, it was like the New York Jets trading Joe Namath to the Dallas Cowboys, where he would back up Roger Staubach. McGovern persuaded himself that Kennedy would value the opportunity to serve in national office while "cooling off" from Chappaquiddick, that Kennedy would not face the same threat of assassination in the number two spot as he would as a presidential candidate (a fear Kennedy had repeatedly expressed), and that the party's urgency in Miami would touch upon Kennedy's sense of duty and inspire him to accept the nomination midconvention. "I thought that once I had that nomination I'd be able to persuade anybody to do anything," McGovern recalled. In other words, McGovern's tendency toward solipsism got the better of him; he thought his own presidential ambitions should and would outweigh Kennedy's fears for his security and obligation to his family as the last surviving Kennedy brother. Publicly, however, McGovern reinforced his empathetic image, telling the press, "I would never sandbag Ted into a position where he felt strained to take [the nomination]." He deemed it "unfair" to put the vice presidential choice to a vote at the convention because doing so would have effectively meant drafting Kennedy against his will.[9]

But wishful thinking and arrogance alone cannot explain the McGovern campaign's lack of planning for the vice presidential choice. Rather, the running-mate selection process also exposed flaws in the dynamics between candidate and staff that the campaign could withstand through the primary and caucus season, but that would ensure failure in a national campaign. A week and a half before the convention, at a July 1 meeting at his Washington residence, George McGovern told Gary Hart that he had had a frank conversation with Kennedy, who rejected the vice presidency in what he interpreted as "final terms." Hart responded by naming ten to twelve alternatives, and McGovern shared six or seven options of his own that he had scribbled on the back of an envelope. At Eleanor's recommendation, Leonard Woodcock, the United Automobile Workers union president, led McGovern's list. This choice seemed an unabashed overture to labor, particularly in view of Woodcock's lack of experience in public office and on the campaign trail, criteria McGovern had previously said were vital to the job. McGovern granted Woodcock an exception because he had demonstrated comparable executive skills as UAW leader. Yet, following their meeting, Hart did not vet the candidates or whittle the list. For one, he had the California Challenge to worry about. He also believed that McGovern considered his choice of running mate personal. Though McGovern surveyed his family members and Senate confidants on the vice presidential options, he seldom sought advice from his staff and refused to delegate responsibility for narrowing the options. As had become his custom when he sensed McGovern "brooding," Hart deferred to his boss's judgment and awaited his pleasure. A "cushion of reserve" had always existed between the senator and his aides, as McGovern's executive assistant Gordon Weil described the dynamic. Whether symptomatic of McGovern's personality, his employees, or both, the campaign's intrastaff communication typically stagnated on questions the candidate considered personal—which, it turns out, were also the campaign's most consequential.[10]

Though he presented himself as hands-off, McGovern divined himself his own campaign manager, often trusting his judgment and experience at the expense of the supposed experts on key decisions. Careful not to repeat the mistakes of 1968, when he had let advisers talk him out of an early presidential bid, this time McGovern seemed to abide by a "God helps those who help themselves" mentality. However, good fortune more than McGovern's own prowess had made this a viable mode of operation through the primaries, and the campaign's top aides doubted the sustainability of McGovern's style of brinksmanship. Their anxiety increased as the convention neared, and the candidate's aloofness intensified as the stakes magnified.[11]

In the midst of the primaries, as the campaign's performance was upending all expectations, Rick Stearns wondered whether McGovern's detached leadership style had avoided scrutiny only because the campaign was achieving its objectives. Under different circumstances, what the press was interpreting as "true serenity and confidence" could have been otherwise critiqued as McGovern's debilitating reluctance to make decisions and haphazard inattention to the campaign's power structure. The McGovern system—if it could be called that—worked through the convention because the team had a clearly defined plan to guide it. McGovern trusted Hart and Stearns's vision for winning the nomination, and the rest flowed from there: Hart managing the organization, and Mankiewicz overseeing its political strategy. With the nominating phase of the mission complete and the campaign lacking a similar road map for the general election, the McGovern dynamic crumbled under the weight of increasingly expansive challenges, colossal pressures, and profound fatigue.[12]

Fred Dutton, the longtime Kennedy adviser and McGovern aide, took a leave from the campaign to get married. When he returned, he found an organization in disarray. Outlining the chaos in a May 30 memo to McGovern, Dutton attributed the campaign's early success to "having shrewdly sensed the public mood and some strong new currents moving." But he warned that coasting could suffice only for so long. The organizational infrastructure and intracampaign communication needed to be raised to presidential caliber. While grassroots organization had galvanized turnout and imbued McGovern with the image of the people's candidate, Dutton believed a national campaign required McGovern to sharpen his tactics. "I have suspected you like the looseness because you keep more control that way," Dutton wrote to McGovern. "But I question whether it best serves you as the operation keeps getting larger and the undertaking more complex."

Dutton warned that McGovern's campaign lacked the finesse of the 1960, 1964, and 1968 Democratic presidential nominees' campaigns and urged the South Dakotan to "clarify the decision-recommending channels to [him], define responsibility more clearly, and begin to make some hard personal decisions about who is really performing at a presidential level." Dutton asked the man averse to firing employees to trim a staff he considered rife with too many "second raters." And, as the convention neared, he said the situation seemed more calamitous.[13]

Another memo from Dutton similarly questioned the sustainability of McGovern's leadership style. "No one except the few who have run for president successfully, and the Caesars of history, have really coped with the scope and subtlety of problems crowding in on you," Dutton explained. "Are you, or those immediately around you, minimizing or maximizing the useful input to you?" he asked, raising particular concern about Kirby Jones, McGovern's inexperienced, though fiercely loyal, press secretary, whom Dutton deemed "the most incompetent any presidential candidate ever had."[14]

"Your executive ability is crucial to the presidency, and it should surely serve your own self-interest if it is going to be up to that challenge later," Dutton explained. "If you feel you cannot make a change for the autumn, how can you when you get through the campaign and go to the White House?" Maybe McGovern was, after all, too nice—or rather too soft, too irresolute—for the presidency. "Making hard, little decisions like this will become more, not less difficult," Dutton continued. "Yet they still go to the essence of the quality of leadership

and the effectiveness of your campaign and potential presidency."
In retrospect, this memo, which was built on experience and packed
with insight, proved uncannily accurate, anticipating dynamics that
would handicap the campaign as it arrived on the national stage.[15]

McGovern eventually heeded the pleas and replaced Kirby
Jones with Dick Dougherty, who would later propose an explanation for McGovern's unflinching self-reliance: "Perhaps . . . there
was a measure of self-hate hidden behind [McGovern's] quiet but
towering vanity, a never-spoken judgment that if a man would work
for George McGovern he couldn't amount to much." In other words,
why should McGovern value aides foolish enough to join his campaign, a candidacy almost everyone else considered doomed and
unworthy of their time? While plausible, Dougherty's assessment
refuses to acknowledge that McGovern must have realized that his
advisers had devised the winning template for a long-shot candidate, outmaneuvering the competition at every stage of the game
up until that point. Perhaps, if McGovern was really as narcissistic
as Dougherty supposed, he never conceded credit for the strategic
vision that brought him this far, imagining it the product of his own
design as the campaign's true manager. Still, if history was correct,
McGovern had reason to revise his relationship with his staff. Despite the exceptionality of this campaign, so defiant of expectation
and teeming with an aura of impossibility, as Dutton warned in his
memo, "No major presidential candidate in modern history has successfully pulled off being both the jockey and the horse—both the
candidate and the man who is also really running the campaign."[16]

Ted Kennedy did not begin the week in Miami Beach, sending his
wife, Joan, and two aides from his Washington office in his place.
On Tuesday, July 11, as Muskie and Humphrey offered McGovern
their concessions, Kennedy spent the morning reviewing files he had
brought up to his family's compound in Hyannisport, Massachusetts,
then spent the afternoon at sea. Rather than commandeering the
Democratic Party as its consensus favorite, Kennedy captained his
brand new fifty-four-foot sailboat, with his sister Eunice Shriver,
his sister-in-law Ethel Kennedy, and seventeen Kennedy children

on board. The press was reporting that all this could change, as Kennedy aides hinted he could arrive to make a last-ditch pitch for party unity. Kennedy did not believe all was lost for the Democrats, expressing optimism that the party could repair itself before November. "We have had trials and tribulations over the last few weeks," he acknowledged in comments picked up by the Associated Press, "but I remember in 1960—we had them then and they were bitter ones—but we got over them," recalling the year his older brother, John F. Kennedy, won the presidency.[17]

Even if Kennedy was guaranteed to reject his offer, the hope remained that asking him could win McGovern previously unconvinced Kennedy supporters, who would appreciate that their man had gotten the call. McGovern had little to lose, other than time, pride, and the stature of a spot on his ticket: time spent obsessing over Kennedy could have been redirected toward investigating more viable vice presidential options, and with each rejection, McGovern dimmed the possibility that a first-tier pick would join the ticket. No one likes being backup, especially not a politician. As time ran out, McGovern dispatched an aide to Hyannisport to appeal to Kennedy—but to no avail.[18]

The history of the vice presidency is riddled with ambivalence, doubt, and most often frustration at the elusiveness of power. As America's first vice president, John Adams, lamented, "My country has in its wisdom contrived for me the most insignificant office that ever the invention of man contrived or his imagination conceived." He added, "I can do neither good nor evil," expressing his feeling of powerlessness, even claustrophobia, as he dwelled in the limbo of the vice presidency when, really, he strove to exercise influence. "My office is too great a restraint upon such a Son of Liberty," Adams wrote in a letter to his wife, Abigail. Thomas Jefferson, the nation's second vice president, said of the role, "[It's] the only office in the world about which I am unable to decide in my own mind whether I had rather have it or not have it," capturing the confusion attendant in the job as it strips political leaders of the legislative or executive power they once possessed, condemning them to a position ostensibly second in power but in reality one constitutionally deprived of much responsibility. Theodore Roosevelt similarly complained that the vice presidency "is not a steppingstone to anything except oblivion." Yet when President William McKinley Jr. was assassinated, for Roosevelt, the vice presidency became a steppingstone to the presidency. Dwight Eisenhower likened the vice presidency to "a kind of coffin," and when asked to name an accomplishment of his own vice president, Richard Nixon, he asked for a week to think about it. Lyndon Johnson said the vice presidency felt like "being naked in the middle of a blizzard with no one to even offer a match to keep you warm. . . . You are trapped, vulnerable, and alone, and it does not matter who happens to be president."[19]

The Constitution prescribed that the vice president "shall be president of the Senate, but shall have no vote, unless they be equally divided." As such, vice presidents long considered themselves members of the legislative branch. Jefferson set the precedent of strict adherence to the doctrine of separation of powers and, for many years, vice presidents resisted encroaching on executive duty because the Constitution also mandates that executive power rests solely in the president. When Woodrow Wilson asked his vice president Thomas Marshall to lead his cabinet sessions while Wilson was away at Versailles, Marshall did so reluctantly, telling cabinet members that he was acting only "in obedience to a request" and "in an unofficial and informal way." Calvin Coolidge was the first vice president to be a regular presence at cabinet meetings, and it was not until Lyndon Johnson served under Kennedy that the vice president received space and staff of his own in the Executive Office Building. Since 1953, which Joel Goldstein, a leading scholar on the vice presidency, identifies as the start of the office's modern era, the post has been more closely aligned with the executive branch, as the presidency itself has expanded in importance. As Goldstein explains, the modern vice president typically chairs various executive-office committees, substitutes for the president as "surrogate head of state" on official visits abroad, and acts as chief spokesman for the administration and as its liaison to Congress. The vice president also now holds a seat on the National Security Council.[20]

But the vice president's status as heir to the president in case of his death or removal has historically infused the relationship between president and vice president with awkwardness and distrust. "The only business of the vice president is to ring the White House bell every morning and ask what is the state of the health of the president," Vice President Thomas Marshall said of the job. Lyndon Johnson echoed Marshall's perspective: "The vice president is like a raven, hovering around the head of the president, reminding him of his mortality." The relationship is an alliance in the shadow of suspicion and rivalry, no matter how compatible and productive the two office holders, individually and collectively.[21]

However, as suggested by Dick Dougherty's talking-points memo, McGovern was willing to relinquish some executive duties to a Vice President Ted Kennedy, letting him coordinate the work of the state, defense, and intelligence departments, indicative of McGovern's desperation to convince Kennedy to join him. The memo bordered on the preposterous by proposing that, when representing the United States abroad in place of the president, Kennedy could become the "number one citizen of the world." And when it predicted that the role would enable Kennedy to serve as "a bridge a decade or so hence to bring about a whole new way of relating to this world," the memo clearly descended into hyperbole, while reinforcing the extent to which McGovern wanted him on the ticket.[22]

Yet running for the modern vice presidency did have several advantages that could persuade the right candidate to accept the calling. For one, it thrust its candidates into the national spotlight as one of only two offices elected by nationwide vote. And with the expansion of new media—television and extended newspaper coverage—the vice president remained in the national consciousness throughout his tenure. The vice president's access to the president could also grant him extraordinary influence on all aspects of the chief executive's job, as later demonstrated by Walter Mondale's and Dick Cheney's integral roles in shaping the policies and priorities of their respective administrations. Furthermore, the vice presidency's importance mounted as the mortality of the president became more real. The White House death of FDR, the attempted murder of Truman, the debilitating heart ailments of Eisenhower, and the assassination of JFK all remained fresh in the nation's memory in 1972. Whether or not such thinking had merit, the public and politicians alike reckoned the vice presidency the best possible training for the presidency.

Ratified in 1951, the Twenty-Second Amendment further enhanced the likelihood of the vice president's becoming president. It limited a president's service to two terms, a restriction that granted the vice president the latitude to contend for the Oval Office without being perceived as disloyal as his partner's final term neared its conclusion. From 1952 through 1972, a vast majority of major-party vice presidential candidates who appeared on the ballot emerged as presidential contenders, exploiting the role's national platform, automatic name recognition, and—if actually elected vice president—freedom to roam the nation unimpeded by the significant legislative or executive duties that bridle senators, congressmen, and governors seeking higher office. From 1923 to 1972, only Herbert Hoover, Dwight Eisenhower, and John F. Kennedy became president without first serving as vice president or vice presidential nominee.[23]

On Wednesday evening of convention week, McGovern asked executive assistant Gordon Weil to survey the rest of his inner circle and provide him a list of their top picks for running mate. Bearing closely cropped dark hair and what Dick Dougherty described as a "well and powerfully made" build, the thirty-five-year-old Weil wore conservative suits and steel-rimmed glasses. He also smoked a pipe. By the time he joined McGovern's Senate staff in 1970, the Bowdoin College grad with a Ph.D. from Columbia had already written five books on foreign policy and economics. But Weil was also the visionary behind McGovern's ill-conceived and much-reviled $1,000-per-person welfare plan, and he could strike staffers as "abrasive," in part out of his apparent status insecurity. Other aides joked about the deftness in which Weil would return right to McGovern's side every time he saw the senator chatting with Dutton. Weil thought of himself as the campaign "heavy." Describing his role for *Life* magazine, he explained, "What I do is represent the staff to the senator and the senator to the staff."[24]

Over the course of the evening, Weil collected the vice presidential preferences of thirteen other aides. Of the fourteen lists total, ten staffers named Kennedy their top pick. As Ted Van Dyk wrote on his slip, "Everything should be done to get [Kennedy]. Frankly, I think our chances without EMK [Edward Moore Kennedy] are long; with him, they're at least even." Eagleton's name found its way onto just five of the fourteen slips.[25]

McGovern did not need any convincing about Kennedy. As he discussed his possibilities with Weil and other aides that evening, McGovern reiterated his supposition Kennedy would not be able to resist the opportunity to help the party in the heat of the moment and that Kennedy was sure to recognize the vice presidency's potential to help him move beyond Chappaquiddick. Some staffers, like Weil, presumed that McGovern had some reason to believe Kennedy would accept, and if not, Weil, for instance, imagined McGovern would say, "We ought to go with so-and-so," after being rebuffed by Kennedy, the contingency plan already thought out by McGovern. Others, such as Frank Mankiewicz, "never thought [McGovern] had a chance" of luring Kennedy in the first place.[26]

At around 9:30 P.M., Scott Lilly—the central states coordinator for the McGovern campaign who had previously worked for Eagleton in the Senate—called the Missourian with a tip, but missed him. Eagleton's administrative assistant Doug Bennet heard that Lilly had called before the senator got the message, and after failing to reach Lilly, he headed to the McGovern trailers and found him. The supposed McGovern insider told Bennet the campaign had narrowed its vice presidential options to three men: Senator Abraham Ribicoff of Connecticut, who had just delivered McGovern's nominating speech, UAW president Leonard Woodcock, and Eagleton. Lilly eventually connected with Eagleton himself as the senator was awaiting an interview with ABC in the network's lounge at the Convention Hall, and he shared the information he had just passed on to Bennet. In his television interviews from the convention floor moments later, Eagleton pulsated with excitement over the vice presidential possibility.[27]

At around the same time, sitting in the McGovern campaign

trailers, Mankiewicz and now-deputy press secretary Kirby Jones picked up a rumor making its way through the convention floor alleging that Eagleton had been hospitalized for a mental problem. CBS reporter David Schoumacher remembered it striking the McGovern aides as merely "one more of the nutty things you hear around the convention," but Mankiewicz sent Jones to see what he could find anyway. He roamed the Convention Hall but turned up nothing.[28]

Nearing midnight, soon after the Illinois delegation voted and formally bestowed upon McGovern the party's nomination for the presidency, the phone rang in the Doral penthouse; Humphrey was on the line. "Thank you so much, Hubert," McGovern said. "You're the first to call and there is nobody I'd rather hear from." Just moments later, Ted Kennedy phoned in. McGovern headed to the bedroom, where he chatted with his Massachusetts colleague for about twenty minutes. There, in relative privacy, he asked the brother of John and Bobby—two of McGovern's heroes—if he would join the ticket as his running mate, now that McGovern was officially the party's presidential nominee. Leaning on Dougherty's memo to guide him, McGovern made the case for Kennedy's candidacy. But Kennedy remained intractable. He told McGovern that passing on the vice presidential nomination was one of the hardest decisions of his political career, but that "overriding personal considerations" ultimately ruled.

McGovern asked his staff to reconvene early the next morning to prepare a list of alternatives.[29]

Late Wednesday night into Thursday morning, when the Eagleton crew returned to the Ivanhoe at around 2 A.M., thirty-three-year-old *Time* magazine reporter and Chicago bureau chief Greg Wierzynski sought an interview with Eagleton in the senator's suite. The request signaled to Eagleton's staff that the possibility of their man's nomination "was beyond the rumors stage." Why else would *Time* make the effort?

As the senator, his staffers, and the reporter chatted about the convention and the prospect of the vice presidency over gin and tonics, Wierzynski monitored Eagleton's alcohol intake. He had heard rumors about a possible drinking problem. Nothing about Eagleton's consumption that night concerned him. However, he did note that Eagleton seemed "very hyped up" and that it seemed he "worked on nervous energy."

The gathering in the senator's suite would subside within the hour. Bennet peeled off first, but he soon phoned back to remind the others that it might prove worthwhile to be somewhat well rested for the day to come. Other than hauling along his portable typewriter just in case he had to draft a last-minute acceptance speech, this was as close to preparing for his boss's vice presidential possibility as Bennet had come.[30]

The Selection

agleton slept late the Thursday morning of the convention, July 13. After ordering a room-service breakfast, he called Ed Filippine, his St. Louis assistant and principal political adviser. Already wearing his brightly colored swim trunks, he told Filippine that he planned to spend the day by the pool, hoping to relax as the hectic convention wound down. But Filippine, an approximately six-foot-tall and fair-skinned family man whose association and friendship with Eagleton dated back to the circuit attorney's office, warned otherwise: taking a swim would mean confronting the press corps and the inevitable barrage of questions about the vice presidency. Instead, Eagleton agreed to "hole up" in his suite for the day with his staff, playing gin with Gene Godley and Bob Maynard, a hefty man from Ohio and legislative assistant to the senator. As for Filippine, Eagleton joked that if McGovern ever did call and name him running mate, he would buy Filippine a blazer worthy of a national campaign to replace the raggedy one he presently sported.[1]

Douglas J. Bennet Jr., Eagleton's thirty-four-year-old administrative assistant, was still splitting time between the Eagleton office and the Democratic National Committee, writing scripts for the con-

The running mates, George McGovern and Tom Eagleton, join forces on the rostrum on the final night of the Democratic National Convention in Miami Beach. DNC chairman Larry O'Brien applauds directly behind McGovern. (George Tames/The New York Times/Redux)

vention proceedings. His position resembled today's "chief of staff," and Bennet had been with Eagleton since the Missourian came to Washington in 1969. Raised in quaint, coastal Old Lyme, Connecticut, the round-faced, brown-haired Bennet had initially avoided politics. His dad had spent a few years as Connecticut governor Chester Bowles's executive secretary and entertained political aspirations of his own, which were blighted when he lost his 1956 congressional bid. A sophomore at Wesleyan University in Middletown, Connecticut, at the time, Doug Jr. abstained from pitching in with the campaign. After college, Bennet picked up a master's degree in history at Berkeley, then headed to Harvard to work toward a doctorate in Russian medieval history. About halfway through his studies, Bennet moved to India, where he spent two and a half years—first as an economist for the Agency for Economic Development, then as special assistant to Chester Bowles, when the old family friend was appointed U.S. Ambassador to India. "I didn't feel that either the traditional academics or the radicals were addressing themselves to any sort of public needs," Bennet recalled of the perspective he forged overseas.

Bennet was a pragmatist and a realist. Those who knew him also described him as wickedly smart. He finished his Harvard dissertation in 1967 and wrote to Hubert Humphrey on a whim, landing a job as the vice president's speechwriter before joining the Eagleton team following Humphrey's 1968 loss to Nixon. He fit in with the rest of the Eagleton crew, but was not as raucous or convivial. Of the men in the junior senator's inner circle, Bennet had the most experience in national politics, first with Humphrey, then, during a leave-of-absence from Eagleton's Senate office in the spring of 1972, as traveling speechwriter for Muskie. He had ascended to traveling campaign director as the Mainer's bid teetered on the verge of collapse. "I'm trying to de-crisis the atmosphere," Bennet told the *New York Times* in April, while still with the Muskie campaign.[2]

Tape recorder in hand, Bob Hardy of St. Louis's KMOX Radio also joined the Eagleton crew in room 605 at the Ivanhoe, as the team huddled in anticipation of McGovern's vice presidential announcement. In addition to Scott Lilly, who phoned in to say that Eagleton remained in contention, reporters, friends, and staffers from the Washington office called throughout the day, every ring raising anticipation that perhaps, this time, George McGovern was on the line. But whenever the well-wishers wondered whether the senator had any news to report, the response was always the same: "No word."[3]

Meanwhile, several candidates mounted formal bids for the number-two spot, arguing that, in the spirit of openness McGovern had fostered, he should leave the vice presidential selection to the convention without putting his own pick in the hat. Contrary to the aims of these advocates of open selection, an open pick would have undoubtedly drafted Kennedy. If he refused to accept, the problems for the Democratic ticket would have compounded.

Unfazed, Senator Mike Gravel of Alaska predicted on the contrary that an open selection would imbue the staid vice presidency with a "character of independence" and "restore the greatness to the office that it hasn't had since Aaron Burr messed it up." He promoted his candidacy as the populist option, promising to work on behalf of everyday Americans. "I'd get out and drive a garbage truck for a day to show how important such work is," Gravel vowed, before adding, "A freely selected vice president could add a little bit of a check and balance to the president," reaching for power beyond the scope of the vice presidency's constitutionally conscribed possibilities and setting up the groundwork for a contentious relationship between the president and his lieutenant.[4]

The former Massachusetts governor Endicott Peabody described himself as "the number one man for the number two job" on his bumper stickers. And his campaign literature depicted him on the steps of the Jefferson Memorial in Washington, DC, suggesting a bond between Peabody—"the first in modern times to run"—and Jefferson—"one of the last to run and become vice president." The pamphlet glossed over the fact that Jefferson had actually aimed for the presidency but ended up as number two only because the rules at that time made the vice presidency a consolation prize for the second-highest presidential vote-getter.[5]

As McGovern waited in his Doral penthouse that Thursday morning, starting at around 8:30 A.M., approximately twenty-one of the candidate's top staffers straggled into the first-floor conference room to debate the merits of the various vice presidential possibilities. In their hazy delirium, they struggled to get started, but, eventually, Mankiewicz called the room to order by ringing his glass with his silverware. "We have three hours to choose the deputy commander of the free world," he told the table of aides, hoping to deliver McGovern a shortlist by midday. They began with the twenty-three names mentioned in Weil's survey the evening before. To pare down the options, Gary Hart read them off and asked the aides to speak up if they objected to a particular candidate's removal. The names ranged from traditional politicians like senators Birch Bayh of Indiana, Frank Church of Idaho, and Gaylord Nelson of Wisconsin, Representative Wilbur Mills of Arkansas, and Governor John J. Gilligan of Ohio, to the more creative, such as university presidents Kingman Brewster of

Yale and Reverend Theodore Hesburgh of Notre Dame, and mayors
Moon Landrieu of New Orleans and Kevin White of Boston.[6]

At the end of June, McGovern pollster Pat Caddell had spearheaded a study to gauge the popularity of a variety of vice presidential possibilities and to evaluate national views on the office. As
expected, Kennedy polled way ahead of the field, but Eagleton ran
near the top on the question of home-state appeal, showing impressive favorability in Missouri and southern Illinois, part of another
crucial swing state. Missouri had been on the winning side of all
but one presidential election since 1892. Kennedy aside, Caddell's
research also revealed that voters were looking for "bright new faces,
not old established politicians," as the *St. Louis Post-Dispatch's* Tom
Ottenad summarized the findings.[7]

CBS News anchor Walter Cronkite was Frank Mankiewicz's top
choice that Thursday morning, even though his name had not made
it onto the list he had given Gordon Weil the evening before. Mankiewicz thought it made sense to pair a candidate whose campaign was
predicated on candor with the man whom a poll deemed the most
trusted in America. Cronkite was revered by Americans across the
political spectrum, even by nonpolitical Americans. Furthermore,
as Robert Kennedy's press secretary, Mankiewicz had been present
at an off-the-record meeting more than four years earlier at which
Cronkite urged the New York senator to jump into the 1968 race for
the presidency, voicing his own inveterate opposition to the Vietnam
War. The McGovern aides around the conference table balked at
Mankiewicz's suggestion, doubting that Cronkite would ever accept
the nomination and noting the embarrassment that would follow
when he turned McGovern down. "Goodnight, Walter," Mankiewicz
whispered, as it became clear that the others considered Cronkite
to be untenable. Yet when McGovern recounted the situation for
Cronkite years later, the newsman said, "I'd have accepted in a minute. Anything to help end that dreadful war."[8]

Weil proposed another creative option not listed the evening
before: Mark Hatfield, Republican senator from Oregon and co-
sponsor of the McGovern-Hatfield Amendment to end the Vietnam
War. With the McGovern campaign pigeonholed at the far left, Weil

thought the campaign "had to do something revolutionary" to make
the McGovern ticket competitive. He found Hatfield a decent man,
a proponent of progressive legislation, and a serious evangelical.
He was Republican in name only, Weil thought. But he was still a
Republican, and the other aides in the room that morning quickly
squelched the concept of a bipartisan ticket.[9]

Gary Hart spoke on behalf of Boston mayor Kevin White. White
was an urban Catholic from a different region than McGovern and
a strong campaigner, as evidenced by his 1967 mayoral victory over
staunch antibusing activist Louise Day Hicks in a city roiled by debates over desegregation. Dick Dougherty, who had covered White
while working for the *Los Angeles Times,* confirmed this impression.
He said White was "personable, young, sensible, with a good record
on the big issues and—in contrast with our man from the prairies
[McGovern]—the mayor of a big city." Mayor White had originally
supported Muskie and, as Gordon Weil's notes of the meeting indicated, he was reputed to be "very attractive personally," "articulate,"
"very moral," a "quick learner," "good with minorities," and a "good
gut liberal." On the other hand, White had lost a campaign for governor in 1970 "because he didn't organize." And as mayor, he was
said to be a "sporadic worker" who "may not make good use of his
time." He also had "a bit of a temper" that had supposedly gotten
him into trouble on various occasions. There was no mention of an
operation White had undergone during his 1970 gubernatorial race
to remove two-thirds of his stomach, in order to treat a perforated
stomach ulcer.[10]

When the aides came to Eagleton's name, Rick Stearns—who
had been vouching for Larry O'Brien—spoke up. He recalled a reporter telling him that if the campaign were to consider Eagleton,
it should be aware of rumors about alcoholism and a family history
of mental illness that surrounded the senator, as Gary Hart remembered Stearns's remarks. Stearns recalled adding that Eagleton himself "supposedly" wrestled with mental illness. Weil remembered
Stearns saying, "Around Missouri, there are strong rumors of alcoholism or mental illness—or both—in his background." Stearns mentioned that he thought the *St. Louis Post-Dispatch*'s Tom Ottenad was

his original source. Other McGovern aides had also heard the drinking rumors. But, at this point in the morning, more than five hours before the 4 P.M. deadline for the vice presidential selection, Eagleton remained a long shot for the nomination, and the discussion around the conference table moved on. South Dakota lieutenant governor and longtime McGovern friend Bill Dougherty vouched for Governor Pat Lucey of Wisconsin, who had been working the convention as a floor leader for the McGovern campaign. And Pierre Salinger, the former JFK press secretary and current McGovern adviser, thought picking Sargent Shriver, a Kennedy relative and the first Peace Corps director, would be a way for the McGovern campaign to channel the Kennedy mystique in the absence of Ted on the ticket.

By noon, the meeting adjourned, and Mankiewicz headed to the penthouse to present the shortlist to McGovern. It bore six or seven names—depending on the report—and was topped by Mayor White of Boston, followed by senators Walter "Fritz" Mondale of Minnesota and Abe Ribicoff of Connecticut, then Lucey, O'Brien, Eagleton, and Shriver. The three names included and excluded in the various reports and recollections of the final shortlist are Mondale, Ribicoff, and O'Brien; Mondale and Ribicoff were personal friends of McGovern's. Since Weil did not have anything else to occupy his time and the campaign lacked much information on Eagleton and White, he decided to do some scouting—entirely on his own volition, Weil insists. He found the *Post-Dispatch*'s Ottenad with Jules Witcover of the *Los Angeles Times* by the door of the first-floor conference room, waiting for the meeting to let out. Ottenad was taken aback by Weil's inquiry about Eagleton's supposed mental illness and said that the *Post-Dispatch*'s 1968 investigation into the veracity of the allegations of alcoholism had proven futile. As it turns out, Stearns had misidentified his tipster—it was Loye Miller of Knight Newspapers, not Ottenad—and Eagleton remained in the picture.[11]

Weil went to his room on the Doral's seventeenth floor to canvass other Missourians and political insiders by phone, and he was told that the allegations of alcoholism could be attributed to "some sort of physiological or stomach problem," which had been identified during one of Eagleton's hospitalizations. Weil's sources added that this condition made Eagleton susceptible to the effects of drinking, even mild consumption, and Eagleton stuck to milk during the 1968 Senate campaign to avoid "potential embarrassment." In his notes, Weil described Eagleton as "reasonably bright and quick" and a "good politician" with "feeling, grasp, understanding, intuition." Furthermore, Weil believed that Stearns's allusion to mental illness in Eagleton's background referred to his family, not to the senator himself. It was easy to imagine, as Dick Dougherty did, that anything damaging about Eagleton would have turned up in his previous four campaigns (three of them statewide), especially his competitive 1968 Senate primary challenge against incumbent Senator Ed Long. Weil did not confront the candidate or his staff with questions about the rumors directly because he did not feel it was his place to let Eagleton know he was under consideration—a feeble excuse, since Eagleton had been widely mentioned in the press as being among the contenders. Weil circulated the information he unearthed about Eagleton, but it did not amount to much.[12]

After receiving the staff's list from Mankiewicz, McGovern spent the next hour calling Democratic leaders and soliciting their opinions. He found Mondale, White, and Eagleton to be the most popular choices. He also summoned representatives of women, black, and labor interests (including congressman William L. Clay of St. Louis) for their views. McGovern uncovered no problems with any of the candidates. A close friend of Mondale's, McGovern decided to offer the vice presidency to him first. But the Minnesotan declined, saying he did not want to endanger his chances at reelection to the Senate, even though an initial scouting report from Stewart Udall, the secretary of the interior in the Kennedy and Johnson administrations who was now working for the McGovern campaign, indicated that Mondale had not previously considered running simultaneous campaigns a concern. Mondale urged McGovern to consider Eagleton instead.[13]

For the moment, McGovern was unsure about Eagleton. At around 1 P.M. a McGovern aide alerted Mayor White's office to telegraph his biography to Miami Beach, and at 1:40 P.M. McGovern called White on Cape Cod to gauge his interest in joining the ticket, without extending a formal offer. "I'd like to have you with me," McGovern told him. White was eager, and McGovern said he would make some "routine" calls and get back to him.[14]

At around 2 P.M. Ribicoff told reporters that he had excused himself from vice presidential contention. "George, I love you, but I can't do it," Ribicoff said he told McGovern. Ribicoff's first wife, Ruth, had died that year, and he was getting remarried before November. Pierre Salinger tried to reach Sargent Shriver at his Washington office but was told that Shriver was on business in Moscow, making his selection impossible.[15]

By 2 P.M. the McGovern team was concentrating on White. Hart asked Stearns to prepare the filing papers bearing White's name and collect the requisite number of signatures. Speechwriter Milton Gwirtzman called Barney Frank, White's closest aide, in Boston, beginning his research for the nominating and seconding speeches he expected to draft.

White phoned one of his best friends, the Harvard professor Sam Huntington, who was vacationing with his wife on nearby Martha's Vineyard. "McGovern wants me on the ticket," White told him. "Get ready for a flight to Miami."[16]

In the next hour McGovern assistant Liz Stevens, who had been working the phones and investigating the various vice presidential possibilities all day, called Ted Kennedy to solicit his views on a Kevin White vice presidency: no objections, she reported. But after talking it over with Mankiewicz, McGovern now doubted that Kennedy would cede the national spotlight to another Massachusetts politician, allowing him a launching pad for presidential contention the next time around, especially if Kennedy wanted to run in 1976 himself, as most suspected he did. Several have proposed that the idea of White was merely a ploy to push Kennedy to reconsider McGovern's offer. If not, the possibility must have seemed a welcome by-product of inquiring about the Boston mayor. Feeling he could not select a Massachusetts politician without a personal call to Kennedy, McGovern phoned his first-choice candidate to personally verify his approval of White and perhaps afford Kennedy one last chance to say "yes" to joining him on the ticket.[17]

According to Kennedy, McGovern again asked him to reconsider the vice presidency, and again he declined. Kennedy said he then approved White's candidacy, but then succumbed to McGovern's insistence that he take another thirty minutes to reassess taking the job himself. McGovern and his staffers, however, recalled Kennedy "hitting the ceiling" about White and asserting that he could not campaign for the ticket as vigorously if White held the number-two spot. They remembered Kennedy *volunteering* to take another half-hour to think about accepting the nomination. Either way, the prospect of a Kennedy on the ticket continued to divert the McGovern campaign, stalling its vice presidential selection process by blurring its focus as time was running out.[18]

To mull over the decision, Kennedy took a walk on the Hyannisport beach with Claude Hooten, an old buddy from his days at Harvard. "I just wanted to beat McGovern up," Hooten later recalled. "It was just so cruel to come at Ted that way, with the line about the good of the country."[19]

While McGovern awaited Kennedy's final decision, the campaign received an alert from John Kenneth Galbraith, a U.S. ambassador to India under JFK and liberal Harvard economist. The Massachusetts delegation, Galbraith reported, was concerned about rumors that White was leading the field of contenders. He said that Massachusetts McGovernites had found the Boston mayor hostile toward them during the state's primary and that he had polled the entire delegation: every last member was prepared to leave the convention in protest if White received the nomination. Galbraith later admitted to having exaggerated the delegation's resentment, but McGovern took his remarks at face value. If Kennedy decided to accept the nomination, the problem was clearly solved. If not—even if Kennedy endorsed White—McGovern would have to look elsewhere, given the Massachusetts delegation's apparent dissatisfaction with White.[20]

Back in room 605 at the Ivanhoe, the convention's closed-circuit channel, DEMO-TV, exhibited the scene in the Doral lobby: reporters milling about and lower-level McGovern staffers waiting by the podium. By 2:30 P.M., the announcer indicated that a press conference on the vice presidential selection was imminent. The broadcaster also erroneously reported that Pat Lucey led the field of contenders. "Well, boys, that's it," Eagleton told the crew of aides and reporters gathered in his suite. "I might as well go down and take a swim." "Hold on, chief," an aide called out. "It isn't over yet. Wait a while for the official announcement." So Eagleton retired to his bedroom to read *Time* and *Newsweek*. At this point, he considered the chance of his selection "a possibility but . . . a distinct improbability." By 2:45 P.M., DEMO-TV reported that the once-impending press conference would be delayed indefinitely. By 3 P.M. the "restrained optimism" that characterized the mood at the Ivanhoe throughout the morning had turned to resignation that their man had not gotten the job—a feeling similar to that after a loss in a close ballgame, as Eagleton aide Bob Maynard described it.[21]

While waiting at the Doral for Kennedy's final response—with the 4 P.M. deadline for submitting his vice presidential nomination fast approaching—McGovern proposed Senator Frank Church of Idaho to his staff. But the aides shuttling in and out of McGovern's suite demurred, citing the similarity of Church's politics and profile to his own. They did not want to forfeit the opportunity to extend McGovern's appeal beyond his base. When Kennedy called around 3 P.M. to confirm that he would not join the ticket, he recommended that McGovern pick Arkansas Congressman Wilbur Mills or Tom Eagleton in his place. Suspecting that a Mills selection would "smack too much of 'old politics'" and frustrate the McGovern faithful, the staff returned to Eagleton. But McGovern resisted. "No, I just don't know enough about Tom," he explained before deciding to ask his "trusted friend" in the Senate, Gaylord Nelson of Wisconsin, whether he would like the nomination. "I know his strengths and he knows mine," McGovern said, choosing to ignore their demographic and ideological similarities as well. "I want somebody I know, somebody I can work with. Let's get Gaylord Nelson on the phone." At 3:05 P.M. a call was placed to Nelson's office, but a secretary told the McGovern campaign that Nelson had stepped away for a moment. When Nelson

returned the call, at 3:35 P.M.—twenty-five minutes before deadline—
he said he preferred his Senate seat to the vice presidency, just as
McGovern had indicated four years earlier when he was rumored
to be a vice presidential contender. Besides, Nelson had promised
his wife he would not run. McGovern remembers Nelson telling
him, "George, I'm afraid you might get elected and then I'd be stuck
with that lousy job." In declining McGovern's request that he take
the second spot as a "personal favor," Nelson added, "The guy who
wants it is Tom Eagleton, and personally, he's the guy I would pick if
I were in your shoes." Though he never said it at the time, as one of
Eagleton's closest friends in the Senate, Nelson knew that Eagleton
had a checkered history of mental health. He did not know about
the shock therapy.

In addition to Kennedy, Mondale, and Nelson, McGovern's
longtime aide John Holum was also vouching for Eagleton, considering his demonstrated enthusiasm for the role a distinct plus. Even
if Eagleton struck McGovern as a bit "superficial" or "a real Junior-
Chamber-of-Commerce type"—as McGovern was to insist after the
campaign—on paper, the young, liberal, border-state Catholic who
enjoyed popularity among blacks, women, and the labor establishment seemed the ideal match. Even more, with the deadline less
than twenty-five minutes away, McGovern and the rest of his staff
thought they needed to abide by the rules and settle.[22]

Just then, McGovern's longtime image consultant, the docu-
mentarian Charles Guggenheim, entered the room. After overhearing the rumors McGovern was leaning toward White, Guggenheim
had tried to nudge the candidate toward his fellow Missourian earlier in the day. He told McGovern that Eagleton projected a "new,
non-political image," whereas the others on his list did not. Guggenheim had come to admire Eagleton while working for his campaigns.
Now, minutes from deadline, McGovern asked Guggenheim whether
he could verify any of the rumors about a drinking problem. Guggenheim said he could not.[23]

At around a quarter to 4, as Kirby Jones slept in the penthouse
sitting room and Rick Stearns slouched in exhaustion at the end of a
long week and frazzled morning of deliberations, George McGovern

made his choice. "I think I'm going to go with Tom Eagleton," he said, then asked a secretary to place the call. It had been no more than a few minutes since Nelson had declined the offer, but the 4 P.M. deadline loomed large—the campaign was conditioned to play by the rules and still paranoid that establishment Democrats would pounce on any excuse, however unreasonable and counterproductive, to strip the nomination from McGovern. As McGovern awaited the telephone connection to the Ivanhoe, he called over to Ted Van Dyk. "What do you really think of Tom Eagleton?" he asked. Eagleton picked up before Van Dyk could respond.[24]

Eagleton was still paging through *Time* and *Newsweek* in the bedroom of his Ivanhoe suite when he heard the phone ring at 3:45 P.M., just fifteen minutes before the deadline. Within seconds, Doug Bennet, Eagleton's top aide, was knocking on his door. "George McGovern is on the phone," he said, motioning toward the living room. As Eagleton rushed to take the receiver, Bob Hardy, the St. Louis radio reporter encamped with the Eagleton crew all day, flipped the switch on his recorder.[25]

"I want to help in any way I can," Eagleton gasped, before breaking for a few seconds.

"I've thought it over carefully, and I think you would make a good contribution to the ticket and in office," McGovern said. "I'd like you to accept the vice presidential nomination."[26]

"I'm flabbergasted, George," Eagleton said, his voice rising in jubilation, "Are you kidding me? Why, ah, before you change your mind, I hastily accept."[27]

The long days of anticipation were past. George McGovern had finally offered him the nomination. The cheers of friends and staff filled the room at the Ivanhoe.

"Oh, my God, George, well, I'm as pleased as I could be," Eagleton continued. "I'm honored, I'm flattered, and, uh, will do whatever I can. I hope I don't let you down."

Precisely thirty-eight seconds into the conversation, Frank Mankiewicz took McGovern's end of the line.

"Frank? God bless you, God bless everybody, and I, I feel that you had something to do with this and thank you very much. Alright, well I have to start working on speeches," Eagleton said.

"No skeletons rattling in your closet?" Mankiewicz asked.[28]

"Right," Eagleton responded, drawing out the word as was typical of his smooth style of speech.[29]

No more than three seconds elapsed between the time Eagleton finished saying he had to work on speeches until he said "right," a narrow window for inquiring about Eagleton's past.

Five more seconds went by as Mankiewicz spoke at the other end of the phone.

"Okay, just a minute, let Bennet, he's got my biographical sketch, let me put him on, will you, so he can read all this pers— What? Yeah, I'll stay here," Eagleton said. "Hold on," he added as he sought Bennet.

"Incredible," an Eagleton aide exclaimed. "Incredible," he continued, emphasizing the first syllable each time. As Eagleton finished speaking with Mankiewicz, euphoria seeped from the Eagleton suite onto the recording of that afternoon's conversation.

"Who is it?" Bennet asked, as he took the phone.

"Mankiewicz," Eagleton said, as shouts of "He's got it! He's got it!" filled room 605.[30]

Recorder still running, Bob Hardy, the KMOX radio reporter, jumped in: "Congratulations, Senator, what's your reaction?"

"Well, I'm flabbergasted."

"You're shaking."

"Well, I can't believe it. As you know we've had a, uh, long vigil here today, and uh."

"Well let's go out on the porch," Hardy said as Eagleton fumbled for words. Meanwhile, Marvin Madeson, an activist from St. Louis with the New Democratic Coalition who had invited himself to Eagleton's "vigil," dashed downstairs to announce the news to the public.[31]

Out on the porch, Eagleton picked up where he had left off, in a hurried, elated pace, "Ah, Bob, you know we've had a long vigil here today in room 605 at the Ivanhoe, and you've been one of the, uh, watchers of what's going on, and I thought once it got to two o'clock that, uh, my star had waned and that someone else had, uh, gotten the call, but, uh, we stayed here just hoping to get some information and, my god, just three minutes ago George McGovern called and he said, 'Tom, I've got a favor to ask of you,' and I said, 'What's that?' He said, 'I want you to be my running mate,' and I think I said something like, 'I hastily accept' before he could, uh, retract it, withdraw it. I'm, I'm honored. I'm pleased. I'm ecstatically happy."

"Tom, it looks like it," Hardy said.

"Thank you, Bob. And thank you for being one of the patient guys, for being around with us because, not only do I respect your profession and your station, KMOX Radio, but you are a good personal friend."

Bob Hardy signed off by wishing the senator "congratulations" and "good luck."

Eagleton sounded almost feverish in his exhilaration, amped up on the adrenaline of the moment. At the same time, he showed his humility, not to mention insecurity, in "hastily" accepting before McGovern could change his mind. To Eagleton, his hospitalizations were a thing of the past, and he strove to keep them that way. If he considered his mental health disqualifying, Eagleton would never have promoted the idea of his candidacy, as he had in a television interview the night before, and in conversations earlier in the week with McGovern advisers Richard Hemenway and Dick Wade at the Convention Hall, and Fred Dutton at Tony Sweet's restaurant.

Whether or not Eagleton intended to share his history of mental illness with McGovern before the campaign publicized his nomination—on the off chance that he ever got tapped—the atmosphere in which he received the call was not conducive to confession. For a man who had concealed his hospitalizations for nervous exhaustion and depression throughout his professional career to suddenly disclose matters he clearly considered private in the presence of his staff, friends, and a radio reporter—recorder in hand—among others, seemed absurd. Yes, Eagleton could have excused himself to take the call. But with the vigil of supporters hovering in the room and the reason for McGovern's call clear—the word already out to the press—it would have taken extraordinary courage for Eagleton to share his deepest secret with a man he hardly knew. As Bennet later framed it, "If someone calls you up on the telephone and says, 'Now I would like you to be my running mate,' you don't say to yourself in that moment, 'Gee, wait a minute. I'd better stop and think about this debilitating disease that I don't have anymore.' You say, 'Great. I'll do it.' And that's exactly what happened."[32]

After finishing the interview with Hardy, Eagleton and his wife, Barbara, went to the bedroom to call Barbara's parents vacationing on Cape Cod, not far from the Kennedy compound in Hyannisport. In their determination to document the jubilation of room 605, *St. Louis Globe-Democrat* political reporter Jack Flach and his photographer barged into the bedroom.[33]

Eagleton and Mankiewicz disputed what followed Eagleton's call to his in-laws. According to Mankiewicz, after Bennet finished his ten-to-fifteen-minute briefing, Eagleton returned to the living room and picked up the phone so that Mankiewicz could resume his questioning: Had Eagleton faced any damaging allegations during his 1968 Senate campaign? Had he caroused in college? Had he entertained any "shady" connections when he practiced law? What were his connections to the Teamsters in St. Louis? Mankiewicz recalled that JFK had passed over another Missouri senator, Stuart Symington, for the vice presidential nomination twelve years earlier, in part because he discovered that Symington had stolen a car with a few friends for a joyride one night while still in high school. Drawing on the Missouri connection, Mankiewicz says he asked whether Eagleton had ever done anything along those lines. Mankiewicz believes he asked up to seven or eight such questions. "Was there anything that was OK in [your] estimation but could be misconstrued?" Mankiewicz said he inquired.

Though both Eagleton and Mankiewicz agreed that Mankiewicz did not ask anything specifically about Eagleton's health, Eagleton insisted that Mankiewicz's account of the events was "100 percent wrong," maintaining that he never returned to the phone that afternoon. "There was one question asked of me, and one question was given. That's all," Eagleton said. Bennet concurred. However, others in the Eagleton camp, such as Bob Maynard, conceded that there was "a distinct chance" that Mankiewicz and Eagleton had continued their conversation. Maynard remembered the concern he had felt upon overhearing Eagleton voice a series of "no" responses through the phone, presumably in reaction to Mankiewicz's queries. Hart remembered Mankiewicz asking "about several possibilities—alcohol, personal relations, business relations," corroborating Mankiewicz's recollection. Eagleton "had every opportunity to tell us there was a problem," Hart said, implying that Eagleton had a moral obligation to volunteer his history of hospitalization, even if no specific question about Eagleton's health was asked. While several other McGovern staffers shared Hart and Mankiewicz's recollection, Gordon Weil took the middle ground in noting the likelihood that Mankiewicz "ran all these points into a single sentence [in the first conversation], eliciting a single negative response from Eagleton." Or, perhaps Mankiewicz asked his vetting questions of Bennet as part of the background interview, and not of Eagleton himself.

Mankiewicz has additionally proposed that the question about skeletons in Eagleton's closet could have been Eagleton's way of synthesizing the overall gist of the questioning. "I asked him if he has *skeletons* in his closet?" Mankiewicz said in a recent interview, leaning on the word skeleton so as to express his disdain for the formulation. "That's interesting," Mankiewicz continued, "because [NBC anchor] John Chancellor . . . called me the next day and said, 'Did you really say that?' I said, 'No, not a chance. I don't talk that way.' I asked Eagleton if there were anything in his records that could hurt us." Either way, no matter how Mankiewicz posed the questions to Eagleton, mere moments before the convention's 4 P.M. deadline for vice presidential selection, word of Eagleton's nomination was uncontainable.[34]

If Mankiewicz did resume his conversation with Eagleton, any inquiry into his past did not come as part of an initial appraisal of a potential vice presidential candidate's fitness for office. Rather, Mankiewicz was quizzing the man already anointed McGovern's nominee, with little opportunity for recourse if something came up. McGovern had already extended the nomination and Eagleton had accepted. At this point, probing into Eagleton's past would have been pro forma. However, Weil likens Eagleton's status at this time in the process to a just-announced multiyear, multimillion-dollar contract for a major league sports star. Such deals are always "subject to a physical." Mankiewicz's questioning was Eagleton's metaphorical physical, Weil said. In another recent interview, McGovern himself scoffed at the practice of even vetting potential vice presidential running mates in the first place. He said he was ashamed at the idea of his team scrutinizing his Senate colleague in this way. Senator John Sparkman of Alabama, who ran with Adlai Stevenson on the 1952 Democratic ticket, later shared with McGovern that Stevenson had not asked him a single question about his past upon selecting him. "I'm a United States Senator," Sparkman told McGovern. "I'm not going to be interrogated by another politician on my personal life and my background."[35]

After his conversations with Eagleton and Bennet, Mankiewicz made his way to a battery of television cameras and reporters gathered at the Doral, awaiting news of McGovern's selection. Mankiewicz launched into rambling remarks about the decision process, comments whose imprecision and unenthusiastic delivery suggested the extraordinary fatigue of the typically eloquent political director. He said that McGovern had "considered very carefully the qualifications of the man to be vice president of the United States, concentrating almost entirely on the question of whether such a man would complement and be an addition to the ticket this year and support the platform and play a leading role in carrying out the mandate of the platform, particularly in reference to the expressed desires of the Democratic voters and the Democratic voters in expressing that platform and the results of the various primary elections and conventions held across the country," seeming to be speaking extemporaneously. Mankiewicz continued, "And [Senator McGovern] has decided on the candidate that he will recommend to the convention because of all those considerations and particularly because he meets the main requirement Senator McGovern set down when he began his consideration, which is a man in whom he would have absolute and complete confidence and in whom he believes the American people would have complete confidence should that occasion arise."

As the McGovern team would affirm time and time again, this, after all, constituted the essential criterion for the vice presidency—fitness to become president, as unscientific a measurement as it may be. "And [McGovern] will ask the convention and those delegates who support him to respect his wishes in this matter to nominate"—Mankiewicz's voice rising as if presenting an Academy Award—"as the Democratic nominee for vice president in 1972, Senator Thomas Eagleton of Missouri."[36]

Rick Stearns had crossed out Kevin White's name atop the filing papers and written in Thomas Francis Eagleton, just in time to meet the convention's deadline.[37]

As Eagleton rode to the Doral to "meet the other guy on the ticket," the forty-two-year-old vice presidential nominee mused aloud, "I wish the old man were alive to see this." Mark Eagleton—who had taken young Tom to all those St. Louis school board meetings, who had provided the coaching and connections to ease his success, who had financed his early political career, and who had sat there, beaming, as his son took the Senate oath—still held a prominent place in Tom Eagleton's sense of himself. "[Your dad] sees it," Ed Filippine confirmed for his boss.[38]

When the Eagleton crew arrived at McGovern's suite—surviving the Doral lobby's crush of delegates and reporters eager to catch a glimpse of the Missourian—the presidential candidate found his nominee "warm and dynamic," calming his worries about the freshman senator. Furthermore, McGovern admired how Eagleton demonstrated a quality that had seemed so rare: a genuine enthusiasm for the vice presidency. Throughout the afternoon, prominent Democrats, such as Senate Majority Leader Mike Mansfield, called McGovern, lauding his pick. In his speech at the convention that night, McGovern labeled his running mate a man of "wide vision and deep compassion."[39]

Jack Perkins reported from the Doral on *NBC Nightly News* that, indeed, Tom Eagleton was not a "household word," but the McGovern campaign did not see that as a drawback. Rather, as Perkins explained, McGovern's "pollsters told him he would be better off

with a man who was not well known than one who was known but
perceived unfavorably by many people." The reporter continued, "So
[McGovern] has a man who is not well known. A man who is not
well known can always get to be known, though. That's the story of
George McGovern in the past six months."[40]

When Eagleton returned to the Ivanhoe and took the swim
he had been longing for all day, three Secret Service agents and at
least one staffer had to tag along. Several members of the Missouri
delegation were lounging by the pool when the running mate and
his security detail arrived. Friendly with their senator, the Missouri
delegates had always called him "Tom." But now, as Eagleton and
his twenty-one-year-old half-brother Kevin took a dip, they were
asking Filippine whether it would be all right to congratulate the
vice presidential candidate and shake his hand. "It was obvious to
me at that moment that a very awesome thing had happened to the
senator," Filippine would reflect.[41]

The Running Mate

In the hours immediately after McGovern picked Eagleton, Marc Howard, a television reporter for the local New York City station, WPIX, heard murmurs in Miami Beach that Eagleton had a history of alcohol abuse. Throughout the spring, Howard had developed a cordial relationship with Frank Mankiewicz, calling him every few weeks or so for updates on the campaign and verification of various stories. So he gave him a ring to check out the report, and Mankiewicz persuaded him not to broadcast this story that evening. Robert Sam Anson, the McGovern biographer, also heard from a source that Eagleton "has some problems." The source told Anson that Eagleton drank a lot. "And I think he's been in the loony bin," he said. Anson knew that several similar allegations were zipping through the corridors of Miami Beach's waterfront hotels, so he reasoned that the general thrust must have some grounding in the truth, even if the specifics were wrong. By 8 P.M. he reached the seventeenth floor of the Doral, where he grabbed Dick Dougherty and Gordon Weil, anxious to pass along what he had learned.

"What you've got is just some bullshit put out by the Republican National Committee," Weil told Anson.

"Well, when that bullshit hits the fan, don't say I didn't warn you," the reporter shot back.

"It's too late now, anyway," Weil said.[1]

The convention's frustration at the last-minute, closed-door nature of the vice presidential selection process stalled its ratification of McGovern's vice presidential pick. McGovern's decision process was typical of the way past presidential nominees had chosen their nominations for running mate, and some delegates hoped to repudiate the perceptibly antiquated process rather than his pick itself. Did the 1972 convention represent an "open convention," a "new day" in Democratic politics? Or was McGovern's running-mate selection process an expression of Old Politics as usual? As a series of overlooked vice presidential hopefuls such as Mike Gravel and Endicott Peabody took the convention's stage to promote their candidacies, they snatched the prime-time television audience McGovern had counted on addressing and surrendered the Democratic Party's best venue for articulating its vision to the nation at large.[2]

Tom Ottenad of the *St. Louis Post-Dispatch* gained access to Eagleton in a makeshift plywood waiting room behind the podium. Chain-smoking while nursing an orange juice, Eagleton gave his hometown newspaper's star political reporter his assessment of the campaign ahead while keeping an eye on the television broadcasting the action from the convention floor. "I don't know the exact timing," Eagleton said, "but I got the impression we're not going to vegetate between now and Labor Day, which has been the traditional starting day," relating the plans for the campaign he gleaned from McGovern and his staff that afternoon. Just yards away, at the Convention Hall podium, Mayor Kenneth A. Gibson of Newark, New Jersey, one of the nation's most prominent black politicians, put forth Eagleton's name for the vice presidency. As a black man, Gibson was a symbolic pick to be Eagleton's nominator, displacing Missouri governor Warren Hearnes in the role at the McGovern campaign's insistence. Gibson described the Missouri senator as a man "committed to the belief that our first national priority and obligation is to one another, be we rich or poor, young or old, black, brown, or white." New Mexico lieutenant governor Roberto Mondragón seconded the nomination of Eagleton, beginning his remarks in Spanish, probably a first in Democratic Party history and another gesture toward inclusion. He was followed by another seconding speech from Debbie Barber, a twenty-year-old speech therapy student at the University of Missouri, Columbia, and a representative of both the youth and the women on the Missouri delegation. Eagleton picked up some of her remarks and noted to Ottenad with a measure of pride in his voice, "I'm the youngest one nominated for vice president in 120 years." However, Barber had her facts wrong. Franklin Delano Roosevelt was thirty-eight to Eagleton's forty-two when James Cox named FDR to his ticket in 1920. Others had also been younger.[3]

Eagleton's concentration returned to the interview, and he answered Ottenad's request for him to define the central issue of the campaign. "Change," he said. "Can we, the Democratic Party, do what Nixon promised to [do] but never fulfilled—bring this country together?" It seemed that McGovern had called upon him to do just that, but on a smaller scale first—bring the Democratic Party together. Eagleton told Ottenad that McGovern had suggested he would have "special responsibilities in the big cities," and be charged with reaching out to the Democratic establishment. Within minutes Eagleton received a call from Ed Muskie, the man who had held Eagleton's role four years earlier and had used the appointment to launch his own presidential ambitions. He had also been Eagleton's first choice for president that year. "Ed," Eagleton said, "if I can end up being half as good a vice presidential candidate as you were, I'd consider myself a success. I hope you'll give us your help this fall." Eagleton was already attacking the task at hand, winning over the party regulars. Hubert Humphrey soon stopped by the waiting room. "Have you got a little acceptance speech?" the one-time vice president and three-time presidential hopeful inquired of Eagleton. Later, as Humphrey was leaving, Eagleton entreated, "You know, I'm going to need some guidance."

"You're going to get it," Humphrey assured him. "Go get 'em."[4]

Meanwhile, Mike Gravel had taken the podium to deliver his own seconding speech to his self-endorsed nomination for the vice presidency. It seemed to be another convention first in a year in which the fictional television character Archie Bunker of *All in the Family;* labor activist César Chávez; Chinese dictator Mao Zedong; U.S. Attorney General John Mitchell's wife, Martha; CBS reporter Roger Mudd; consumer advocate Ralph Nader; and famous pediatrician and People's Party candidate Dr. Benjamin Spock were all among the names submitted for consideration during the vice presidential roll call. *Newsweek* called the evening "a comic interlude, a burst of silliness on the part of the delegates whose taut bonds of decorum and discipline seemed suddenly to snap, now that it didn't make a difference." But the litany of nominating and seconding speeches had real implications. McGovern's acceptance speech was pushed late into the night, depriving the candidate of the prime-time audience he needed.[5]

The commotion over Gravel's seconding speech caught Eagleton's attention, and he called over his thirty-year-old press secretary, Mike Kelley, who had flown to Miami that evening. Kelley was of middling height, and had dirty-blond hair and an Irish complexion. The son of a newspaper reporter, Kelley had started working as a copyboy for the *Kansas City Star* while still in college, eventually becoming a reporter. He was a straight shooter and had a wry sense of humor. "Hey, what's Mike Gravel doing? Is he hanging me?" Eagleton asked him. Kelley filled him in, then Eagleton resumed recounting his late-afternoon discussion with McGovern for Ottenad, the *Post-Dispatch* reporter. "We agreed that a vital ingredient to success is a massive, intensive voter registration drive, directed to the young and the blacks in the major cities," Eagleton recounted. Eagleton clearly brimmed with excitement for the vice presidency and appeared to have forgotten the joke about two brothers he had shared in 1965, while lieutenant governor of Missouri, the state-level approximation of vice president: "One of [the brothers] went to sea, and the other became the vice president. And neither of them has been heard of since."[6]

Eagleton's nomination also thrilled the Missouri delegation, and its distress over McGovern's candidacy appeared to have evaporated. Though the delegation had withheld the majority of its votes from McGovern on key planks earlier that week, it now threw its unanimous support behind the McGovern-Eagleton ticket. Governor Hearnes, who had previously resisted McGovern and resented Eagleton for abandoning Muskie on the California Challenge, now took pride in his fellow Missourian and felt gratified by his state's new-found influence—even if he was disappointed that the McGovernites had deprived him of his seconding speech. "History has a way of repeating itself," Hearnes proclaimed as he cast the state's votes, recalling Missourian Harry Truman's service as vice president before becoming commander in chief. Even Alabama, the dominion of Governor George Wallace, principal antagonist of the party's liberals, seemed to play along with the idea of Democratic unity. "If Governor Wallace was casting these thirty-seven votes, he would want them all to go to Senator Eagleton," the Alabama state Democratic chairman announced just before 1 A.M. However, on this last night of the convention, some McGovernites had assumed the role of spoiler, delaying the roll call with the litany of pet nominations and seconding speeches, and voting for—among others—Frances "Sissy" Farenthold of the Texas House of Representatives, a move intended as retribution for the McGovern campaign's betrayal of the women on the South Carolina Challenge.[7]

Finally, about an hour and twenty minutes into the roll call, at around 1:50 A.M., after the Texas delegation cast its votes, Larry O'Brien introduced a motion to halt the voting and hand the nomination to Eagleton by acclamation, a symbolic gesture in the direction of party unity. For the first time all week, the Missouri delegation unfurled its state banner and waved it in celebration, finally content with the party. The arena erupted in a resounding—if delayed—ovation of song, dance, and apparent reconciliation among the Democratic Party's various factions.[8]

In the VIP box where Barbara Eagleton watched with her two children, who had arrived in Miami that evening, the running mate's son Terence tossed a handful of confetti overhead. Reporters and cameramen had been keeping them company all night, and Barbara seemed entirely equal to the role of vice presidential wife. Though immaculate in presentation, she predicted, "I don't think it will be a 'What are you wearing?' and 'How are you doing your hair?' kind of campaign."[9]

As Eagleton waited backstage, eager to live the moment when "Tom Who?" became "Tom Eagleton," he reflected on his life up to that point. "Eagleton, you are a mighty lucky kid," he thought. "You lucked into circuit attorney of St. Louis. You got some good breaks and became attorney general of Missouri. By happenstance and fate you became U.S. senator from Missouri. Now you are being nominated for the second-highest office in the free world." Eagleton knew he had enjoyed a charmed rise to his spot on a national ticket. "God has been good to you," Eagleton acknowledged. "I hope God gives you the strength and courage to do the job for which you are being nominated."[10]

Governor Hearnes, Senator Stuart Symington, and representatives Leonor K. Sullivan and William Clay of St. Louis congressional districts—all Missourians and each an influence on Senator Eagleton's political career, Old Politics and New Politics alike—accompanied the vice presidential candidate to the podium for his speech. His face dripping with sweat and his hands quivering in a combination of excitement and nervousness, Eagleton accepted his party's vice presidential nomination. "From the people who promised to bring us together, we have gotten deception and more mistrust," he said, pointing to the failings of the Nixon administration. "From the people who promised the lift of a driving dream, we have a sodden mound of shattered hopes. We have an electorate so jaded by gimmickry that their healthy skepticism about politics and politicians has escalated into a total lack of confidence in the administration," he said. Eagleton promised to restore "dignity to the second highest office in the United States" and to steer clear of the "cheap rhetorical attacks that divide our nation," a not so subtle jab at Vice President Spiro T. Agnew, known for his fear mongering and divisiveness. Looking ahead, Eagleton implored the convention before him, "Let us conduct ourselves and our campaign and, indeed, our lives, so that in later years men may say 1972 was the year, not when America lost its way, but the year when America found its conscience." He told the convention that, for him, the nomination capped a year rife with political surprises. Just as few people had suspected that Mc-Govern would rise to the nomination, his own ascent was, as he had described it, "a distinct improbability." As applause interrupted his delivery, Eagleton smiled broadly. He said he dedicated his address to M.D.E., leaving those who knew him to realize that he meant his father.[11]

Ted Kennedy had flown down to Miami to partake in the show of unity, reveling in the crowd's affection for him, "the best living tradition in this party today," as one delegate phrased it. Banners bearing portraits of his two deceased brothers hung above the convention floor. "Democrats are united by heritage, by conviction, and unyielding opposition to Republican leadership," Kennedy affirmed, attempting to connect the McGovern campaign to the party of years past and fitting the South Dakotan squarely in the Democratic tradition. "In 1948, Hubert H. Humphrey proclaimed a dedication to the equality of all races, and Harry Truman took this to the people. And George McGovern would do the same. Lyndon Johnson promised we shall overcome. And, beginning next January, under the leadership of George McGovern, we shall overcome." The crowd concurred, rising in ovation, another fleeting moment of unity in a year characterized not only by surprises but also by division.[12]

When he arrived at the podium at 2:48 A.M., McGovern began with self-deprecating humor. "I assume that everyone here is impressed with my control of this convention in that my choice for vice president was challenged by only thirty-nine other nominees. But I think we learned from watching the Republicans four years ago as they selected their vice presidential nominee that it pays to take a little more time," he said—a sure applause line, as Democrats of all stripes reviled Agnew.[13]

According to the Nielsen ratings, an average of 17.8 million homes—or approximately 71 million Americans—watched the convention during prime time that week. On Thursday evening, the night of McGovern's address, 17.4 million homes tuned in during prime time, but only 3.6 million televisions remained on by the time McGovern spoke. Despite the chaos of Chicago, even Humphrey had gotten to address the nation in prime time in 1968.[14]

McGovern's speech resembled a sermon, showcasing the preacher's son's propensity for outlining America's choices in moral terms and for drawing from the Bible to affirm the rightness of his cause. "In Scripture and in the music of our children we are told: to everything there is a season, and a time to every purpose under heaven. . . . This is a time for truth, not falsehood," he proclaimed. "Truth is a habit of integrity, not a strategy of politics. And if we nurture the habit of candor in this campaign, we will continue to be candid once we are in the White House." Who could have foretold that doubts about Eagleton's candor and McGovern's own were soon to become his campaign's greatest liability? "From secrecy and deception in high places, come home, America," McGovern said, launching his speech's most memorable refrain. And, in a conclusion that amplified his trademark moralism, McGovern prayed, "May God grant us the wisdom to cherish this good land and to meet the challenge that beckons us home." In addition to the task of bringing America home from its war in Indochina, from its excessive military spending, from its unjust tax laws, from its prejudices, and from all other ills that plagued the nation, it seemed that McGovern would require godlike wisdom to overcome the unique challenges of his own campaign.[15]

As McGovern spoke, Bennet watched the broadcast from the ersatz plywood waiting room, preparing himself for the task at hand by drawing upon the lessons of his past campaigns, Muskie's included. "First, having been in some poorly organized campaigns, I meant to make this one really work well," Bennet recalled of his thoughts. "And, second, I would make every effort to avoid the kind of clash between the presidential and vice-presidential staffs which seems to have developed in the past."[16]

Back in the Convention Hall, standing at the center of the podium, McGovern and Eagleton clasped their hands and raised them above their heads like Olympic gold medalists, inspiring the crowd to roar in celebration of their union. Eagleton was glowing.

Before the exhausting convention adjourned at 3:26 A.M., Kennedy, Humphrey, Muskie, New York Congresswoman Shirley Chisholm, and Scoop Jackson all joined McGovern and Eagleton on stage. The party leaders—once rivals, now apparently compatriots—linked arms in unity and bowed for the convention audience as the band played, "Hail, Hail, the Gang's All Here." Democrats of all stripes—black, white, northern, southern, urban, suburban, young, old, blue-collar, white-collar—joined in singing "Happy Days Are Here Again."[17]

With a dizzying week of official convention proceedings complete at long last, the McGovern and Eagleton teams returned to the Doral Hotel to meet, greet, and continue the party. Doug Bennet and Gordon Weil landed in the same elevator up. When the door opened on the seventeenth floor, Weil urged Bennet to follow him to his room first, before joining the festivities on the Starlight Roof. He told Bennet that the campaign had selected Eagleton despite rumors that he had been hospitalized for alcoholism. As Bennet remembered it, Weil did not ask whether the allegations were true, which he took to mean that, even if they were, the campaign felt that they would not hurt the ticket. Weil recalled telling Bennet that it would be best for the campaign to know everything relating to the rumors so that it could prepare the appropriate response should the information surface in the press. Bennet clarified the situation, telling Weil that, yes, the vice presidential nominee had been hospitalized—but for "fatigue and depression," not a drinking problem. "Oh, well that's a relief," Weil said. "We knew we were right. He hadn't had a drinking problem." Bennet withheld details of Eagleton's treatment, other than to state the general cause. While he knew his boss had been hospitalized and treated with shock therapy, nothing about his behavior during the three years Bennet had been working for the senator suggested that depression continued to plague Eagleton. "I'd never seen any evidence of a disability of any kind," Bennet explained four years later. Eagleton had "conquered it. It was in his past. . . . Nothing triggered in my mind the possibility that this was a problem." With such benefit of distance and time for reflection, Bennet added, "Now, obviously, that's one of the colossal failures of political judgment, I guess, of all time."[18]

Before 4 A.M., the two men joined the party down the hall,

and Weil updated Mankiewicz on his conversation with Bennet. As Eagleton prepared to leave the Starlight Roof, Mankiewicz caught him at the door. "We ought to talk about that health problem," Mankiewicz said.[19]

Perhaps fatigue, or the seeming impossibility of Eagleton's selection, explains why Mankiewicz forgot to mention in the staff meetings that morning that he knew Eagleton had been hospitalized twice for "nervous breakdowns." Back in June, about a week before the Missouri state Democratic convention, Scott Lilly, the former Eagleton staffer and current McGovern aide, had proposed to Mankiewicz the idea of spreading a rumor that McGovern was considering naming Eagleton his running mate. Given Eagleton's popularity in his home state, Lilly believed this ploy would entice more Missourians to embrace McGovern and thus facilitate greater representation of McGovernites on the state's delegation to Miami Beach. In seeking the campaign's permission to enact this scheme, Lilly volunteered to Mankiewicz that, contrary to the rumors, Eagleton did not have a drinking problem. However, Lilly said only that Eagleton had received psychiatric care during two hospitalizations—after victorious but trying election campaigns in 1960 and 1966. Mankiewicz approved Lilly's plan. Lilly had not known about Eagleton's 1964 hospitalization or his treatment with electroshock, and thus neither did Mankiewicz.

Yet Mankiewicz also later recalled that, a few weeks before the convention, a friend and fellow board member of his sons' private school had warned him not to let the campaign nominate Eagleton. "I just saw [Eagleton] at a press conference," the man, a respected Washington psychiatrist, told him. "And he has a pronounced tremor in his hands. And the way he kept answering questions suggested to me he's got trouble," the psychiatrist continued. "Oh, shit," Mankiewicz recalled thinking at the time. In the exhaustion and bustle of the convention, both omens slipped from Mankiewicz's mind the day the campaign went about selecting its number two.[20]

When a prominent Democrat read in the papers that morning of increasing speculation that McGovern would pick Eagleton, he called the candidate's staff, hoping his knowledge that Eagleton had been twice hospitalized for psychiatric care would preempt the selection of the Missourian. After several attempts to contact someone in the McGovern organization, the man finally reached Anne Wexler, an old friend and aide high in the campaign. Wexler confirmed receiving the report and said she passed it along to Rick Stearns, who denied ever getting it, saying that he was napping when Wexler supposedly told him. In the end, the message never reached McGovern.[21]

When the Democratic informant heard that McGovern had chosen Eagleton, he called the campaign back: "What in the name of God are you smoking up there?" he asked.[22]

The Investigation

Late nomination night, after fêting Eagleton's selection and the end of the convention with the McGovernites at the Doral's Starlight Roof restaurant, the Eagleton crew returned to the Ivanhoe, stopping by the senator's suite for a final nightcap. Greg Wierzynski, the *Time* reporter who had dropped in the previous night, told Bob Maynard of Eagleton's staff that he had heard rumors about Eagleton's hospitalizations. When Ed Filippine returned to his room, he found a message awaiting him from St. Louis County Democratic chairman Dr. Martin Greenberg, marked "important." Filippine returned Greenberg's call and found out that *Time* was investigating a tip that Eagleton had been hospitalized in 1964, 1965, and 1967—for exhaustion, for drinking, and for "a breakdown of some sort," respectively. *Time* also checked with Johns Hopkins, whose public relations representative told the reporter that he could not find records indicating whether the senator had been a patient of the hospital. But indeed, the magazine had reason to inquire: on September 21, 1966, the *St. Louis Post-Dispatch* had reported that Lieutenant Governor Eagleton was seeking treatment there for a "gastric disturbance." As it turns out, *Time* had another lead: the 1968 memo crafted by young

Miami Herald reporter Clark Hoyt poses with the story that won him a 1973 Pulitzer Prize (AP/Wide World Photos)

reporter Jonathan Z. Larsen, which noted that Eagleton "sinks into depressed states so severe, that, according to friends, he has taken shock treatments to get himself out of them." Upon learning of Eagleton's nomination, Wierzynski asked his staff in Chicago to review the bureau's files on Eagleton, and they uncovered Larsen's dispatch. But it was just a report for the file, and it came with a disclaimer, "We have not been able to confirm any of this."[1]

When Doug Bennet learned about *Time*'s inquiries on Friday, July 14, he called Frank Mankiewicz. No need to fret, Mankiewicz assured him. Given what Mankiewicz knew about Eagleton's past that Friday afternoon—that the Missourian had been hospitalized after one campaign, maybe two, early in his career—the McGovern political director believed he had devised the perfect preemptive damage control: before Eagleton's scheduled appearance on *Face the Nation* that Sunday morning, Mankiewicz would plant a question with one of the show's panelists inquiring about Eagleton's stamina. "I am such an energetic campaigner," Mankiewicz imagined Eagleton would respond, "that I once ran myself right into the hospital for exhaustion." Such an answer would allow Eagleton to cast his hospitalizations on his own terms. And with that, Mankiewicz left the next morning for some postconvention rest and relaxation at Henry Kimelman's house in the Virgin Islands.[2]

Fifty-year-old Brooklyn-born and -bred Kimelman was McGovern's finance director, but in truth, he was also a primary reason for his nomination. After attending business school at Harvard and marrying into wealth, Kimelman went to the Virgin Islands to manage a hotel owned by his father-in-law. In addition to pursuing real estate investments, in time, Kimelman established his own company, the West Indies Corporation, and it became the biggest importer and distributor in the region, selling hundreds of goods through a network of stores under its aegis. Kimelman had a "business brilliance that ooze[d] from him," a *Miami Herald* reporter wrote. Physically tall and tan with a full head of dark brown hair, Kimelman looked "movie star handsome," resembling a mix of George Hamilton and Cary Grant. Before launching his candidacy, McGovern doubted his ability to raise enough money for a presidential campaign, but Kimelman had told him not to fret. "I'll make it possible," he assured him. Kimelman was not only McGovern's chief fund-raiser, and among his closest personal friends, he was the campaign's lifeline, writing it loans when money was tight.[3]

After speaking with Mankiewicz, Bennet called Eagleton and the running mate's brother Mark to update them on the situation. Eagleton was already in Kansas City for a previously scheduled address before the annual convention of the National Audio Visual Association. He had left Miami earlier that afternoon, but not before attending two unity breakfasts and stopping by Abercrombie and Fitch to buy Filippine the spiffier sports coat he had promised he would get his aide if nominated, considering it unlucky to renege on his word. As Bennet was becoming the link between the McGovern and Eagleton operations, he asked his boss whether there was any additional background information that might prove useful for him to know. There was not, Eagleton vowed.[4]

As Eagleton sat for an interview in his Kansas City hotel later that evening, one reporter noted that he seemed on his way to re-covering from the "extremes of exhaustion and euphoria" that had characterized his last twenty-four hours in Miami Beach. When he delivered his keynote address that evening, Eagleton scrapped his prepared remarks and somewhat ominously implored the crowd to pray. "I ask you to say a couple of prayers, not that I'm going to get killed, or anything," Eagleton said. "But I've been a very lucky young man, blessed with wonderful parents and good friends who helped me get elected as a pink-cheeked twenty-six-year-old with a choir-boy look when, frankly, there were better, more qualified men in the race. I'm in the big league now, and I hope I can meet the test. So say a prayer, however you pray, that I'm equal to the task that's been imposed on me."[5]

The next morning, Saturday, July 15, Gary Hart and Doug Bennet, still in Miami Beach, met for a briefing on campaign issues and logistics. By the afternoon, Hart was in St. Thomas, where he joined Mankiewicz at Henry Kimelman's house, blessed with vistas of Charlotte Amalie Harbor. "That's how excited they were [about reports of the running mate's hospitalizations]," an Eagleton aide would later crack. Then again, Hart and Mankiewicz had not known that the vice presidential candidate's medical care had included shock therapy, and Bennet did.[6]

Eagleton returned to Washington from Kansas City on Saturday, and McGovern aides Ted Van Dyk and John Holum joined him at his Chevy Chase home to help him prepare for his *Face the Nation* appearance the next morning. Meanwhile, Eagleton staffers Gene Godley, Mike Kelley, James Murphy, Ed Quick, and Doug Bennet, who had just arrived from Miami, charted the campaign's course of action. They decided to send Murphy to the Mayo Clinic in Rochester, Minnesota, and to Barnes Hospital in St. Louis to secure Eagleton's medical records. The McGovern aides in the next room were unaware of the investigation. By midnight, as he had promised, Eagleton called Mankiewicz in the Virgin Islands. Hart listened in to the conversation. "Tom," Mankiewicz began, "I don't know about the integrity of these lines so I think we ought to sort of talk in generalities." Eagleton reiterated what Mankiewicz already thought to be true—that a grueling campaign schedule apparently had led him to be hospitalized. "That's it?" asked Mankiewicz. "Yes, nothing very serious," Eagleton confirmed. Mankiewicz continued, "Tom, let's suppose I'm [Nixon special counsel] Chuck Colson in the White House, and I have these medical records and I say, 'Look here, Mr. President.' Tom, what does the president see? What do the records say?"

"Exhaustion, probably depression, maybe melancholy."

Eagleton withheld the specifics of his treatment, perhaps out of concerns about the lines. The terms "depression" and "melancholy" were vague enough to suggest a condition of any degree of severity. Eagleton's explanation perplexed Hart, Mankiewicz, and Mankiewicz's wife, Holly, who had joined the McGovern aides on St. Thomas. The term "melancholy" especially baffled Mankiewicz. "Tom," he said. "We don't use words like that anymore. Melancholy? That's a nineteenth century disease. I think what it's now called is depression." At the recommendation of Eagleton's staff, Mankiewicz agreed that the vice presidential candidate should not volunteer his history on *Face the Nation* the following morning.[7]

Eagleton's press secretary Mike Kelley made him go to church before his taping on Sunday, and Eagleton's *Face the Nation* appearance went well. Bruce Morton and Barry Serafin of CBS News and Marquis Childs of the *St. Louis Post-Dispatch* sat on the show's panel that morning. None of them brought up the rumors. Neither did the candidate.

After the show, Eagleton, Hart, and Mankiewicz resumed their phone conversation, and the McGovern aides continued to press Eagleton for details about his psychiatric care. As he had done the night before, Eagleton avoided mentioning shock treatment. But the "loose ends" in his account raised Hart's and Mankiewicz's suspicions nonetheless. If the convention had not been so draining, perhaps the aides would have immediately packed for Washington, where they could question Eagleton in person, uninhibited by fears of Nixon wiretaps. "But it was so great being down there [in the Virgin Islands], and we'd only been there such a short time," Mankiewicz later confessed.[8]

For Knight Newspapers and its bevy of regional dailies across the nation that included the *Charlotte Observer,* the *Detroit Free Press,* the *Miami Herald,* and the *Philadelphia Inquirer,* Thomas F. Eagleton was largely an unknown entity. While Washingtonians knew Eagleton as chairman of the Senate Committee on the District of Columbia, charged with oversight of the nation's capital city before it received the right to home rule, he lacked the national name recognition of a Kennedy or a Muskie. So before jetting off to northern Michigan for his postconvention vacation, Knight's Washington bureau chief Bob Boyd dispatched twenty-nine-year-old *Miami Herald* correspondent Clark Hoyt to St. Louis to prepare what he believed would be a routine profile of the man McGovern had picked for his ticket, scuttling Hoyt's own plans for some postconvention respite with his wife.[9]

Hoyt neatly parted his dark, sideburned hair and wore glasses with thick frames and large, circular lenses. He was a stocky young reporter who looked like someone who had played football in prep school, as indeed he had, at the Hill School in Pennsylvania. He came from a middle-class background and was not much of a student, but he found his place in the machine shop, fascinated by the mechanics of car engines. He also cofounded a short-lived magazine with a classmate, Norm Pearlstine. After graduating from Columbia with a degree in English, he landed a summer internship on Capitol Hill with Democratic senator George Smathers of Florida. The stint soon became a full-time job as Smathers's speechwriter and press assistant. But with a couple of years in the role, Hoyt had become frustrated with office work and found himself fascinated by journalism. He started spreading word among congressional staffers and reporters that he wanted to join the press. When the *Miami Herald* reporter who covered the Smathers office in DC, Rose Allegato, landed a job as executive editor of the *Ledger* in her hometown of Lakeland, Florida, she invited Hoyt to join her, and he jumped. Two years later, in 1968, Hoyt took a job with the *Detroit Free Press,* but a Detroit newspaper strike kept him from reporting, so he detoured back to politics, working on the unsuccessful Senate campaign of former Florida governor Leroy Collins. After a few years covering politics in Detroit, Hoyt returned to Washington as the youngest DC correspondent for the *Miami Herald,* another paper in the Knight family.[10]

As Hoyt flew from Miami to St. Louis on Saturday, July 15, John S. Knight III—the twenty-seven-year-old grandson of the patriarch of the Knight Newspapers syndicate—received a call from a man who would identify himself only as "a McGovern supporter." Young Jack Knight listened patiently at his office at the *Detroit Free Press,* where he had been training to write editorials for the newspaper group. The caller claimed to know that Eagleton had a history of mental illness and had received electroshock treatment for a "manic-depressive state with suicidal tendencies." He believed Republican operatives knew this background history and would probably release it late in the game—when it would be too late to correct—if the Democrats did not act soon.[11]

"How do you know this?" Jack Knight asked the mysterious caller, whose voice quivered on the other end of the line. "We have to be able to verify it—can you give us names or anything?"[12]

The caller lacked specifics, but promised to get back to Knight with more information soon.

The caller said he chose the *Detroit Free Press* because he considered it a responsible newspaper, capable of handling the story with care.[13]

As it turns out—if Boyd's theory on the caller and his identity is correct—the caller could not offer more details at that time because he did not have any himself. He had obtained the information second-, even thirdhand in the first place, having overheard the nephew of a female Barnes medical assistant or nurse seated nearby in the restaurant of an Ann Arbor, Michigan, country club, discussing what his aunt had told him about Eagleton.[14]

Another theory on the caller, which *St. Louis Post-Dispatch* Washington bureau chief Dick Dudman later shared with Mike Kelley, is that a young doctor became concerned after seeing reference to Eagleton's electroshock in his medical records. He wanted to know what the treatment meant and started asking around "to bone up on psychiatry." As Kelley's notes recount it, "one of the people [whom the young doctor] asked let [Eagleton's medical history] slip to a young man, a non-doctor," who was also a McGovern supporter and "feared those Republican doctors would blow the whistle." The McGovernite non-doctor thus called the *Detroit Free Press*, "then got cold feet." Kelley, for his part, could not recall what he meant by "cold feet." His scribbles on a U.S. Senate memorandum pad also indicate that the young doctor's "father-in-law [wrote] Agnew or staff at the White House."[15]

A third recollection comes from David Cooper, a former assistant city editor at the *Detroit Free Press* who had done some digging into the tipster's identity as the mystery continued to nag him. Cooper remembers finding that the caller was the college-aged son of a Republican physician or psychiatrist, the patriarch of a prominent Detroit Jewish family. The father had gotten word of Eagleton's treatment from friends of his from St. Louis, and his son—a McGovernite—called the *Free Press* after overhearing his father discussing what he knew, feeling that someone should act before it became too late. The *Post-Dispatch* later reported that "a prominent Detroit man" had written a friend on Agnew's staff with the news, and the vice presidential staffer soon followed up with him by phone. At first the Agnew adviser told him that the administration would not leak Eagleton's treatment, but the aide soon called back to say the news would break the following day.[16]

While these three theories differ in their specifics, they bear a common strand: a young Michigan McGovernite called the *Detroit Free Press* after hearing the gist of Eagleton's treatment from a friend or relative with connections to the St. Louis medical community, fearing its repercussions on McGovern's candidacy.

When Hoyt landed in St. Louis that Saturday, he rented a car and drove straight to the *St. Louis Post-Dispatch* offices to start his research. Hoyt asked to review the paper's clips on Eagleton—a standard preliminary for journalists acquainting themselves with previously unfamiliar subjects. A *Post-Dispatch* editor set Hoyt up alone in a room and delivered him stacks of white envelopes stuffed with the paper's Eagleton clips, yellowing on the aging newsprint.[17]

As a leading figure in St. Louis and Missouri public life, Eagleton received a nearly constant stream of press chronicling his activities in office, so it seemed odd to Hoyt that there were significant gaps in the *Post-Dispatch*'s coverage. Hoyt found short blurbs that corresponded with these gulfs. One, "Eagleton Is in Hospital," dated December 17, 1960, reported that the circuit attorney had checked himself into Barnes, stricken by a virus that was "complicated by hard work in his successful campaign for the office of attorney general." Another notice, "Eagleton Has Check-Up," from December 28, 1964, disclosed that "Attorney General Thomas F. Eagleton entered Mayo Brothers Clinic at Rochester, Minn., yesterday for some tests." He had just won election as lieutenant governor in November, and the notice reported that Eagleton had lost fourteen pounds in the two weeks preceding his hospitalization. The pattern was making itself clear: two successful elections, two hospitalizations. Later, Hoyt found a third news item, from September 21, 1966. This one did not coincide with an election victory. It said the lieutenant governor was "admitted to Johns Hopkins University Hospital, Baltimore, with a gastric disturbance." He was there for some tests, Eagleton's law office said.[18]

Hoyt also discovered a Sunday magazine story that portrayed Eagleton as high-strung, referencing a tremor in his hand and alluding to rumors that the politician had a drinking problem. Hoyt took note of these leads and set off for the Howard Johnson's hotel in downtown St. Louis, where he was staying. There, he checked in with Knight's Washington bureau. News editor Davis "Buzz" Merritt answered the phone and told Hoyt about the call Jack Knight had received in Detroit. After speaking with Merritt and phoning Knight himself, Hoyt confirmed that he should dig deeper into Eagleton's medical history, even as the paper awaited specifics from the caller.

The anonymous tipster called back the following day, Sunday, July 16, and provided Jack Knight the name and address of a doctor who supposedly had been present while Eagleton received shock therapy at Renard Hospital in St. Louis, sometime between 1961 and 1963, dates that were irreconcilable with the *Post-Dispatch* clippings. Knight passed the doctor's information along to Hoyt, and as he drove his rental car sixty miles south of the city to the doctor's house in Bonne Terre, Missouri, Hoyt rehearsed in his head how he would introduce himself.[19]

Hoyt had reason to be nervous. Not only was he inquiring about confidential information—details intended to be kept private, between doctor and patient—but this information regarded a major political figure in Missouri in his moment of national ascent. Hoyt knew that publishing the details of the senator's past could derail Eagleton's political ambitions. Yet Hoyt never doubted his mission to uncover the truth. To Hoyt, the idea that Eagleton had needed shock therapy suggested that he had suffered a seriously debilitating depression. Hoyt reckoned shock therapy "almost a medieval kind of thing . . . a treatment of last resort, for somebody who was extremely far gone." The prospect of someone with the propensity for this kind of incapacitating illness occupying an office a heartbeat away from the presidency frightened him. For Hoyt, the truth about Eagleton's medical history was no longer a private matter but one of national importance, even necessity.

Eagleton's doctor, an anesthesiologist who had since retired, lived in a gated community, but the guardhouse sat empty as Hoyt approached it on this Sunday, permitting him entry into the private enclave. Hoyt knocked on the front door of the physician's house, and Eagleton's doctor—a woman—greeted him.[20]

"Hi, my name is Clark Hoyt, I'm from Knight Newspapers in Washington, DC," he began, "and I'm here to ask you about the time you were present when Senator Eagleton received electroshock therapy at Renard Psychiatric Hospital in and between 1961 and 1963." He sensed himself racing through the lines that he had practiced on the drive over.

As he spoke, Hoyt watched the color drain from the doctor's face.

"I can't talk to you about that," said the doctor as she slammed the door shut.

Though Hoyt was completely unsuccessful in obtaining specifics, from that moment onward, he knew that Eagleton had received shock therapy. Still, this tacit confirmation was not sufficient corroboration for publication. Over the next few days, Hoyt continued compiling information for his profile of the vice presidential candidate. He interviewed Eagleton's Aunt Hazel, who remembered young Tom sitting on the bench next to Judge David F. Fitzgibbon, whom Aunt Hazel worked for as chief parole officer. Hoyt tried to get in touch with Eagleton's brother, Dr. Mark Eagleton, but failed to make contact, which—as Hoyt recalled—turned out to be a blessing in disguise, at least from his perspective as a journalist.[21]

On Monday, July 17, the day after Eagleton's *Face the Nation* appearance and just five days into the Missourian's candidacy, Hart checked in with McGovern-Eagleton Washington headquarters, and as his campaign assistant Marcia Johnston was reading off his messages, she paused. "Oh," she said, "we got this crazy call at the switchboard that was taken down by a volunteer before I came in this morning." Susan Garro, a high school student who was working for the campaign over her summer recess, had spoken with an anonymous "McGovern supporter," who said that a relative of his had worked at Barnes Hospital in St. Louis in the 1960s and knew of Eagleton's treatment at the hospital, which included shock therapy. To Garro, it was not clear whether the informant was calling long-distance, but he struck her as nervous. It also sounded like someone was hovering over him as he spoke. When Johnston finished relaying word of the call to Hart, he and Mankiewicz rolled their eyes and tapped their foreheads in bemusement; with each passing day, Eagleton's mental health history had grown more problematic. They wondered what else their last-minute pick might have hidden from the campaign in his exuberance for the nomination.[22]

The anonymous caller phoned the Washington office again on Tuesday, this time reaching Mankiewicz's secretary, Pat Broun, and sharing the name of his original source, a female Barnes medical assistant. The anonymous caller said that when his source, the medical assistant, checked the hospital's records to verify her memory of Eagleton's treatment, which she believed had occurred sometime between 1961 and 1963, she could no longer find the senator's file. The informant also told Ms. Broun that he had called the *Detroit Free Press* with this tip. Later that day, Susan Garro, the McGovern volunteer who answered the original call from the tipster, relayed the developments to Eagleton's office. Neither Bennet nor Mike Kelley was available, but Bennet's secretary left the following message on his call pad: "Man called [McGovern's] office saying he had access to St. Louis hospital files saying between '61–63 Eagleton was given electroshock treatments for a manic depressive disorder. . . . Said he had also contacted Knight Newspapers on it." Bennet wondered whether Jim Murphy's attempts to secure the records had backfired by reminding the hospital staffers in St. Louis of Eagleton's visit. However, the inaccuracy of the caller's dates relieved Bennet's concern that Murphy's visit to Barnes had led to the tip. Hart and Mankiewicz arranged to meet Eagleton for breakfast on Thursday morning, when they would be back in DC, presumably refreshed from the convention by then. There, they could "grill him."[23]

Upon discovering the Larsen memo in *Time*'s files indicating that Eagleton had received electroshock, Chicago bureau chief Greg Wierzynski sent thirty-two-year-old reporter Burton Pines down to St. Louis for a scouting mission similar to the one Hoyt was undertaking for Knight. Pines's task: to investigate Larsen's allegations that Eagleton had received shock therapy. Wierzynski remembered thinking at the time, "Electroshock is a pretty drastic treatment, and if a man is nominated for a post that is the proverbial heartbeat away, you get antsy about it." Unlike Hoyt, Pines did manage to connect with the senator's brother. When they met, Pines found Dr. Mark Eagleton Jr. to be an exceedingly nervous man, who was nonetheless prepared for *Time*'s visit and ready to discount the rumors the magazine had picked up. A practicing radiologist at Barnes Hospital with a medical degree from Washington University in St. Louis, Dr. Eagleton took Pines to Barnes and showed him the room where he said his brother had been treated—for exhaustion, not depression, and not with electroshock, according to Dr. Eagleton. Pines began his reporting with a few names of Eagleton intimates and, through referrals, ended up speaking with a few dozen associates of the running mate. "From nobody did I get any indication that [Senator Eagleton] was a troubled person," Pines recalled. He found this particularly convincing given the competitive political climate in Missouri. Today, Pines believes the Eagleton network of close family and friends had concocted a web of deception that shielded the full extent of Eagleton's condition and treatment from the public, the press, and political opponents alike. "Certainly his family and those around him were lying," Pines concedes now. But at the time—as he frames it—"I wasn't in any position to draw judgment."[24]

Over the course of *his* week in St. Louis, Hoyt, however, connected with Missourians of both parties who shared new details about the senator's past. Both a Republican involved with the Committee for the Reelection of the President (CREEP) and a player in St. Louis's Democratic circles disclosed that Eagleton had received treatment for some type of nervous breakdown at the Menninger Clinic in Topeka, Kansas, in January 1965. Hoyt also had the name of a nurse believed to have been present for at least one of Eagleton's treatments, but he could not track her down. Hoyt believes that this nurse was the original tipster who passed the information along to the anonymous caller from the Detroit area. Hoyt also spoke with another medical professional who brushed him off with something like, "I can't talk to you about it, but you're on the right track." This response, like that of the door-slamming doctor, reaffirmed Hoyt's conviction that Eagleton had been less than forthcoming about his past.[25]

Senator Eagleton, meanwhile, remained in full-fledged campaign mode, beginning the task of tempering labor's opposition to McGovern's candidacy and winning over big-city voters. On Wednesday, July 19, seven days into Eagleton's candidacy, the AFL-CIO's executive council decided not to endorse either McGovern or Nixon for president, but Eagleton said he was undeterred: "I'm not going to give up hope until such time as Meany tells me categorically that under no circumstances would he support the McGovern-Eagleton ticket."[26]

It was McGovern's fiftieth birthday, and the presidential candidate—vacationing on Sylvan Lake in South Dakota's Black Hills—headed to Mount Rushmore just a short drive away. South Dakota Governor Richard Kneip had declared July 19 George McGovern Day, and, pacing before reporters and supporters gathered at a Mount Rushmore lookout spot, McGovern took questions and signed autographs. He also posed for pictures with the busts of four of the nation's greatest presidents hovering overhead. "We're here for a fitting," Dick Dougherty, McGovern's press secretary, chuckled a bit sheepishly among the newsmen trailing the candidate from photo op to photo op that week. Wearing a cowboy hat, McGovern hopped atop a horse named Big Red and posed for the cameras. An Oglala Sioux Native American shared with McGovern advice first imparted by Abraham Lincoln, one of the presidents enshrined on Mount Rushmore: "Be like a postage stamp—stick to it till you get there," the man told McGovern.[27]

At 8:30 A.M. on Thursday, July 20, Eagleton and Bennet joined Hart and Mankiewicz in the Senate Dining Room as planned. Over breakfast, the vice presidential candidate faced an hour and a half of direct questioning from McGovern's top aides. It may seem odd that the McGovern aides would select the relatively public venue for cross-examining their running mate, but their pointed questioning elicited Eagleton's most accurate account of his mental health history yet. The running mate divulged, albeit with hesitancy, the details of all three hospitalizations. Exhausted from his winning campaign for attorney general of Missouri, in 1960, Eagleton had spent December at Barnes Hospital, in the Renard Psychiatric Division. Other than his specification of Renard, Eagleton was recounting little information that could not be found in the *Post-Dispatch* news clips. A couple of months after winning the lieutenant governorship, he had voluntarily hospitalized himself again, this time for a few days, from December 27, 1964, to January 1, 1965, at the Mayo Clinic, where he supposedly received treatment for stomach problems related to exhaustion. This, too, coincided with the aftermath of an election campaign. Hart also remembered Mankiewicz cracking in December 1971, as the McGovern campaign struggled to make headway in the polls, that more suicides occur around Christmastime than any other time of year. It seemed as if Eagleton's depression could have had something to do with the holiday season and not purely postcampaign depletion.[28]

Eagleton's professed need to revitalize himself also surely resonated with the McGovern team, as it would have with anyone who knew the punishing schedule of a political campaign. Just a few days later, Dougherty—unaware of potential problems with Eagleton's medical case history—was to write a memo to McGovern and several of the other staffers recommending that they avoid scheduling media events from Saturday afternoon to Monday morning in order to afford McGovern some rest and let him rejuvenate for the week to come, the exception being appearances on Sunday morning television shows like *Meet the Press* and *Face the Nation*. Such hiatuses would also give the press a break. "Better spirits, better tempers, all around," Dougherty wrote. If Eagleton learned to allot himself time for rest, as he said he had, perhaps he would be just fine this time around.[29]

But in 1966, from September 20 to October 21—neither an election year nor during winter—Eagleton returned to the Mayo Clinic, suggesting to Mankiewicz that his condition was not, in fact, predicated on overwork on the campaign trail or necessarily exacerbated by Christmastime blues. During each hospitalization, Eagleton said, rest had been his primary form of treatment. Only when the McGovern aides asked Eagleton directly—"Anything else, anything like shock therapy . . . ?"—did the running mate reveal that he had received shock treatments during two of his three hospitalizations: Barnes in 1960 and Mayo in 1966. He added that he had not received much, submitting that he continued to take medication as needed. "But don't worry," he said. "They're in Barbara's name." To Mankiewicz, this was little source of comfort.

Mankiewicz remembers learning later that Eagleton had been taking Thorazine, the brand name for chlorpromazine, one of the first psychotropic drugs ever developed. The medication was used primarily to treat schizophrenia. Mankiewicz also remembers discovering that the diagnosis in Eagleton's medical records listed "paranoid schizophrenia with suicidal tendencies." He is not sure exactly when he first heard this diagnosis and would not share who gave him this information, but he believes it is reliable.[30]

Then, at the Senate Dining Room breakfast, Hart reminded Eagleton that the Committee for the Reelection of the President

(CREEP) would probably locate the senator's medical records; he believed that John Mitchell, the CREEP chairman and U.S. attorney general, who had authority over the FBI, would probably use the Bureau to investigate Eagleton's past if it had not done so already. Thus it seemed reasonable to Hart that Eagleton warn the McGovern campaign of everything that might come its way. Eagleton said he understood the campaign's predicament, and though he said he had never seen his medical records himself, he believed his doctors would cooperate with the McGovern staff. Eagleton promised to bring the records to South Dakota on Tuesday, July 25, the day he planned to visit McGovern in the Black Hills. Eagleton assured both Hart and Mankiewicz that he did not want to hurt the man who had put him on the ticket.[31]

It seems Hart and Mankiewicz had the right intuition: the Nixonites were on the case. On July 15, 1972—two days after Eagleton's nomination to the ticket—President Nixon's personal secretary Rose Mary Woods wrote to Sam Krupnick, a longtime Nixon supporter from St. Louis and the owner of the Krupnick and Associates advertising agency. Before closing, Woods wondered whether Krupnick knew anything about Eagleton and asked what he made of the Missourian's nomination. "About the Tom Eagleton picture," Krupnick wrote near the top of his July 19 response. "I think McGovern made a bad blunder." Then, he proceeded to outline three angles of inquiry:

First, Krupnick described Eagleton's father, Mark, as "a political conniver of a very unsavory nature." He had heard that Mark boasted of his willingness to devote a million dollars to securing Tom's election to the Senate—which, in truth, was far less than what True Davis had dispensed on his own primary campaign against Eagleton. Yet Krupnick continued, "Mark's loose ethical conduct extended even to his domestic life," noting reports that Mark Eagleton Sr.'s will stipulated that half of his estate go to his widow and the other half to his secretary, who Krupnick had heard was his longtime mistress.

Second, Krupnick passed along rumors that Eagleton had cycled in and out of St. Louis's Malcolm Bliss mental hospital, a public institution, over the years, afflicted with "acute alcoholism." Eagleton "still has a whiskey voice," Krupnick related, seemingly speaking from firsthand knowledge. "He came by it honestly."

Third, Krupnick believed that there was a "very strong likelihood" that Eagleton had connections with corrupt labor bosses and their associates who could have helped him capture the vice presidential nomination. Krupnick recommended further digging.

It should be noted that, while they are not certain of every allegation in Krupnick's letter, Ruth Herbst and Dorothy Dubuque, who worked as secretaries for Tom and Mark Eagleton Sr. during parts of the time period in question, reported in interviews and correspondence with the author that they find nearly all of Krupnick's assertions either wrong or inconceivable.

Krupnick added that he considered Eagleton "a very bright and articulate young man. Photogenic, too." But he suspected that the Missourian's selection would backfire on the Democratic ticket as more details emerged about his past. He inserted "one more thought about Tom Eagleton" before ending his three-page letter. "He's a very impetuous person," Krupnick declared. "And the combination of his drinking and his impetuosity got him into serious trouble at home." Krupnick also wrote that he had received a call from "Bob" that week. Krupnick did not provide Bob's last name, but all indications point to H. R. "Bob" Haldeman, the White House chief of staff, or Robert Mardian, assistant attorney general. Krupnick noted that Bob would be stopping over in St. Louis on Friday night, July 21, probably to conduct additional reconnaissance on Eagleton on his way to the West Coast for the weekend.

That Sunday, July 23, Pat Buchanan got hold of Krupnick's letter. Woods had presumably passed it along to the young White House aide who had worked for the conservative *St. Louis Globe-Democrat* after completing his journalism degree at Columbia. Buchanan responded to Krupnick's letter by firing off a memo to Nixon counsel Chuck Colson: "Let's get together and make a determination as to how we can get this material investigated fully—and then gotten out of here," he wrote. "Also, the timing. Perhaps it should come rolling out, in the fall or in October." Buchanan imagined that Nixon's team could spring it on McGovern in the critical weeks before the election. Colson scrawled a handwritten note on Buchanan's memo: "Pat—no need to talk about it; I've already taken care of it."[32]

On the Thursday of Eagleton's breakfast meeting with Hart and Mankiewicz, July 20, a week into the Missourian's candidacy, Mc-Govern interrupted his vacation in the Black Hills to return to the Senate to cast the deciding vote on the minimum wage bill. When in DC, McGovern learned from Hart that he and Mankiewicz had met with Bennet and Eagleton that morning to discuss Eagleton's mental health. But Hart did not convey any urgency. Judging from Hart's presentation of the matter, McGovern gathered that the consequences of Eagleton's unspecified revelations about his history of medical treatment were, if not insignificant, certainly not insurmountable for the campaign. As McGovern would argue in retrospect, however, he should have stayed in Washington, where he could have confronted the situation with the "best-qualified" advisers at his disposal and his running mate on hand. No one conveyed alarm to him; no one insisted that McGovern stay in Washington. Hart and Mankiewicz's lack of urgency is puzzling, particularly given their mutual acknowledgment that Eagleton's history posed a serious problem for the campaign. As Mankiewicz had gasped that morning, upon learning Eagleton's therapy had included electroshock, "This word 'shock.' Boy, that's a tough word for the public."[33]

Though most medically oriented psychiatrists have considered electroshock therapy the most effective means of treating severe depression, the treatment has faced two fundamental obstacles to its widespread acceptance. First, no one has concluded why electroconvulsive therapy (ECT) works; ECT's inexplicability has long aroused suspicion and enabled proponents of rival therapies to discount it. Second, its similarity in name and appearance with the electric chair invites a link between the two procedures in the popular imagination, leading some to presume ECT to be a horrific, life-threatening procedure; some have believed that shocking the brain means burning it. As Phil Zeidman, who served as executive director of the 1972

Democratic Platform Committee, said of the impression of electroshock in a recent interview, "It's an assault on the senses."[34]

Professor Ugo Cerletti of Italy performed the first electroshock
treatment in 1938, and the procedure's arrival in the United States
a few years later coincided with the popularization of Freudian
psychoanalysis and its emphasis on sustained talk therapy. Following the teachings of Sigmund Freud, psychoanalysts promoted a
situational understanding of mental illness, viewing neuroses as
"reactive" to life experiences. They believed depression, for instance,
was rooted in unconscious hostilities, residual anger or ambivalence
over loss, or other early childhood experiences. Shock therapy, conversely, appeared to have no philosophical or logical underpinning
other than its proven success rates and its practitioners' speculation that mental illness is "endogenous," determined by a person's
brain chemistry and disconnected to external life circumstances and
events. In 1972 psychiatry was fraught with opposition between these
two perceptibly irreconcilable visions.[35]

A doctor performs shock therapy by sending a short jolt of
electricity through the patient's brain, inducing convulsions that,
when the procedure is successful, somehow improve the patient's
outlook. The seizure is the vehicle of electroshock's efficacy. As the
procedure typically was practiced in the 1960s, anesthesia, muscle
relaxants, and oxygen tanks had made electroshock painless and
relatively safe. In the intervening years, adjustments in electrode
placement and pulse type have made ECT even safer and more effective. Placing both electrodes on the right side of the brain instead
of one on each side has reduced memory loss, which already was
relatively minor. Today the risk of amnesia from ECT is about equal
to or less than the risk in open-heart surgery. Further, new titration
procedures have helped tailor dosages for each individual, additionally increasing efficacy. Outcomes tend to be best when followed up
with a combination of medication and talk therapy.[36]

Still, while there are several hypotheses about ECT's efficacy,
in the 1970s—as today—no one could conclude exactly why electroshock worked. The treatment implied a chemical basis of mental
illness that challenged psychoanalysts' educations and professional

value, contributing to the suspicion, and even passionate opposition, surrounding the procedure. The most effective treatment for certain types of depression contradicted psychoanalysts' belief that mental illness stems from an unconscious mind that is disconnected from the brain and its chemistry. Although today divisions have faded within psychiatry, psychoanalysts have always recommended ECT sparingly—as a method of "last resort," a stop-gap solution reserved for those instances when continuing psychoanalysis alone risked a patient suicide. In part because today's psychotropic medications are significantly improved, many professionals still resist using ECT. In 1972 psychoanalysts argued that ECT interfered with psycho-analysis by disrupting a patient's memories, the exploration of which they considered essential to the efficacy of psychoanalysis and, thus, eventual rehabilitation. Yet medically oriented psychiatrists believed ECT's interruption of unhealthy emotional and behavioral patterns explained precisely why it worked. The 1950–52 *Biennial Report* of the California Department of Mental Hygiene described electroshock therapy as "[unscrambling] twisted emotions," an understanding of ECT that persisted long thereafter. Another hypothesis grounded in neuroscience and gaining traction by 1972 suggested that ECT spiked the brain's levels of serotonin and norepinephrine, the neurotrans-mitters that psychiatrists believed to drive mood.

Crusaders in the antipsychiatry movement of the 1960s cam-paigned to curtail electroshock, prompting new regulations. In-deed, some doctors employed electroshock inappropriately—to fight schizophrenia, morphine addiction, and homosexuality, as well as to punish and control unruly mental hospital patients. These were conscious misapplications of the treatment that gave fuel to the cam-paign against it. But these abuses were the exceptions, not the rule. From 1938 to approximately 1970, many psychiatrists, neurologists, and family doctors safely performed electroshock outside the con-fines of hospitals, often in the form of quick "maintenance" treat-ments. In the fifties and sixties, the zenith of electroshock usage in the United States, approximately 300,000 Americans received the treatment each year.[37]

The antipsychiatry movement also grew out of 1960s New Left

counterculture and targeted ECT as a brutal implement of government repression, of societal standardization, exploiting the procedure's consternating appearance in vilifying it. Psychoanalyst
Thomas Szasz's influential *The Myth of Mental Illness* propounded the
notion of mental illness as an invention of modern society, depicting
psychiatrists as complicit in the governmental conspiracy to suppress
individuality. An array of films, including *Three Faces of Eve* (1957),
Splendor in the Grass (1961), and *Pressure Point* (1962), promoted talk
therapy as a rational, individualistic means of self-improvement as
opposed to the supposedly baseless, impersonal, and torturous ECT
alternative. The influence of Ken Kesey's 1962 novel *One Flew over
the Cuckoo's Nest* was especially profound. The best-seller described
the electroshock machine as "a device that might be said to do the
work of the sleeping pill, the electric chair, and the torture rack" as
wardens of state mental institutions deployed electroshock to pacify
their most unruly patients. Kesey's electroshock rendered its victims
unable to think clearly or to recall past events, and it trapped them
in a "foggy, jumbled blur" that often lasted more than two weeks.
"No one ever wants another" ECT treatment, the novel's narrator
said, hardening the public's aversion to ECT and branding the treatment with a stigma that persists to this day, compounded by the
Oscar-winning film adaptation of the book. Despite electroshock's
acceptance in certain psychiatric circles, particularly in the early
sixties—which was when Kesey wrote *Cuckoo's Nest* and Eagleton
received his treatment—the novel cultivated the perception of ECT
as "almost out of vogue and only used in extreme cases nothing else
seemed to reach, like lobotomy." The novel also popularized a sensationalized portrayal of ECT, depicting a version of the treatment
that was already anachronistic at the time of the book's publication,
after Eagleton had already undergone his first treatment. By the
1960s most ECT practitioners were using anesthetics and muscle
relaxants, minimizing the pain and the danger of broken bones, but
without purging those specters from the public imagination. Millen
Brand's 1968 best-seller *Savage Sleep*, Doris Lessing's 1971 *Briefing for a
Descent into Hell*, and the 1971 American edition of Sylvia Plath's *The
Bell Jar* reinforced Kesey's portrayal of electroshock—as a harrowing,

scarring procedure. Interestingly, Barbara Eagleton had just finished reading *The Bell Jar* before arriving in Miami Beach. "Electroshock is simply something you don't go around talking about at cocktail parties," Tom Eagleton explained.[38]

But shock therapy was not always so taboo, especially in the pre–*Cuckoo's Nest* era at Barnes Hospital, where Eagleton first received treatment. Barnes was an affiliate of Washington University in St. Louis, whose researchers and doctors subscribed to a medical model of mental illness. Psychiatrists who suspected a biological basis of mental illness gravitated toward the Midwest and places like Washington University and the University of Iowa, where they could pursue their study free from the domination of psychoanalysts who had long ruled psychiatry departments at the elite East Coast universities. Washington University was one of the first universities to name a full-time chairman to its psychiatry department, Dr. Edward Gildea, and he established a program that united psychotherapy with investigation into the biological underpinnings of mental illness. When Gildea retired, Dr. Eli Robbins was named chairman, and he focused the department on biological psychiatry, with an emphasis on establishing definitions and diagnoses for the different types of mental illnesses and tailoring treatments accordingly. As clinicians, doctors who trained at Washington University and practiced at Barnes did not share the suspicion of ECT rampant elsewhere in the country. They considered ECT an effective procedure, and doctors saw little point in dawdling with other treatments for conditions they believed to be ECT-treatable, especially in the early 1960s. The psychotropic drugs available—Monoamine oxidase inhibitors (MAOIs) and tricyclics—were toxic, slow, and encumbered with side effects, from sexual dysfunction to hypertension, and sometimes even fatal strokes. Further facilitating ECT's adoption, most private insurance companies covered thirty days of inpatient psychiatric care, allowing time for a full course of ECT treatment. It was also not uncommon for people, mentally ill or otherwise, to disappear to the hospital for a few weeks to ward off a variety of ailments. Furthermore, for people in the public eye, inpatient ECT had the advantage of sheltering a depressive at his or her most vulnerable state.[39]

While electroshock's reputation had waned in the years since Eagleton's therapy, the public also seemed to have become more accepting of mental illness in general during this period. For example, a 1967 Louis Harris poll found that most Americans would seek a psychiatrist's help if a relative became mentally ill. "The day has passed when a person requiring professional help is looked upon as 'crazy' or 'mad' or 'out of his mind,'" Harris summarized. Most believed mental patients could successfully rehabilitate. The 1954 arrival of chlorpromazine, marketed by Smith Kline and French as Thorazine in the United States, certainly helped. But reformed attitudes toward mental illness in general did not equate to acceptance of electroshock, or of patients who had undergone the treatments, with ECT already in its post–*Cuckoo's Nest* remission.[40]

Thus, McGovern's senior aides' postponement of their discussion of how to approach Eagleton's mental health history is confounding, particularly given their professed concern. Perhaps Hart and Mankiewicz detected in McGovern an eagerness to return to the Black Hills. Perhaps they felt they could use the extra days for reflection. Perhaps their own exhaustion kept them from charting a more strategic course of action. Perhaps they wanted to wait until they had McGovern to themselves, hoping to reestablish their authority over the campaign. Whatever the reason or reasons, Hart and Mankiewicz, apparently perceiving that their influence was slipping, seemed reluctant to press McGovern on Eagleton.

On July 20, the day of the aides' breakfast meeting with Eagleton, and with McGovern in town to vote on a bill to raise the minimum wage, the candidate announced—with his vice presidential running mate, Tom Eagleton, standing by his side—that Larry O'Brien, the Old Guard pol ousted as DNC chairman just six days earlier, would join the campaign as its chairman. In announcing O'Brien's new position, McGovern said he expected O'Brien would act as the campaign's "foremost consultant on . . . overall policy and strategy," which—if taken at face value—compromised Hart and Mankiewicz's jurisdiction over the campaign, even though McGovern claimed otherwise. Some reporters interpreted this as a deliberate affront to McGovern's supposed brain trust. "I'm sorry I didn't have time to discuss this more fully with you," McGovern whispered to Hart before his press conference with O'Brien.[41]

McGovern's staff had angered him the day after the convention by failing to relay word that New York State Democratic Chairman Joseph Crangle had called to urge him to reinstate the big-labor favorite, O'Brien, as party chief. Instead, he ended up appointing Jean Westwood and Basil Paterson to the top jobs. McGovern had promised the DNC chairmanship to both O'Brien and Westwood, the slender forty-eight-year-old Democratic committeewoman from Utah, who had closely cropped blonde hair and looked like an elementary school librarian. Westwood's career in national politics had begun when she joined the PTA of her children's school, and she boasted loyalty to McGovern since 1968. However, by promising the DNC chairmanship to both Westwood and O'Brien, McGovern had lodged himself in a bind. In the end, the day after the convention, McGovern rescinded his offer to O'Brien within an hour of having extended it to him. Mankiewicz, Hart, and other top campaign aides, unaware their boss had already told O'Brien he wanted him to continue as DNC chair, recommended that McGovern use the chairmanship as substantiation of his New Politics values, a symbol of progress on behalf of women. They argued that O'Brien, conversely, embodied the status quo, and McGovern also sensed Westwood's anguish at the prospect of not getting the post. So he handed her the job. Then, at the Democratic National Committee meeting later that day, McGovern also backtracked on his nomination of Pierre Salinger as vice chairman when Charles Evers, the black civil rights activist, objected and proposed picking a black man for the position—another symbol to complement Westwood's appointment. Evers recommended Basil Paterson, and the notion gained momentum. McGovern soon amended his endorsement of Salinger, saying either man was fine with him. A disappointed Salinger bowed out before the committee could vote.[42]

The day after McGovern named O'Brien campaign chairman, Friday, July 21, a *New York Times* article quoted a McGovern "senior adviser" as dismissing O'Brien's new post as "largely honorary"—a comment taken by the press as evidence of the bitterness within the McGovern organization, the simmering tensions between Old and

New Politics, and between veteran and youthful campaign advisers. This was at a time when the press was already rife with speculation of an intensifying power struggle, even a standoff, within the McGovern organization.[43]

In this context, the candidate, his wife, his staff, and his press corps left Washington at around 12:30 P.M. that July 21, without any discussion of Eagleton's history. About halfway through the flight to South Dakota, Hart and Mankiewicz joined George and Eleanor McGovern in the couple's compartment. The aides leaned in, lowered their voices, and recounted their conversations with the vice presidential candidate.

"What does this mean?" McGovern asked after the aides presented Eagleton's full history as they understood it.[44]

Despite Mankiewicz's delay in relaying the information, to him, Eagleton's three hospitalizations and two treatments with electroshock therapy meant that McGovern should remove his running mate from the ticket as soon as possible, but he should do so in a way that would make it seem as if Eagleton was withdrawing on his own volition. Though it is unclear whether he told McGovern at the time, Mankiewicz had polled nineteen psychiatrists since learning of Eagleton's illness; he began with four or five whom he knew and spoke to others on referral. The consensus was clear: Eagleton's case history and course of treatment implied manic-depression, and a manic-depressive could handle any job but the presidency, the professionals had told him.[45]

To Hart, lingering questions about Eagleton's history demanded professional validation of his fitness for office. As Hart saw it, the campaign needed to consult Eagleton's personal doctors and scour his medical records, which Eagleton had promised to deliver when he stopped by South Dakota on Tuesday, already scheduled to meet with McGovern on his way west for his first campaign swing. "You owe that to the country," Hart told his boss. If professional opinion concluded that Eagleton was competent enough to remain on the ticket, the running mate should stay. If not, McGovern had a scapegoat—the professional assessment that said Eagleton must go. "Those [medical] records and what they contained could prove to be

McGovern's salvation, not his ruin," Hart remembered thinking at the time. He considered the proper response to be a "clinical question, not a political one." Unlike Mankiewicz, Hart had not yet made up his mind. Still, he suspected that a medical assessment based on the records themselves would require Eagleton's departure. And he imagined this—a medical decision—would be more defensible than a simply political calculation.[46]

McGovern resisted drawing any conclusions: he wanted to hear Eagleton's story from Eagleton himself. As his O'Brien appointment implied, McGovern was starting to show signs of doubting his top staffers and their judgment. Or maybe he just really did want Eagleton's perspective. But it also seems that McGovern—now aware of the Eagleton case history, shock therapy included—should have sensed the urgency of the situation and summoned his running mate to the Black Hills ahead of schedule to give the campaign extra days to reflect and deliberate. Despite his top aides' warnings that this development might require he drop his running mate, McGovern—as uncomfortable with confrontation as ever—still believed he could avoid the issue. Hart and Mankiewicz might have insisted that the campaign confront the Eagleton situation at once, but they lacked the political capital to do so.[47]

Speaking with McGovern privately for the first time since the convention, Hart found him "distracted, even disconsolate," on the plane to South Dakota. Hart asked McGovern why he, the victor—the Democratic Party's nominee for the presidency—seemed so glum.

"I can't explain it," McGovern responded. "Eleanor and I have both been kind of blue since Miami. It's been kind of a letdown emotionally."[48]

While on the ground in St. Louis, Clark Hoyt kept in constant contact with his editor Bob Boyd, who was still vacationing in northern Michigan. The two journalists knew that Knight's corporate psychologist, Byron Harless, was reaching out to his peers in St. Louis and elsewhere on background, and his reluctance to pull them off the case implied that their story had grounding. As the reporters accumulated more evidence, they became increasingly confident in the veracity of the anonymous caller's assertions and decided to craft a memo outlining what they knew. Thursday night—the same day Eagleton, Bennet, Hart, and Mankiewicz had met in the Senate Dining Room for breakfast and McGovern had named O'Brien his campaign's chairman—Hoyt sat at his desk in his Howard Johnson's hotel room in St. Louis, tense as he pecked at his typewriter, distilling the information he had compiled through the week. The far-reaching reverberations of his scoop, personal and political for Eagleton, for McGovern, and for the nation at large, weighed heavily on him.[49]

A knock on the door broke Hoyt's concentration. He opened it to find a towering police officer standing there, his uniform neatly pressed and gun tucked in his holster. "Oh shit," Hoyt quaked. "They're going to do something to me."

"Do you have a [red Chevy sedan] in the parking lot?" the policeman inquired.

Someone had hit-and-run the reporter's rental car, and the officer had come to deliver the news. Relieved in a way that must have surprised the policeman, Hoyt thanked the officer and resumed typing.[50]

Eagleton Memo

1. A Mr. X telephoned John Knight and, in a series of conversations, said Eagleton received shock treatment for an acute manic-depressive condition, with suicidal tendencies, at Renard Hospital, St. Louis, some time between 1961 and 1963. He said he is a McGovern-Eagleton supporter who wanted to "warn McGovern" before this information could be used in a smear campaign.

2. Mr. X gave us the name of a physician who was allegedly present during the treatment. The physician refused to discuss the matter with us in any detail but tacitly confirmed it.

3. A Kansas City political reporter said he heard repeated rumors that Eagleton, at some point during his term as attorney general (1961–1965), had to slip away to St. Louis to "dry out."

The reporter discounted the rumors at the time because he came to know Eagleton well after 1965 and never saw any evidence of a drinking problem.

4. Independent of the above information, a top Missouri Republican leader connected with the Committee for the Re-Election of the President volunteered that Eagleton was treated for nervous exhaustion or a nervous breakdown at the Menninger Clinic in January, 1965.

5. A leading St. Louis Democrat, who said he is a friend of Eagleton's, also told us Eagleton was treated at Menninger Clinic in January, 1965, for a nervous breakdown. He said there was a relapse in 1967.

6. Three psychiatric sources—all of whom were connected with Renard and/or Menninger's in the 1960s—tacitly confirmed that they knew Eagleton had been treated. Citing professional ethics, all refused to discuss specifics of his case. But each indicated, even before we said it, that he knew exactly what we were calling about. All used phrases such as, "I can't deny it. . . ."

7. Newspaper clippings indicate Eagleton suffers periodically from a "gastric disturbance." He was hospitalized in December, 1964, at Mayo Clinic and again in September, 1966, at Johns Hopkins University Hospital.

8. Eagleton told the Kansas City reporter in 1968 that he suffered from a "nervous stomach."

EAGLETON'S HEALTH is certainly going to become an issue before the campaign is over.

The rumor mill in St. Louis, in both Republican and Democratic circles, is humming, and a reporter doesn't have to be in town long to get an earful.

The Committee for the Re-Election of the President is

clearly in possession of some information, and we know that
at least one other news organization, Time Magazine, has been
investigating and may still be.

Bob Boyd and Clark Hoyt
Knight Newspapers[51]

Hoyt and Boyd reasoned that they had a professional responsibility to give Eagleton the opportunity to respond. Yet they suspected
he would deny it, stall indefinitely, or, at best, respond only after
conferring with McGovern and his aides. They knew Eagleton was
scheduled to arrive in South Dakota from Washington late Monday,
and the reporters concluded that they should be on the scene a couple
of days earlier, on Saturday, affording them some time to try to cor-
roborate the story with the McGovern campaign first.[52]

McGovern intended to find postconvention sanctuary at the wood-
paneled Sylvan Lake Lodge in his home state's Black Hills National
Forest. Between TV-ready photo ops—like that atop Big Red in front
of Mount Rushmore—and tennis lessons with a pro whom he had
flown in from Washington, McGovern planned to regroup his staff
and retool for the fall campaign. The anonymous senior adviser's
crack in the *Times* that O'Brien's appointment was "largely honorary"
still irked McGovern on Saturday, and he vented his disappointment
at the staff meeting first thing that morning. "I want this stopped,"
he announced. "I don't know who all these 'senior advisers' are who
know what's on my mind better than I do myself. I don't want to
know. I'm just telling all of you that I'm not going to put up with any
more of it." He continued: "So from here on out nobody is to talk
to the press for this campaign except myself and Dick Dougherty,
and that's that."

Just hours after McGovern reprimanded his staff for its habit
of inside leaks, a story about McGovern's rebuke of his aides had
hit the wires.[53]

By nightfall, tension appeared to have subsided. Camp McGovern capped off its first day of strategizing since the candidate's return
from Washington by gathering in the Sylvan Lake Lodge lobby for

The McGovern high command strategy session at the Sylvan Lake Lodge near Custer, South Dakota, Saturday, July 22, 1972: clockwise from left, Rep. William Clay of Missouri, congressional delegate Walter Fauntroy of the District of Columbia, Frank Mankiewicz, Eleanor McGovern, George McGovern, Gary Hart, Stanley Greigg (sitting in on behalf of Larry O'Brien), and DNC chair Jean Westwood (AP/Wide World Photos)

some postdinner song. John Holum, a longtime McGovern aide from South Dakota, strummed his guitar that Saturday evening, and the candidate joined in with the rest of his staff, humming folk classics like "Amazing Grace," "Shenandoah," and "This Land Is Your Land." The Reverend Walter Fauntroy, the District of Columbia's at-large delegate to Congress, who was black and had joined McGovern's circle after folding his own presidential bid, belted out "There Is a Balm in Gilead." And the whole crew joined in for a resounding rendition of "We Shall Overcome"—a hymn emblematic of the McGovern campaign and its New Politics, but one whose title also invoked the daunting task ahead. On the one hand, the campaign needed to overcome intrastaff and intraparty tensions. And on the other—though only four people on the McGovern team in South Dakota knew it at the time—it seemed that the campaign would also need to overcome the legacy of its vice presidential candidate's history of depression and electroshock treatment.[54]

When the two Knight reporters met in Rapid City, South Dakota, on
Saturday, eager to discuss how to proceed with what promised to be
the biggest story of the summer, they stumbled across *Chicago Sun-
Times* columnist Bob Greene at the rental car station. "Come on, ride
with us," they volunteered, though neither Knight reporter wanted
to make small talk. Boyd and Hoyt patiently waited until they arrived at the Hi-Ho Motel in Custer to review their memo one last
time and plot their course of action. They would visit Mankiewicz
first and then, if necessary, confront McGovern.[55]

The Disclosure

On Sunday, July 23, the running mate's tenth day on the ticket, Eagleton was still in Washington, on ABC's *Issues and Answers*, accusing Nixon of pursuing "an election-year schedule" for withdrawing the nation's troops from Vietnam. In South Dakota, McGovern also took to the airwaves, appearing on *Face the Nation* and referencing his running mate throughout the program. And it was there, in South Dakota's Black Hills, where Knight Newspaper reporters Bob Boyd and Clark Hoyt found Frank Mankiewicz alone in his Sylvan Lake log cabin, with the fireplace lit on the cool summer day. The reporters handed over their memo and, though riddled with factual errors, it laid bare Eagleton's potential to damage the campaign. "The rumor mill in St. Louis, in both Republican and Democratic circles, is humming, and a reporter doesn't have to be in town long to get an earful," they had written. Mankiewicz later was to remember that Boyd and Hoyt's July 23 memo had alleged that Eagleton had been treated for "severe manic depressive psychosis with suicidal tendencies." The version of the memo found in McGovern's papers verifies this: "Eagleton received shock treatment for an acute manic-depressive condition, with suicidal tenden-

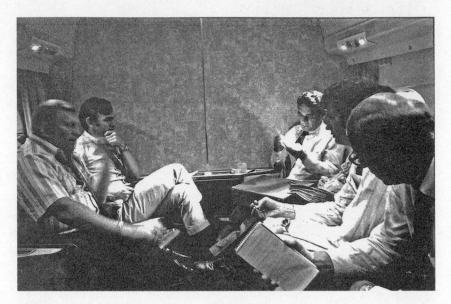

Aboard a Braniff Airlines chartered Lockheed Electra propjet, the Eagleton crew huddled en route to Rapid City, South Dakota, from Washington, DC, late Monday night
into early Tuesday morning. From left, Jerry McDougal, Doug Bennet, Tom Eagleton,
Gene Godley, and Bob Harris. "The damn engines caused so much vibration that
the first-class section was in the tail," recalled AP reporter Brooks Jackson, who was
traveling with the vice presidential candidate. (Personal collection of Gene Godley)

cies." The copy of the memo found in Eagleton's archives, however,
does not include "suicidal tendencies." This phrase appears crossed
out.[1]

    After reading through the document, Mankiewicz said he was
not convinced. "There's no proof here of anything," he said. No one
had furnished the medical records, no one had provided any evidence. Yet Mankiewicz did concede the seriousness of the matter:
"Eagleton is on his way out here, we'll produce him for an interview
with you, and we'll get you his medical records, we'll clear this all
up," he said. Mankiewicz thanked the reporters for speaking with
him first and promised to follow up soon. As Eagleton had assured
him, the records were on their way.[2]

    With time for reflection running short and concerned that the
reporters' memo related a history of mental illness more serious than

Eagleton had suggested, Mankiewicz visited George and Eleanor McGovern that night. "Let's get rid of this guy," he told the couple in their cabin. Mankiewicz felt duped by the vice presidential candidate's dishonesty, anxious about the impending public reaction, and responsible for guaranteeing Eagleton's fitness to serve. But McGovern held firm. As before, he wanted to hear from Eagleton himself.

Mankiewicz called Doug Bennet to share the substance of the Knight memorandum, which Mankiewicz described as rife with "lurid" details, and to see whether he could get anything more out of him. Bennet assured Mankiewicz that the memo cited the wrong dates and, in some cases, the wrong place of treatment. And he repeated yet again that Eagleton did not have a drinking problem. Still, Mankiewicz reiterated his desire to see the records himself, so after checking with Eagleton, Bennet asked Jim Murphy and Ed Filippine to try to collect them from Barnes and Mayo in time for Tuesday's meeting in South Dakota. Other than that, Bennet did not make much of Mankiewicz's phone call, and he prepared for Eagleton's stop in South Dakota as it was originally conceived: as an opportunity for the running mates and their staffs to meet in person and start planning for the fall campaign. He still expected the meeting to focus on questions about scheduling, budget, and how Eagleton could be most strategically deployed. "Who is responsible for Chicanos and other minorities?" for instance. As Bennet summarized for Eagleton in a memo outlining issues for discussion, "The point [of the meeting] is to try to precipitate decisions in each of these areas where, apparently, decisions have not been made," making no reference to decisions about the senator's mental health history.[3]

On Monday, Boyd and Hoyt checked in with McGovern's press secretary Dick Dougherty every few hours about when they could interview Eagleton. "Soon," Dougherty would reply each time, unaware of why they were so desperate to talk with the running mate, even by phone. The reporters believed, as Mankiewicz had promised, that they would receive a private session with Eagleton so that he could clarify the specifics of his treatment and answer the inevitable questions about his fitness to serve. They expected that the campaign would hold a press conference only after their article ran in the Wednesday or Thursday morning editions of Knight Newspapers nationwide.[4]

That night, Dougherty found Mankiewicz in his cabin, just as he was telling Fred Dutton, another one of McGovern's older, more experienced advisers, about the Knight memo. "As I assume you've guessed, Richard, there is more than a little truth to those Eagleton rumors," Mankiewicz told Dougherty when he arrived.

"Unbelievable," Dougherty responded.

"But true, alas. At least true enough to hurt. You know? A little shock treatment."

"Jesus Christ," Dougherty said, shaking his head in the swirl of astonishment and anxiety that engulfed him.

"That was exactly my response," Dutton jumped in, "Oh, boy, oh, boy, oh, boy!"

Mankiewicz told Dougherty and Dutton that Tom and Barbara Eagleton and the rest of the vice presidential candidate's traveling party would be arriving at the lake later that night. The Eagletons had a breakfast meeting planned with the McGoverns in the morning, around 8 A.M., and Mankiewicz said they would decide what to do from there.

Before the three aides dispersed for the evening, Dutton said, "I'll tell you one thing. If [Eagleton had] pulled this on a Kennedy, we'd find his body at the base of the cliff in the morning."[5]

When Eagleton arrived in the Black Hills shortly after midnight, he asked his two envoys, Murphy and Filippine, to join him in his cabin to "talk about the records." Documentation of their conversation does not detail their discussion. Bennet's reference to this meeting seems purposefully ambiguous: it is not clear whether "talk about the records" implies that they talked about the content of the records that Murphy and Filippine had recovered and Eagleton had not yet seen, or whether it means Eagleton merely sought an update on their efforts to get the records, which had been unsuccessful.[6]

Before breakfast on Tuesday, the Knight reporters Bob Boyd and Clark Hoyt returned to Sylvan Lake from their motel in nearby Custer, itching for their private session with the vice presidential candidate. When they checked in with Mankiewicz, he told them that Eagleton had arrived late the night before and had not yet met with McGovern. He also answered their request to see the medical records: they would not be released, he told them.[7]

At 8 A.M., Tom and Barbara Eagleton joined George and Eleanor McGovern in their cabin for breakfast. It was July 25, the second anniversary of the death of Tom's father and twelve days since the birth of Tom's own candidacy. After eating, McGovern proposed that the running mates head to a separate cabin and talk in private. Eagleton, however, preferred the presence of their wives. "George and Eleanor, I want to give you the full background on my health," he said. And McGovern agreed to stay put, handing Eagleton the two-page memorandum from the Knight reporters. As Eagleton dissected the memo's inaccuracies and shared his own account, McGovern scribbled notes on a yellow legal pad, interrupting only occasionally to request that Eagleton specify his dates. After noting the three hospitalizations Eagleton had already accounted for with Mankiewicz and Hart—their reason, dates, location, and treatment, underlining *electric shock* both times the phrase occurred—McGovern wrote: "Menninger charge totally false—; Never at Menninger—; Never at Johns Hopkins—." The exchange lasted between fifteen and twenty minutes. "That's not too bad," McGovern concluded when Eagleton finished. "Tom, I think we can handle this situation." And with that, McGovern and Eagleton called in their aides—Dougherty and Mankiewicz of McGovern's staff, and Bennet and Kelley of Eagleton's—to plot how best to proceed.[8]

George, Eleanor, and Barbara remained at the table, which had been cleared of all but Mrs. Eagleton's cup and saucer. Tom sat across the room, in the middle of the sofa, with the aides finding seats to his left. McGovern fiddled with an unlit cigar, and Eagleton lit another cigarette. Then he summarized the preceding conversation for the aides.[9]

"I've also told George," he added, "that if he wants me to, I'll get off the ticket this second, this minute, this hour, [this day], this week—any time that he concludes my presence on the ticket is an embarrassment or a hindrance to his chances of election." But there, in the intimacy of cabin 22, McGovern affirmed his support for his running mate. "I'm prepared to stand by him in this," McGovern said. "I think we can ride it through."[10]

With more time for reflection, perhaps McGovern could have anticipated the backlash that would follow. There was a reason his running mate's history of depression and treatment with shock therapy had attracted the press's interest and inspired his own staffers' concern. But in cabin 22, McGovern and Eagleton did not speak politician-to-politician, or as a boss to his subordinate. Miles away from Washington, and with their wives by their sides, the running mates spoke man-to-man, teammate-to-teammate. One wonders whether Eagleton anticipated that the wives' presence would give the conversation a tone of intimacy that would work to his advantage. That morning, the candidates also spoke couple-to-couple, family-to-family. Eagleton stressed his recovery, emphasizing a desire to put his past behind him. And he apologized for failing to publicize his bouts of depression and treatment with electroshock in the midst of the proudest moment of his career, his selection to the ticket. McGovern extended his compassion to the freshman senator, channeling the same yearning to help those in need that characterized his politics. Reacting as a person rather than a politician, McGovern resolved to help his partner confront his demons, forgetting his own pragmatic, politically expedient self for the time being.

Though few knew it at the time, McGovern's daughter Terry had been wrestling with her own case of clinical depression. Like Eagleton, McGovern kept this detail hidden. However, McGovern revealed to his aides nearly two years later—and to the general public after Terry's 1994 death from depression and alcoholism—that his feelings for his daughter and her condition had shaded his judgment in evaluating the political ramifications of Eagleton's case. "I could not in effect punish [Eagleton] for being a victim of depression," he wrote. As Mankiewicz later understood, when the candidate sat across from his running mate that morning, telling Eagleton that he could not handle the vice presidency would have been equivalent to McGovern telling his daughter, "You're not fit."[11]

And though he never said it, Eleanor's experience with depression must have also figured into McGovern's thinking. According to Blue Cross insurance claims left in George McGovern's papers, Eleanor McGovern had received treatment for "nervousness, depression" in spring of 1970. Billing records from the University of Virginia show that Eleanor had been treated by two medically oriented psychoanalysts and professors, one of them Terry's psychiatrist. A few years later, Eleanor wrote about her bouts of depression in her memoir. The private division of the university's clinic also billed George McGovern himself for thirty-one "one hour psychotherapy sessions" between July 14 and September 15, 1971. It is, of course, conceivable that these bills were for family therapy regarding Terry.[12]

Concurrently, McGovern's younger brother, Larry, was embroiled in his own battle with alcohol addiction, cycling in and out of treatment centers. Larry would call upon his older brother for financial support as he squandered cash on ill-conceived business ventures and struggled to hold onto a steady job. McGovern's conversations with Terry's doctor, Vamik Volkan, had led him to understand alcoholism as being closely tied to mental illnesses such as depression. McGovern's attentiveness to Larry fluctuated, but he funded his brother's treatment bills and usually sent him extra money, until December 1971, when McGovern told Larry it had to stop. "It is not good for either one of us for this financial dependence to go on year after year, and I know if you are going to ever be well enough, you've got to sever this dependence on me," McGovern wrote, clearly coming to terms with a complex mix of emotions, signing off, "with affection."[13]

McGovern could additionally empathize with Eagleton's compulsion to disguise his actual whereabouts and the true nature of his hospitalizations, fully conscious of public discomfort at the thought of a potentially sick man in elected office—no matter the ailment, physical or mental. When McGovern had felt faint at a campaign stop in Sioux Falls during his 1962 run for the Senate, his aides had driven him to a hospital in neighboring Iowa, fearful of causing a stir. The candidate had checked in as G. Stanley McGovern instead of George S., and—as Eleanor filled in for her husband on the campaign trail while he lay bedridden for two weeks fighting this recurrence of hepatitis—McGovern's campaign fed the press a white lie. McGovern had "a mild kidney infection," his campaign explained.[14]

There were yet more skeletons in McGovern's closet, which may have also enhanced his empathy with Eagleton. In the 1940s McGovern had fathered an illegitimate child, a daughter, in Terre Haute, Indiana, while training for army service overseas. As the McGoverns sat with the Eagletons in cabin 22, Eleanor knew nothing about her husband's sixth child. McGovern would tell her that fall, when his campaign learned that Republicans—and supposedly the *St. Louis Globe-Democrat*, Pat Buchanan's old paper—were waiting to break the story. CREEP never released this dirt during the campaign, but Bob Haldeman let it slip at a Watergate hearing the following year, putting forward the campaign's abstention from using this sordid detail as evidence of the Nixon campaign's fair play.[15]

So McGovern made up his mind about Eagleton—the Missourian was here to stay—and no one could persuade him otherwise. In fact, that morning, his staff did not even bother trying. This was one of those decisions McGovern seemed to consider personal. Indeed, it was more personal than any of them understood.

Furthermore, as Bennet later described the meeting's backdrop, the cozy confines of cabin 22, it was "not an environment in which it's easy to make a cold, calculated political decision." Instead, the group of politicians, wives, and strategists focused on timing. "This information should be made public, and it should be made public by me," Eagleton said assuredly. "The sole question is whether we do it here and now—today—or whether we do it on some other date in the near future at a forum which might be more suitable." Kelley and Mankiewicz urged postponing the announcement until Eagleton had finished his trip west and McGovern had concluded his South Dakota vacation, when both candidates had returned to Washington, where they could confront the fallout of the announcement together. To them, it seemed wrong to launch Eagleton's first campaign trip with this news and then burden the vice presidential candidate with the inevitable questions to follow in isolation from McGovern, his staff, and the Democratic organization. Since Hoyt and Boyd's memo was laced with inaccuracies, Kelley and Mankiewicz anticipated that the reporters would require at least a few days to complete their fact-checking before publishing their scoop, buying the campaign some time to determine the most efficacious course. Still, they could not gauge *Time* magazine's progress, and Mankiewicz had said the *Manchester Union Leader* was also on the case. Dougherty argued that they did not want to risk being preempted by the press and thus caught on the defensive. The *Manchester Union Leader*'s conservative bent and a flair for the dramatic made matters more urgent, whether or not the paper was really investigating.[16]

As the candidates huddled with their wives and top aides inside cabin 22, the Knight reporters paced at the edge of the woods surrounding it, with the Secret Service agents standing guard in the trees. Over the course of the two-hour meeting between the candidates, Hoyt would periodically dart into the woods to urinate, unable to contain his nervous bladder. Occasionally the gingham curtains covering the windows of the cabin would ruffle; it seemed to Hoyt that some anxious candidate, wife, or aide was keeping a suspicious eye on them.[17]

Inside, on the issue of timing, both Eagleton and McGovern proved united and uncompromising. Eagleton reiterated his "strong preference" to reveal his history to the public that day, eager to march forward and begin his campaign with a clear head. McGovern agreed. For better or worse, the decision was made. They would call a press conference after the meeting, Eagleton would divulge his case history, and McGovern would emphasize his support for his running mate. Mankiewicz suggested that the campaign "clam up" after the vice presidential candidate told all. He hoped that the campaign would force the press to move on by refusing to entertain further questions about Eagleton's mental health. If the campaign could not delay the announcement until both candidates had returned to

Washington, stiff-arming the press seemed the next-best option. It was as close to strategizing as they came.[18]

"I have some bad news for you," Mankiewicz told the Knight reporters when he emerged from the cabin. "We've decided that [Eagleton] can't [meet with you], that he's going to hold a press conference right now and announce it."

Boyd and Hoyt did not try to hide their disappointment.

"I can't help it," Mankiewicz said defensively. "This is something where he's just going to announce it, and there can't be some reporter forced him to. Your consolation prize—you'll have an exclusive interview with [Eagleton] right after the press conference because he's going to be leaving here immediately to fly away out on the campaign trail. And you could ride with him and get an interview."

"We're sorry," Dougherty chimed in, "but we understand the *Manchester Union Leader* has the story and you can imagine how they'd handle it. We've got to break it ourselves, and right away."

As the McGovern aides left, Dougherty speculated, "I wonder if Boyd wouldn't like to kill us."

"I wouldn't be at all surprised," Mankiewicz replied.[19]

Throughout the Democratic presidential candidate's two-week vacation, the press corps had bunkered up eight miles down the road at the Hi-Ho Motel in Custer, a "tourist paradise" replete with kitsch antique and Native American souvenir shops. Until that Tuesday morning, the reporters had mirrored their subject's holiday activities: they canoed, played tennis, and traversed the park roads, admiring the beauty of the landscape from their cars. For the most part, however, the reporters relaxed around the motel's swimming pool, admiring the beauty of the bikini-clad "Secret Service lady" from lounge chairs. About once a day, Dougherty drove down from the Sylvan Lake Lodge and updated the reporters on McGovern's tennis game and lunchtime diet from the motel parking lot. "It was dull stuff," Dougherty later described, "but the writers, like the cameramen, needed to justify their existence—and their expense accounts—to editors at the home office." The reporters returned the favor at night, socializing with McGovern and his staffers in the lodge, savoring their nightcaps together.[20]

On that Tuesday morning, July 25, the campaign summoned the reporters encamped at the Hi-Ho to Sylvan Lake for an 11:30 A.M. press conference that everyone presumed would be a routine photo op of the presidential candidate and his running mate, together for the second time since the convention. Journalists engaged in small talk with McGovern-Eagleton staffers as they awaited the candidates in the pine-paneled auditorium next to the lodge.[21]

After finishing with Boyd and Hoyt, Mankiewicz headed to the auditorium and found a phone resting on a poker table toward the back of the room. He crouched under it for some privacy and dialed Gary Hart, who had left South Dakota for Washington on Sunday. "You aren't going to like this," Mankiewicz whispered, "but I am standing here, and the senator and Tom Eagleton are going to be here in a couple of minutes to hold a press conference."[22]

"What?!" Hart shot back.

"Yeah. I've got a phone here in this hall where they're holding the press conference and there are just a couple of phones and I won't be able to talk very long because in about two minutes every reporter in the Western Hemisphere is going to be heading for these two phones, but in the meantime I'm going to stand here talking to you with a smile on my face like I'm very pleased with what is about to happen even though it's really a disaster and I'm sure when you hear what's going to happen you'll agree it's a disaster. . . ."

"Frank, just tell me what the hell is going on," Hart said, trying to get a grip.

"Well, what's going on is that George McGovern is just now walking up in front of all these reporters to tell them that Tom Eagleton has this problem, but that he's his running mate all the way. . . ."

"Frank—no, no, can't you stop it? We were going to talk it over. We were going to discuss it."

"Yeah, I know, we were, weren't we?"

"What about the records? What did the records show?"

The running mates and their wives pose in the Sylvan Lake Lodge auditorium at what was supposed to be a routine press conference, July 25. Barbara and Tom Eagleton at left, George and Eleanor McGovern at right (AP/Wide World Photos)

"I don't know. He didn't bring them with him. They said the hospitals wouldn't let them out or something like that."

"What did Eagleton tell him? Why is he so sure?

"I don't know," Mankiewicz said. "They met by themselves, and I wasn't there. He said he's made up his mind and that's the way it's going to be."[23]

Bob McNeely, a McGovern campaign photographer in town for Eagleton's arrival, had scheduled a brief photo session with the two candidates following their morning meeting. It was his first chance to find the running mates together since the convention and the last opportunity to do so before Eagleton was to take off for the West Coast. Unsuspecting, McNeely met McGovern and Eagleton in the entryway to the auditorium. But it quickly became apparent that something was amiss. McGovern and Eagleton seemed preoccupied, and Eagleton was especially cold. McNeely could not get the candidates to pose or smile.[24]

Eagleton looks on as the presidential candidate addresses reporters. McGovern press secretary Dick Dougherty observes from the side of the stage, at the lower right-hand corner of the photograph. (AP/Wide World Photos)

Just past noon, George and Eleanor McGovern and Tom and Barbara Eagleton emerged through the door of the wooden assembly hall. Eagleton wore a blue-and-white checkered sports jacket over a dark shirt. As he mounted the podium, his hands shook. As he spoke extemporaneously, his voice bore what one reporter described as a "nervous edge."[25]

Rumors, Eagleton described, are "part and parcel" of political campaigning, and rumors, he acknowledged, had followed him throughout his political career, from the St. Louis Circuit Attorney's Office to the United States Senate. In turn, the vice presidential candidate aspired to offer the public "as complete a picture" as he could about his personal health. He deemed concern about a candidate's fitness for office a "legitimate" worry, and he said it was one he would quell by telling the truth. On three occasions over the previous decade, Eagleton had hospitalized himself for "nervous exhaustion and fatigue," he disclosed, relying on this euphemism to describe what happens when "an intense hard-fighting person" drives himself too hard, as he did while campaigning to become attorney general in 1960.

"Part of the manifestation of my fatigue and exhaustion relates to the stomach," Eagleton described. "I am like the fellow in the Alka-Seltzer ad who says I can't believe I ate the whole thing." Eagleton would suffer a similar—if not the same—ailment two more times, and these experiences taught Eagleton about himself, more specifically about his need to "pace" himself at work and on the campaign trail. "All of us live our lives, I guess, in the attempt to learn more about ourselves. . . . In many respects we are our own worst enemies, and it took these experiences, these tough experiences, for me to learn a little bit about myself," he explained. Eagleton said he learned to make Sundays his day of rest, setting aside time to relax and watch the St. Louis football Cardinals and the Kansas City Chiefs, his favorite National Football League teams. Doing so had kept him in "good, solid, sound health" since 1966, he said.

A question-and-answer period followed the vice presidential candidate's remarks. No, McGovern had not known about his running mate's history before selecting him for the ticket. Still, the presidential candidate insisted that this information would not have affected his selection of Eagleton. Instead, he emphasized the "good judgment" his partner had demonstrated in seeking psychiatric help when he needed it. "I have watched [Senator Eagleton] in the U.S. Senate for the past four years," McGovern affirmed, and thus said he considered Eagleton's problems a thing of the past. "As far as I'm concerned, there is no member of that Senate who is any sounder in mind, body, and spirit than Tom Eagleton."

Indeed, Eagleton had undergone two physicals at the Bethesda Naval Hospital—one Friday and a follow-up on Monday—after the receipt of the Boyd and Hoyt memorandum. The doctors had checked "everything from toenails to dandruff," Eagleton said, injecting some levity into the tense atmosphere. "I am two pounds overweight and have half a hemorrhoid." The doctors had found no condition that would impair his judgment, he said. Calling his affliction "depression" for the first time, Eagleton described his melancholy as the by-product of the upset stomach that his exhaustion had spawned. As he explained it, his fatigue caused his stomachache, which precipitated his melancholy.

After an outfit change, the running mates amble through the woods on the grounds of the Sylvan Lake Lodge resort. Within the hour, Eagleton would depart on his trip west. (AP/Wide World Photos)

No, "Alcohol was not involved in any iota," Eagleton vowed, categorically refuting the rumors that had plagued his career.

By now, the reporters started to wonder why the campaign had called the press conference. Nothing Eagleton had said seemed to merit much concern.

Then, the press inquired about the specifics of his treatment, which—as Eagleton admitted when asked—had included psychiatry, sleeping pills, the occasional tranquilizer, and electroshock. Though his voice trailed off as he spoke it, that word, "electroshock," got the press's attention. The reporters asked him to elaborate.

"At that time, [electroshock] was part of the prescribed treatment for one who is suffering from nervous exhaustion and fatigue and manifestations of depression," Eagleton explained. He said he occasionally took tranquilizers when overtired, but he could not remember the name of the medication, calling it just "a little blue pill."

When asked whether he would release his medical records,

Eagleton demurred. They were meant for communication between medical professionals—not for public consumption.

"You have seen here today a demonstration of the candor and openness you're going to get from Senator Eagleton and me," McGovern summarized, emphasizing his campaign's mantra to restore honesty to the White House. "We have no secrets. We have nothing to hide." McGovern, it seems, imagined that the press would find Eagleton's sincerity refreshing, accept his explanation as the whole truth, and thus redirect its focus to the campaign's other, more substantive issues.[26]

After the press conference, ABC News anchor Harry Reasoner bet another reporter that Eagleton would not last more than a week. Many disagreed. *Rolling Stone*'s Timothy Crouse later recalled the prevailing sentiment in the Black Hills: "Eagleton had seen a shrink, so what?" But it had not stopped reporters from knocking over chairs as they sprinted for the phones.[27]

Tom and Barbara Eagleton returned to their cabin to change before taking off for Los Angeles. George and Eleanor McGovern stopped over to say their goodbyes. McGovern rested his hand on Eagleton's shoulder. "Tom," he said. "I have even a higher respect for you than I did before. The way you handled yourself at that press conference proves to me that you are even more of a man than I ever knew. I am proud of you and proud to have you on the ticket." Like a father to a son who has made a show of courage, McGovern conveyed his approval. The admiration was mutual. They were in it together. They were the ticket. They were a team.[28]

In the car to the Rapid City airport from the Sylvan Lake Lodge that crisp summer afternoon, Mike Kelley rode next to the driver up front. In the back row, the Knight reporters sat to the left of Eagleton, with Hoyt in the middle, pressed up against the candidate in the tight sedan. This interview was their "consolation prize," and Boyd left the questioning to Hoyt. The reporter spent most of the forty-minute ride asking Eagleton about his early years for the profile he was writing on the vice presidential candidate—the reason his editors had sent him to St. Louis in the first place. "My father was the idol of my life," Eagleton told Boyd and Hoyt.[29]

The conversation inevitably returned to the issue at hand: Eagleton's delayed disclosure of his mental health history and its implications for the campaign. In their article, which ran in the next day's papers, Boyd and Hoyt described Eagleton as "relaxed and at ease." Though his hands shook and he was sweating profusely, drenching the checkered sports jacket that he had worn to the press conference, Eagleton appeared to the reporters to be in possession of himself.

"I've been living with it for twelve years," Eagleton said of his history of depression and electroshock therapy in between tokes of his cigarette. "It's been a millstone around my neck. I always knew it was going to come out someday."

Eagleton said he did not volunteer his history to McGovern or Mankiewicz upon his selection to the ticket because "it was a very brief conversation. I didn't think that this was a disqualifying factor, and I still don't. . . . Maybe the public will. . . . We'll just have to wait and see."[30]

From the passenger seat, Mike Kelley grunted in annoyance at Hoyt's inquiry, but Eagleton diligently answered every question the reporter posed. As Eagleton finished one cigarette, he would pull another from his box of Pall Malls, lighting it with the butt of the depleted cigarette, which he would then flick out the car window. Hoyt feared turning his head to find the South Dakota forest in flames.

Hoyt wondered what had necessitated Eagleton's electroshock, and the running mate explained, "My doctor asked me if I was willing to have shock treatments. I said, 'You're the doctor.' He said it was worth trying, so I had it."

The treatment worked, Eagleton insisted. His irritability faded, and he learned to pace himself, to relax. "I can go to Bethany Beach [in Delaware] and take some good books," he explained. "I'll sit on the beach and relax. I'll have a nice lunch and dinner and do nothing. I couldn't do that in 1960. I had to be moving. As I get older I've learned to roll with the punches. I never blow my cork at a negative editorial now the way I used to. As a younger person I was less resilient."

Amid the questioning on specifics, Eagleton admitted, "I

never was at Johns Hopkins. It was a ploy . . . a mild attempt to be diversionary."

In their article the next day, Boyd and Hoyt reported that, "although suicidal tendencies sometimes develop in cases of severe depression, Eagleton said he had never become so depressed that he had considered it."[31]

When Hoyt asked him how he would have responded if he had handed Eagleton the memo of allegations before giving it to the McGovern campaign, Eagleton said, "I guess I would have told you the truth . . . but I probably would have tried to stall until, say, Thursday, so I could talk with Senator McGovern first."[32]

"One has a private life that should be just that," Eagleton reflected. "Even if you're in politics, you would like to have some kind of private life. But now that I'm in the national fishbowl, my private life is almost nil. I'm not saddened by that. It's natural."

As the car approached the airport, Hoyt flipped his notebook shut. "Well, I really don't have any more questions."

"Thank god," said Eagleton, exasperated, slumping down in his seat in relief.[33]

Though Hoyt believed that Eagleton severely miscalculated the seriousness of his mental health issue, the young reporter admired Eagleton's relative composure through their car ride; he respected his courage.[34]

Upon arriving in Rapid City, Eagleton and his team boarded their propjet for the flight to Los Angeles. The plane became a physical and metaphorical bubble—detaching Eagleton and his staff from all but their own reactions to the disclosure of just a little over an hour before.

Eagleton downed about three drinks over the course of the long flight. "It was part of his self-medication," recalls Bob McNeely, the McGovern photographer who had joined the Eagleton crew for the trip west. Everyone present, including McNeely, thought they had gotten over the worst of it, that they had jumped in front of the story and quashed it before it blew up. "It will blow over," they said, "we'll focus on the politics," "I think we got past it."[35]

The Aftershock

Soon after the Eagletons left Sylvan Lake, McGovern wanted to hit the tennis courts. As he was preparing to head out, Tom Ottenad, the top political reporter for Eagleton's hometown *St. Louis Post-Dispatch*, approached McGovern for an interview, and the candidate invited Ottenad along for the ride to his tennis lesson. As they made their way through the woods to the courts in nearby Custer, McGovern recounted how he had discovered Eagleton's problems, starting with the late-night party at the Doral Starlight Roof, the night he selected the Missourian in Miami Beach. McGovern said his aides' initial findings had not worried him, but as reports continued to pile up, he realized that he should check them out with Eagleton himself. Even now, as he spoke with Ottenad, McGovern questioned whether Eagleton's medical history had merited the press conference hours before; he said his running mate's health issues did not seem too significant to him. "I have complete faith in the fairness of the American people," he told the reporter, and Ottenad would write that McGovern seemed "totally relaxed and undisturbed" throughout their interview. But the journalist warned against extrapolating anything from the presidential candidate's serenity. "The South

Eagleton addresses the media upon arrival in Los Angeles. Brooks Jackson of the Associated Press takes notes in the lower right-hand corner of the photograph. (AP/ Wide World Photos)

Dakotan has rigid control and seldom shows any sign of strain," Ottenad explained.[1]

When he had gone to call in the Eagleton news after the press conference, Carl Leubsdorf of the Associated Press had to wait forty-two minutes before he could get out his headline because the AP's Chicago bureau chief was in the middle of taking transmission of the hog and corn prices from the Chicago Mercantile Exchange. For Leubsdorf, the only comfort was that the rival UPI reporter had the same problem. Still, feeling somewhat disappointed in himself, even though he had done all he could, Leubsdorf felt the "best thing to do would be to get some quotes," as he recalled it. He lingered around cabin 22 and spotted McGovern and Ottenad leaving for their car-ride interview. Leubsdorf hopped into his own car and trailed them to Custer. When they arrived, Leubsdorf asked McGovern whether he could interview him on the way back. "You know how he was,"

Leubsdorf later said of McGovern. "If he saw a reporter he knew, and the reporter asked him a question, he'd go right ahead and answer it." Naturally, McGovern agreed to the one-on-one, and Leubsdorf dashed to the Hi-Ho, grabbed his tape recorder from Greg Harrington, another AP reporter, and made it to the tennis courts in time for the interview.[2]

A hailstorm broke out as McGovern and Leubsdorf drove back to the cabins, with McGovern recounting for Leubsdorf his meeting with Eagleton. His running mate had "just said 'If this is embarrassing to you in any way, don't feel any obligation to keep me on,'" McGovern recalled. "I thought it was ridiculous even to bring it up, and I think he did it as kind of a courtesy gesture." McGovern continued, "I don't think he felt there was any grounds for his withdrawal. I certainly don't." Leubsdorf asked McGovern how he expected the public to react to Eagleton's disclosures. "We'll have to wait and see," McGovern said, a comment seemingly at odds with his message to Ottenad, but much less apprehensive than the commentary of others high in the campaign apparatus. "Well, it certainly isn't a plus, is it?" cracked Mankiewicz, who had returned to DC. "Obviously, we would prefer not to have to deal with" the political problems likely to result, he acknowledged. "I think we're in for a couple of tough days," Mankiewicz forecast in the *Washington Post.* "There could be a considerable backlash," he speculated in the *New York Times.* "A lot will depend on how the Republicans react," he told the AP.[3]

President Dwight Eisenhower once told Richard Nixon that every president should have "his S.O.B.," and there was no mistaking that the forty-five-year-old former Boy Scout from California, Harry Robbins Haldeman, was Nixon's. As Haldeman put it, he was even more—Nixon's "pluperfect S.O.B.," or, in the president's words, his "Lord High Executioner." Haldeman had begun his career at the J. Walter Thompson advertising agency, working his way up to become a vice president in the firm's Los Angeles office, where he oversaw the accounts of 7-Up and Walt Disney Productions. Over the years, he took time off to work on Nixon's early campaigns and eventually joined Nixon full-time, managing his run in 1968. By the time of the 1972 campaign, "the personality of Richard Nixon had been Haldeman's chief intellectual preoccupation for ten years," wrote Teddy White. White also discerned that the president felt "most at ease" with Haldeman. As White House chief of staff, Haldeman essentially acted as "traffic manager," filtering what and to whom the president paid attention. Haldeman awaited Nixon's beck and call and executed the president's orders. As the historian Stanley I. Kutnik described him, Haldeman was a "loyal, efficient instrument of [Nixon's] wishes."[4]

"Clark," Haldeman bellowed through the phone when CREEP director Clark MacGregor picked up his call from the White House.

"Bob," MacGregor acknowledged.

"Hi, I just wanted to be sure, the president wanted to be sure . . . that you've seen the Eagleton news, I assume," Haldeman began, clearly excited and maybe even giddy to discuss the revelation.

"No, I have not."

"You haven't?" Haldeman inquired, surprised.

"I've been closeted here for an hour and a half."

"Oh Jesus," Haldeman said, dishing some quick sympathy before getting on to the juice. "Well, Eagleton went out and had a press conference today and announced that he had been hospitalized three times."

"Ah."

"For mental disorders."

"Yep."

"That he had electroshock treatment and psychotherapy."

"Yep."

"And, uh, that he had not told McGovern this, and McGovern had not known it when he nominated him."

"Yep."

"That's a rather devastating blow."

"It sure is," MacGregor confirmed. "I'm not sure whether you knew this, Bob, but I knew that this was the case, and I had seen his face sheet. I think I indicated it to you."

A "face sheet" is a medical cover letter or abstract, encapsulating the relevant information about a patient's medical history and treatment on a single page.

"Right," Haldeman said, suggesting that he had also previously known what the McGovern-Eagleton campaign had just disclosed, before continuing, "Now this is all between '60 and '66. Have you seen anything that he's been hospitalized since '66?" he asked.

"No, I haven't," MacGregor said.

"Okay. Because there's some report that he was also in Johns Hopkins after, in the last year or two."

"That I do not know."

"And [Eagleton] left that out. And if that's true, then he," Haldeman said, searching for the word, "he lied."

As Eagleton told Boyd and Hoyt, he had never received treatment at Johns Hopkins. Rather, in 1966, his office only told the press that he was there, when he had in fact been at the Mayo Clinic. If Haldeman was right, then, yes, Eagleton had lied; it is surely conceivable that Eagleton had sought treatment at Johns Hopkins in the three and a half years preceding his nomination to the ticket, while serving in the Senate and living in Chevy Chase, Maryland, just an hour from Baltimore. Yet when a *Time* reporter had been investigating, the Johns Hopkins public relations representative said no records existed, though the hospital official might have been concealing the truth from the prying journalist.

MacGregor corrected Haldeman, clarifying that he had previously believed Eagleton's last hospitalization was in '67, but—presuming the running mate's comments at the press conference that afternoon were accurate—MacGregor adjusted his story. "I guess it was '66," he said, continuing, "Yea, it was the '66 hospital face sheet that I saw."

"Okay, well he was in three times," Haldeman said.

"I don't think we should make any comment, should we?" Mac-Gregor asked.

"Well, what the president wants everybody to say is that the president has given instructions he never, none of us ever have any comment on a personal matter."

"Right," MacGregor said.

"And, that it should be . . . Make the point, that the president has instructed all of us that he's always had the policy never to comment on a personal matter in a campaign."

They agreed.

MacGregor said he would call Frederic Malek, deputy campaign director, and tell him to pass along the word from above to everyone at CREEP headquarters: they should all keep quiet.

"Put the lid on. Right. Good," Haldeman assented.

"Will do," MacGregor said, wondering aloud, "I think [Eagleton's history of mental illness] had to come out . . ."

"Sure it did," Haldeman said, speaking over MacGregor's words.

"I think Eagleton knew that medical teams were probing and that this information was leaking. But it is an absolutely devastating thing," MacGregor said.[5]

The McGovern and Nixon organizations had the same inclination: both campaigns originally planned to "clam up" and deny reporters' requests for further commentary. The difference: the White House followed through, whereas the McGovernites did not. The Democrats waited to gauge public reaction, and McGovern's and Mankiewicz's confessions of ambivalence—to waiting and seeing—additionally seemed to grant insiders permission to vent in the interval.

Wasting no time, Haldeman placed a call to Vice President Spiro Agnew, who, it turned out, was away from the office. Then he tried Senator Bob Dole of Kansas, chairman of the Republican National Committee. Haldeman wanted to make sure the president's order to resist commenting on Eagleton got to all the chains of command. After conferring about the news and their strategy with Dole, Haldeman predicted, "This one will take care of itself."

"I think it will," Senator Dole agreed.[6]

Soon, the vice president called back.

"Hi Bob, how are you?" Agnew asked Haldeman.

"Very good, sir. Have you got, seen the story on Eagleton?"

"Yes, I have," the vice president said.

"Okay. The president just wanted me to check with all of our key people and, uh, to be sure you covered with all of your people the, the point that we make absolutely no comment on any personal matter, you know, and . . ."

"I had figured that anyhow," Agnew interrupted.

Their conversations dragged on, with Haldeman justifying his call. Finally, the vice president said, "I had a letter I had turned over to be checked out from the chief of psychiatry at the hospital in St. Louis, in Missouri." Word of Eagleton's hospitalizations had found many channels to the White House. This tip from the chief of psychiatry at an unidentified St. Louis hospital—presumably Barnes, although potentially Malcolm Bliss, where St. Louis Republican Sam Krupnick alleged Eagleton had sought care in his letter to Nixon's secretary—has not been previously reported.

"I assume the press was digging to the bottom of it without any stimulus from us," offered Agnew.

"That's right," Haldeman assured him. "They were already on it, which is why [Eagleton] had to make this move today anyway," overeagerly skirting the suggestion of Nixonian fair play.[7]

Haldeman jotted down a few notes on his legal pad that afternoon: "Find out when the [Eagleton appointment] was," probably referring to the doubts he had raised with MacGregor about when, exactly, Eagleton had been a patient at Johns Hopkins, if Eagleton had even been to Johns Hopkins at all. Then Haldeman added one final instruction to himself: "Destroy [Eagleton], the pipsqueak that he is."[8]

Contrary to the Eagleton crew's expectations, his South Dakota press conference had not sufficed, and the running mate's revelations certainly had not blown over during his journey west. In fact, the impact of the disclosure only seemed to intensify. The CBS and NBC evening news broadcasts both led with reports on Eagleton. ABC's nightly news broadcast, which aired a half-hour earlier than the others and thus had a shorter turnaround time, included the Eagleton news toward the end of the program. And when Eagleton's propjet arrived in Los Angeles, the running mate was mobbed by reporters firing off questions about his past and its implications for the future, something more akin to modern-day Hollywood scandal culture than the media environment of the 1970s. Confronting the barrage of reporters, television cameras, recorders, and microphones awaiting him, Eagleton adhered to the campaign's agreed-upon strategy and gracelessly brushed away the questioning, leaving the impression that he had something to hide. As Brooks Jackson, the Associated Press reporter traveling with the vice presidential nominee, remembered, Eagleton seemed "wired." He was "tense and shaking" and "vibrating like a tuning fork."[9]

In an interview with Robert Abernethy at the NBC studio in Burbank, Eagleton continued to rebuff inquiry into the specifics of his illness. "You called what happened 'nervous exhaustion,'" Abernethy summarized. "Wasn't it also a rather severe depression?" But Eagleton refused to clarify: "There's no sense in being redundant and replowing the ground that was very thoroughly considered by a press conference," he said. "I've made up my mind I'm not going to be redundant and repeat and repeat and repeat." But Eagleton missed the point. Though he had shared more information about his past than ever before, the press was still confused by the language he had used to describe his illness. Was Eagleton's ailment simply exhaustion combined with a bad stomach? If so, why did it require shock treatment? Or, was it serious depression? In South Dakota, Eagleton had never addressed these specifics, and his resistance to sharing more details appeared to contravene the very candor that McGovern had said the disclosure represented.[10]

Barbara and Tom Eagleton attended separate functions that evening before meeting for a taping of the *Merv Griffin Show*. At a meet-and-greet with Beverly Hills Democrats at the home of Maurice and Adrienne Halls, Barbara was asked about the conversation in which she and her husband had decided that Tom would not reveal his history of mental illness if selected. "To be perfectly honest, I can't remember when we talked," Barbara said. "But I must say it was a wise decision."[11]

At 11 P.M. in Los Angeles, the end of a very long Tuesday for the Eagleton team, Mike Kelley alerted reporters that the vice presidential candidate would hold a press conference at his Century Plaza Hotel at 8:30 the following morning. According to Bill Gruver, a longtime Democratic advance man working for the McGovern campaign in

Los Angeles, the last-minute announcement led the media to suspect that the running mate was about to withdraw. But the next morning, Eagleton appeared "fully in command of the situation" and "handled himself beautifully," despite the lengthy questioning, hot weather, and some signs of nervousness, as Gruver reported back. While Eagleton was not going to withdraw, he did announce a switch.[12]

Eagleton said that he decided that he should answer reporters' questions after reviewing television clips and newspaper treatment of his refusal to speak. But while he may have felt more comfortable with the revised "open" strategy, as he responded to the press's inquiries in Los Angeles, he failed to distinguish between the details that needed to be disclosed and those better left unsaid. For example, Eagleton recalled the weight loss, "irascibility," and "depression of the spirit" that had compelled him to seek medical assistance. "As my son says, 'You're down in the dumps,'" Eagleton related, explaining that he had stayed there longer than normal. But this illustration failed to allay concerns about Eagleton's ability to maintain his composure at all times. Furthermore, his admission to still taking "an occasional—very sporadic—tranquilizer" whose name he could not remember did not seem to help. Further, he had not yet made his doctors, William Perry and Frank Shobe, available to verify his fitness for negotiating the challenges of the vice presidency and, if need be, the presidency. Backpedaling on his assurance that the doctors would release statements soon after his disclosure, Eagleton was now saying that he would call them to "discuss with them the kind of statement they can or should make" only after he had returned from Hawaii, the next stop on his trip. He said his doctors would provide "honest" statements, but the delay did not inspire confidence.[13]

However, when it came to intracampaign dynamics, Eagleton was even more forthcoming. And in this regard, transparency proved particularly misguided. For example, Eagleton's admission to reviewing with Barbara whether or not he should inform McGovern of his past mental illness if he were chosen for the ticket fostered the perception of Eagleton as a political operator who had purposefully deceived McGovern in his effort to secure the nomination. The same goes for his confession that, yes, the report of his visit to Johns

Hopkins instead of Barnes had been a ploy, meant to be diversionary. But he had justification: "When you need rest, one of the things you need rest from is the press." Still, the press—and public—seemed to find the concept of rest incompatible with vigorous presidential campaigning. And Eagleton continued to insist otherwise, vowing to run a "full and complete" campaign while assuring "an adequate amount of relaxation" to keep him going. "I'm going to bear up under it," he assured. "In a way, I think it is going to strengthen me in this task." The balance would not change once in office, he promised. Eagleton said past presidents had made it their policy to get rest. But while the rigors of campaigning explained two hospitalizations, they could not account for the third, in 1966, which Eagleton attributed to "a hellish amount of work" as lieutenant governor, directing an education conference for Governor Hearnes.[14]

Perhaps most injurious to Eagleton's prospects, he continued to reiterate his willingness to leave the ticket if that would be in McGovern's best interests, echoing the leading man's "wait and see" approach. "If my visceral feeling is that my candidacy is untenable and is negative insofar as the McGovern ticket is concerned," Eagleton said, "I'll not even wait for McGovern to give me the word. I'll give the word myself." By reinforcing the idea that he could leave the ticket, Eagleton legitimized that possibility, making it seem more conceivable in the minds of the press, the public, and the McGovern staff alike. The *New York Times* headline the next day—"Eagleton Hints He'll Quit Race if Polls Are Negative"—further slanted the media narrative toward the prospect of his withdrawal. In comments to the *Post-Dispatch*, however, Eagleton abdicated responsibility for deciding whether he should bow out. "I told [Senator McGovern] that although I have been in excellent health for the past six years, if it appeared that my presence on the ticket would be in any way an impediment or a hindrance, that was a decision Senator McGovern could make and I would abide by," he said.[15]

The McGovern staffer on the ground in California, Bill Gruver, reported back to the campaign that the press had turned on the running mate since his medical disclosure; their friendliness toward the vice presidential candidate had given way to distrust. One thing was certain: "In the past twenty-four hours, Tom Who has become a household word," as Eagleton joked at a "unity" breakfast at the hotel later that morning.[16]

At the Executive Office Building in Washington that Wednesday morning, Bob Haldeman and the president debated whether to hold a news conference the following day. They had no special occasion to mark, but Haldeman had his reasoning: "It's the fact that you're there running the damn government, while they're out there running around deciding who they're going to have on the ticket or not. It's a good contrast," he explained.

The conversation meandered, but Haldeman and Nixon eventually returned to the McGovern-Eagleton disclosure.

"He's unstable," the president said of Eagleton.

"He's unstable," Haldeman echoed, continuing, "What could be worse, what could be scarier than a guy in here who isn't in full command of everything? And, the grueling nature of the job is very clear to the American people. The hard work, and all of that. They know what great shape you're in, and they know you get tired. They know it's tough, the mental pressure, and all that. It has to scare them to death."

As Nixon and Haldeman had determined the previous day, they would refuse to comment on Eagleton's health. Still, the Republicans had another inviting line of attack: Eagleton's premeditated decision not to tell McGovern about his mental health history up front and his admission to having fed a diversionary tale to the press in 1966. These revelations combined to saddle the running mate with a credibility problem, not merely a medical problem. "That's a very clear thing to all people," Haldeman explained. "That's the line that we all tell our children all the time. If you tell one lie, then people are never going to know when you're gonna tell another. . . . And that's just logged in there. They can't undo that at this point, at any time." In Haldeman's estimation of it, no matter how Eagleton tried to explain his behavior, he was a confirmed liar and a drag on McGovern's claim to credibility.

"If this campaign gets rough a ways down the line, we'll start putting signs in [Eagleton's] crowds," Haldeman proposed, thinking one step ahead. "We'll start shouting some hecklers out. . . ."

"The way I would put it out is not about his sanity," Nixon said.

"His honesty," Haldeman concurred.

"But the lie," Nixon added, flipping the emphasis to the negative.

"Sure" Haldeman said, posing a hypothetical challenge: "'Why did you lie to McGovern?'"

"'Why did you lie to McGovern?'" Nixon said, this time echoing Haldeman.

"'Why did you lie to . . .'"

"'Why did you lie to McGovern about your health?'" Nixon jumped in.

"'If you lied about your health, what else are you lying about?'" Haldeman proposed.

"They've got a big problem," the president finally said of the McGovernites. "They've basically got a problem."

"That's right," Haldeman assured him.[17]

Reporting on his one-on-one interview with McGovern the previous afternoon, the *Post-Dispatch*'s Tom Ottenad wrote in Wednesday's afternoon paper that the Eagleton revelations posed "a number of the most serious political problems." First, Ottenad said the news "raises the prospect of an ugly campaign," predicting an ensuing cycle of mudslinging if the Republicans dwelled on questions about Eagleton's mental health. Ottenad speculated that the Democrats would respond with reports of Nixon's visits with a psychiatrist in the 1950s. Second, Ottenad believed that "hostile attacks" on Senator Eagleton would soon follow and ultimately distract from the real issues of the campaign, such as the Vietnam War and the economy. And third, Ottenad wrote, the disclosure "may raise the question of whether the Missouri senator can continue on the Democratic ticket." The *Miami Herald* and others made that question more tangible by printing an AP brief on the process for replacing a member of the national ticket. According to the "Call for the 1972 Democratic National Convention," should the presidential or vice presidential nominee resign, die, or suffer an incapacitating disability between the convention and the election, the Democratic National Committee would assume responsibility for selecting a replacement. The 150 core members of the 303-member DNC would vote for the new nominee with the weight of each member's ballot proportional to the population of his or her state; the candidate who received the majority would become the party's new nominee. In his article, Ottenad added that "McGovern and his advisers do not expect the situation to reach such an extreme point," but the inclusion of such information and quotations from staffers surely led readers to believe otherwise.[18]

Ottenad also included in his article commentary from Mankiewicz and other insiders. "How much of a blow it will be remains to be determined," said an anonymous but well-placed source. "It is impossible to gauge what the public reaction will be. I'm romantic enough to believe that the public is much more generous and kinder than we tend to think." But even in such public display of optimism, the message was still plain: Eagleton's revelations were guaranteed to bruise the ticket; the only question was how seriously. When Dougherty let slip, "Senator McGovern's position—as of now—is to stick with Senator Eagleton," reporters pounced, inquiring what exactly "as of now" meant.[19]

Carl Leubsdorf's report of McGovern's "wait and see" comments stunned Gary Hart when he saw them hit the wires back in Washington. As Leubsdorf presented McGovern's commentary, it could seem Eagleton's fate hinged on the public's reaction.

Carl P. Leubsdorf
AP Political Writer

CUSTER, S.D. (AP)—Rejecting Thomas F. Eagleton's offer to quit the Democratic ticket, Sen. George McGovern says he wants to "wait and see" the reaction to his running mate's revelation that he received psychiatric care and shock treatment.

Hart immediately called the Black Hills, anxious for the campaign to discredit the AP story and reaffirm McGovern's support for Eagleton so that McGovern would not seem disingenuous after just having proclaimed his running mate would remain on the ticket.[20]

Dick Dougherty was at the Hi-Ho fielding reporters' questions in the makeshift pressroom when the phone rang. A reporter picked up the phone. It was McGovern, he said, before handing the phone off to Dougherty.

"Dick, I'm Goddammed mad at Leubsdorf," McGovern hollered when Dougherty got on the phone. "He's written a story—Gary Hart just called and read it to me—saying that I'm waiting to see if Eagleton stays on the ticket. I want you to get out a denial right now. I want you to say the story is absolutely false."

"Oh, Jesus, I wouldn't," Dougherty said, as the other journalists in the room listened in, intent on picking up some nugget of infighting. "He's a good reporter," Dougherty continued, referring to Leubsdorf.

"I don't give a damn," McGovern retorted. "I never told him any such thing."

"Alright, I'll get something out. I'll say the story's misleading . . ."

"False. Say it's false. Say it's just not true."[21]

Dougherty was in no position to push back. The journalists in the room would have picked up on the tension and woven such palace intrigue into their articles, as the griping and power struggles among McGovern's top aides had been the object of their curiosity before the Eagleton news. If Hart had called Dougherty about the Leubsdorf article instead of going directly to McGovern, it would have been a whole different story; they could have found a way to tiptoe around the matter in private. But in the reporters' presence— with McGovern riled up and insistent—Dougherty had no choice but to heed his chief's command. Dougherty crafted a statement explaining that the AP story had given the wrong impression about McGovern's stance; the candidate was standing by Eagleton, as had been previously stated, and he did not need to "wait and see" to determine whether or not to keep him. According to Dougherty, the language of his statement was clear and innocuous.[22]

Dougherty read his statement to the reporters in the Hi-Ho, and just as he was handing it to his assistant to type and tack on the press room bulletin board, the phone rang. It was McGovern again.

"Dick, I want you to put in the statement that not only is that [Leubsdorf article] wrong but that I'm a thousand percent behind Tom Eagleton," he said.

"Oh, no. Oh, dear," Dougherty gasped.

"Yes, I do," McGovern rebutted.

"Are you sure?"

"You're damned right I'm sure," he said. "A thousand percent."

"Okay," Dougherty said, relenting; he believed he had no choice.

Dougherty put down the phone and called out to the reporters, "The senator wants added to the statement that he is behind Senator Eagleton a thousand percent," voicing the line that would prove enduring, the signature phrase embodying McGovern's mismanagement and symbolizing the embarrassment to come. As written and delivered to reporters, replacing the first message on the bulletin board, the statement from George McGovern characterized the AP story as "utterly untrue. I am 1,000 per cent for Tom Eagleton and have no intention of dropping him from the ticket. This is what I said yesterday and I am repeating it to assure no misunderstanding on my position."[23]

Reflecting on the series of unfortunate events, Dougherty later concluded that the candidate meant what he said at the time. Perhaps 1,000 percent was a slight overstatement, but McGovern felt wholehearted support and a "genuine compassion" for Eagleton, despite his running mate's disappointing lack of candor up front. Dougherty explained, "The McGovern intelligence, while of high order, is not without great patches of liberal mush of the sort which allots sympathy equally to the rapist and the raped." Dougherty may have packed his language with an unseemly amount of bite, but his analysis gnaws at the essence of McGovern's problem; he habitually allowed compassion to trump strategy. As Leubsdorf understands it, "They created a problem where they could have easily finessed it."[24]

Regardless of McGovern's affirmation, Dougherty would continue the strain of pessimism that day: "We've had reports from some of our financial people that this is dismaying news for fund-raising," he revealed. Hart said that McGovern's inner circle had considered alternatives to keeping Eagleton, but deemed his full disclosure and continuation on the ticket the campaign's best option. Meanwhile, hundreds of McGovernites kept the switchboard abuzz at the Mc-Govern headquarters in Washington that afternoon and throughout the week, literally crying in outrage, frustration, and disappointment that Eagleton's revelations had unquestionably shattered McGovern's chances, devaluing what was for many of them nearly two years of hard work on behalf of a candidate and a cause they believed in.[25]

Hart met with reporters in Washington, explaining the events that had led to Eagleton's disclosure and attempting to clarify and reaffirm McGovern's stance. He said the campaign had preempted the possibility that Knight Newspapers or another news organization could report Eagleton's health history so that the McGovern-Eagleton campaign would not be left in the uncomfortable, potentially "hurt-ful" position of "making revelations after the fact." Hart also in-sisted that the campaign had known Eagleton's "full record" before receiving the Knight memo and said that he thought (erroneously, as it turned out) that Eagleton had shown McGovern hard copies of his medical records. More damagingly, however, Hart said that the campaign, before it had selected Eagleton, had heard rumors that he had battled alcoholism and had been hospitalized. Hart admit-ted that the campaign had failed to ask Eagleton or his staff about the allegations due to "shortness of time." This excuse did not speak well of the campaign's organization, care, or prudence. At best, Mc-Govern's selection of Eagleton seemed sloppy, which did not augur well for his decision making in the White House.

In response to the question of whether McGovern would still have chosen Eagleton had he known the whole truth, Hart affirmed, "That is the senator's position." After a pause, he added, "Mine also," seeming to distance himself from the decision while asserting it. Hart could not say for certain whether Eagleton's history would have an impact on his ability to serve in office. "Perhaps it does, perhaps it doesn't," he said, suggesting that this consideration no longer mat-tered and thus adding to the damage; the issue surely mattered to the public, which could be expected to resent such willful disregard of the qualification Mankiewicz said mattered most the afternoon of Eagleton's nomination: capability to be president. After all, the selection of the man who could assume the most powerful position in the universe—a selection on which the fate of the nation might one day hinge—is hardly a task that should be taken lightly. In confirming the capabilities of a man who might become the most important person in the world, "perhaps" is not a good enough answer.

Hart denied that the campaign's diligence in choosing a vice presidential candidate was "inadequate," but he admitted that the selection process had been imperfect. He had one proposal for revising the system: delaying the vice presidential nomination for two or three days after the convention. "You really do not have the time, if you are up against a closely contested nomination, to give the vice president uninterrupted consideration," he said of the current system. And therein lies another of Hart's thinly veiled contradictions: he was questioning the mechanics of the selection process at the same time he was claiming that McGovern would have arrived at the same vice presidential pick regardless.[26]

Hart also validated the place of the candidates' health in political discourse by demanding that Nixon and Agnew submit their medical records for public evaluation along with Eagleton's and McGovern's. "This is not a one-way street. There is a point beyond which some reciprocity is involved," Hart said. If Hart had known that McGovern's full case history included thirty-one visits to a psychologist just two summers earlier, it seems unlikely that he would have raised this issue. In any event, the White House refused to budge. "The president made it quite clear and has directed that there be no comment on personal matters," Nixon press secretary Ron Ziegler affirmed. "The individual citizens will decide for themselves on this issue and they need no assistance from me," added CREEP director Clark MacGregor. The next day, when reporters brought the question to Nixon himself, his answer was consistent. "The issues that divide the opposite side and this administration are so wide—in fact, the clearest choice in this century—that we must campaign on issues," the president explained. As to Hart's request that Nixon disclose his medical records, the president reminded the reporters that he had opened his records in 1968, and that his doctor had continued to share them every year since. Nothing new to report there, Nixon said. Besides, the question of whether he could handle the presidency should be clear enough, the president explained. "Considering what I have been through, some fairly stern crises and rather extensive travel, I don't think anybody could question the state of my health," he said.[27]

Yet something ticked Nixon off: MacGregor had disclosed that he had known about Eagleton's hospitalizations since the 1968 Senate race. Upon learning of MacGregor's comments, the president howled, "He's a goddamn liar!" in the Executive Office Building that afternoon. Nixon feared that admitting to prior knowledge of Eagleton's problems would incite speculation that CREEP had leaked the news. "Did [MacGregor] say he knew about it and told me?" Nixon snapped rhetorically at a group of top aides. "He didn't tell me a goddamn thing! . . . Clark knows he didn't talk to me," the president railed. "He knows it. I knew nothing. I think he talked to Haldeman. Haldeman was aware, he knew something to the effect that [Eagleton] was a manic-depressive. But there was nothing, nobody told me before that yesterday that he had ever been in a hospital. Nobody."

The evidence indicates otherwise: Nixon discussed Krupnick's letter with his secretary, Rose Mary Woods, in the Oval Office on Friday, July 21.[28]

In truth, Nixon's mental health was not as crystal clear as the president tried to make it seem. Questions about Nixon's psychiatric care surfaced in 1968, when syndicated columnist Drew Pearson learned that the Republican presidential nominee had received treatment from Dr. Arnold Hutschnecker, a New York psychiatrist, while serving as vice president during the Eisenhower administration. It was believed that Nixon had visited Dr. Hutschnecker's Park Avenue offices as recently as 1961. When Pearson phoned to investigate, Hutschnecker called his treatment of Nixon a "very delicate matter," which he could not discuss any further. But Hutschnecker let it slip that Nixon "did have a problem—not standing up under great pressure." This was exactly the type of issue that made people skittish about Eagleton. Pearson's reporting partner, Jack Anderson, proceeded to check out the story with the Nixon campaign, which resoundingly dismissed the allegations. And Dr. Hutschnecker soon called Pearson back to clarify that he had treated Nixon "for a brief period when he was vice president, but only for problems involving internal medicine." The doctor seemed to be under pressure to retract his initial offhand comments. Pearson refrained from publishing the story before the election, but he recounted his findings in a speech to the National Press Club on November 13, days after Nixon won. When the story surfaced in the papers, Nixon's staff discredited the allegations yet again. They said that Nixon had been treated for exhaustion, not a mental problem—echoing Eagleton's approach. Indeed, Hutschnecker had certifications in both internal medicine and psychiatry. But the intermingling of mind and body was what fascinated him most. By the time Nixon saw him in the 1950s, Dr. Hutschnecker had concentrated his practice almost exclusively on psychotherapy and psychosomatic medicine. Pearson could not help but wonder, he told his National Press Club audience, "why Nixon would go up to New York to consult a doctor for internal medical problems when we have some excellent doctors here in Washington."[29]

More recent reporting has confirmed that, indeed, Nixon conferred with Hutschnecker throughout the course of his life, first meeting with the doctor in 1951. He was "a little nervous, irritable, and not sleeping so good," Dr. Hutschnecker told Anthony Summers of Nixon's first visit. Summers interviewed Hutschnecker in 1995 in preparation for his book *The Arrogance of Power: The Secret World of Richard Nixon*, published in 2000. "I gave [Nixon] a mild sedative and told him to come back in two weeks," Hutschnecker recalled of the first session. The doctor and others indicated that Nixon's affliction included depression. Pat Nixon said her husband was "more depressed than . . . ever" in the beginning of 1956, the year Nixon campaigned for reelection to the vice presidency, according to their daughter, Julie Nixon Eisenhower. And in 1960, during Nixon's presidential campaign against Kennedy, a businessman who had served alongside him in the military told a *New York Times* reporter that the candidate "had severe ups and downs, and it was not easy to pull him up when he fell into depression." He said that Nixon was currently in one of those slumps. Another Nixon colleague, Leonard Garment, later disclosed that Nixon grappled with "powerful depression" throughout his life. FBI agent Mark Felt—revealed in 2005 as the anonymous source "Deep Throat" from Bob Woodward and Carl Bernstein's Watergate investigation—told the *Washington Post* reporters that Nixon had been "having fits of dangerous depression" as recently as a year or so before the 1972 election. Hutschnecker, for his part, was relatively circumspect. "He didn't have a serious psychiatric diagnosis," the psychiatrist told Summers of his patient. "Nixon wasn't psychotic. He had no pathology. But he did have a good portion of neurotic symptoms."[30]

Although Nixon initially resisted opening up to Hutschnecker, he eventually grew comfortable enough to vent with the therapist, who believed that his patient's "sharp intellect and outward self-confidence masked 'deep-seated inhibitions,'" according to Summers's account. "Nixon was an enigma, not just to me but to himself," Hutschnecker said. Nixon's father had abused his wife and sons, but Hutschnecker thought Nixon's mother's religiosity had the deepest impact on the president's development. Devoted to his mother, Nixon felt "trapped" into going through the motions of praying each day in order to satisfy her, the psychiatrist explained. "Fear was a virus that infected Nixon's life, that he never recovered from—fear that he would be regarded as weak," Hutschnecker explained, "What would Mama think? What would Daddy say? . . . I believe that the image of the saintly but stern face of his mother defeated him more than any other factor. . . . His mother was really his downfall."[31]

In the aftermath of the 1968 Pearson revelations, Hutschnecker wrote an article for *Look* magazine, affirming that he saw "no sign of mental illness" when he treated the man now occupying the Oval Office. He vouched that Richard Nixon possessed "not only the strength but the imagination and clarity of goal that [Hutschnecker] thought were prerequisites for a successful leader." The doctor described four personality categories that characterize the different human responses to stress: (1) "the strong, excitatory type"; (2) "the lively" type; (3) "the calm-imperturbable" type; and (4) "the weak, inhibitory" type. Hutschnecker explained that people classified as type one and type four are most likely to crack under stress, and that "men of type two represent the most desirable leaders because they show a controlled reaction." When he wrote the *Look* article in 1969, Hutschnecker anticipated that Nixon might "turn out to be a type two leader, the controlled, adjusted personality." But by the time of his 1995 interview with Summers, Dr. Hutschnecker conceded that Nixon had proven to be type one; the president released his aggression to make himself feel better, Hutschnecker explained.[32]

Nixon also experimented with psychotropic drugs. In 1968 Jack Dreyfus, founder of the Dreyfus Fund and a Nixon friend, provided the president-elect with Dilantin, a medication that was believed to help circumscribe "fear, worry, guilt, anger and related emotions, irritability, rage, mood, depression, violent behavior, hyperglycemia, alcohol, anorexia, bulimia and binge eating, cardiac arrhythmia, muscle disorders." Dreyfus gave Nixon one thousand hundred-milligram pills to start with, and he supplied the president with another thousand capsules when his initial allotment ran out, as he sometimes took two pills per day. Nixon refused to get a proper prescription. "To heck with the doctor," he told Dreyfus. Newer, more efficacious drugs with fewer side effects have since supplanted Dilantin as a top treatment for anxiety and the other ailments the drug was believed to alleviate.[33]

In the days before e-mail, the fastest way other than a telephone call for McGovern and Eagleton supporters to express their opinions to the campaign was by sending a telegram. But with the campaign vacationing at the remote Sylvan Lake Lodge, the only telegraph machines were in the press room of the Hi-Ho, where reporters could intercept the cables as they came in. This set-up provided journalistic snoops undistorted, real-time access to the same information as the campaign and thus limited the campaign's ability to downplay the issue of Eagleton's mental health and to fudge the statistics. As Bob Boyd reported in the Knight syndicate papers on Thursday, by mid-Wednesday, approximately fifty telegrams had arrived for the campaign in South Dakota, and they ran two-to-one against Eagleton.

Boyd sampled the reaction in his article. "Since you have con-

ceded election to Nixon by selection of a psychotic running mate, I
would like a refund of money contributed when you were a viable
candidate," a Democrat from California wrote to McGovern, voicing
the presumption that Eagleton's revelations had destroyed McGovern's candidacy. While a few saw Eagleton's disclosure as a display
of "honesty and courage" meriting "deepest admiration, respect,
and confidence," others emphasized Eagleton's dishonesty in not
telling McGovern about his mental health history up front. Eagleton's
"unconscionable, puerile, rapacious duplicity is reprehensible and
incompatible with your bold, principled and visionary primary campaign," wrote a couple from Philadelphia. Others merged distaste
at Eagleton's behavior with anger at his apparent reckless disregard
for the campaign's hard-earned viability. "As a twenty-two-year-old
worker for your candidacy in Rockland County, New York, I believe
I speak for many of us," read one telegram. "We did not work for
your candidacy for four years to see it thrown down the drain by
Eagleton's incomprehensible actions. I sympathize with his problem
but I do not want him ever as my president." The volunteer did not
specify why, exactly, he would never want Eagleton in the White
House. Was it because Eagleton had concealed his history of mental
illness and was thus deemed untrustworthy, or was it because of the
mental illness itself? The young New Yorker's dispatch skirts the
specifics, yet it captures the McGovern campaign's bind as it went
about deciding on Eagleton.[34]

While the campaign assumed that Eagleton's history of mental
illness would upset the American citizenry—repelling voters from
the McGovern ticket and thereby negating months, even years of
hard work—most staffers and voters felt uncomfortable castigating
Eagleton simply because he had suffered from an illness he claimed
to have overcome. As Gary Hart later explained, there was an impression of "personal understanding, but political intolerance" both
inside and outside the McGovern organization. Philosophically, the
McGovern campaign wanted to believe Eagleton, but staffers imagined that most Americans harbored primitive understanding of
mental illness, and this worried them. Still, this was all conjecture,
based on anecdotal information and little, if any, hard data. No one

knew for certain how Americans felt about mental illness. As NBC's David Brinkley cautioned, Americans "may be more sophisticated on the subject than Washington realizes since it often underestimates the American people in many other ways." In comments that aired on *Nightly News*, Howard Metzenbaum, a Cleveland millionaire and early McGovern supporter, expressed the quintessential McGovernite sentiment that Brinkley described: "Unfortunately the American people do not comprehend the nature of psychiatric treatment. And if they did, I don't think that it would be necessary that Eagleton [withdraw]." Metzenbaum distanced himself from the supposedly unsophisticated masses, whom he presumed to be fearful of a Tom Eagleton vice presidency.[35]

Yet no one knew how Americans *should have* felt about mental illness in the Oval Office. The state of science and psychiatry provided no universally satisfactory answers to the questions of whether someone with a history of depression and electroshock could be confident of avoiding relapse through the extraordinary strains of the presidency and successfully perform in office; psychiatrists and other medical professionals could not agree whether, in fact, a depressive could ever entirely recover. Some believed that electroshock left the treated patient no more susceptible to depression than anyone else. Other, more psychoanalytically oriented professionals, did not consider electroshock curative, or merely "pace" preventative. Some also believed that the likelihood of depression only increases with age. Rife with division, the psychiatric community could not definitively tell the American public what to believe.

Both the McGovern campaign and the nation—as it appeared to its staffers eyes, colored by their own internal doubts and anxieties—found themselves caught between what they *wanted* to believe (what seemed "sophisticated," to use Brinkley's term), and what they *could* believe given the constraints of psychiatric knowledge. Thus if the campaign were to drop Eagleton, it needed to satisfy both those fundamentally averse to voting for someone with a history of mental illness on the ticket and those morally uncomfortable with the prospect of disqualifying someone based merely on a history of mental illness. Most of those pleading for Eagleton's withdrawal—

in telegrams and letters, in newspaper and television editorials—
sidestepped the politically fraught insinuation that someone with
a history of mental illness could never be vice president. Rather,
they censured Eagleton because he appeared to have deliberately
deceived McGovern by neglecting to mention his past condition
when he was selected. Most people believed that Eagleton's willful
omission demonstrated a lack of character and "seriously bad judgment." A Gallup poll commissioned by *Newsweek* revealed that 80
percent of Americans thought Eagleton "should have told George
McGovern . . . about his past before accepting the vice presidential
nomination." Only 28 percent admitted to deeming his mental health
history disqualifying in and of itself.[36]

When the nation's leading newspapers began editorializing on
Eagleton—starting with Thursday's *Los Angeles Times, Miami Herald*,
and *Washington Post*—most would focus on the running mate's lack
of candor rather than on his health. They also emphasized the exceptionality of the presidency, conceding the ability of someone with a
history of depression to take on any job, but making an exception for
commander in chief, with the particular strains inherent to the Oval
Office. These editorialists pontificated on the value of reincorporat-
ing the mentally ill into society, and they expressed the need to erase
the stigma attached to mental illness. They explained that mental illness was, for the most part, just as treatable as physical impairments.
The *Post* editorialist, for example, argued that to believe otherwise
meant succumbing to "unenlightened taboos." And the writer for the
Los Angeles Times called it "honorable, not shameful," to seek treatment. Yet at the same time, the *Post* considered Eagleton's treatment
with electroshock to be "rather beyond the mere seeking of psychiatric care." And the newspaper's editorial board did not believe the
vice presidency to be like any other job; after all, three of the nation's
previous five presidents had moved to 1600 Pennsylvania Avenue
by way of the vice presidency. Thus the position of the *Post* was that
the severity and unpredictability of Eagleton's case of depression
combined with the unparalleled responsibility of the presidency
made Eagleton a problematic candidate. The editorialists all ignored
the melancholy endured by such iconic American and British leaders

as Abraham Lincoln and Winston Churchill while in office, though the newspapers referenced such examples in explanatory sidebars accompanying their news coverage of the Eagleton disclosures. And they failed to discern the contradictions in their argument. Is it honorable to seek some treatment, but not others (like electroshock)? Is it okay to seek psychiatric care, but shameful to receive treatment?

For the most part, however, the editorials emphasized the "remarkably bad judgment" Eagleton had demonstrated in his failure to disclose his condition, as the *Post* framed it. The writer for the *Herald* deemed Eagleton's actions incompatible with a campaign "pegged to candor and credibility." The newspapers also stressed the need to return to the issues, ducking responsibility for the role the news media had played in dictating the tenor of campaign conversation. By focusing on Eagleton's mental health, the newspapers were making his illness into the distraction from the real issues that they lamented it to be.[37]

Meanwhile, the *St. Louis Post-Dispatch*, among others such as the *Arkansas Democrat* and *Milwaukee Journal*, came to Eagleton's defense, speculating that the Missouri senator "presumably felt he had been cured for six years" and thus considering his past mental illness a nonissue. The *Post-Dispatch* editorialist viewed Eagleton's record of service on behalf of Missourians as indicative of his future performance, whether as senator, vice president, or president. Looking back on Eagleton's long career, the writer argued, "It is an unusually distinguished record, and it merits confidence," also noting a perception that sympathy for Senator Eagleton's dilemma overshadowed the condemnation of his critics. But Eagleton's status as homegrown hero and the relative acceptance of electroshock in St. Louis likely shaded the paper's view.[38]

Beyond the opinion pages, the Eagleton situation provoked the nation's leading newspapers to examine the facts behind electroshock. Accompanying their coverage of the Eagleton revelations were explanatory articles that debunked common misconceptions about depression and the treatment of choice for the condition at the time and the place Eagleton received care, electroshock. These articles' reporters typically noted the prevalence of depression in the general population; legitimized electroshock as an effective, even standard treatment for this common ailment; identified Eagleton as a prime candidate for electroshock; and evaluated competing theories about depression and electroshock therapy, both of which psychiatry still struggled to understand.

Though by the 1970s doctors typically recommended electroshock only for the most severe cases of depression, the mainstream media acknowledged disagreement within psychiatry about depression and divergent philosophies about when to prescribe electroshock. Of course, the term "depression" could suggest a range of feelings from the "down in the dumps" mood that Eagleton described at his Los Angeles press conference, to chronic lethargy, and a massively incapacitating state of mind, like that later captured by the novelist William Styron in his 1990 memoir *Darkness Visible*. "With their minds turned agonizingly inward, people with depression are usually dangerous only to themselves," Styron wrote. "The madness of depression is, generally speaking, the antithesis of violence. It is a storm indeed, but a storm of murk. Soon evident are the sloweddown responses, near paralysis, psychic energy throttled back close to zero. Ultimately, the body is affected and feels sapped, drained."[39]

A *Los Angeles Times* reporter inferred that Eagleton suffered from the type of depression found in "compulsive hard workers who drive themselves to exhaustion." Writers at the *New York Times, Washington Post,* and elsewhere concurred, citing medical professionals to legitimate this conclusion. Eagleton's depression may have been just as debilitating a disease as the one Styron later described, but in 1972 the nation's major newspapers cast his condition as nothing particularly unusual, especially among the ambitious set. In the *New York Times,* for instance, Dr. Francis Braceland proposed that Eagleton probably had suffered a "success depression," suggesting that he must have felt "a dizziness and an aloneness on the heights which he [had] attained," almost trivializing it. And the newspapers identified this form of depression as the type that electroshock treated best.

Indeed, blaming Eagleton's depression on hard work seemed to mitigate the stigma of his illness. If overwork was the culprit of Eagleton's depression and electroshock expiated it, surely he could stifle recurrence by "pacing" himself, as Eagleton insisted he had learned to do since his last hospitalization in 1966. In response to Eagleton's disclosures, the American Psychiatric Association affirmed that "countless thousands of people" had resumed their predepression lifestyles after completing their treatment, offering "compelling evidence" that the public should regard depression as similar to any other illness. In this vein, asserting his total recovery, Eagleton dismissed his illness as no more significant than a "broken leg or a broken arm." One psychiatrist quoted in the papers cited two politicians whom he had treated with electroshock about twenty years earlier and who had since scaled the Washington hierarchy depression-free. Media coverage also minimized or dismissed the drawbacks to electroshock that critics alleged, like brain damage and memory loss. Most of the articles concluded that, given Eagleton's fast-paced, high-octane lifestyle, ECT must have appealed to the young, ambitious politician as a therapy that offered reliable success rates without the outlay of time and money that psychoanalysis and newfangled drug programs required.[40]

According to a diagnosis Senator Eagleton received in January 1983 from Dr. Frederick Goodwin, he suffered from bipolar II disorder. People afflicted with bipolar II cycle between depression and hypomania, the tempered form of the full-blown acute mania found in people with a bipolar I diagnosis. The depressions of bipolar II patients tend to be more severe than the transient feelings of sadness and despondency that most people experience at various points in their lives, often for identifiable reasons.[41]

People suffering from the depressions that are typical of bipolar II patients lapse into protracted periods of feeling worthless, emotions that collude with physical symptoms, such as unceasing fatigue and difficulty getting out of bed, or insomnia, often at random. Their diminished appetites usually translate into weight loss, and the afflicted no longer find joy in activities that once evoked happiness. Experiencing profound loss of self-esteem, some may even contemplate suicide. The intensity and duration of these symptoms can vary, but they typically last two weeks or more.

During the hypomanic phase, the afflicted abounds with enthusiasm for life, brimming with "flight of ideas," good cheer, and frivolity. Self-doubt is unthinkable. Confidence pervades. The mind races from thought to thought. Creativity thrives, and one often bursts with eagerness to share observations, interrupting others and talking at a feverish clip. Sleep becomes an option, no longer a requirement. Yet this exuberance can tip into irrationality and impulsivity, spawning wild spending sprees, ill-conceived business agreements, even misguided sexual relationships.

Periods of normalcy called "euthymic intervals" punctuate the polar depressive and hypomanic episodes, and these remissions vary in length and can last as long as decades. It is worth noting that, in psychiatry, there are few, if any, perfect diagnoses. Professionals may disagree about what degree of severity qualifies someone as bipolar to begin with, and bipolar II in particular.

Most twenty-first-century professionals believe that mental illness stems from a combination of biology and life experiences, yet they argue about the proportions and about why some events trigger episodes and similar experiences do not. Some psychiatrists insist that mental illness should be considered a physical disease just like any other. Such psychiatrists believe that just as some people get heart disease no matter how strict their regimen of exercise and diet, some people are genetically susceptible to mental illness, irrespective of their life experiences. Medication, talk therapy, and regular sleeping habits can stabilize mental illness, but psychiatrists adamant about a purely biological basis of mental illness say there is no foolproof preventative. Other professionals believe that mental illness is entirely environmental—the product of life experiences, particularly early-childhood socialization—and they reject the notion of a biological underpinning of depression. At the extreme of the psychoanalytic camp, Dr. Peter Breggin, the founder of the Empathetic Psychiatry movement, for example, rejects the concept of a biological basis of mental illness as "totally unfounded," dismissing it as a "speculation that serves power and money," such as the drug companies. He even argues that psychotropic drugs are counterproductive, actually instigating depression instead of appeasing it.

Electroconvulsive therapy similarly evades consensus, remaining the object of ire, suspicion, and claims of abuse. Critics of ECT say that it causes memory loss, and they dwell on the lack of a conclusive explanation for its efficacy. Yet despite the expanded and much improved arsenal of psychotropic medications, ECT still occupies a niche in psychiatry for those instances when all else has failed or a quick recovery is crucial—for suicidal patients, for example—or when psychotropic drugs risk interfering with concurrent medications or biological processes, as in pregnant women and the elderly. As new practices (like individualizing dosage and electrode placement) and technologies (brief and ultrabrief pulse sine wave stimulation, magnetic seizure therapy, and focal electrically administered seizure therapy) have diminished side effects, some doctors have begun to have more confidence in ECT and similar procedures. More than one hundred thousand people, many of them suicidal, receive electroshock treatment in the United States each year. Approximately thirty-five thousand Americans commit suicide each year, hardly any of whom had received shock treatment.

Of course, Eagleton received electroshock therapy in the pre-Lithium era, when doctors had limited pharmacological options, and the drugs that did exist were hampered by significant side effects. Since Lithium's approval by the Food and Drug Administration in 1970, bipolar disorder has become much more manageable and seldom requires ECT to alleviate. In the 1990s, for example, Eagleton was able to control his condition by taking Lithium, Tegretol, Buproprion (marketed commercially as Wellbutrin), and Restoril. Lithium and Tegretol are mood stabilizers; Buproprion is a nontricyclic antidepressant that is also believed to help users fight nicotine addiction; Restoril is a sleeping aid. The combination of these four drugs had by then become a fairly typical regimen for people diagnosed with bipolar II. In other words, the emotional distress that mandated Eagleton's treatment with electroshock in the 1960s probably would not have necessitated ECT today. On the other hand, given the pitfalls of treatments available in the 1960s, it seems that Eagleton's ability to overcome his depressions relatively quickly and forge a successful political career despite his history of mental illness can be attributed, at least in part, to ECT.[42]

Most psychiatrists surveyed for this book believe that bipolar II disorder can be controlled with a combination of psychotropic drugs, talk therapy, and indeed adjustment of one's "pace." Still, there remains a certain amount of unpredictability to bipolar disorder, for which no single measure is a guaranteed preventative. Nonetheless, most of the current professionals interviewed for this book are confident that a bipolar II diagnosis is not disqualifying, especially if the most recent signs suggest the disease is not affecting functionality, as seemed to be the case with Eagleton. He performed ably in the Senate, and his aides who did not know about his past never suspected depression.

Furthermore, in the post-Watergate era, increased awareness of the fallibility of our leaders seems to have made many Americans, particularly the psychiatrists and psychologists surveyed for this book, less fearful of mental illness in the Oval Office. Lyndon Johnson's paranoia and Richard Nixon's dubious mental states are both widely known, and America elected George W. Bush fully aware of his history of alcohol abuse. A 2006 Duke University study of the thirty-seven U.S. presidents in office from 1776 to 1974 determined that 49 percent of them met criteria indicative of a psychiatric disorder. Twenty-four percent experienced depression, and 8 percent are suspected to have been bipolar. A recent book by the director of the Mood Disorders Program at the Tufts University Medical Center, Dr. Nassir Ghaemi, *A First Rate Madness: Uncovering the Links between Leadership and Mental Illness,* goes so far as to suggest that some mental illness may actually be beneficial in our leaders, especially in times of crisis. Dr. Ghaemi argues that traits associated with bipolar disorder, like realism, resilience, empathy, and creativity are conducive to effective leadership, especially in periods of emergency. "For abnormal challenges, abnormal leaders are needed," he writes.[43]

"I want George McGovern in the White House and I wouldn't do anything to keep him from obtaining that goal," Eagleton said Wednesday afternoon upon his arrival in Hawaii, the next stop on his western swing. He reiterated that he would withdraw if his candidacy ended up proving incontrovertibly harmful to McGovern's chances. "I wouldn't wait for McGovern. I would pull out myself," Eagleton promised, echoing lines he had used in California.[44]

But everything changed as he spent more time in Hawaii. The once conciliatory and subservient running mate gave way to a tenacious Eagleton, invigorated with a newfound determination to remain on the ticket at whatever cost, even if it meant dragging down George McGovern's candidacy along with him, as it seemed to some. Yet, the Hawaiian crowds showered Eagleton with adulation, and the vice presidential candidate's busy schedule seemed to provide him welcome distraction. Locals treated him to a native dance demonstration that afternoon, and Eagleton handily picked up the routine, with poise and good humor.[45]

In the audience, Eagleton spotted a barefooted and seemingly indigent boy no more than ten years of age and invited him to come along for his afternoon activities. The Secret Service called the boy's parents for their approval, and the boy hopped into the limo with Eagleton and the rest of his party. "I'd like you to meet my friend," Eagleton would say as he introduced the boy to members of Hawaii's political elite.

"It's just the kind of guy [Tom] was," explained Gene Godley, who oversaw the Hawaii trip for Eagleton. "Here he was, a candidate for vice president, and he saw this little boy who did not have anything to do except hang around the edges, and he adopted him for the day and brought him along with us. . . . Tom was such an egalitarian."[46]

With forty-five minutes to spare between the dancing event at the shopping center and a scheduled meeting with fourteen labor leaders at his hotel, the Hilton Hawaiian Village on Waikiki Beach, Eagleton decided to take a swim. Sporting flashy orange swim trunks and encircled by Secret Service agents, Eagleton took a dip in the Pacific. As he headed back to land, a heavyset older woman swam over and embraced him "in the affectionate bear hug of a loving aunt," as Eagleton described it, before the Secret Service agents could stop her. "Eagleton," the woman said. "You're a good kid. They're giving you a hell of a going over. Hang in there kid!" According to Eagleton, the woman's support vanquished any remaining self-doubt.[47]

Recounting the scene in his unpublished memoirs, Eagleton explained, "You see, politics is still an imprecise science. You can have computers and professional pollsters and all the rest. In the final analysis, a politician gets a feel[ing] in his gut which tells him whether he is right or wrong. He gets a feel[ing] in his gut after a speech. Even though his staff says, 'You wowed 'em, champ,' a good politician can feel in his gut whether he did or not." On that swim in the Pacific, a world away from the pine-paneled auditorium on Sylvan Lake, Eagleton felt that the public was with him.[48]

But then there was Jack Anderson.

Back in Washington, Eagleton's administrative assistant Doug Bennet heard rumors alleging that Eagleton had recently been arrested six times for drunken driving, three of the incidents in DC. At around 3 P.M. that Wednesday, Bennet heard from Charles Ferris, chief counsel to Senate Majority Leader Mike Mansfield, that NBC was ready to break the story on that evening's *Nightly News*. DNC general counsel Joseph Califano had told Ferris that NBC anchor David Brinkley had called to give the heads-up on the story. At least two similar rumors heard that day seemed to have originated with NBC staff, and the network's clout gave them additional heft. Bennet promptly called WRC-NBC, the network's Washington affiliate, and left a message for the news director, condemning the rumor mongering and declaring the allegations "entirely untrue." Bennet also expressed disappointment that the folks at NBC would spread gossip. The news director soon returned Bennet's call and said that, after further digging, the network could not substantiate the allegations and would withhold the story. In a memo to Mike Kelley, Eagleton's press secretary, Bennet ended: "I would like to see Brinkley get a fat lip."[49]

The Muckraker

At around 11 A.M. in Washington on Thursday morning, July 27, exactly two weeks after McGovern named Eagleton his running mate, Bennet heard that a station in the Mutual Broadcasting System radio network was previewing a report by Jack Anderson, the Pulitzer Prize–winning nationally syndicated columnist. Apparently Anderson was claiming to have "located" evidence of Eagleton's history of drunk driving, Photostats of the citations that seemed to undercut the running mate's insistence that he had no history of alcohol abuse. In addition to his column, "Washington Merry-Go-Round"—which appeared in 965 newspapers worldwide—Anderson's reach extended to his own television programs, and he boasted a reputation as a diligent and fearless reporter, the scourge of the Nixon administration. Upon hearing of the broadcast, Bennet immediately dialed Hart and Mankiewicz. "We're all going to have to be very strong about this," he asserted. "There is no drunkenness and there are no arrest records."[1]

Off in Hawaii, shortly after 6 A.M. Hawaii-Aleutian Standard Time, Eagleton's press secretary Mike Kelley awoke him. "Chief, you won't believe this," he began, "but Jack Anderson has just made a radio broadcast in Washington in which he says you have been arrested for eleven major automobile offenses, six of which involved drunken driving."

"Shit, pure unadulterated shit," Eagleton responded. "He's a god damned liar."[2]

After hanging up with the McGovern aides, Bennet had dialed Eagleton in Hawaii to confirm what he had assured Mankiewicz and Hart. Indeed, when he connected with Eagleton, the running mate dismissed Anderson's allegations as groundless, so Bennet called back the McGovern campaign. "Are you absolutely sure?" Hart demanded, still apprehensive about Eagleton's guarantee. The McGovern campaign had been through this before; Eagleton and his staff had dodged the details about the senator's history of mental illness, and Hart wanted to be certain McGovern had the facts before deciding how to respond. But Bennet insisted, "This is our chance to hit this thing head on. Let's kill this once and for all." Bennet believed the McGovern campaign should capitalize on the accusations, using them as a jumping-off point for vigorously defending the running mate from a treacherous reporter's slime. But Hart did not trust Bennet and Eagleton. To clear his head, McGovern went canoeing.[3]

The Anderson accusations deepened the rift between the McGovern and Eagleton staffs by disentangling their objectives. Armed with firsthand knowledge that Anderson's report was false, Eagleton could disparage the reporter for his shoddy, vindictive reporting and avow his determination to prevail. The fight to discredit Anderson energized Eagleton because, as he explained it, the charges cut to "the depth of [his] political competence." If left unchallenged, they could halt his public career: he would be seen as not only a depressive and a drunkard, but a dishonest one at that.[4]

Eagleton scrapped his scheduled breakfast meeting with the Hawaiian governor, opting instead to document his driving record and prepare to refute Anderson's charges before the press. Over the phone, Bennet read Eagleton a statement he had drafted for him, and Eagleton took it down. Eagleton sharpened up the language and soon called Bennet back. In the new version, Eagleton chided

Anderson for propagating a "damnable lie," phraseology proposed by Gene Godley. But Bennet pushed back: "Don't do anything that sounds intemperate," he said, fearful of the candidate's appearing angry, emotional, or unstable; Bennet thought the risk of feeding such perceptions would only exacerbate the problem. But Eagleton was adamant.[5]

Speaking from just a few notes jotted on a sheet of yellow legal paper, Eagleton forcefully defended himself to the reporters, hardening his resolve to remain George McGovern's running mate. "I'm all the more determined after this Anderson business to remain on the ticket and campaign for the office of vice president and to be elected vice president of the United States," he barked. "That is my intention, and I am going to persist and pursue it as vigorously as I can." Eagleton's anger toward Anderson gave his voice an edge, as he declared that the allegations "absolutely reek[ed] of politics." They represented exactly the type of rumors that had hovered around the St. Louisian upstart throughout his political career. "I want to set the record straight," Eagleton said. "And I want to give the unvarnished context." When responding to questions about his medical records, Eagleton had revealed specifics only as they were asked and skirted requests to see the documents themselves. But now, as he marshaled evidence in his defense—evidence stemming from complete, undoctored, traceable driving records—he was forceful and clear, in stark contrast with his previous lack of forthrightness. Traveling with the vice presidential candidate, Loye Miller of Knight Newspapers identified Eagleton's changing persona in a news analysis piece the following day: the man who was "taut and nervous" immediately following the disclosure handled "endless, highly personal questions [in Honolulu] with patience, aplomb, and apparent candor." Perhaps Eagleton had learned from the experience of the past few days, finding directness the most efficacious course. But it seems his newfound vigor came at least partly from the reality that, this time, he had less to hide and even more to lose.[6]

Eagleton cited two blemishes on his driving record, both of which had "absolutely no connection, direct or indirect, with alcohol." The first episode had occurred on March 11, 1962, right around

9:30 P.M., which Eagleton said he remembered because he was rushing to make it home to Jefferson City in time to catch the 10 P.M. newscast on the radio that evening. "Do you know why I was driving?"
he asked rhetorically. "I was bringing back twenty-four rolls from a
bakery in St. Louis that my wife wanted for a party that day at our
home in Jefferson City." Eagleton remembered driving seventy-five
or eighty miles per hour in a zone posted for sixty-five or seventy.
In fact, he had been driving eighty-five in a sixty-five zone, according to the *St. Louis Post-Dispatch*'s fact-check of Eagleton's defense—
a discrepancy, but a slight one. The *Post-Dispatch* also checked with
the apprehending officer and confirmed that alcohol had not figured
into the arrest. Eagleton had paid a $35 fine, plus $11 in processing
fees.[7]

The second incident had occurred during an "icy rainstorm,"
as Eagleton made his morning commute from St. Louis to Jefferson
City, on December 11, 1963. "I put my brakes on to make a turn and
damaged my left fender and grill," he explained. The *Post-Dispatch*'s
review of the Missouri State Highway Patrol records indicated that
his car had skidded on ice just past noon on a detour off of Interstate
70 in Warren County, along the route from St. Louis to Jefferson City.
Only a minor difference in the time of the accident—early afternoon
instead of morning—distinguished the two versions. The officer who
arrived at the scene confirmed for the *Post-Dispatch* that Eagleton
"had not been drinking."[8]

Still, the newspaper's investigation into Eagleton's driving record did turn up one former trooper in the Highway Patrol who said
that he, too, had stopped Eagleton for speeding—on three separate
occasions before 1966. The former official said he knew of other
troopers based in Jefferson City and Kirkwood who had stopped
Eagleton along the Jefferson City–St. Louis route, too, but had similarly declined to ticket Eagleton or report the incident because of his
role in state government. While the *Post-Dispatch*'s review confirmed
that no record of drunk driving existed, it could not verify that Eagleton had an otherwise spotless driving record. The Associated Press,
meanwhile, unearthed four violations in the record books as opposed
to the two Eagleton identified in his public rebuttal of Anderson's

charges: the first on July 27, 1948, when Eagleton was eighteen, and the second on February 19, 1954. Both were for negligible fines. Still, George Phipps, the assistant superintendent of the state highway patrol, validated Eagleton's rejection of Anderson's charges, explaining the department could not find records of the sort Anderson was alleging to exist. While the AP and *Post-Dispatch* reviews suggested the possibility Eagleton had avoided arrest only because of his high status in state office, Eagleton's ability to co-opt the story and seize the offensive—to grab Anderson by the collar as he was attempting to push him down even farther—proved more critical.[9]

The Anderson allegations enabled Eagleton to morph from treacherous campaign spoiler to sympathetic, national victim, with the guts to pick himself up and defend himself from a man spineless enough to hit him while he was down. Eagleton spoke deliberately as he presented his case to more than one thousand delegates to the Retail Clerks International Association convention in Honolulu later that day. "If I was determined to remain on the ticket yesterday—and I was so determined—I am doubly determined to stay on it today," he said, continuing to slam Anderson's charges as "a damnable lie." After he reminded the cheering audience that Harry Truman was also a Missourian, attendees shouted "Give 'em hell, Tom!" paraphrasing a battle cry associated with the thirty-third president. Eagleton continued to invoke Truman. "I hope I have some small measure of the guts that he possessed," he said. "I'm a stronger, better person than I was seventy-two hours ago. It takes a little adversity to find out what kind of person you are. It takes a little adversity to find out who your friends are. I don't know what the future will hold for me. But I am going to hang tall. I am going to stay in there," he pronounced. "You didn't invite me here to make a Perry Mason case for the defense. . . . I don't ask for your sorrow or your pity. I ask for your support for Senator George McGovern." As he finished his speech, the audience rose to grant him a lengthy ovation, chanting, "Ea-gle-ton. Ea-gle-ton. Ea-gle-ton," as they stood in place. Flashing a broad smile, Eagleton "clasped his hands like a prize fighter and waved," as one reporter described it. The Retail Clerks International convention endorsed the McGovern-Eagleton ticket through standing acclamation, giving the Democrats their first endorsement by an entire union convention since McGovern and Eagleton had joined forces in Miami Beach. Eagleton left Hawaii believing he was transcending controversy about his past and zeroing in on an essential task of the campaign: securing the support of organized labor—in this case, the 650,000 members of Retail Clerks International.[10]

Campaigning in California, Barbara Eagleton similarly called Anderson's assertions "preposterous" and vowed that they were "absolutely not true." Looking "poised and relaxed in the storm of national inquiry into her husband's medical history and arrest record," as reported by the United Press International wire service, Barbara said she would be "very disappointed" if her husband had to withdraw. "Yes, we will stay in the campaign," she maintained, though conceding, "I'm kind of distressed that things have gotten to this point."[11]

Meantime, while the presidential candidate remained personally supportive of Eagleton—affirming in private when the two men talked on Thursday, "Don't worry, Tom. We'll get this all behind us"—the McGovern campaign simultaneously pondered whether the benefit of standing up for its running mate outweighed the risk of appearing foolish should Anderson substantiate his allegations with hard evidence. Given Eagleton's track record of abridging the truth, McGovern staffers were inclined to believe Anderson, a Pulitzer Prize winner who swore by his source's reliability, regardless of whether he had seen the Photostats firsthand. Following Eagleton's rebuttal, Anderson returned to the airwaves, correcting the language he had used in his original broadcast of the charges. He revised his initial pronouncement, "We have now located Photostats," to "We have traced—but have not seen," admitting he lacked the hard evidence he previously said he possessed.[12]

McGovern's crew in South Dakota jettisoned his own beleaguered candidacy that day and headed to Custer's Harney Theatre, immersing itself in the current film *The Candidate* and the fictional candidacy of Bill McKay. In the movie, Democratic operatives convince a young, idealistic son of the former governor of California to run for the U.S.

Senate. Played by Robert Redford, McKay shuns "machine-type politics," insisting on saying what he feels, doing what he wants, and going where he pleases. A civil rights and environmental lawyer, McKay champions the expansion of welfare, busing, environmental regulation, and abortion rights against a Republican incumbent who taps into the public's fears of a collectivist state and disdain for so-called "welfare chiselers." But McKay's blend of idealism, candor, and guts earns him considerable support. "Credibility," McKay tells audiences, "depends on whether you mean what you say." McKay's unabashed moralism channeled the South Dakota senator in the Custer audience that day.[13]

But as fame goes to McKay's head and his consultants impress upon him the need to reassure California's suburban voters, his once-refreshing humility, sincerity, and compassion soon fade. Behind the scenes, viewers see McKay cheat on his wife and abuse his staff. The public also notes his changing persona. ABC anchor Howard K. Smith appears in the film, lamenting the new Madison Avenue McKay. In the beginning of the campaign, McKay "seemed different," Smith says. He bore a "frankness and directness" too uncommon among politicians. But as the campaign progressed, "those early hard statements are turning into mush," Smith complains. "Once again, it appears virtue is too great a strain for the long haul of the campaign." Though McKay loses his good nature and the adoration of the audience, his good looks and charisma win him the Senate seat, which—in truth—was the goal.[14]

At Harney Theatre that Thursday afternoon, a smattering of patrons—presumably McGovern staffers—applauded when one character blurted out, "Politics is bullshit." Laughter continued throughout the showing. But McGovern did not enjoy the film. It featured "some of the sicker side of politics," he lamented. His reaction was not surprising; the movie's message would unsettle anyone attempting to balance ideals and politics. In McKay, one wonders whether McGovern saw his own transformation—a reflection that repulsed him. As the movie meditated on the commercialization and superficiality of American politics, it laid bare McGovern's own internal struggle to balance his sense of rightness against his sense of prudence and political acuity. His staff's supposedly strategic pressure to dump Eagleton contradicted McGovern's moral instinct to keep him.[15]

McGovern approached the Eagleton decision like a sailboat headed down a bay, wrote Bill Greider of the *Washington Post*. The candidate tacked one way, and then moved the other, befuddling reporters about the intended direction of his vessel. Some would call McGovern's technique "keeping your options open," and it would seem proponents of New Politics such as McGovern should have derided this strategy as Old Politics maneuvering. But in truth, beneath the candidate's apparent decency lurked "a cautious tactician."[16]

As Anderson was vehemently propounding his charges, McGovern heard from his campaign finance chairman Henry Kimelman that donations had slowed since Tuesday, the day of Eagleton's disclosure. It signaled a loss of confidence in the organization. Top contributors to the campaign, who had pledged between $3 million and $4 million in loans to set up the joint McGovern-Eagleton campaign and launch its first postconvention direct-mail drive, had been calling in to renege on their commitments. In the seventy-two hours since McGovern and Eagleton's press conference in South Dakota, approximately 90 percent of these donors had withdrawn their commitments or hedged them with the condition that "the Eagleton thing" must be resolved. News of the crumbling confidence seeped into the press.[17]

Deeply apprehensive, Dick Dougherty asked McGovern whether he remained committed to keeping Eagleton. "I'm afraid we can't," McGovern responded. Reason, ambition, and pragmatism finally undermined McGovern's commitment to his running mate. "For now though," McGovern told Dougherty, "until we can see what to do, I want you to keep telling the press I'm staying with him." If the dynamic had been different, Dougherty might have pleaded with McGovern to halt the charade and urged him to tell Eagleton and the public how he truly felt. Nonetheless, while ostensibly reassuring the press that McGovern stood by his running mate, as the candidate had instructed him, Dougherty could not help but admit that the campaign entertained "concern" about the ongoing impact of the running mate's revelations. Another top aide similarly conceded to the press that matters were "at a furious boil" inside the McGovern camp, ultimately leaving the press—and the public—with a mixed message and underscoring the campaign's own disingenuousness.[18]

Later that day, McGovern issued a stop-talk order to his staff: "I have made my support for Senator Eagleton clear, and I want no further comment on the matter by anyone connected to the campaign other than Senator Eagleton or myself." Yet Gary Hart told NBC, "The official position of the campaign is that Senator Eagleton is our vice presidential candidate and will remain so," with "official" being the operative word. McGovern is "not going to put his finger up in the wind and reverse his decision," said Mankiewicz with characteristic gusto. Yet—as the comments of Dougherty and the other campaign aides implied—behind closed doors, McGovern was surely exploring his options.[19]

That day, Mankiewicz's secretary Pat Broun recorded at least two calls from self-proclaimed manic-depressives voicing apprehension about someone of Eagleton's psychological makeup potentially becoming president. Conveying one caller's sentiment, Broun noted on her call pad, "Eagleton does *not* know his own limits. Sympathetic but believes TE's ambition greater than his judgment." In a letter dated July 26, three California congressmen wrote that keeping Eagleton on the ticket meant a "political disaster" come November. As Californians, they knew Nixon's capabilities, and they predicted that the president's "caustic tactics of smear, whisper, doubt, and innuendo [would] run rampant as a result of this new issue." Another call memo came with the note from Broun, "Frank—this sums it up." Relating comments from the McGovern campaign coordinator in Middlesex County, New Jersey—and a vastly different outlook from the support the running mate was receiving in Hawaii—a campaign receptionist had written: "Eagleton thing a disaster, has cut off money, ruined volunteer force, everyone demoralized."[20]

A "responsible Republican" had also tipped the McGovern campaign that its rivals were preparing lists highlighting federal regulations that forbade someone with Eagleton's history of mental illness from becoming a private in the Strategic Air Command, for instance. Mankiewicz shared this intelligence with McGovern. That Thursday night, burdened by escalating pressure to drop his running mate, McGovern queried two prominent psychiatrists himself.[21]

Dr. Wilfred Abse of the University of Virginia, whom McGovern had consulted about his daughter Terry before institutionalizing her in 1969, told McGovern that he could not predict Eagleton's future mental health with any certainty. But he advised McGovern not to risk the chance that Eagleton might relapse. McGovern looked to Dr. Karl Menninger for a second opinion. The Knight reporters' July 23 memo indicated that, according to a leading St. Louis Democrat, Eagleton had received treatment for a nervous breakdown at Kansas City's Menninger Clinic in January 1965 and again in 1967, an allegation that Eagleton denied. When they spoke, Menninger warned McGovern that he could not diagnose Eagleton's condition from afar, but that he recognized the campaign's public relations quagmire: "Millions of Americans are so frightened by mental illness that they will not support you for the presidency in the knowledge that your vice president has had a history of mental problems," Menninger acknowledged. "On the other hand, if you now ask Senator Eagleton to resign from the ticket, millions of other Americans will turn against you for persecuting a man who has suffered mental instability." As McGovern distilled it, he was damned no matter what he decided. "As for the interest of the nation," Menninger continued, "you can afford no risks, and I would therefore hope that you would ask Mr. Eagleton to step down."[22]

Hart remembered one of the doctors speculating that someone with Eagleton's profile, his case history, would have harbored "suicidal tendencies," a detail that was alleged in Boyd and Hoyt's memo and that surely would have added to the campaign's difficulty if reiterated publicly. A late-night conversation McGovern had with his family in cabin 22 reaffirmed the complexity of his decision. Of McGovern's five children, two now thought Eagleton should withdraw from the ticket, including Terry; three thought he should remain. Eleanor—convinced by Menninger's assessment—believed that Eagleton should go.[23]

On the plane ride from Hawaii back to California, Eagleton took a break from watching Charlie Chaplin's *City Lights* to field a few questions from Loye Miller, the Knight Newspapers reporter traveling with the campaign. "I would have to rate the last forty-eight hours as a mixture of the most intriguing days of my life and perhaps the most perplexing," Eagleton reflected. He said that sharing his mental history on national television was the hardest experience of his life, other than confronting the death of his father. For "most individuals, as you go through life, you have times of sadness, times of anguish and personal family matters and the like, and my life has been no more immune than any other American citizen's."

Eagleton tried to put it all in perspective. As he often told himself, he was a lucky guy, but—like all people—he also had bouts with misfortune. Eagleton's life seemed to vacillate between highs and lows more exaggerated than most people experience, from the pinnacles of triumph to the depths of despair. Miller called his Hawaiian jaunt with George McGovern's running mate "a strange, almost psychedelic mixture of joy and tribulation."[24]

The Tablehopping

Press secretary Mike Kelley has likened Eagleton's vice presidential candidacy to "being in the middle of a hurricane," and the morning of Friday, July 28, helped illustrate why. When Eagleton awoke at Del Webb's Townhouse motel, yet another pitfall awaited him: a *New York Times* editorial calling for the vice presidential candidate's voluntary withdrawal. Like the *Los Angeles Times* and *Washington Post* before it, the *New York Times*—the nation's most influential newspaper—refrained from labeling Eagleton's history of mental illness alone as grounds for his removal, arguing instead that his departure would allow the campaign to return to "the issues that should concern the American people." Mocking McGovern's hyperbolic Black Hills suggestion that no one was sounder in mind, body, and spirit to be president than Tom Eagleton, the paper maintained that, "regrettable" though the case might be, the state of scientific knowledge in 1972 left Eagleton's prospects of future mental illness unpredictable. Even if pacing himself had proven rehabilitative and preventative for Eagleton as senator, the *Times* reasoned, "Unfortunately no president since Calvin Coolidge has enjoyed the luxury of a world geared to so personal a need." The sarcasm of that comment fed the perception of Eagleton as victim and provided the vice presidential candidate another opportunity to demonstrate resilience.[1]

Powerful San Francisco mayor Joseph Alioto visited Eagleton in his suite at the Del Webb that morning, just before the scheduled unity breakfast at the Hilton. Though he had previously been disenchanted with McGovern, Alioto told Eagleton, "If McGovern had good enough sense to pick you for the vice president, I've got enough sense to support that ticket." He announced the endorsement when he spoke at the breakfast, and Bennet called Hart to share word of the new supporter: "At least Alioto hasn't been frightened," he gloated.[2]

In his own address before the cross section of Democrats in attendance at the breakfast that morning, Eagleton capitalized on the *Times*'s criticisms by painting the media as the assailant, "I have to disagree with the *Times*'s editorial because I think this discussion will run its course," he said. "The best proof of how it will run its course is the fact that (a) I will stay in the race and (b) I will remain as aggressively healthy as I am today." Instead of a campaign to defend his credibility, the race became a test of Eagleton's perseverance—that he had cured his depression and that he could withstand the injustices heaped against him by those insensitive to the plight of people with histories of mental illness. William Smith, a lawyer from Pennsylvania, whom Eagleton did not know, sent him a $5,000 campaign contribution. The attached note read, "I don't like to see people pushed around." Eagleton had also received a telegraph from Eunice and Sargent Shriver that morning. "Don't quit," the Kennedy in-laws wrote. "Make this into a plus for the people of this country. You are a great candidate. Your record is superior in every way. Please don't give up." Senate Majority Leader Mike Mansfield and McGovern's first vice presidential pick, Ted Kennedy, also phoned to lend their support. But not all signs were so encouraging. When Eagleton left a television studio, two picketers awaited him. The woman's placard read, "Save McGovern's race, not Eagleton's face."[3]

Later that day, Eagleton sat down in his hotel suite with three *Time* magazine staffers and, serenely dragging on his Pall Mall cigarettes, reflected on the events of the previous two weeks. As the interview came to a close, he said, "I know that there are some people on the McGovern staff who want me off. I understand their thinking. If I had given a year and a half of my time and money, and all my heart and soul, and now here's a guy who comes in at the last minute and he is put on the ticket, I can see how a guy in the splendid isolation of South Dakota could feel that I should go," conceding empathy with the view he step down, albeit maintaining that such a view was misguided. Eagleton continued, "But I haven't been in South Dakota. I have been in Los Angeles and Honolulu and San Francisco, and I feel a different mood." He explained, "Politics isn't a science like physics, where you put things in a beaker and measure them. What makes or breaks a politician is how he perceives the public pulse, the public mood. I'm confident as I can be that the public is with me. I'm not living in a dream world. I know the stakes are high, but I firmly believe it."[4]

The presidential candidate began Friday at Custer's annual Gold Discovery Days Parade, celebrating the start of the gold rush in the French Creek Valley almost one hundred years before. Sporting a buckskin jacket and a brown Stetson hat, McGovern told reporters, "Let's just talk about the Discovery Days Parade." A Lincoln Town Car served as McGovern's steed, and several times along the parade route he stopped and dismounted to shake hands with the locals. "That wasn't a bad parade for a hick town," a local businessman said afterward. "But there were more politicians than there were horses."

"It only seemed that way," a *New York Times* reporter quipped.[5]

After the parade, McGovern spoke with an old friend from his days in South Dakota politics, soliciting an outsider's view of the Eagleton situation. McGovern's pal confided that others thought it inconceivable Eagleton could help the ticket. "Yes, I guess he's got to go," McGovern reportedly agreed. "But he's got to [be the one to] do it."[6]

That afternoon, the McGovern staff distributed to the press a preview of the speech the candidate would deliver at the South Dakota Democratic Convention in Aberdeen the next evening. McGovern expected the following paragraph to signal his shifting outlook: "I do not know how [the Eagleton situation] will all come out, but I do know that it gets darkest just before the stars come out. So I ask for prayers and your patience for Senator Eagleton and me while we deliberate on the proper course ahead." Not everyone within the Mc-Govern campaign endorsed this strategy. But the ones who objected were back in Washington. "What the hell's going on?" Mankiewicz asked Hart when they both learned what McGovern had scripted. "Here we are standing solid as a rock, and somebody's digging out the foundation [in South Dakota]," he said, though perhaps overesti-mating their own loyalty to what had been the campaign's "official" position. Mankiewicz immediately called McGovern, who told him that he believed he could not change his stance on Eagleton without first giving the public and his running mate some warning, how-ever faint the signal. Thus, with the Aberdeen speech embargoed until after its delivery the following evening and thus unprintable in the press, McGovern felt in even more of a rush to show Eagle-ton's detractors that he valued their concerns. He hatched a plan. But it seems only Mankiewicz foresaw how the press and the public would receive it.[7]

With Eagleton increasingly committed to remaining on the ticket, Dougherty was the one who suggested signaling through the press that his continuation might not be the best idea. Averse to direct confrontation, McGovern was intrigued. "Would it make any sense if I had a talk with Jules Witcover?" he proposed. The respected *Los Angeles Times* reporter had written a book about Spiro T. Agnew and had spoken with McGovern about the vice presidency several times over the past few years. Witcover "was talking to me more as a historian than anything else," McGovern told Dougherty of their past meetings, expressing his fondness for the journalist. "Anyway, I remember telling him that if, by some wild chance, I ever got the presidential nomination I would damned well avoid the messy way vice presidents had been picked in the past. I think Jules will re-member that." Recognizing the positives, Dougherty did not object.[8]

Back at the Hi-Ho Motel in Custer that Friday afternoon, *News-week*'s Dick Stout and *Time*'s Dean Fischer were finishing their weekly reporting in the makeshift pressroom—copy was due in New York that night—and they watched as a McGovern press aide scurried to find Witcover, who soon darted into the room short of breath and picked up the phone.

Witcover was a "tall but unprepossessing man of forty-five," as *Rolling Stone*'s Timothy Crouse described him. His loose skin under his "weak chin" sagged like a frog's goiter. Respected and well liked on the press bus, Witcover was known to be a "compulsive" hard worker. As Witcover spoke with McGovern, Stout and Fischer could hear that he had agreed to meet the candidate at 6 P.M. that evening. "He just wants to talk," Witcover told the curious newsweekly-men. "Has something to do with the last chapter in my Agnew book. We've talked about it before." Unconvinced, Fischer and Stout pressured Witcover into agreeing to update them after meeting with McGovern. Meanwhile, they headed to the Sylvan Lake Lodge for dinner and were surprised to find other reporters there, too. McGovern had stopped socializing with the press after Tuesday's press conference, preferring to dine with his family in the solitude of cabin 22. But tonight, Dougherty had given a few reporters the heads-up that they should be there, and word got around the press corps.[9]

In the lodge's Lakota Room, adorned with a Native American–style mural recounting "The Legend of the White Buffalo," reporters feasted on buffalo steaks as an organ blasted 1940s hits. After dining with his family, McGovern started making the rounds, first approaching a table of newsmen from the *Chicago Daily News*, the *Washington Post*, and United Press International. "Are you fellas glad to be getting home?" he asked, starting with small talk as the reporters wondered whether it would be appropriate to bring up Eagleton. But it soon became apparent that that was the candidate's intention as well. McGovern seemed "relaxed and confident," according to the *Post-Dispatch*'s account of the evening, as he emphasized the importance of public opinion in shaping his running mate's fate and explained to the table of journalists that the decision of whether Eagleton would continue on the ticket was no longer "entirely," but only "to a great extent" Eagleton's own. This meant, of course, that McGovern would also have a say in determining whether his running mate remained his partner.

McGovern said three considerations weighed on his mind that evening. First, he needed an unbiased assessment of Eagleton's mental health. Did Eagleton—as some had suggested—risk relapsing into similar bouts of depression that would necessitate similar hospitalizations and thereby hinder his ability to function in office? Second, did Eagleton's presence on the ticket help or hurt McGovern's candidacy? Which strategy—keeping him or removing him—would earn McGovern more votes in November's election? And third, should Eagleton have disclosed his history of mental illness before accepting the number-two spot on the Democratic ticket? Could the public trust Eagleton?

McGovern also divulged the reasoning behind his initial decision to back Eagleton. Rather than an instinctive, personal decision that stemmed from empathy for his running mate, McGovern portrayed his continued support as a more cerebral, political calculation; it was contrived not to offend people who suffered from mental illness, their family members, and others sympathetic to the plight of the mentally ill—a group that comprised a growing segment of the population, he explained. And now, when it appeared that Eagleton's presence on the ticket would hurt his chances at the presidency, McGovern was beginning to rescind his backing, each stance manufactured to generate maximum support for his own candidacy. Contrary to Mankiewicz's claim, it seemed that McGovern had, in fact, held his finger up in the air, detected which way the wind was blowing, and adjusted his position accordingly. In this election he could not afford to alienate any segment of the population, McGovern said. Even if polls indicated 99 percent of voters supported Eagleton, McGovern explained that the 1 percent who opposed him could prove enough to decide the election.[10]

When McGovern left the first table, the reporters there debated the ethics of quoting from a "casual dinner conversation." Soon their notepads came out, and they began reconstructing the candidate's words before ducking out to the telephones in the lodge lobby. "No point arousing all those other reporters," reflected the *Post*'s Bill Greider, who had been seated at the first table. McGovern, it turned out, would fill the others in, too. After stopping by the CBS group, he headed to Fischer and Stout's table. Knight Newspapers' Bob Boyd and Doug Kneeland of the *New York Times,* who were stationed at another table, wandered over. Kneeland had overheard the commotion as McGovern made his way through the room, and he could no longer stand waiting to hear what the candidate was sharing.[11]

In the next day's papers, the reporters revealed not only McGovern's message but also his method. Kneeland wrote in the *New York Times:* "Tonight's unusual casual conversations . . . which seemed to have been carefully arranged by aides who had dropped hints to a number of reporters that it might be wise to be on hand at the lodge for dinner, were interpreted by most of those present as designed to send a message to Mr. Eagleton." As Kneeland described it, McGovern paced the Lakota Room, "studiously repeating" himself to each table of reporters. "It slowly dawned on us," the *Post*'s Bill Greider would later reminisce, "that we were the ones who were being used."[12]

The *Post-Dispatch* found McGovern's son Steve at the Rapid City Airport; he said he thought it was "very likely" Eagleton would leave the ticket. "My father thinks it, too," he added. Mankiewicz, however, was now holding firm back east, insisting that discussion had halted among "decision-level staff"; Eagleton was here to stay, he had told the *New York Times* in a comment printed alongside word of McGovern's tablehopping.[13]

In the next morning's *Los Angeles Times,* Eagleton's fate was described in starker terms. "McGovern Wants Eagleton off Ticket," read the page-one headline. Reaction to Eagleton's disclosures, wrote Jules Witcover, "has been so negative that Senator George S. McGovern is convinced that Eagleton must withdraw from the Democratic ticket, the *Times* has learned." And everyone in the Black Hills knew why Witcover could pack his words with so much certainty; McGovern had probably been even more frank in his conversation with the reporter. Witcover reiterated McGovern's preference to let Eagleton decide his own fate, yet he described the presidential candidate as positive that his running mate would soon recognize his own liability to the ticket, a few days removed from his fantastical, maybe even delusional, reception in Hawaii. "If not," Witcover continued,

"McGovern is going to have to make the decision for him, and as of now, [the *Times*] has learned, that decision will be for Eagleton to go." With Eagleton campaigning in California, McGovern seems to have pointedly chosen Witcover as his messenger. In case Eagleton missed the other stories, he was sure to catch Witcover's in the *Los Angeles Times*.[14]

To McGovern's chagrin, Eagleton's history of mental illness had broken the last week of July, when—as *New York Times* media columnist Steven Roberts wrote—"the rest of the world's newsmakers seemed to have retreated to their porches with pitchers of martinis." Roberts explained that "when news is slow, [reporters] grab for what is available. From a single word, even the inflection of a voice, they can and do manufacture the major stories of the day." Yet after McGovern's tablehopping stratagem, the press appears to have accurately portrayed his intentions. As Greider of the *Washington Post* observed a few days later, "What McGovern did was either very slick or very clumsy. The people who watched still are not quite sure which." The *New York Times*'s James Naughton was more directly critical: "Senator George McGovern appears to have undone most of his effort over the past [eighteen] months to establish an image as an unusually candid presidential candidate." Three days after stressing 1,000 percent support for his running mate, Naughton wrote, McGovern had compromised his credibility when he "began orchestrating an attempt to persuade Mr. Eagleton to withdraw from the ticket." Knight's Bob Boyd called McGovern's strategy "devious," noting that he could have just picked up the phone and conveyed his feelings to Eagleton directly. His resistance to confrontation implied weakness. Was this how he would behave in the Oval Office, avoiding honest dialogue with allies and enemies because it was difficult? In convincing himself that Eagleton doomed him, McGovern sabotaged himself.[15]

McGovern called Hart late that evening to tell him about his tablehopping experiment, and Hart supplied his end of the information exchange with news that Eagleton had scheduled two television interviews for Sunday, one on *Face the Nation*. McGovern asked Hart

to suggest that Eagleton cancel them, and Hart immediately phoned
Bennet to convey that the campaign preferred Eagleton to limit his
television exposure that weekend. Bennet resisted, believing that
the appearances were vital to sustaining Eagleton's momentum. In
fact, Bennet could not believe Hart was even inquiring. "Whose instruction is that?" he asked Hart. "That's not part of the company
policy around here. We agreed that we'd take every advantage, every opportunity, to make [Eagleton] look good. Why shouldn't he
go on?" Bennet was responding so forcefully because—as he later
admitted—at that moment, he finally realized that the McGovern
campaign had made up its mind and changed its stance on Eagleton:
the McGovernites were protecting their man's best interest at the
expense of Eagleton's redemption. As Hart later explained, the campaigns "were beginning, at some points, to work at cross purposes."[16]

The Sunday Shows

T he next morning, Saturday, July 29, desperate to preserve his boss's national candidacy, Bennet telecopied his proposed
strategy from Washington to San Francisco, where Eagleton was
campaigning. "We have reached the crunch," Bennet declared. "Further speculation and uncertainty can only damage the credibility
of the ticket." He recommended that, in speaking with McGovern,
Eagleton acknowledge the backlash he had provoked, apologize,
then emphasize his belief in the transiency of the mental illness
controversy, predicting that his departure would, conversely, only
exacerbate the problem, alienating "the Aliotos of the world," whose
support was essential to McGovern's chances of victory. Bennet then
proposed that Eagleton affirm upon landing in Columbia, Missouri,
on his way east, "It will be McGovern-Eagleton in '72," imagining
that McGovern could arrive next, his presence irrefutably confirming the unity of the ticket. Bennet suggested releasing the medical
records later in the day, confident that McGovern's demonstration
of solidarity with Eagleton would crowd out from the news cycle
the publication of the medical documents. With his place on the
ticket now reconfirmed, Eagleton would use his Sunday-morning

Jack Anderson and Tom Eagleton exchange a few words after their *Face the Nation* taping on Sunday morning, July 30, 1972. (AP/Wide World Photos)

appearance on *Face the Nation* to refocus the campaign on the issues. But Bennet's advice did not interest Eagleton, and it probably would not have swayed McGovern; Eagleton already knew what he wanted to say.[1]

McGovern called Eagleton that morning in his San Francisco hotel room. The vice presidential candidate was chatting with his wife, Barbara, and aides Gene Godley, Mike Kelley, and the crew's advance man, Dale Ledbetter, when the phone rang. McGovern had tried to reach Eagleton before going tablehopping but had not connected with his running mate. After reiterating his support for Eagleton, McGovern told him that the events of the last few days and the "intense pressure" from his supporters had forced him to question the prudence of sticking with him. McGovern was giving Eagleton an out, but Eagleton refused to bite. McGovern said they should meet Monday on their return to Washington; he said they would reassess their predicament there. Then, McGovern read Eagleton the third paragraph from the bottom of his planned Aberdeen speech—the one where he asks for the people's prayers as he and Eagleton deliberated on the course ahead. "That's beautiful, George," Eagleton said. "I wish I had written it." Either the coded language eluded Eagleton, or he simply heard what he wanted to hear. Eagleton later described himself as a "blunt, sometimes abrasive soul who liked to hear it direct and to the point."[2]

But it is likely Eagleton did, in fact, understand what McGovern meant, as the news coverage of McGovern's tablehopping in the morning papers made it clear how the leading man felt. "When I read [the coverage], it became somewhat apparent to me that the 1,000 percent support had perhaps dropped a little," Eagleton later conceded. "But I thought I had a fighting chance and so I made my case."[3]

In private, Eagleton was furious. "Screw McGovern!" he yowled in his hotel room when he hung up. "I'm going to tell everyone he's a no-good son of a bitch."[4]

"Sit down and shut up!" Barbara snapped at her husband, arguing for restraint. "If you handle this right, you could be the senator of Missouri for the rest of your life. If you don't, you won't be able to make a living." Barbara Eagleton was as committed as anyone to seeing her husband's candidacy prevail, but she now offered the voice of reason and gave him the support, the guidance not to self-destruct.[5]

Eagleton measured his temperament but nonetheless chose to ignore McGovern's message. Before leaving California for Missouri, he told reporters, McGovern "did not mention to me any conversation he had with reporters last night." He repeated, "All [McGovern] said to me was he was for me 1,000 percent." While McGovern may not have described the tablehopping incident in full, he had conveyed its basic message; Eagleton should have acknowledged that McGovern could no longer back him 100 percent, let alone 1,000. Eagleton "sure can't take a hint!" a McGovern aide complained to the press.[6]

As McGovern attempted to let the Eagleton issue decompress and Eagleton and his staff clung to their "wave of popular support," the absolute lunacy of Anderson's allegations began to surface. On Friday, July 28, Anderson had made his "unimpeachable," "totally reliable" source available to the *New York Times,* and the resulting article ran in the paper that Saturday. The source had agreed to be interviewed under the condition that the *Times* identify him only as a "former high official from Missouri." In 1968, during Eagleton's run for the Senate, a man had approached this unnamed official "at a political rally somewhere," a place he could also no longer pinpoint. Nor could the source remember the man's name. "It was the only time I ever did see the guy," the source told the *Times*. The man "said that he was a state trooper and that he was off duty—he had on civilian clothes—and he said, 'There's some violations here in this envelope about Tom Eagleton [that] I think you would find to be very interesting.'" The source recalled discovering nine to eleven traffic citations stuffed into the envelope. "Speeding, and there was reckless, careless driving, and intoxication on several," said the source. The source had no proof because—for a reason he did not share—he had shredded the Photostats of the tickets. When asked whether the citations could have been forgeries, he replied, "There's always that possibility." Anderson then admitted to the *Times* that he, too, had been unable to authenticate the citations or confirm his source's recollections before publicizing them on national radio. "I wanted to score a scoop," he told the paper.[7]

In the *Washington Post* that morning, gossip columnist Maxine Cheshire also discredited Anderson. Like Anderson, Cheshire had a policy of not revealing her sources, so she admitted that she could not verify having spoken with the same individual as Anderson. Yet Anderson's and Cheshire's contacts bore uncanny similarities. Each reporter described the source as a former high official from Missouri and a Democrat, whose informant was in the Missouri State Highway Patrol in 1968. As Cheshire traced her source's allegations, documenting her reporting methods in her article, she discovered that the evidence backing her source's charges was flimsy at best. The only citation she found was one Eagleton had admitted to receiving, for driving twenty miles per hour over the speed limit on March 11, 1962. Cheshire contacted the officer who had apprehended Eagleton, Trooper James Laffoon. He confirmed that alcohol did not figure into the transgression. "Look, [Eagleton] didn't have to get [the ticket] reduced from drunk driving to speeding," Laffoon asserted. "He could have made it rough on me and gotten the whole thing covered up, if he had wanted to. He was the top law enforcement officer in the state." Laffoon said Eagleton acted like "a perfect gentleman" during the incident and paid his fine like any law-abiding citizen. Laffoon had never heard of another officer stopping Eagleton—neither for speeding nor for drunk driving. "The Anderson charges, in short, are a classic example of precisely the type of reporting practices that have brought the news business under increasing attack," Cheshire summarized. That Sunday, Anderson and Cheshire's source disclosed his identity on the CBS *Evening News*. He was William True Davis, one of Eagleton's opponents in the three-way Democratic primary in the 1968 race for the U.S. Senate; Davis was now chairman and president of the National Bank of Washington. He said he had tipped Anderson and Cheshire "without realizing it might be made public without verification." Around Washington, AP reporter Brooks Jackson recalled recently, Davis was known as "something of a sleazeball with that slick little villain's moustache of his."[8]

The Anderson episode had all started on the morning of Wednesday, July 26—the day after Eagleton's disclosures in South Dakota—when Brit Hume, one of Anderson's assistant reporters, had swung by his office upon arriving at work.

"It seems to me that this Eagleton press conference left some questions unanswered," Hume began. He said he had scoured the papers that morning and had an idea.

"Oh?" asked Anderson, curious.

"Well, in a separate interview with the Knight papers, [Eagleton] said something about still taking some 'little blue pills.' I wonder if they are barbiturates and, if so, what kind. That raises questions about when they were prescribed and if they were prescribed by a psychiatrist. . . . You can't tell how the press will react. They may decide to drop the subject. They might press it all the harder. But if they drop it, there might be an additional story there."

Anderson was intrigued. "Why don't you go after it?" he said.

Hume started digging. So did Anderson, who remembered that Eagleton's two opponents in the 1968 Democratic primaries had each consulted him on whether to exploit the rumors of alcoholism that surrounded the lieutenant governor. Senator Ed Long had even asked Anderson to undertake the investigation on his behalf. But Anderson declined in 1968, explaining that he sought dirt on a politician only if the alleged misdeed seemed to interfere with his ability to perform his job, echoing the philosophy of the *St. Louis Post-Dispatch* and other leading newspapers in Missouri at the time. The question was different now, as proof of the allegations would challenge Eagleton's credibility. Anderson reached Davis by midafternoon, seeking confirmation. Davis recalled seeing as many as eleven Photostats of Eagleton's traffic tickets, and he said that a prosecutor in one of the two counties directly north of Jefferson City might have the hard copies.

"God, it's a hell of a story," Hume affirmed when Anderson told him about True Davis's information. "Eagleton has denied over and over that he's ever had a drinking problem."

Anderson assured Hume that True Davis had "never misled [him] before," and, since he had some errands to run, asked Hume to reach the prosecutor in one of the counties north of Jefferson City whom Davis had suggested.[9]

Hume was never able to nail down evidence of drunk driving, and every source he spoke with—including the Calloway County prosecutor, Gene Hamilton—mentioned the 1962 speeding incident that Eagleton acknowledged. Hume did hear persistent speculation that Eagleton had a drinking problem and that charges could have been dismissed because of Eagleton's status as attorney general. But there was no proof. As Hume explained in retrospect, "plausibility and provability are not the same." Anderson remained undeterred. "When a guy like True Davis says he saw those Photostats, there's obviously something to it," he said. "Someone's going to get this story, so I'm inclined to move ahead with something [on my radio program] so we don't lose it," he continued. The year after winning the Pulitzer, it appears that Anderson was propelled by "the hot breath of other newsmen on [his] back." Anderson's original radio script on Eagleton, prepared for him by a copywriting assistant, included a report that newsmen were "streaming into St. Louis" to investigate "rumors" that Eagleton had been "stopped for drunken driving," but that nothing other than a speeding ticket had turned up thus far. Anderson crossed out this line and decided to announce instead that he had "located" evidence of Eagleton's drunk driving.[10]

Anderson's broadcast attracted a barrage of scrutiny, especially from his colleagues in the press, some of whom may have enjoyed the chance to rebuke a rival and recent winner of the Pulitzer Prize. But Anderson refused to back down. He disclosed to his staff—which was growing increasingly adamant that he apologize to Eagleton— that Davis was not his only source. Anderson shared that he had spoken with two Missouri state troopers who said the tickets had been expunged from the official records, but that the officers who arrested Eagleton had copies of the documentation. Anderson said that Senator Long, whom Eagleton had defeated in the 1968 Democratic primary, had also told him that someone on the Long campaign staff had received Photostats of the arrests. But while this information led Anderson to believe the allegations would be substantiated with time, it did not excuse his brazen pronouncement that he had "located" the records when in truth he had only heard about them.[11]

Indeed, the story of Eagleton's drunk driving probably stemmed from confusion between Tom and his brother, Mark, who was known around St. Louis as a prolific partier more than for his prowess as a radiologist. Mark had reportedly started accumulating gambling debts by the time he was twelve, and in his middle age, the older Eagleton brother ran in the same circle as legendarily "raucous," and "fun-loving" St. Louis Cardinals broadcasters Harry Caray and Jack Buck. But Mark still drove down to the Bootheel once a week for pro bono work taking X-rays for the region's indigent population, a route that could have taken him on the roads where the officers claimed to have stopped Eagleton. When Mark was asked by a friend whether Anderson could have mistaken his drunk driving citations for Tom's, Mark replied, "Name a date. Name a time." Within a few years, while still in his forties, Mark fell victim to a stroke that confined him to a nursing home for the rest of his short life.[12]

Looking back on Anderson's refusal to give in, Hume reflected on his boss's behavior: "It seemed that Jack had an upside-down reaction to his own success. Instead of feeling more secure, [Anderson] felt more compelled. And once he had slipped, it was more difficult than ever to accept the humiliation of admitting the error."[13]

Perhaps the foiling of Anderson's accusations and the ensuing sympathy for Eagleton undercut McGovern's resolve. Perhaps the editorials slamming the veteran journalist in the Saturday papers did it. Or maybe it was talking to Eagleton, hearing his voice and his perspective that Saturday morning. Whatever factors compelled McGovern to backtrack, the candidate revealed an inability to grasp the ramifications of his vacillation. "Rumors and reports of any decision having been reached on this question [the Eagleton decision] are misleading," McGovern told the press on Saturday, the day after his tablehopping. "Senator Eagleton and I had a lengthy conversation this morning and I assured him I'm still backing him as the vice presidential nominee of the party." McGovern said he planned to meet with Eagleton on Monday to evaluate the running mate's future on the ticket, but added that he considered change a possibility and not necessarily an inevitability.[14]

However, in word and deed, McGovern's colleagues and staff—and even McGovern himself—indicated otherwise. In comments to another reporter, the candidate said, "I'm with Eagleton all the way until he and I have a chance to talk," suggesting that the support could—and probably would—end Monday, at what Knight framed as an impending "showdown" between the two candidates. McGovern also underscored the importance of having a ticket that inspires "trust and confidence at a time when the country seems to have lost faith in its leaders and institutions," as the *Miami Herald* interpreted his remarks. These comments clearly undercut Eagleton, whose candor was under close examination by the American people, and whose stability was also in doubt. McGovern admitted that leading psychiatrists had not been able to assure him that Eagleton would be able to handle the inevitably intensifying pressures of the campaign and the office of the vice presidency. While McGovern had not yet spoken with Eagleton's doctors themselves, this disclosure did little in the way of generating confidence in Eagleton's fitness. One senator who was close to the South Dakotan seemed to speak for the rest of the campaign when he told the *New York Times*, "The general conclusion is that there is no way the ticket can recover from this." Meanwhile, the McGovern team canceled a large order of McGovern-Eagleton campaign buttons. DNC counsel Joseph Califano sketched a brief on the procedures for selecting a new vice presidential candidate, and the committee postponed a fund-raising mailing. It was not, finance chairman Henry Kimelman said, "the right psychological moment" to launch a fund-raising drive. The campaign lurched in uncertainty.[15]

In Washington, Hart said Senator McGovern's "position has been the same for the last several days: he's behind Eagleton 1,000 percent," reiterating McGovern's historic blunder of a line—stretching its relevance, extending its harm to the campaign, and contradicting his earlier impression. Then Hart hedged: "Any evaluation is based on how the outlook looks at the time," implying that the situation could change. "No rational human being—certainly no rational candidate for president—is going to foreclose anything absolutely. New information can intervene; discussions can intervene; public opinion can develop. A lot of things can happen," he said.[16]

Meanwhile, Hart kept pressing Bennet for Eagleton's medical records and even considered sending another McGovern aide, John Douglas, to St. Louis, or going there himself to examine Eagleton's records and interview his doctors. Bennet told Hart that one doctor had agreed to accommodate the visit if he received a call and written permission from Eagleton, but Bennet soon called back to inform Hart that the doctor had changed his mind. Bennet said Eagleton would call McGovern about the situation as soon as possible. "You mean Senator Eagleton wants Senator McGovern to tell him that he wants me to talk to the doctors?" Hart inquired defensively, reading the Eagleton team's hesitancy as evidence of doubt that McGovern had authorized such a trip, but also reluctance to have the campaign review the records. Whether or not it was ever sent, a memo Bennet composed on Saturday afternoon and telegraphed to California for Eagleton to review on the plane to Missouri confirms these suspicions. "It is clear that time is not on our side," Bennet wrote. "It will reduce rather than increase our options."[17]

With each passing day, the McGovern staff came closer to securing Eagleton's records, and though he did not say as much, Bennet's concern suggests that he believed that the records, once obtained, would guarantee Eagleton's removal. As reported in the *St. Louis Post-Dispatch* the next day, Dr. Frank Shobe, Eagleton's doctor at St. Louis's Barnes Hospital, met with two of Eagleton's associates—probably James Murphy and Al Stephan, both lawyers—on Saturday afternoon. They came bearing a letter from Senator Eagleton granting the doctor permission to discuss his treatment with them, and only with them. According to the newspaper account, Dr. Shobe refused, saying that medical ethics require Eagleton be present at such a review. But perhaps that was only what Dr. Shobe told the press. Maybe he had, in fact, shown the Eagleton lawyers the records, which increased their fear of examination by McGovern's aides.[18]

By then—or by Monday at the latest—Mankiewicz received a letter from Dr. John Arnold Lindon of Los Angeles, dated July 27, speculating on the records and their language. "Chances are with a history of three hospitalizations and two courses shock treatment that the diagnosis, or probable diagnosis, on the hospital records of Senator Eagleton would state 'manic-depressive psychosis,'" Dr. Lindon wrote. It was not a soothing term. "Hospital records," he continued, "unfortunately, though supposedly confidential, are *notoriously* easy to get to, and I am certain that they have already been photocopied or filmed by many, many enthusiastic Nixon supporters among the doctors or the other staff at the hospital." Dr. Lindon said that a decision to keep Eagleton on the ticket would be indicative of "some wild masochistic impulse" on the part of the McGovern campaign. Though, like Lindon, Mike Kelley had never seen the records themselves and did not know whether others in the campaign had obtained or reviewed them, he explained the campaign's caginess in a recent interview. Medical records are generally "not all pure, clean diagnoses and rational statements," Kelley observed; often they contain inaccurate preliminary nurses' notes and doctors' incomplete thoughts, especially at university-affiliated research hospitals. Terminology can also vary from hospital to hospital, he explained. In essence, what was "manic-depressive psychosis" at one institution could have been considered mild to moderate depression at another.[19]

Thus, no matter what the Eagleton campaign knew, in his memo Bennet advocated a "preemptive strike." He thought that Eagleton should accept McGovern's invitation to determine his own fate and reiterate to the nation "the ticket will be McGovern-Eagleton in 1972," ending all speculation. This strategy was similar to what he had recommended that morning. It would reinforce the notion that Eagleton was not waiting to decide whether to remain in the race—that determination had already been made—and Bennet envisioned this plan as a way to "checkmate" the McGovern staff, which seemed increasingly eager to drop Eagleton. If, however, Eagleton thought that he should withdraw, Bennet advised him to blame his departure on the "irreconcilable" tensions with the McGovern camp. As Bennet outlined the situation, Eagleton had survived the medical issue, had weathered the Anderson accusations, and had converted uncommitted voters such as Alioto into McGovern-Eagleton supporters. A *Time* magazine poll indicated that only 5.2 percent of voters would switch their vote to Nixon because of Eagleton's presence on the ticket. Eagleton's team portrayed the poll, along with a concurrent survey in *Newsweek,* as proof that the Missourian's former mental illness scared few, while the McGovern staff pointed to the results as evidence that Eagleton hurt the ticket—losing 5.2 percent or more of voters in a close race might wreck McGovern's chances. Yet Bennet's tone substantiates the complaints McGovern staffers leveled at the Eagleton organization in general: the running mate's staff appeared to place Eagleton's interests above McGovern's. Language such as "preemptive strike" and "checkmate" implies that Bennet viewed Eagleton in competition—if not at war—with McGovern and his staff.[20]

That evening, as McGovern was in Aberdeen asking South Dakota Democrats for their prayers, Eagleton was back in Missouri—unaccompanied by McGovern as Bennet had hoped, but revved up all the same. On the plane, Eagleton scribbled out his "Airport Speech to Roaring Middle America at Columbia Airport," writing, "I will not let the *New York Times* and the *Washington Post* knock me off this ticket!!!" He pointed his animus toward the media instead of McGovern. Then, Eagleton doodled the word "ROAR" in large caps, pumping himself up for his performance upon arrival.[21]

Eagleton was right to anticipate a crowd: anywhere from five hundred to fourteen hundred people (depending on the estimate) met his plane at the Columbia County airport, waving placards bearing slogans like "We Love Eagleton" and "Tom Eagleton and George Who?" While gratifying, the signs underscored the Thomas Eagleton–versus–George McGovern mentality; the two men were increasingly seen as rivals more than teammates. "As I went through the crowd, someone said, 'Don't quit, Tom,'" Eagleton told his supporters when he arrived at the platform. "Well, I've got a little Webster's dictionary on the plane and just drew a line through the word 'quit.'" The crowd did roar in support of its home-state hero.[22]

After a day spent crisscrossing South Dakota by chartered plane— from Sylvan Lake, to his hometown of Mitchell, to Aberdeen—McGovern unveiled new campaign rhetoric alongside his plea for the audience's prayers "before the stars come out."

"I seek for America a new horizon, where the goals of the people and the acts of the government meet one another," he said.

"A new horizon of peace and opportunity on which the barriers to achievement have been felled and no American need live in the shadow of joblessness and poverty.

"A new horizon where the air is clear, not only of smoke and fumes, but of suspicion and fear and deception. Where the clouds of war have passed and the sun will rise each day on a people at peace whose sons have come home from war."[23]

The crowd of thirteen hundred attending Governor Warren Hearnes's annual birthday bash and Democratic fund-raiser at the Ramada Inn in Jefferson City that evening greeted Eagleton with a three-minute standing ovation. "It's hot in here tonight," said the vice presidential nominee, "and Eagleton perspires even on Christmas Eve. But I'll tell you one thing," he continued, riffing off of another famous Truman line. "I can take the heat and I am going to stay in the kitchen." But as Eagleton's enthusiasm waxed, McGovern's confidence waned. "Does [Eagleton's previous psychiatric treatment] in any way impair his capacity of leadership?" the presidential candidate asked reporters on his chartered jet back to Washington. "Does it arouse anxiety in a public that already is nervous and uptight about its national leadership? Does it damage our chances of winning the election? These are all things I frankly cannot answer." McGovern now admitted that he wished he had known about Eagleton's history of mental illness before he had selected the Missourian. "I really don't know at this point whether he's a plus or minus," McGovern said wistfully.[24]

Then the candidate wandered over to Jules Witcover and took a seat beside him. "I guess Tom didn't get the message, did he?" McGovern said, with a look of despondency drooping down his face, alluding to the quotations he had planted with the *Los Angeles Times* reporter during their one-one-one the previous evening.

"No, he didn't," Witcover agreed.[25]

Eagleton arrived in Washington at 2:30 A.M. that night, with *Face the Nation* scheduled for the following morning. The senator had been lying in bed for three hours unable to sleep when he reached for the phone at 7 A.M. to dial Bennet and Kelley. Bennet urged Eagleton to call aide Jim Murphy as well, citing additional conversations that Murphy had supposedly had about the medical records, but not indicating with whom. Murphy rebuffed repeated requests for comment for this book. As Eagleton's lawyer, he cited attorney-client privilege as his reason for not wanting to talk.[26]

When the staffers arrived at Eagleton's Washington house, they found their boss shaking. In the small hours, Eagleton had finally confronted the full newspaper and editorial coverage of the previous week, and he had begun to panic. Barbara was similarly deflated. Furthermore, *Face the Nation*'s producers had replaced Jim Naughton of the *New York Times* on the roundtable's panel with Jack Anderson, heightening the show's importance for Eagleton and contributing to his worry. Though the producers promised Eagleton's team that Anderson would not launch new charges, Murphy, who probably had the most information about the records and had been in Washington for most of the previous week and thus bombarded by the anti-Eagleton media coverage, believed that the senator should cancel his appearance. Kelley, who had traveled alongside the vice presidential candidate and grown energized by his popular support, remained adamant that Eagleton should take the opportunity to present his case, though he was justifiably peeved by *Face the Nation*'s last-minute panel change. Eagleton interrupted their scuffling. "Come on. I'm in trouble. I need help," he said.[27]

Bennet and other staffers had prepared a detailed briefing that sketched answers to questions Eagleton was likely to receive that morning. If the panelists asked him for his reaction to the editorial opposition in the press, Bennet recommended Eagleton remind them that 85 percent of editorials were against FDR, 65 percent against Truman, and 80 percent against JFK, advising him to add in conclusion, "I don't know what the Eagleton count is, but I'm really more interested in how I stand with the voters." Still trembling, Eagleton got dressed, and headed to the studio.[28]

On *Face the Nation*, which was to air from 11:30 A.M. to 12 P.M. Eastern Standard Time, Senator Eagleton met the public's most pressing questions. He wore a dark tie over a crisp white shirt and spoke with a steady voice and measured delivery.[29]

Did Eagleton plan to stay on the ticket? "I intend to stay on. I think I'll be an asset to the ticket," he affirmed.

Did he expect that his meeting with McGovern scheduled for Monday evening would confirm that he would remain on the ticket? "Well, I'll not try to crystal ball what will be the ultimate outcome," Eagleton replied. "Your question was did I intend to stay on the ticket. The answer to that is yes, and I said it because I think I'd be an asset to the ticket." He proceeded to describe the "warm, cordial, supportive" receptions that greeted him throughout his swing out West. "I don't live in a house of self-delusion," he explained. "I'm a pretty pragmatic politician and I can pretty well tell the response of people."

How could Eagleton justify staying on the ticket, given the press reports suggesting that McGovern expected his running mate would voluntarily withdraw? "The only thing I can testify to that's direct are my conversations with Senator McGovern himself," Eagleton explained. "On each of those occasions [the last being the previous morning], he has indicated that he is standing with me, standing by me—whatever the phraseology might be—supporting me, and urging me to continue as the vice presidential candidate. I take his word at face value." Nonetheless, Eagleton said he would not stand "pig-headed" in discussing the situation with McGovern and expressed the hope that their meeting on Monday night would prove "a free exchange of ideas" that would produce a "joint decision." "This is a partnership," he reminded viewers.

Then Anderson spoke. "I've always told my reporters, senator, that a fact doesn't become a fact for our column until we can prove it. Now I violated my own rule, and I want the nation and you to know that I violated it," Anderson confessed before recounting his shoddy journalism. "I went ahead with a story that I should not have gone ahead with, and that was unfair to you, and you have my apology."

"Well, let me say, Mr. Anderson, that the true test of moral character is, I guess, to admit when one makes a mistake," Eagleton replied. "I'm not going to sit in moral judgment on you, and you, in turn, I guess, won't sit in moral judgment on me. But it takes quite a man to get on a nationwide television network to say he made a mistake, and I commend you for your courage." Intentional or not, he seemed to be referring to himself as much as Anderson. Just five days earlier, Eagleton had appeared on national television to admit that he had not warned McGovern about his history of mental illness before accepting the nomination.

Then, as he had done at the press conference that Tuesday and again throughout the week, Eagleton emphasized the speciousness of the rumors that implicated him as an alcoholic. "I can tell you, with all the candor that I can summon, and on any number of Bibles that we could put on this table, I've never been arrested for drunken driving, charged with it, issued a summons for it, in any way, shape or form," he maintained.

If Eagleton stumbled, it was when George Herman, a panelist from CBS News, hinted at the tranquilizer that Eagleton had
mentioned earlier in the week. Could Eagleton provide specifics?
"No, I—I'm not ducking you," Eagleton began, giving the opposite
message. "I said it was a blue pill, but I haven't—I didn't look at the
pill or anything to see the name—I don't remember the name." As
Eagleton fumbled his response to questions about this still-elusive
detail, Anderson segued into defending his resistance to retract his
story. "I cannot in good conscience do that," Anderson said.

"I don't quite get the apology and then the no-retraction business," Eagleton said, baffled. Maintaining his composure, Eagleton
pushed the point and sent Anderson on the defensive as the columnist struggled to justify his refusal to retract the story, his hands
fidgeting and his face quivering. Suddenly, the stocky man looked
weak next to a calm, gracious, and relatively fit Eagleton. "I think the
story has been so thoroughly discredited," Eagleton concluded, "that
. . . it leaves me in a puzzlement as to why you can't retract a story
you shouldn't have promulgated in the first place. . . . That doesn't
seem to be quite equitable to me." Eagleton the lawyer, Eagleton the
"nail-them-to-the-wall-style" Senate debater, channeled reason as he
stifled Anderson. The reporter appeared vindictive, even malicious,
in his refusal to back off.[30]

As his half-hour cross-examination came to a close, Eagleton
defended his response to Mankiewicz's fateful question about skeletons in his closet. "I'm not trying to make a case as a Philadelphia
lawyer or as a nitpicking semanticist," Eagleton told the nation,
adapting the rhetoric he had delivered to various news outlets over
the preceding week. "What's a skeleton to Eagleton? A skeleton is
something that's dirty, filthy, corrupt, illegal, sinister. There's nothing
about having been fatigued and exhausted and being in a state of
mild depression that I find sinister, dirty, or ugly," he said. Even more,
he turned his experience into a positive. "At least I had the courage
to seek out medical treatment, the best that was available, and try
to do better." If someone from the McGovern team had asked him
about his medical past in advance, he said he would have disclosed
his full case history.

As Eagleton soared, George Herman, one of the CBS moderators, asked a question that seemed designed to bring him down. "Senator," the reporter said matter-of-factly, "this is a television program, and everybody watching you can see that you're perspiring considerably and that your hands have a slight shake to them." By all accounts, Herman's assessment was an exaggeration, but it channeled oft-repeated critiques of the running mate, as the press had appropriated Eagleton's sweat as evidence of his ongoing instability. It irked Mike Kelley, for instance, that every time Eagleton wiped his brow at a press conference, the cameramen would furiously start clicking away.

"Right," Eagleton interjected as Herman spoke on *Face the Nation*.

" . . . like many guests whom we've had on this program under the spotlight," Herman finished his sentence. "Now I'd like your comment, because people in this context are going to look at your perspiration and your slight tremor and they're going to say what . . ."

"Well," Eagleton jumped in. "The lights in the studio are less than cool, and they—you know, they focus in on the guy getting the third degree with the lights," he explained in his defense. "But I feel very comfortable and very relaxed," Eagleton continued. "In fact, I'd like to go on for another half-hour if we could."

Then came the moment when Eagleton transcended the McGovern campaign. Barry Serafin, the other CBS News panelist, asked the senator whether his performance that morning, and over the previous week, demonstrated an ability to defuse stress.

"These last five days," Eagleton began, "have been about as much stress as one could be under, one being a politician. But I've weathered this week very well, and I think it's been a successful week for Tom Eagleton in any event, because he's his own man." With those three words—his own man—Eagleton separated himself from McGovern and the presidential campaign. In his attempt to salvage his political career, Eagleton showcased his tenacity, earning the respect and admiration of legions of citizens previously unacquainted with the junior senator from Missouri. Whether or not he could stay the course, Eagleton would emerge from the week a winner.[31]

The reaction to *Face the Nation* seemed to suggest that Eagleton and his staff had a better sense of the country's mood than the Mc-Govern team. The CBS News bureau in New York City received 368 calls regarding Sunday's show. All were complimentary toward Eagleton. The Los Angeles affiliate received 354 calls. All but one viewer appreciated Eagleton's performance. And of the more than 500 calls to CBS's DC bureau, nearly all were favorable toward the senator from Missouri. Callers jammed the switchboard at the Western Union headquarters in Washington. "I can't remember anything quite like it," said operations manager John Woodward. Company policy forbade Woodward from revealing the substance of the telegraph messages, but he did share, "You can rest assured that when something like this happens it's the people who want to help, who are supportive, that call and come in. It's the ones who have been touched." Most of the telegrams were addressed to McGovern, with others going to Eagleton and the Democratic National Committee.[32]

According to Eagleton's office, by early afternoon it had received five hundred telephone calls, only twenty-seven of them critical. One telegram read:

> Please disregard my previous telegram urging you to with-draw. Your performance on *Face the Nation* has satisfied me of your stability, integrity, and resoluteness under fire. While you owed it to Senator McGovern to reveal your previous health problems, you have admitted your error in judgment, just as I now admit mine. I am now convinced that on balance . . . you will be an asset rather than a detri-ment to the ticket.[33]

As Eagleton drove home from the CBS studio, justifiably proud of his performance, he heard on the radio that Jean Westwood and Basil Paterson, the newly anointed chairpersons of the Democratic National Committee, had appeared on NBC's *Meet the Press*. "It would be the noble thing for Tom Eagleton to do to step down," Westwood said. Paterson agreed. Westwood believed Eagleton's withdrawal would allow the campaign "to change the focus . . . from personality to issues." "Let us go on about our business," she protested, adding that she had conferred with McGovern before voicing her opinion—her *personal* opinion, as she stated, not necessarily McGovern's—on the program. Yet she seemed to speak with McGovern's tacit, if not explicit, approval. Had McGovern opposed Westwood's views when she spoke with him just eight minutes before she went on the air, he could have requested that she keep quiet; after all, he was the party's national candidate, the man who had nominated Westwood chairwoman. Later, McGovern disputed charges that he had sanctioned her remarks, but others like Dougherty subsequently reported that Westwood spoke "on [McGovern's] instructions."

Bennet was particularly irritated by Westwood's comments because, at a briefing session the previous afternoon, she had assured him that she would not address the situation at all, which did not please Bennet either. He wanted Westwood to make a strong statement on Eagleton's behalf. But saying nothing was certainly better than what she ended up telling the nation. Either way, Westwood's comments managed to further estrange Eagleton from the ticket, and the optics were disastrous: as Eagleton persevered on CBS, the Democratic leaders smothered his hopes on NBC. To borrow Bennet's assessment, Westwood, Paterson, and—by extension—the McGovernites, had exposed themselves as "pious liars, bubbling amateurs, [and] callous limousine liberals" in their determination that Eagleton must withdraw.[34]

The Precedent

T wenty years earlier, another ticket had loomed on the brink of destruction. Republican presidential candidate General Dwight David Eisenhower confronted widespread doubts about his running mate and nearly heeded calls for his nominee's removal. In an irony that escaped few in 1972—certainly not McGovern and Eagleton, and definitely not the press—it was Richard Nixon whose fate lay in jeopardy that fall of 1952. The thirty-nine-year-old junior senator from California was, like Eagleton, a dark horse when Eisenhower picked him to join a campaign similarly predicated on integrity and candor.

At a campaign stop in Iowa, on Thursday, September 18, 1952, Eisenhower railed against the "crooks and cronies" undermining Washington, vowing that with his election, "the experts in shady and shoddy government operations [would] be on their way back to the shadowy haunts and subcellars of American politics." Corruption was also on Nixon's mind; speaking at a rally the previous evening, he had announced that the incumbent Democratic "administration is going to go down in history as a scandal-a-day administration because [every day] you read about another bribe, you read about another tax fix, you read about another gangster getting favors from the government." But, just hours after Eisenhower spoke that Thursday, the afternoon *New York Post* ran the headline, "Secret Nixon Fund: Secret Rich Men's Trust Fund Keeps Nixon in Style Far beyond His Salary." The article was actually typical tabloid fare. Nixon used the $18,000 fund to cover travel and campaign expenses he could not afford out of pocket, and it was neither secret, nor illegal, nor unique to the vice presidential candidate. However, even the faintest whiff of corruption meant trouble, provoking cries for the running mate's removal. For nearly four days, it seemed likely that Nixon would leave the ticket, especially after the editorial pages of conservative newspapers, such as Eisenhower's favorite *New York Herald Tribune*, began advocating for his withdrawal. At every stop on his West Coast campaign swing, the press badgered Nixon for more details, and Nixon fully obliged. Meanwhile, Eisenhower refused to comment on his running mate's status as the one-fund controversy quickly turned into a three-ring circus.[1]

Before the candidates had set off on their separate campaign expeditions, Eisenhower's and Nixon's top aides had outlined a system of frequent and direct, level-to-level coordination between the counterparts in each of their staffs. However, as controversy erupted over Nixon's secret fund, Eisenhower resisted phoning his running mate, foreshadowing McGovern's behavior twenty years later.[2]

And like Eagleton, Nixon attacked his critics head-on, but with even more forthrightness as he left no allegation unanswered. Nixon artfully deflected the charge that he had misused the funds for his own enrichment, explaining that, to the contrary, the extra money enabled him to keep his constituents informed about his important initiatives, like the fight against communism, without eating into his taxpayer-allotted money. He also sanctimoniously stressed that while the wife of Democratic presidential candidate Adlai Stevenson collected a government salary, his own wife, Pat, remained off staff payrolls despite her tireless work on behalf of his office. He similarly noted that his conscience prevented him from collecting legal fees to supplement his federal income, though several of his peers did just that.[3]

As pressure mounted on Eisenhower to drop his running mate, he met with reporters on his eighteen-car campaign train for a not-for-attribution bull session. The event was a sort of precursor to McGovern's tablehopping. "Of what avail is it for us to carry on this crusade against this business of what has been going on in Washington," asked Eisenhower, "if we ourselves aren't as clean as a hound's tooth?" The comment seeped its way into the newspapers as coming from the "highest authorities." Meanwhile, on the other hand, Eisenhower's team enlisted the Los Angeles–based law firm of Gibson, Dunn and Crutcher and the Price Waterhouse accounting firm to verify the legality of Nixon's activities. By Monday afternoon, these investigators would clear the vice presidential candidate.[4]

As with McGovern and Eagleton, part of Eisenhower's reluctance to contact Nixon could be attributed to his lack of familiarity with the senator before selecting him. But reticence is a flimsy excuse, especially coming from men who might conceivably reside in the White House. Finally, at 10:05 P.M. on Sunday, Eisenhower phoned Nixon from his stop in St. Louis. The running mates traded pleasantries about their campaign progress before Nixon announced, "I'm at your disposal. . . . I want you to know if you reach a conclusion either now or at any time later that I should get off the ticket, you can be sure that I will immediately respect your judgment and do so."[5]

Eisenhower, in turn, left the decision to Nixon, who decided to take his case to the American people. Republican groups doled out $75,000 to purchase national television and radio airtime, scheduling Nixon's address for Tuesday, September 23, following the popular *Milton Berle Show*. That day, before the broadcast, three of every four telegrams Eisenhower had received urged Nixon's withdrawal. Moments before showtime, Governor Thomas Dewey of New York, a confidant of both men on the ticket, finally reached the running mate by phone. He said he had polled the campaign and party sentiment and determined that Nixon should bow out. In substance and implication, Dewey's remark was not unlike the comments of Democratic chairpersons Jean Westwood and Basil Paterson on *Meet the Press* in 1972, as Dewey's advice to Nixon appeared to come from above. After speaking with Dewey, Nixon "looked like someone had smashed him," said Representative Patrick J. Hillings of California, a friend of the running mate.[6]

But Nixon rallied and proceeded with the broadcast as planned, recounting his modest upbringing and meditating on the value of hard work. Nixon told of the pay-your-own-way, up-by-the-bootstraps ethos that had been the foundation of his rise to national prominence.[7]

After outlining the charges against him, Nixon succinctly refuted them. "I say that it was morally wrong if any of that $18,000 went to Senator Nixon for my personal use," Nixon explained, speaking in the third person—a style Tom Eagleton was sometimes to adopt. Nixon continued, "I say that it was morally wrong if [the fund money] was secretly given and secretly handled. And I say that it was morally wrong if any of the contributors got special favors for the contributions that they made."

He went on: "Not one cent of the $18,000 or any other money of that type ever went to me for my personal use. Every penny of it was used to pay for political expenses that I did not think should be charged to taxpayers of the United States."

Later in the speech, Nixon did concede to accepting one personal gift of questionable value to his job. Before leaving on his campaign swing out west, he received notice from Baltimore's Union Station that a package awaited him. "It was a little cocker spaniel dog in a crate that [a man] sent all the way from Texas. Black-and-white spotted," Nixon told the nation. The donor had heard that Nixon's daughters longed for a puppy. Nixon continued, "And our little girl—Tricia, the six-year-old—named it Checkers. And you know the kids love that dog, and I want to say this right now, that regardless of what they say about it, we're going to keep it."[8]

The performance wowed Eisenhower and the public alike. The presidential candidate celebrated Nixon's courage as unparalleled, and—coming from an army general—this meant a lot. "I am not ducking any responsibility," Eisenhower had previously said. "I am not going to be swayed by my idea of what will get the votes. . . . I am going to say: Do I myself believe this man is the kind of man

America would like to have for its vice president?" Though he initially withheld judgment, Eisenhower went with his instinct, and
his verdict was now clear: Nixon was here to stay. "We like Dick!"
roared the crowd at the Eisenhower rally in Cleveland, where they
watched the running mate's broadcast. Nixon's so-called Checkers
Speech prompted a swift reversal of fortune for the vice presidential
candidate. Viewers jammed phone lines and telegraph switchboards
nationwide. Of the two million telegrams that the campaign received
following Nixon's broadcast, 99.6 percent were positive. Nixon had
rehabilitated himself and won the support of Eisenhower and his
country alike.[9]

Nixon finally joined Eisenhower the next evening, in Wheeling,
West Virginia, where the presidential candidate's campaign train
had stopped, and Eisenhower was there to greet him at the airport.
"You're my boy," Eisenhower beamed.[10]

The Decision

At McGovern's request, Eagleton spent Sunday afternoon, July 30, 1972, trying to track down Dr. Frank Shobe of Barnes Hospital. The running mate's staff had gathered at his Chevy Chase house, with television trucks and news crews swarming the neighborhood. Though the Eagleton aides had been thrilled with his *Face the Nation* appearance, *Meet the Press* had forced them to confront reality and prepare for Eagleton's resignation. "The question was [now] not whether to get out, but how," Bennet recalled. Eagleton's departure had become a "fait accompli."[1]

Ted Van Dyk, the McGovern insider friendliest with Bennet from their days together on Humphrey's staff and similarly most sympathetic toward Eagleton, called to emphasize the inevitability of Eagleton's withdrawal. He suggested that the two candidates meet before their highly anticipated "showdown" the following evening. "Otherwise, the time between now and Monday night will be the most miserable in your lives and ours," Van Dyk said.[2]

By 4 P.M., Eagleton had not reached Shobe, who he later discovered had been away for the day. He called McGovern to explain his inability to produce the records. The McGovern team interpreted

Eagleton and McGovern cross paths and trade glances in the Senate Caucus Room, where they held their final press conference as running mates, Monday evening, July 31. (AP/Wide World Photos)

Eagleton's difficulty as self-made. However, Bennet's wife, Suzie, wondered whether Shobe was intentionally avoiding Eagleton's calls because he had "grossly overtreated" Eagleton's case and was now trying to cover up his misapplication of electroshock. This explanation affords Eagleton more benefit of the doubt than the McGovernites would concede.[3]

It was day seventeen of Eagleton's candidacy. "Tom, maybe we could meet somewhere tonight," McGovern proposed when the running mates spoke on the phone. Eagleton agreed.[4]

While Eagleton's staffers had pragmatically resigned themselves to their boss's withdrawal, some still held hope. Mike Kelley told Bennet that he wondered whether Murphy, who had visited Shobe and probably viewed at least some of Eagleton's records, was being overpessimistic about Eagleton's prospects. Bennet thought this was a possibility; Murphy had previously indicated that, as a longtime friend, he was more concerned with Eagleton's "well-being as a man" than with his political career. For a second opinion on the records, Bennet called Al Stephan, one of the Eagleton associates and lawyers who had accompanied Murphy to Barnes Hospital. But Stephan reinforced the sense of Eagleton's peril. Stephan said that while Eagleton had accurately described his symptoms and treatment, he suspected the doctors' medical language would frighten the public. Though he originally supported Eagleton's continuation on the ticket, Stephan said he had since "reversed his position 180 degrees."[5]

Meanwhile, at McGovern's Japanese-style house in northwest DC, the McGovern team also deliberated, assessing how Eagleton had affected, and would continue to affect, the campaign. Henry Kimelman, the finance chairman, reiterated that the fiasco had forced him to delay a fund-raising mailing. Westwood verified that every state delegation but Missouri's would confirm any replacement McGovern picked. Hart remained focused on the medical records. "The only way [Eagleton] could stay on is if you see those records and convince yourself," he warned McGovern. "Otherwise, the burden is on him and you have no choice." Mankiewicz feared the Eagleton issue would dominate the campaign through the fall. Furthermore, he was convinced that CREEP had access to the medical records. "I couldn't believe . . . that a campaign in which [Nixon aides] Murray Chotiner and Bob Haldeman had anything to do with wouldn't use every trick they could," he later recalled. Furthermore, he found it suspicious that Eagleton's team had failed to produce the records since he first requested them ten days earlier. What was Eagleton hiding?[6]

By 9:30 P.M. the television crews had finally left Eagleton's driveway, and at 9:45 Eleanor McGovern called Eagleton to report that her husband had escaped the press encamped in front of their place. At that point, Eagleton, Bennet, Kelley, and their Secret Service escorts headed to Kimelman's mansion for the running mates' clandestine encounter. The Eagleton party arrived first, after a fifteen-minute drive, condemning the men to "anxious, but pleasant" small talk with their host in his library as they awaited McGovern. The South Dakotan had stopped on his way over at the house of Senate Majority Leader Mike Mansfield, who had said in a phone call to Eagleton and on a national television appearance earlier that week that he believed Eagleton should continue on the ticket. Now McGovern wanted Mansfield's private take on Eagleton. Mansfield said he respected the junior senator both personally and professionally, and that the disclosures had not changed a thing. He still felt that way. Then McGovern asked Mansfield whether he would be interested in assuming the vice presidential spot if Eagleton withdrew. Mansfield declined, preferring his work in the Senate.[7]

About a half-hour later, McGovern showed up at Kimelman's with Mankiewicz and Hart. The staffers left the two candidates in the library, heading upstairs to mix scotch and sodas and watch the eleven o'clock local news. McGovern and Eagleton were now alone for the first time since they had shared the Senate steam bath for forty-five minutes in the spring of 1969.

McGovern complimented Eagleton on his performance on *Face the Nation*. Eagleton responded by sarcastically congratulating McGovern on Jean Westwood's "hatchet job" on *Meet the Press*.

"Tom, believe me, I had no idea what she was going to say," McGovern said.[8]

"Don't shit me George," Eagleton replied.

McGovern smirked.

Then he asked Eagleton for his perspective on the campaign and for his thoughts about his viability on the ticket. In their first face-to-face meeting since cabin 22 six days earlier, the running mates talked for an hour and a half. Eagleton described his perception of growing popular support and his conversion of establishment politicians to the McGovern cause. The Old Guard, after all, was the constituency the campaign needed most. McGovern, in turn, cited the newspaper editorials adamant that Eagleton resign and recounted conversations with colleagues in the Senate and elsewhere. For example, McGovern told Eagleton that Senator Walter Mondale of Minnesota, a friend of both men and an early proponent of Eagleton's selection, had called McGovern every day since the disclosure to press for Eagleton's withdrawal. Mondale believed that Eagleton hurt the presidential ticket and—more important, it seemed—Eagleton threatened Mondale's own chances at reelection to the Senate by dragging down the Democratic slate. "Tom," McGovern said, "I know you have gone through hell for this week, but so have I." Eagleton said he understood.

As their discussion of their various options waned, Eagleton concluded, "George, you probably won't win with me, but you can't win without me." McGovern agreed to sleep on it.[9]

On the car ride home, as we have seen, Eagleton recapped the conversation between the two candidates for his staffers. McGovern is "in a struggle between his heart and his staff," he assessed.

"Chief," Bennet said. "If that is the contest, you lose."[10]

Still, Eagleton held onto that glimmer of a chance that he could somehow make his way as a running mate. Ever realistic, Barbara Eagleton warned otherwise.[11]

If his running mate's plea prompted McGovern to doubt his intention to drop Eagleton from the ticket, a letter McGovern received the following morning, July 31, seems to have preempted any reconsideration. In his memoir, McGovern reprinted nearly in full the letter sent to him by Arthur Schlesinger Jr., which suggests that Schlesinger's advice weighed heavily on the candidate that day. Schlesinger, a close friend of McGovern's, had been a special assistant to President Kennedy and was a preeminent historian of the American presidency.

Schlesinger called Eagleton's behavior "inexcusable" and wrote to McGovern, Eagleton's "betrayal of you and his party is the essential issue, not his psychiatric history." As a historian, Schlesinger buttressed his argument with support from the past, though he keenly avoided Kennedy's hidden struggle with his own debilitating and distracting medical conditions such as Addison's disease. "I have the fear," he wrote, "that [Eagleton] has reread [Nixon's book] *Six Crises* and is determined in the manner of Nixon in 1952 to make it impossible for you to divest yourself of him," referring to the president's account of the Checkers Speech. "If this is so," Schlesinger continued, "it certainly relieves you of any personal obligation toward him." Schlesinger also compared McGovern's predicament to that of President Kennedy during the Bay of Pigs crisis. "I well recall the pressure JFK was under to justify a bad decision by escalating his commitment," Schlesinger wrote. "He declined to do so. Instead, he cut his losses; and obviously this was the right thing to do." From one historian to another, Schlesinger advised McGovern to heed this lesson: McGovern should admit he had erred and fix his mistake, not further entangle himself with Tom Eagleton. "Better a surgical excision than a running sore," Schlesinger warned. Schlesinger also noted a few others who felt that McGovern should act, including John Kenneth Galbraith and Dick Wade, the CUNY professor and New York campaign organizer who had run into Eagleton at the Convention Hall in Miami Beach nearly three weeks earlier and vouched for the Missourian's spot on the ticket.[12]

A few days later, Schlesinger reflected on Eagleton in his personal journal. He wrote that the running mate's behavior in the days following the revelations of electroshock therapy repulsed him. He found his television appearances "appalling: voluble, compulsive, filled with self-regard and generally oblivious to the issues of the campaign." In his journal, the historian also recorded his impression of Eagleton as "a man on the manic phase of a manic-depressive cycle. He could not stop talking about himself—and he incessantly referred to himself in the third person: 'Eagleton' believes this or that." Eagleton's self-righteousness perturbed Schlesinger, as it had other McGovern loyalists.[13]

A memo from McGovern aide Ken Schlossberg distilled for the candidate that the only thing that "really mattered" was the perception of his comport in managing the crisis, and it was not looking good. Schlossberg identified the Jack Anderson fiasco as the game changer and explained that Eagleton's exposure of McGovern's mixed messages in its aftermath compounded the damage. "The press is now playing this story as a struggle between you and Eagleton," Schlossberg observed. "It is absolutely the worst kind of political press for you to be getting." Schlossberg saw the situation as the public probably interpreted it, providing McGovern a perspective he seemed to lack. "The longer you fail to confront [Eagleton] directly," Schlossberg wrote, "the more you will appear to be engaged in a 'back-door political stab in the back operation' against him."[14]

McGovern spent most of the day in Louisiana, along with more than half of his colleagues in the Senate, attending the funeral of Democratic Senator Allen Ellender. Eagleton decided to stay in Washington, where it seems good humor and the encouragement of a growing number of fans were helping him cope. "Hang in there," supporters wrote him in letters and telegrams. "Don't quit," they said. "In every way, ten words or less, I was told to persist," Eagleton recounted. One caller, the district attorney of Boston and Suffolk County, Garrett Byrne, suggested that Eagleton dump McGovern instead of the other way around. "That's my new thing," Eagleton joked with the reporters he had invited to his office. "I'm going to consider dropping" McGovern, he said. Eagleton soon retracted that statement, clarifying that he had spoken "in jest—J-E-S-T." Though the journalists could not hear Byrne's end of the line, they could deduce that he had gone on to say that he would pray for Eagleton's longevity on the ticket. "A rosary isn't enough for the vice presidency," Eagleton bounced back. "This needs a novena," referring to the Roman Catholic practice of intensely praying for nine consecutive days when conditions demand such devotion. Leafing through a book on his desk, *Not Exactly a Crime: Our Vice Presidents from Adams to Agnew,* Eagleton pulled out humorous passages to entertain the journalists watching him answer calls. "Needless to say, I won't be needing this much longer," Eagleton said of the book. "Or maybe I might? Who knows?"

"Keep the faith, baby," Eagleton exclaimed into the phone as he spoke with Representative Ronald V. Dellums of California. Then, he called Governor Warren Hearnes of Missouri, who had pledged $5,000 to the Eagleton vice presidential campaign at his birthday dinner in Jefferson City two nights before, to tell him to "keep your God damned $5,000." Predicting the likely outcome of his scheduled encounter with McGovern, he told Hearnes, "The axe falls in three hours."[15]

That afternoon, Eagleton also crafted a handwritten note to Ted Kennedy, who had vouched for his nomination and continued to support him. "I sincerely believe that adversity makes a person much stronger!" Eagleton wrote to the man McGovern had so badly wanted in Eagleton's place. "You and your family have faced adversity and tragedy time and again. Yet each time, you emerge as the strong person you are. Through the years, I've had remarkably good luck insofar as getting more than my share of breaks. This past week has truly tested me and, without bragging, I've survived the travail." Eagleton returned to the perspective he had expressed in Kansas City the day after receiving the nomination: in the grand scheme of things, Eagleton was a lucky guy. He thanked Kennedy for phoning in his support to California, and affirmed, "I started out my political career as a Kennedy man, and I am still 10,000% in the Kennedy corner."[16]

Meanwhile, young CBS reporter Lesley Stahl had stationed herself before the desk of receptionist Janice Carter in the entryway to Senator Eagleton's suite of offices. As Carter fielded calls throughout the day, Stahl strained to catch a few words, then peppered her with questions about who had called and why. The reporter even tailed secretary Ruth Herbst to the ladies' room in her zeal to score a scoop. Now, grasping Stahl's intent and unwilling to let her intrusion continue, Mike Kelley set a chair outside the office door and told her he wanted to make her "as comfortable as possible" there, letting it slip that the secretaries might receive a call they did not want her to know about. "Calls?!?" Stahl asked. "What phone calls?!?"[17]

By day's end, McGovern and the rest of the senators had returned to the Capitol for a series of roll calls, which ended at around 6:45 Monday evening. As the session let out, the running mates motioned to each other and met in the cloakroom. Senator Gaylord Nelson was there as McGovern and Eagleton greeted each other. It was not a coincidence. Senator Nelson was a fishing and bridge buddy of Eagleton's, as well as a confidant of McGovern's. It was he who had ultimately recommended the Missourian back in Miami Beach after turning the job down himself, and McGovern had looked to the Wisconsin senator for advice all week.[18]

Before taking off for Senator Ellender's funeral that morning, McGovern had spoken with Nelson, who told him that he considered Eagleton's continuation on the ticket untenable. Nelson stopped by Eagleton's office later that morning, presumably to prepare the running mate to relinquish his post. Senator McGovern asked Nelson to come along that evening to the meeting between running mates as an impartial adviser. Knight Newspapers described Nelson's role as "a cushion, a go-between." McGovern's need for a mediator hinted at a lack of courage to face Eagleton one-on-one. It suggested that McGovern feared Eagleton, or severely dreaded confronting the situation. Dick Dougherty later explained to reporters that McGovern had requested Nelson's presence "in order to make a heart-breaking chore easier," reinforcing the impression of McGovern as cowardly and as weak. But after the election McGovern told Dougherty that he had invited Nelson at the recommendation of a psychiatrist, who warned that lack of a comforting but impartial third-party presence at the meeting increased the likelihood of an "adversary setting," a situation in which Eagleton would dig in and push back, as he had done at their clandestine meeting the night before.[19]

From the cloakroom, the three men headed to the Marble Room, a formal, senators-only reading room off the Senate floor. "I feel very good," Eagleton told reporters as he passed them. "I felt very good all day," he tried to assure them. In the privacy of the Marble Room, Eagleton phoned his psychiatrists—first Frank Shobe of Barnes, then a doctor from the Mayo Clinic, who preferred to remain nameless at the time, but probably was Dr. Maurice Martin, the hospital's head of adult psychiatry, who had helped treat Eagleton. The running mate turned the receiver over to McGovern each time, stepping back to afford him some space.[20]

The doctors confirmed all the doubts McGovern had about his running mate's fitness for office. Dr. Shobe acknowledged that Eagleton could probably weather the pressures of the campaign and the vice presidency, but when he was asked about the presidency, he submitted, "I don't like to think about that prospect." Dr. Martin expressed amazement that Eagleton had managed to hold up thus far, surviving four years in the Senate and the tumultuous week since his psychiatric history was revealed. McGovern asked about the vice presidency. "That would make me most uncomfortable," the psychiatrist replied. A vow of confidentiality forbade McGovern from ever sharing with Eagleton or anyone else precisely what he had learned that evening, but McGovern later disclosed that the conversations made him feel that he had no choice. The national interest required Eagleton to go.[21]

In 1976 McGovern biographer Robert Sam Anson published an article in *New Times* magazine, partially based on background conversations with three of Eagleton's mental health professionals. According to Anson at the time and in a recent interview, one doctor rated Eagleton's likelihood of relapse as "twenty times greater than the average patient in a similar situation." The two others would not quantify a probability, but they underscored that depressions tend to increase with age.[22]

In the Senate Marble Room that midsummer evening, after McGovern hung up and the verdict seemed clear, Eagleton reiterated the Black Hills promise that he seemed to have forgotten. "George," he said, "if my presence on the ticket causes you any embarrassment or is a hindrance or is an impediment, I shall step aside."

"Yes," McGovern said, finally delivering to Eagleton, directly, the response he had been fumbling all week. At last, McGovern had overcome his personal instinct, ultimately acting on what now seemed in his campaign's and the country's best interest with a one-word utterance. To McGovern it had been painful, but, in the end, undeniably necessary, given the judgment of science.[23]

Suspecting the inevitable though remaining in denial, Eagleton had come prepared with two copies of a "joint statement" attributing his withdrawal to the need for the campaign to return to the issues and a desire for "party unity." Speaking through clenched lips, Eagleton warned McGovern that if he or anyone on his team ever so much as hinted that doubts about his health had figured into the decision, he would fight McGovern "right through to November." Eagleton had a career to protect, and here he held the upper hand because McGovern lacked the legal authority to drop him. Though McGovern had tapped Eagleton, the delegates to the Democratic National Convention had officially nominated him, and authority for his removal rested with the Democratic National Committee. So Eagleton trapped McGovern, forcing him to assent to his statement about the "joint" decision that Eagleton must go. The "party unity" claim was especially specious, as allegiances in the Eagleton debate largely fell according to the Old Politics–New Politics divide, and Eagleton's departure was likely only to exacerbate such tensions. McGovern was condemned to justify his running mate's removal as a political decision rather than a medical one. Surely, the truth would have reflected more kindly on McGovern's actions than the course Eagleton obliged him to accept.[24]

Soon, Jim Murphy and Frank Mankiewicz arrived in the Marble Room, and they helped Senator Nelson edit the candidates' official statements. Before the nearly two-hour session concluded, Eagleton had to express his feelings one more time. "George," he said. "I know the decision is made and it won't be unmade." Yet he continued, "Sometime between now and the election I'll bet you will have second thoughts about my getting off the ticket. A time will come when you will wish I was still on the ticket. The time will come when you would prefer to have this election be conducted as a referendum on my health rather than be a referendum on Nixon's Vietnam policy."[25]

Eagleton and McGovern emerged from the Marble Room just past 8:30 P.M. As they trudged down the long, underground corridor that connected the Capitol to the Senate office buildings, Eagleton looked "red-eyed and visibly nervous," according to one observer. He draped his arm over McGovern's shoulder, telling him within earshot of the press that they had reached "the correct decision, the only decision—it will prove to be the right one in the long run." Eagleton seemed to be reassuring himself as much as McGovern, who needed little convincing anymore. At the end of the passageway, the running mates raised their clasped hands and waved to the onlookers, almost as they had done when Eagleton joined McGovern on stage in Miami Beach eighteen days earlier. When they released their grip, McGovern headed to his office, and Eagleton toward his own.[26]

Senate aides, campaign workers, and the press corps crammed into the majestic Senate Caucus Room of the Old Senate Office Building. Two Kennedy brothers had launched their White House bids in the ornate, Beaux Arts–style room, and McGovern had used it twice to do the same. Twenty-six microphones and eleven television cameras awaited the running mates under the room's marble, chandeliered ceiling. About an hour later, McGovern and Eagleton arrived, embraced by the warm gleam of the television lights and the ovation of the candidates' staffs. "Self, don't let those cameras catch you with your head down," Eagleton muttered to himself as he paced toward the Caucus Room that evening.[27]

As Senator McGovern disclosed the decision at around 9:45 P.M., Eagleton forged a smile. "Senator Eagleton and I have met this evening to discuss his vice presidential candidacy," McGovern announced. "I have consistently supported Senator Eagleton. He is a talented, able United States Senator, whose ability will make him a prominent figure in American politics for many, many years," he said, evoking the crowd's applause. "I am fully satisfied that his health is excellent. I base that conclusion upon my personal conversations with his doctors and my close personal and political association with him," McGovern continued, compromising accuracy. "In the joint decision that we have reached tonight, health was not a factor. But the public debate over Senator Eagleton's past medical history continues to divert attention from the great national issues that need to be discussed." McGovern honored his running mate's privacy at the expense of his own image, maybe even his campaign. Though the audience could not perceive it at the time, McGovern was the same man he had been eighteen days earlier, still decent in his own way.

"Senator Eagleton and I agree that the paramount needs of the Democratic Party and the nation in 1972 are unity and a full discussion of the real issues before the country," McGovern told the audience in the Caucus Room and watching live on national television. "Continued debate between those who oppose his candidacy and those who favor it will serve to divide the party and the nation.

"Therefore, we have jointly agreed that the best course is for Senator Eagleton to step aside."

When Senator Eagleton took the podium, he admitted the difficulty of the decision, emphasizing the outflow of support he had received the preceding week. Yet in the end, he said, he ultimately recognized that he had become a distraction from the real issues of the election—the war and the economy, for example. "My personal feelings are secondary to the necessity to unify the Democratic Party and to elect George McGovern as the next president of the United States," Eagleton said, reiterating McGovern's explanation.

When he finished his prepared remarks, George McGovern's first running mate said he wanted to add a "personal" sentence or two. He ended: "I said sometime during the week that there used to be a TV show called 'That Was the Week That Was,' and this was the week that really was. No one could have been finer to me, more considerate, more genuinely concerned and interested in me as a person and in my welfare as a politician that the man that I'm proud to call the next president of the United States, George McGovern."[28]

Three times Eagleton was interrupted by thunderous applause, the whistles and howls of the crowd. And each time, Eagleton smiled, feigning contentment. The Reverend Jerome Wilkerson, a close friend from Missouri who presided at Tom and Barbara's wedding and had flown in to offer Eagleton his support, noticed tears welling in Eagleton's eyes as he spoke—full of pride yet evidently stinging with disappointment.[29]

"This is definitely not my last press conference, and Tom Eagleton is going to be around for a long, long time," the senator vowed.

During the Q-and-A that followed, McGovern said, "Few men . . . in the history of American politics have been under more pressure than Senator Eagleton has this past week, and he's held up well. He maintained his poise, maintained his dignity, and I'm very proud of him." The audience erupted in sustained applause.[30]

As Eagleton later sat down to collect his thoughts on his short-lived vice presidential campaign, he described his own feelings: "I wasn't defeated—I had done nothing wrong—I had lived and experienced emotional setbacks—but I was not ashamed—I had committed no crime—I was my own man!"[31]

When Eagleton returned home that night—still a senator, but no longer a running mate—he found Barbara on the telephone. He kissed her, and as he told her about the day's events, he kept it all in perspective, declaring that he was at peace with McGovern's decision.

Barbara had been hoping her husband would withdraw. She was eager for the press to move on. "I think a presidential election is too important to spend three months talking about what happened six years ago," she said later that week. Barbara yearned for her life to return to normal, for the questions to end, for the reporters and camera crews circling her house to go away. She knew it would all eventually stop, and, "Well, I was right," she sighed, sitting in a living-room easy chair with her bare feet tucked under her body, seemingly at ease as she answered a journalist's questions. "Everyone asks how did I stand it. How was I so cool?" Barbara said. "My only response is that obviously I hadn't been sitting around being waited on all my life. We've had problems to deal with. And every time you deal with one, and it's behind you, you're better able to cope."

The Eagletons may have looked like the picture-perfect American family, without a care in the world: handsome and extraordinarily successful husband; beautiful and capable wife; white, colonial-style home in an affluent suburb; a son and a daughter, and a dog named Pumpkin. In reality, the Eagletons were much like any other family. They had problems, they confronted challenges, and they endured. "So the news of Tom's health that came as a shock to everyone was hardly a shock to me," Barbara reflected. "I've already been there. It was horrendous in 1966, but it isn't now."[32]

Nearing midnight the night her husband withdrew from the ticket, Barbara threw a party. Tom told her he was going to bring around twenty people over, and sixty-five showed up. "I love that spirit she showed," Father Wilkerson, the priest who had married the Eagletons, said of Barbara. "Her reaction was—'We're going to have a party.' It was such a kind of strong, joyous answer to adversity." And it appeared to have relieved her husband. Tom especially appreciated that two Republican senators, his good friends Marlow Cook of Kentucky and Ted Stevens of Alaska, stopped over that evening. Stevens came lugging a twenty-pound frozen Alaska salmon over his shoulder. As Mike Kelley told a reporter, "This isn't any wake. We're all looking toward the future. And I think [Senator Eagleton] has one hell of a good future ahead of him." A woman who worked in the Eagleton Senate office noticed that Kelley's eyes were red and asked him whether he had been crying. Stunned, "That's interesting," Kelley responded. "There wasn't any reason to cry." His eyes must have been swollen in exhaustion, he said. Looking back on it all, he says now, "Not before, or since, have I ever been so proud of anyone." Later on at the party that evening, Eagleton told Father Wilkerson that the day of his withdrawal was the happiest of his life.[33]

The next day, Tuesday, Senator Eagleton awoke at 6 A.M. for a CBS television interview. "I'm not bitter," he said on air, "and I'm not going to get bitter. . . . I did the job, I took the heat, and I endured. I endured very well." Eagleton tendered his official resignation letter to the Democratic National Committee later that morning. "The world will go on and so will I," he said, before meeting with McGovern for a private and reportedly cordial breakfast.[34]

Then it was back to business for Thomas Eagleton. Though, for fifteen minutes, he sat at the front of the chamber, facing the other senators, overlooking them from the presiding officer's chair. Serving as president of the Senate is part of the vice president's official job description. In 1972 the job typically fell to the Senate's president pro tem, Senator James O. Eastland of Mississippi, when Vice President Agnew was absent. Today Eastland ceded the post to Senator Eagleton for a short while, and the onetime vice presidential candidate performed the role ably.[35]

"Mr. President," McGovern called out for Eagleton's attention when the Missourian was seated in the presiding officer's chair. McGovern was trying to speak on an amendment he had proposed to trim $4 billion from Richard Nixon's $100 billion Pentagon budget. The South Dakotan said the "reckless war in Indochina" and Nixon's oversized arms budget were "the real sources of inflation." Eagleton soon returned to his usual post and spoke in favor of his old ticket mate's amendment. "America must be strong militarily," Eagleton told his colleagues. "But a nation weakened from within is just as endangered as one threatened from without," he argued. Later, when he came to the line in his prepared remarks, "Nineteen seventy-two is a strange year for the American political system," he paused, and added, "Parenthetically, I guess I can say that again," eliciting compassionate laughter from his peers before he continued with his speech. McGovern's amendment failed to pass, thirty-three votes to fifty-nine—another setback for the presidential nominee. But Eagleton was already making his way back to the life he knew before being tapped by McGovern, the life of a legislator—prepping proposals, meeting with constituents, brokering compromises in committee meetings, and forcefully voicing his conscience on the Senate floor.[36]

For Eagleton, the Senate had always been the goal, "my be-all and end-all," as he told reporters. "Anything beyond that is blind luck, happenstance—like getting picked in '72," he said. Eagleton believed he emerged from his fling with the vice presidential candidacy much the better, unencumbered by his secret and more confident in his ability to handle pressure. He approached the Senate with renewed concentration and expressed eagerness for his 1974 reelection campaign. "I'm going to run like hell," he said, and, "I'm going to win." His only immediate worry was for his thirteen-year-old son Terry, off at camp in Pennsylvania. He hoped the other boys were not picking on him. Eagleton also brushed away questions about whether he would accept a cabinet appointment should McGovern win; he said the commissionership of baseball was the only way to woo him from the Senate. "I think to get paid $100,000 a year to attend ball games is a job I'll really like," he explained. Eagleton resisted disparaging McGovern, reserving criticism for the candidate's aides. "My conversations with the senator were always very candid and forthcoming," Eagleton said, "but I suspect that one or two of his staff were too busy backgrounding reporters that Eagleton was going to get off the ticket." Eagleton said he still refused to make his doctors available for public comment on the state of his health, explaining that he wished to respect the integrity of doctor-patient confidentiality so crucial to psychiatry. He told the talk show host Dick Cavett that he was not bitter, remarking, "I think I ended up with more friends after [my candidacy] was over than when I started." Cavett volunteered that he, too, had experienced occasional spells of depression ever since graduating from Yale in 1958. In fact, he battled bipolar disorder and was to receive ECT the following year, later becoming one of the treatment's more prominent proponents. "It was like a magic wand," he wrote of ECT in a 1992 *People* magazine article.[37]

On Wednesday, in a speech to the Senate, Majority Leader Mike Mansfield drew lessons from the previous week: "We might well ask ourselves, within the Senate and without, who among us could have stood up at all under an ordeal of this kind? Let alone with [Eagleton's] decency and dignity. Let alone with his unfailing sense of humor." Mansfield described Eagleton as a "dedicated and able Senator" before his immersion in the "pressure chamber" of public scrutiny. And he affirmed that the junior senator from Missouri had emerged all the better for his brush with the national spotlight—as a "senator who towers in courage, strength, sensitivity and wit." Indeed, Eagleton had survived the country's penetrating scrutiny of not only his basic character, decency, and capability, but also his emotional well-being and deepest secrets pertaining to it. Mansfield wondered what good might come from the Eagleton ordeal and reasoned that perhaps experiences such as those of the previous week serve "to remind us that men and women in public life are not gods but humans." In the pre-Watergate era, this seemed a truth too often glossed over. "Sometimes . . . I think too much is asked of those who dare to offer themselves for election to the highest offices of the nation," Mansfield continued. "In the ruthless search to find out everything about one senator, it is to be hoped that, as a nation, we may have found out a little more about ourselves."[38]

Some of the lessons of the preceding days could be found in the letters sent and received in the month that followed. On August 1, Henry Kimelman wrote to tell McGovern that he had confirmed himself as "a man of deep compassion, understanding, and humanity—who at the same time possesses the quality of great moral leadership." Kimelman took McGovern's wavering, hesitation, and careful evaluation of the situation to be evidence of strength of character rather than opportunism. Kimelman saw a man who cared deeply for his running mate and for his country. In the end, McGovern had judged the best course for the nation, and he acted accordingly.[39]

Philip M. Stern, another McGovern backer, evaluated the candidate's actions from a relatively detached perch—unlike Kimelman, from beyond McGovern's inner circle. Stern began his letter by recalling his early doubts about McGovern in the spring of 1970 and went on to reminisce about the McGovern he had come to admire in the early parts of the campaign: the McGovern of "a strength, a stature—maybe even a greatness." Stern described that ineffable quality: "I saw it clearly in the McGovern of June and early July, 1972: a man whose *own* personal beliefs, whose *own* instincts, whose *own* style had made fools of the conventional 'wise men'; a man who seemed to be following his *own* clearly perceived plan to win in July and to pursue the best chance of surprising the pundits again in November." He longed for that George McGovern to return from his "brief partial eclipse" of forgetting who he was. McGovern was faltering because he had lost a grip on his judgment, an instinct that had previously served him so well. As the stakes rose, perhaps a certain insecurity had emerged. But Stern urged McGovern to return to being himself, or at least his better self. "Do and say only what feels comfortable to *you*," Stern advised. "Above all, trust your own instincts, as you did with the SDSers in the lobby of the Doral. Your instincts are right and good, as people will come to know. And they are your greatest asset."[40]

Two days after Eagleton's withdrawal, Richard Nixon wrote a note to the Missouri senator's son Terry. The president's letter evinced sympathy and understanding for the Eagleton family predicament, as well as respect for Tom's decision to dust himself off and keep fighting for the Democratic cause, even if Nixon and his policies were inevitable targets. The president told Terry he wanted to share a lesson:

> Politics is a very hard game. Winston Churchill once pointed out that "politics is even more difficult than war. Because in politics you die many times; in war you die only once."
>
> But in those words of Churchill we can all take some comfort. The political man can always come back to fight again.

What matters is not that your father fought a terribly difficult battle and lost. What matters is that in fighting the battle he won the admiration of foes and friends alike because of the courage, poise, and just plain guts he showed against overwhelming odds.

Few men in public life in our whole history have been through what he has been through. I hope you do not allow this incident to discourage or depress you.

Years later you will look back and say, "I am proud of the way my dad handled himself in the greatest trial of his life."[41]

The experience of the eighteen-day vice presidential campaign left Doug Bennet disillusioned with politics, or "jungle warfare," as he now termed it. He took a sailing trip to recover and pondered a new career, perhaps a return to academia. "How is the market for Russian medievalists?" he asked friends. Though Bennet's disappointment in the outcome of the ordeal was palpable, he took solace in his faith that the McGovern campaign had blundered and that, maybe, Eagleton had been spared. "The truth is that Big George needed Eagleton," Bennet wrote in a letter to a friend, "but his henchmen managed to set him up so he couldn't keep him."[42]

Bennet's commentary underscores a crucial failing of the McGovern-Eagleton organization: it never became one campaign, unified by more than just a hyphen. Rather, it was two separate organizations, serving two separate candidates, with two separate agendas and disparate ambitions. With their goals disentangled and the organizations emotionally and physically miles apart, the campaigns worked against each other instead of forging a course that could have proven politically beneficial for both men. "In the final days . . . we had all-out, delightfully uncomplicated jungle warfare—the kind where scruples don't count and survival is everything," Bennet wrote in a letter to the distinguished historian Carl E. Schorske, who had taught him at Wesleyan. Writing at the end of August, with a bit more distance, Bennet wrote of the whole affair, "Regretting the experience would be like regretting an earthquake, although I am fully prepared to accept whatever accountability may be ours. What I do very much regret is missing our opportunity to help bring this year's campaign to bear on some real issues," referring to what mattered most. In his letter to his old professor, Bennet continued, "I hope you are still doing with Voltaire and Goethe and Ravel what you did for me at Wesleyan. You always managed to set a new universe before us just as I, at least, was beginning dimly to understand the last one. That perspective more than anything else makes me continue to believe there is room for reason in this maelstrom."[43]

The Aftermath

On October 7, 1972, sixty-seven days after he withdrew from the ticket, the Missouri junior senator returned from out of state ahead of schedule at the presidential candidate's request. McGovern had asked Eagleton to join him at a rally in the parking lot of a shopping center near St. Louis. Eagleton obliged, and the former running mates hit the campaign trail together for the first time all year. "No matter what others may think," McGovern told the crowd sprawled across eighty-five hundred cars that filled the concrete expanse, "there will always be a special bond between the Eagletons and the McGoverns that is only possible when two families go through a difficult and heart-rending experience together." McGovern conceded that he had stumbled at times in his handling of the matter, "but if there were mistakes," he said by means of justification, "they were honest mistakes of the heart." McGovern continued, "To those who are troubled that a presidential candidate could back his chosen running mate 1,000 percent and then ask him to step down a week later, I can only say that in politics as in life, compassion must sometimes yield to more reflective and painful judgment."[1]

McGovern proclaimed, "To those who object to a presidential candidate publicly changing his mind, I say that a leader who would rather save face than respond to new insight is no leader at all—he is a disaster—as witness our sad experience in Vietnam." He never specified what "new insight" he was referring to with regard to the Eagleton affair, but the ambiguity intimated that McGovern was privy to more than he let on. "I took the hard course that I believe was in the national interest—a course that was only possible with Tom's respect and cooperation."[2]

That evening the Eagletons, Ed Filippine, and Mike Kelley joined McGovern and Mankiewicz for a 7 P.M. dinner in McGovern's suite at the St. Louis Chase Park Plaza Hotel. The Truman Day festivities were to begin at 8:30 P.M. downstairs. After posing for photographs in McGovern's living room, the group settled into the private dining room. Over the course of the meal, Eagleton expressed his disappointment at several comments the press had attributed to McGovern associates. Their remarks implied that the truth about Eagleton's health had precipitated his departure from the ticket, and not simply a desire for party unity and the need to return to the real issues of the election, as they had said at the final press conference on July 31. Eagleton had a political future to protect, and it irritated him that a story in that morning's *New York Times,* for example, quoted a top McGovern donor, Miles Rubin, as saying, "To make public what really happened goes against what George McGovern stands for." In his comment, Rubin elaborated, "George McGovern went out of his way to protect Eagleton's name and reputation." The implication: McGovern was too decent to jeopardize Eagleton's career by revealing the whole truth about the state of Eagleton's mental health. McGovern and Mankiewicz both apologized to Eagleton for Rubin's remarks, and Mankiewicz promised to correct Rubin and the staffers' tones in the press; McGovern insisted that he always rebuffed press inquiries about Eagleton, but members of the Eagleton team said that the coverage indicated otherwise. McGovern asked them to let him know any time they felt he had breached their pact.[3]

Then McGovern told Eagleton and his staffers that the Eagleton situation continued to haunt the campaign—a fact they surely already knew. McGovern asked Eagleton whether he would say that he, too, had considered leaving the ticket to be the right decision and not merely one he had been pressured into accepting. Eagleton refused, still adamant that he would have bolstered McGovern's standing in the polls. Eagleton told McGovern that in his speech that evening he would note their disagreement on the decision to leave the ticket, but would emphasize that he accepted McGovern's perspective and supported his candidacy. Before their conversation ended, McGovern again proposed a stronger endorsement of the decision, and Eagleton continued to resist. "You know, George," Barbara Eagleton said, "Tom is now the most popular politician in America."[4]

Washington Post reporters traversing the country in preparation for a mood-of-the-country story published in the paper earlier that week had found overwhelming sympathy for the junior senator from Missouri. They also discovered respect for his judgment. "There was a shrewd appreciation that pressures can build on any man—and [Americans] admire someone who has the character to recognize his problems, seek help, and surmount them," one of the *Post* journalists, Haynes Johnson, wrote, summarizing the findings. Perhaps the voters would have felt differently had Eagleton remained on the ticket, but most seemed to acknowledge that mental illness could touch anyone's life, even their own; Eagleton may have received shock treatment, but he had proven his resilience under extreme pressure, and his triumph was inspiring.[5]

Though Eagleton's history of mental illness ultimately foreclosed his chance to stay on the ticket, the Eagleton affair repudiated the notion that a former electroshock patient could never serve in office. Concurrent medical considerations aside, Eagleton himself began to dismantle such presumptions. Yes, there was the inevitable outpouring of anxiety expressed by some that failure to disclose past psychiatric care might cost someone a job. But the grace with which Eagleton confronted rejection and the courage he demonstrated in overcoming his disappointment worked to invalidate the perception of the current or formerly mentally ill as emotionally weak, erratic, or untrustworthy. For example, Matthew Troy, the outspoken

Queens County, New York, Democratic leader, who had declared in July that he would not vote for McGovern if Eagleton remained on the ticket, saying that he would not feel safe if "some unstable person" became president, now wrote to Eagleton to apologize for the "terrible injustice" of questioning his competency. In addition to improving public perceptions of the mentally ill, Eagleton humanized electroshock patients, and his resilience on the campaign trail compelled Americans to question their sensationalized *Cuckoo's Nest* understanding of ECT. Lamentably, the poignant and provocative Academy Award–winning movie adaptation of *One Flew over the Cuckoo's Nest* the following year seems to have set back the process of ECT normalization that Eagleton had begun.[6]

At the Truman Day Dinner following the former running mates' meeting in McGovern's hotel suite, Eagleton addressed what had been termed "the Eagleton backlash" before a crowd of fifteen hundred of St. Louis's leading Democrats. "I want you to know that I have the fullest, most unqualified faith in, and belief in George McGovern that one human being can possess on this earth," he said. Yet he made clear that this faith did not extend to McGovern's decision about his future on the ticket that final evening of July. He recalled their discussion in the Senate Marble Room the night of July 31, describing it as the deliberation between "two rational, mature people in politics." Eagleton said he argued his case, but that McGovern remained uneasy about the prospect that Eagleton's presence on the ticket might divert attention from the crucial issues facing voters, and this view prevailed. When it came down to it, as the presidential candidate, McGovern "had the right to make" this decision. While Eagleton accepted the decision, he refused to promote it.[7]

But the campaign never centered on the issues. Through their inability to stop discussing it, both McGovern and Eagleton helped ensure that the Eagleton affair remained in the national dialogue, diminishing the chances that the campaign would ever be decided on policy. Though McGovern may have made the right decision based on his understanding of the medical issue—and perhaps even the right political decision—his management of the decision ultimately undermined his campaign. In initially reaffirming his support for his running mate, McGovern had initially met the public's expectation of compassion and reasserted his qualities of integrity and decency. Besides, in the course of auditioning for a job that rarely affords second chances, it would have seemed imprudent to admit fallibility, and dropping Eagleton in South Dakota would have branded McGovern as both callous and incompetent. By being himself, McGovern originally avoided this mistake. But then the campaign and the media—cocooned in its already insular Black Hills bubble—fed off each other's presumption that the nation could never stomach the running mate's past, ratcheting up the sense of crisis and forcing McGovern to reconsider his decision. In the end, it appeared to many that the seemingly backhanded and spineless manner in which McGovern compelled Eagleton to withdraw probably hindered McGovern's shot at the presidency more than keeping Eagleton would have hurt it, in large part because it ultimately contradicted the public's expectations of his behavior.[8]

Yet for some reason McGovern continued to flaunt his "credibility," though pollsters now considered it among his biggest liabilities, far greater than his supposedly radical stands on the issues. "There will never be a time when I am sneaking around advocating something in secret behind closed doors that I am ashamed to defend in public," he told a Cleveland audience that October. But no one seemed to buy it. Seventy-two-year-old Santos Hernandez, a lifelong California Democrat, for example, picked Nixon that year. "I can't vote for that son-of-a-bitch McGovern," he said. Voters considered McGovern two-faced, untrustworthy, an opportunist, and a flip-flopper. "Seldom has the public perception of a major political figure changed so rapidly," the *Washington Post* declared. By October polls showed that most voters found Richard Nixon to be "the more sincere and trustworthy" of the two candidates. While 5 percent more Americans preferred Democratic control of Congress to Republican, Nixon led McGovern 59 percent to 31 percent in an October poll.[9]

Even on the war, which was supposed to be the Democrat's most penetrating advantage, McGovern, imperiled by his moralism, could never manage to seize momentum. A comprehensive review of 1972 survey data by Princeton political scientist Stanley Kelley

Jr. found that judgments of the candidates' competency in general and capability to satisfactorily usher in the end of the Vietnam War in particular added 8 percent to Nixon's tally. By late summer, the president was believed to be successfully deescalating the conflict in Southeast Asia, and a Daniel Yankelovich, Inc., survey found that Richard Nixon—not George McGovern—was now considered "the peace candidate." Fifty-two percent of Americans believed McGovern had made the wrong decision on Eagleton. *New York Times* columnist Tom Wicker wrote in November that the Eagleton affair "may well have been the most damaging single blow ever to fall upon a presidential candidate." Whether McGovern should have kept Eagleton or not, one thing was clear. Wicker wrote: "It would be hard to find anyone, even in the McGovern camp, who thinks the matter should have been handled just as it was." The Eagleton affair hastened the unraveling of George McGovern the saint.[10]

The 1972 election is often misread as a vast cultural realignment, with Nixon's forty-nine-state victory taken as evidence of the country's rejection of New Deal government. Conservative political scientist Jeane Kirkpatrick described the 1972 contest as "a cultural class struggle with Richard Nixon cast as leader of the free masses and George McGovern as the spokesman of an embattled revolutionary elite." Ben J. Wattenberg, coauthor of *The Real Majority,* similarly viewed the election as "a referendum on the so-called cultural revolution," involving questions of defense, welfare, race, and style. Wattenberg said that, in the end, Americans voted "no" on the "New Politics" that George McGovern embodied, and historians liberal and conservative alike have embraced this thinking. But this is too reductive a view of 1972. In this election—as in all elections—Americans voted not just on platforms but on people; they voted for a leader, not simply on issues.[11]

As Stanley Kelley documented in his book *Interpreting Elections,* the Eagleton affair was instrumental in shaping the electorate's eventual views of the candidates as people. While the Eagleton case in and of itself ultimately swung 0.5 percent of voters Nixon's way, according to Kelley's postelection analysis of the marginal impact of various criteria on voting outcome, it probably influenced overall judgments of candidate competency, which alone granted the president an additional 6.4 percent boost, as Kelley argues. He believes the Eagleton affair indelibly tainted voters' perception of McGovern and his campaign, resulting in the general distrust reflected in other metrics. Two and a half times as many people voiced aversion to McGovern's character than those who deemed him "too liberal," which Kelley takes as evidence that personal judgments counted more than policy distinctions.[12]

A poll conducted by Cambridge Survey Research, the McGovern-employed and Pat Caddell–led company that so brilliantly discerned the mood of the electorate through the primaries, asked voters to choose which candidate each of a series of adjectives evoked. Nixon dwarfed McGovern in association with "strong" and "sneaky," while McGovern outscored Nixon by the largest margin on "foolish." As *New York Times* columnist Anthony Lewis explained, the poll verified that McGovern's problem was not his ideology but his personality. "It is a capability gap," he said, adapting the term "credibility gap," which McGovern had long used to deride his opponents. "In the crucial period after the convention, under the impact of the Eagleton affair, many voters came to the conclusion that [McGovern] was not competent," Lewis wrote. First McGovern botched his original vice presidential pick, flip-flopping his way through an embarrassing week of sticking with him, then cutting him loose. Then he settled in for the humiliation of rejection after rejection as he struggled to find a replacement, before eventually landing Sargent Shriver. It no longer seemed to matter that Nixon had chosen a malignant Spiro Agnew as his vice president and had blundered far worse on his first two Supreme Court nominations. (According to Lewis, one of his picks for the Supreme Court had been "the most grotesquely unqualified choice in memory," and both were rejected by the Senate.) Nixon was president, and he ran not as himself but as "the president." The term itself promised competence, and the president benefited from this veneer of prestige and detachment from political mudslinging that was believed to accompany the post, leaving the election to become a referendum on McGovern, his credibility, his capability, or his lack thereof. As John Herbers of the *New York Times* wrote, "It is Mr. McGovern who has become *the* issue in the campaign."[13]

Political memory can be terribly simplistic. Senator Eagleton has been reduced in the popular imagination to the running mate McGovern dropped because of his treatment with electroshock, his name often bringing to mind in those who lived it vague memories of "skeletons in your closet" and "1,000 percent." McGovern, conversely, has often been reduced to a joke, dismissed as the delusional champion of hopeless, radical policies and politics, the candidate who relinquished every state but Massachusetts and lost the popular vote 61 percent to 38 percent in a presidential gambit that never had a chance. The reality is more complicated than that, with each player experiencing a constellation of feelings over the years—often complex and understandable—as they have tried to come to grips with Eagleton's eighteen-day spot on a national ticket.[14]

Epilogue

In the aftermath of the campaign, Eagleton complained of being the McGovernites' scapegoat for their loss. McGovern himself said the Eagleton affair was "the saddest part" of his whole run. "Many people never forgave me" for dropping Eagleton, he reflected in a television interview with Dick Cavett. "I thought I was acting in the national interest but many thought I was not." Then, in March 1973, McGovern allowed the journalist Joe McGinniss to spend some time with him in South Dakota, and the resulting magazine piece appeared to have caught the senator with his guard down, throbbing with resentment toward Eagleton. "I didn't like [Eagleton] one bit," McGinnis quoted McGovern as saying. "He had always seemed superficial to me. He had no dignity, no reserve. And there was always this nervousness to him." McGovern recalled the ferocious taunts he confronted at an exhibition football game at RFK Stadium shortly after dropping his running mate and described the pang he felt upon hearing that Eagleton had received a standing ovation when he was introduced at a Kansas City Chiefs game the following week. "Well, my blood just ran cold," McGovern reportedly told McGinniss. "To realize the terrible injustice. That a man who had not leveled with me was being given credit as an All-American type. While I was being treated like a bum." Upon publication of McGinniss's article, McGovern denounced it as a "disreputable and shoddy piece of journalism" and said the reporter had fabricated his quotations. McGinniss, meanwhile, attested to his article's veracity, calling McGovern's sensitivity a function of his insecurity upon seeing how his words looked in print.[1]

Reporters never stopped needling McGovern, pushing for the full story behind Eagleton's withdrawal; they kept begging to know what really had happened. McGovern refrained from spilling the whole truth, but as former staffers such as Dick Dougherty, Gary Hart, and Gordon Weil began to write their campaign memoirs, he decided to set the record straight. He scribbled a letter on a white sheet of paper and affirmed what they probably suspected: his conversations with Eagleton's doctors had disqualified his running mate.

Despite McGovern's pain, resentment, and understandable anger toward Senator Eagleton, McGovern found perspective, evincing sympathy for Eagleton and his predicament. McGovern asked his own aides to use what he shared only "for [their] own guidance," keeping it private for the sake of Senator Eagleton and his career. "I ask you to remember that while Senator Eagleton did us a great injustice, he is still a talented [public] man with a promising career in the Senate, who is doubtless waging a difficult private battle to maintain his emotional balance," McGovern wrote. "There is nothing to be gained either in hurting his Senate career or his private rehabilitation."

For McGovern, the Eagleton case was deeply personal, and not just because of its implications for his deepest professional ambitions. The decision tested his feelings about his daughter Terry, and his faith in her future. He told his advisers this was "perhaps a central reason why I first reacted so strongly in support of Senator Eagleton even though I shared your consideration that he was not candid with us at the Miami convention." McGovern went on, "I continue to feel that judgments about [Eagleton] must be tempered by the knowledge that he carries a heavy emotional burden that may serve to explain his original failure to disclose his medical history to us and his subsequent efforts to appear as a political martyr while we bore the brunt of the criticism and the public indignation and confusion toward me."

For McGovern, the dismantling of his credibility was perhaps the Eagleton affair's most personally devastating consequence. "Never before in my public career has either my honesty or my decency been questioned," McGovern continued. "It must be one of the strangest paradoxes of political history, that the press somehow managed to convey the impression that my credibility and decency were on trial—not Senator Eagleton's," he wrote. As he was forced to insist that health had not factored into the "joint decision" that Eagleton must depart, McGovern had undermined his public reputation as a man of character and his private confidence in himself as a man of candor.[2]

Gary Hart said that the decision on Tom Eagleton's future with the campaign could have been made on three possible bases: the personal, the political, and the factual. McGovern's compassionate reaction—his instinctive empathy and care for his running mate—represented the personal course. Then, as the circumstances changed, he was compelled to reconsider his position and frame it in political terms, placating the fund-raisers and addressing the need for the campaign to return to the issues. In truth, however, McGovern's decision was a factual determination: the doctors led him to doubt Thomas Eagleton's stability, and McGovern deferred to their judgment. In the end, he had made not only a political decision but also a medical one, but he had no choice but to explain it as simply political, setting up the perception of the candidate as a disingenuous schemer. Hart also believed this was devastating. "The tragedy was in confusing an issue of national leadership and security with personal and political considerations," he wrote. In reflecting on McGovern's behavior, Dougherty assessed it as noble and self-effacing: "One has to believe, as I do, that McGovern risked the loss of his chances for the presidency in order to save the career and possibly the life of the man who had wronged him."[3]

McGovern's resentment was still raw when he recounted the Eagleton affair in his own memoirs, *Grassroots*, a few years later.

McGovern said he found the events surrounding his vice presidential pick "painful" to retell and admitted to harboring "conflicting
emotions" about the affair. At the conclusion of his chapter on the
episode, McGovern invoked Eagleton's comment that dismissed his
short run as "one rock in th[e] landslide." "Perhaps that is true," he
acknowledged. "But landslides begin with a single rock."[4]

Senator Eagleton's eighteen-day foray into presidential politics did
not define his political career, but it has dominated our memory of
it. Upon his retirement from the Senate fourteen years later, he told
the *Kansas City Star* that he was sure his obituary would lead with
his brief interlude as McGovern's running mate. Thinking wishfully,
he later wondered whether his role in bringing professional football
back to St. Louis might eclipse his vice presidential candidacy as
the defining moment of his career. Like McGovern, Eagleton could
accept the events of July 1972, but he could never entirely get over
them.[5]

    Following Eagleton's withdrawal, the running mates served
another eight years together in the Senate. Over time, the two men
began to trade correspondence. In December 1980, soon after George
McGovern lost his Senate seat in an election year that saw the ascen-
dance of Republican Ronald Reagan to the White House, Eagleton
sent him a handwritten note on a U.S. Senate memorandum pad:
"Just a short, personal note to wish you the best of health and happiness in the years ahead. You have brains and guts—two things in
increasingly short supply in American political life." It was typical
of the missives he would write to friends and colleagues throughout his life—warm, noble, to the point—though this one lacked his
trademark humor. At the same time, on this particular note, one
could not help but notice the letterhead: "United States Senate"—
a reminder of who would remain in office come January, and who
would not.[6]

Though McGovern left the Senate, he could never shed his presidential ambitions—or that craving for a voice, to make a difference.
He had little staff and meager funding, but as he ran for president

again in 1984, he had a platform. After McGovern appeared on ABC's *Nightline* that June, well after his withdrawal from the race, Eagleton wrote him again and told his old running mate, "Both what you said and how you said it was *absolutely first-rate.*" He also used the letter to comment on McGovern's abortive but worthwhile bid for the presidency. "When you embarked on your campaign, I frankly thought you had flipped. I viewed it as a hopeless tilt against numerous strong winds," Eagleton conceded. "I was *dead wrong* (as were lots of others). . . . You didn't win the nomination, but you won the soul of the campaign," Eagleton told him. "Some men turn bitter after defeat; a few turn better. You are one of the latter." He signed off "with admiration."[7]

Regarding the eighteen days that molded their relationship, McGovern and Eagleton each eventually came to impart empathy and respect for the other man, and for his position, at least in public. When Eagleton left the Senate in 1986, McGovern said of the Missourian, "I think he's one of the best senators that I served with for the eighteen years I was there. . . . He brought a certain passion to it that I always admired." And looking back on the Eagleton affair from the vantage point of 1986, McGovern mused, "I still don't know yet after all these years what the proper course was to follow on the matter, because there isn't any answer that had a happy ending." Eagleton agreed: "It was heads you lose, tails you lose," "an impossible situation." And he allowed, "I think [McGovern] did the right thing from his point of view. If he had done otherwise it would have hurt him." At the same time, Eagleton felt that he, too, did what was "right and correct" under the circumstances. He said, "I have no second thoughts or second-guessing." Recognizing that there were no easy answers, the more circumspect McGovern speculated, "I guess only history and providence will make the final judgment."[8]

In an April 2006 interview with the *New York Times*, McGovern had arrived at a resolution. "If I had it to do over again, I'd have kept him." He explained, "I didn't know anything about mental illness. Nobody did," he said, though in truth, McGovern had known at least something about mental illness from his experiences with his daughter Terry. A year later, McGovern told Carl Leubsdorf the same thing but added, "A lot of people have suffered depression, including me." Four years later, in a June 2011 interview in preparation for this book, McGovern's feelings were consistent. "I think in retrospect we might have been better off to stay with him," McGovern told me. He imagined an alternative media strategy, in which the campaign said, "Yes, yes [Eagleton] had suffered from depression. So did Abraham Lincoln, so did Winston Churchill. And we're going to keep an eye on this. If we see any evidence of the senator being ill, we'll deal with it." Clearly having replayed these events many times, he continued to reflect:

> I think that probably would have been better, but I don't know. I know there were millions of people who would have felt nervous about that decision, just as there were millions of people who didn't like it when we asked him to step down. So it was kind of one of those things politically, it's a lose-lose proposition no matter which way you go. . . . I thought, on balance, we shouldn't take a chance. You only have one vice president and one president. You shouldn't take a chance. But I'd say in retrospect, I think politically, we'd have been better off staying with him.[9]

I asked McGovern to clarify: did he mean to say he should have given more weight to the political considerations?

"Not only the political, but also Senator Eagleton's situation. He had been a successful politician in Missouri, even while he was going through this depression," McGovern told me. "I think if I had been thoroughly informed on the nature of depression, the best thing to do would have been to stay with Senator Eagleton but keep an eye on his mental health which would be very easy to do because he'd be sitting next to me in the White House. And that's probably what I would have done with the knowledge I have now," he said. "But I have to tell you," McGovern continued:

> Some of the best psychologists in the country disagree with me on that. They tell me they thought I did the right

thing. But in the last analysis, I had to make the decision, and I couldn't depend on a psychologist or psychiatrist telling me, and all I am telling you is I know a lot more about depression now. I wrote a book, a biography of Abraham Lincoln, I know how it affected him throughout his adult life. So knowing what I know now, I probably would have kept him. And I think we would have done better in the general election, but I don't know that.

Later in our conversation, George McGovern the veteran statesman shared perhaps the best analysis, or justification, of all: "Politics is an uncertain enterprise," he said, "and you just have to do what you think at the time is your best way to go. And that's what I did."[10]

As the 1992 election approached, McGovern grappled with the idea of another run. Of course, 1972 loomed large, and he took the measure of its implications for his present. He jotted a memo to himself on scraps of paper and called it "Why I May Run for President in 1992," making his case for another try. He began by noting that, though he had suffered the ignominy of losing forty-nine of fifty states in 1972, just eighteen months later polls showed that, if the election were held then, he would have trounced Nixon by as great a margin as the president had defeated him. "So it has always seemed to me," McGovern reasoned, "and I suspect to many other Americans, that if there was 'a debacle' in 1972, it was the Watergate cover-up," which ultimately wrecked Nixon's presidency. McGovern said two other facts had further encouraged him. First, history had proven him right on so many of the stances he had taken during that campaign. And, second, the members of the "McGovern Army" who captured the party's nomination on his behalf were no longer young and considered radical. Rather, they had become the establishment, rising to positions of power and authority, in government and elsewhere, locally and nationally. This was the generation that the 1972 McGovern campaign had helped to define. "I cannot walk down any street in America, or ride on an airplane, or visit a restaurant, hotel lobby or public building without being told by strangers that the high point of their political experience was working in the '72 campaign," McGovern wrote. "Frequently they say, 'If you run again, I'm with you.'"[11]

After the 1972 election, Gary Hart turned his ambition inward and focused on his own political career. He unseated a Republican incumbent to become the junior senator from Colorado in 1974. Ten years later, he ran for president, pitting himself against the man whose campaign he had helped run, among others. McGovern said at the time, "Gary Hart has no peer in the United States Senate on foreign and nuclear arms issues." But he added wryly that Hart should stay put in the Senate and "leave the White House to us former senators who are unemployed and really need that job." Though neither man captured the Democratic nomination that year, Hart's bid set him up to enter the 1988 contest as the widely touted front-runner. As rumors of his womanizing circulated soon after he announced his candidacy in April 1987, Hart sat down for an interview with E. J. Dionne Jr. for a *New York Times Sunday Magazine* interview, published the first weekend in May. "There's no reward for being candid," Hart explained. "In fact, there are penalties for being candid. People say, 'Why are politicians such conniving, calculating S.O.B.s?' It's because who knows what oddball thing you say is not going to come back fifteen years later to be some profound insight into your character." Then he uttered the words that would become to Gary Hart what "1,000 percent" was to McGovern. "Follow me around," he said. "If anybody wants to put a tail on me, go ahead. They'd be very bored." On a tip, the same newspaper company that confronted the McGovern campaign about the Eagleton allegations took Hart up on his challenge. The *Miami Herald* staked out the candidate's Washington townhouse and caught the married Hart with young and blonde Donna Rice. This time, a skeleton in Hart's own closet derailed *his* presidential ambitions. Just as in 1972, Hart entertained the illusion that an American presidential nominating contest could center exclusively on the issues. He pleaded for the public and the press to turn their attention "away from what is temporal, sensational and irrelevant to the real challenges confronting our nation and our world." However, his public comments failed to take into account, as David Broder did, that "what was at issue here was Hart's truthfulness, his self-discipline, his sense of responsibility to other people—indeed, his willingness to face hard choice and realities." This, Broder explained, had implications for governance. George McGovern clipped Broder's article, and scribbled in the margins, "Good piece. Tough but honest." In another article that McGovern cut out and underlined, A. M. Rosenthal wrote, "We need leaders who see things clearly, starting with themselves. Mr. Hart showed himself unable to see himself at all. Thus, in the end, Gary Hart disqualified Gary Hart from being president of the United States."[12]

Frank Mankiewicz lost a run for Congress in 1974 and returned to public relations until he became president of National Public Radio in 1977. In 1983 Mankiewicz left NPR and advised Hart on his 1984 campaign. Like the candidate himself, Mankiewicz bemoaned the press's fixation on the minutiae of the campaign intrigue at the expense of the issues. Mankiewicz still works in Washington and is vice chairman of Hill and Knowlton, the international public relations powerhouse. Interestingly, Douglas Bennet succeeded Mankiewicz as president and CEO of NPR, spending ten years in that position. Then, from 1995 until his retirement in 2007, he was president of his alma mater, Wesleyan University, an institution he always cherished. One of his sons, Michael Bennet, is the junior senator from Colorado, a post that once belonged to Gary Hart.

Rick Stearns, mastermind of the McGovern campaign's field organizing in the caucus states and parliamentary maneuverings at the convention, is currently a federal district court judge in Massachusetts. Ed Filippine of Eagleton's team is also a federal district court judge, in the Eastern District of Missouri. Gene Godley eventually became assistant secretary of the treasury under President Jimmy Carter and is now a partner in the Washington office of white-shoe law firm Bracewell Giuliani. Jim Murphy serves "of counsel" at Bryan Cave. Mike Kelley tired of politics and tried his hand at the restaurant business, owning and operating Swensen's Grill and Ice Cream franchises in the Kansas City area. But he found his heart was not in it, and he eventually returned to journalism. As top editor at the *Las Vegas Sun,* he led the newspaper to the 2009 Pulitzer Prize for Public Service for its exposure of rampant safety violations during the Las Vegas Strip building boom that contributed to the deaths of twelve construction workers in an eighteen-month period. Two others at the heart of Eagleton's eighteen-day run won Pulitzers: Bob Boyd and Clark Hoyt, for discovering the story that ultimately led to the running mate's withdrawal.[13]

Nearly forty years later, Boyd and Hoyt reflected on the story that earned them their profession's highest honor, and neither regrets pursuing the lead. "The question [was] whether someone who was the proverbial heartbeat away from the presidency would suddenly, through some tragedy, become the president and then undergo extreme stress and then have a crash at a moment, at a highly inopportune moment for the country, and be dysfunctional, or unfunctional," Hoyt reasoned. "And so I never doubted that it was appropriate that we ask the questions, and I never doubted that [Eagleton's] medical history was an important part of his qualifications for high office. I would say that would not be the case for someone running for senator or lieutenant governor or attorney general of Missouri, but I think when you're talking about the vice president of the United States, the bar changes."[14]

As Boyd recalled, "Clark and I felt that the voters of the country ought to know that this man who could be a heartbeat away from the presidency had had a serious problem. I'm not sure what he told [Missourians], but it wasn't the truth."[15]

As for Richard Nixon, Bob Haldeman, and the Republican operatives inside the White House and at the Committee for the Reelection of the President headquarters, they may have secured a landslide, but they lost their dignity in the process—whether or not they played a role in the leak. In August 1974 the president resigned amid the Watergate scandal, and many of his top aides did so even earlier, his administration and our memory of it forever stained. The day before the 1972 election, the Associated Press reported that Johnson-era U.S. Attorney General Ramsey Clark remembered seeing as deputy attorney general in 1965 reference to Eagleton's treatment in his FBI file. The Missouri lieutenant governor was being considered for an assistant U.S. attorney general post, and intensive background checks of prospects were standard practice. The same day the *St. Louis Post-Dispatch* revealed that Agnew had known about Eagleton's medical history before his disclosure, though the vice president's office denied these allegations. In May 1973 the *Washington Post*'s intrepid Watergate reporters Carl Bernstein and Bob Woodward suggested that White House domestic affairs chief, John D. Ehrlichman, had received Eagleton's medical records "several weeks before the information was released to the news media." And in *All the President's Men* they quote Deep Throat's explanation of E. Howard Hunt Jr.'s leak-plugging operation, the "Plumbers," that worked for the president's campaign. "That operation was not only to check leaks to the papers," Deep Throat told the journalists,

> but often to manufacture items for the press. It was a Colson-Hunt operation. Recipients include all of you guys—Jack Anderson, Evans and Novak, the *Post* and the *New York Times,* the *Chicago Tribune.* The business of Eagleton's drunk-driving record or his health records, I understand, involves the White House and Hunt somehow. Total manipulation—that was their goal, with everyone eating at one time or another out of their hands. Even this press.[16]

"Yeah, yeah, anonymous source," Frank Mankiewicz said dismissively when I asked him about the identity of the leaker. "Chuck Colson or Pat Buchanan, that's what I always thought," he said, adding that a well-placed source corroborated these suspicions for him. Colson and Buchanan's correspondence regarding the letter that Sam Krupnick had sent to Rose Mary Woods—Colson's "I've already taken care of it," for example—seem to substantiate this theory. Convicted "Plumber" obstructionists Egil Krogh Jr. and G. Gordon Liddy, whose Special Investigations Unit broke into the office of Pentagon Papers leaker Daniel Ellsberg's psychiatrist, did not return my request for comment. Neither did Buchanan or Colson. When asked by e-mail whether he knew anything about Nixon administration or CREEP involvement in the leak, deputy CREEP director Fred Malek replied, "No idea now or ever."[17]

Just because the Republicans had information on Eagleton's medical case history does not mean they leaked it to the media. And even if they did leak it, it seems likely that word of Eagleton's treatment and hospitalization, already percolating in Miami Beach even before the Missourian was selected, would have made its way to the press anyway. Mike Kelley also remembers Matt Reese, the outside political consultant on Eagleton's 1968 Senate campaign, sharing with him that he had disclosed the information. But Kelley cannot recall with whom Reese said he shared it. To Hoyt, whether the phone calls that helped tip him off to the Eagleton story were part of a dirty trick is irrelevant. He told me, "What matters in the end is that it is true, and I would argue with you that we handled it responsibly no matter where the information came from."[18]

In the end, history emancipated the McGovern agenda, freeing it from the shackles of its "radical" label. McGovern believed that most all McGovernites and indeed most Americans could now see the prudence of his platform. "We were right in denouncing the Vietnam War as a major disaster and calling for immediate U.S. disengagement," McGovern observed in his 1992 notes.

> We were right in contending that America was exaggerating the military challenge to the country while underestimating the economic challenge from abroad. . . . We were right about the danger of environmental pollution, educational mediocrity, and declining productivity. We were also right in calling for reform of the tax system, welfare, healthcare, and defense. Needless to say, we were right in worrying about Watergate and corruption in the Nixon administration. Indeed, the platform of 1972 seems amazingly in tune with the needs of today.

McGovern may have been right about the issues, but his fatal flaws had not changed. He was still moralistic and ambitious, unrelenting in his desire for the Oval Office. And though the Eagleton affair gave him another layer of perspective and experience, it seems likely that the same qualities that foiled him in 1972 would have unraveled him once more when confronting the tests, personal and political, bound to encumber his campaign, as all campaigns. In the end, all elections—especially presidential elections—are about people. Every election measures the public's relationship with the personalities and images of the various candidates. McGovern would have to leave 1992 to another man with ties to his 1972 campaign, Bill Clinton. The man from a town called Hope got his start in politics and worked alongside his future wife, Hillary, campaigning for the decent man from South Dakota.[19]

In 1984 Eagleton hoped to write a book profiling vice presidential candidates on losing tickets throughout American history. "They Ran, Too," he had planned to call it. Eagleton outlined his idea in a memo to his aide, Jack Lewis, "The *purpose,* thus, is to humanize the obscure guy, to place [the losing vice presidential candidate] in the context of his political times as a force, as a matter, as a consideration, as a factor. It's the crass *humanity* of the guy that I want. If he had human *shortcomings,* human *idiosyncrasies*—that's what we want. If he said *humorous* things, that's what we want. Did he die broken hearted?" When Eagleton retired from the Senate in 1986, after eighteen years in Washington, his Republican colleague from Missouri John Danforth said, "What has set Tom Eagleton apart from the rest of us is not his intellect and his energy, as impressive as they are. It is his moral passion, his capacity for outrage, his insistence that justice be done, that wrongs be made right."[20]

Eagleton left the Senate at age fifty-seven, disillusioned with the partisan squabbling that defined life in the modern legislature. He said the Senate was "in a state of chaos," and he had no interest in toiling in a chamber ruled by ascendant doctrinaire archconservatives like Jesse Helms of North Carolina. He was also sickened by the amount of money—and time in fund-raising—that had become necessary to get elected. Eagleton looked forward to a new career, teaching politics, law, and international business at Washington University in St. Louis and at the St. Louis University School of Law. "I've seen some people stay in the Senate for way, way too long, far beyond their physiological and psychological endurance," he explained. "There is something about power that causes people not to want to surrender it. Power becomes an addiction. I didn't want to end up like that. I think I could have gotten reelected, but why try to go on and on and on if your juices tell you it's time to try something new?" Yet he said his retirement did not mean he would quit loving politics. "My God, you can't devote your whole life—eighteen years in the Senate, thirty years of active politics, and then all my growing and formative years of wanting to get into politics—you can't dismiss all of that from your bloodstream," he explained.[21]

Two years after his retirement, Tom Eagleton returned to Capitol Hill. He was one of just two senators—one Democrat and one Republican—invited to deliver a commemorative address in the original Senate chamber on the occasion of the legislature's bicentennial. It was a tremendous honor. In his speech, Eagleton reminded the senators gathered that day, "The government's life force—what makes it work and endure—is our capacity to accommodate differences and to find a way beyond parochial, partisan, and ideological concerns to live together as a free nation." He continued, "We remember the poet Yeats' very gloomy assessment: 'things fly apart; the center will not hold.'" Eagleton said that, excluding the Civil War, the opposite has been true in the case of the United States. "The center has held because of our understanding of the importance of compromise," he explained. "Without some accommodation and compromise, our government cannot function, and we will not be able to preserve the values we hold in common and in trust for future generations."[22]

Eagleton died in 2007, age seventy-seven. The year before his death, when his health had begun to deteriorate, he composed a letter that he wanted distributed to mourners at his funeral. He titled it the "Thomas F. Eagleton Farewell Address." "This is my last audience and, thus, I think I am entitled to the last word," he began. Quoting Lou Gehrig, he continued, "I consider myself the luckiest man on the face of the earth," as he had reminded himself so many times before. He thanked his "wonderful, understanding" wife, and he apologized to his two children for not spending as much time with them as he would have liked, telling Terence and Christy how much he loved them. He recalled his devoted mother—a "saint"—and his father, whom he had idolized. "In the Senate, I tried my best to express and vote my conscience," Eagleton wrote, though he did admit to succumbing to "several 'hold your nose' votes." In 1973, the year following his withdrawal from the presidential ticket, he had handwritten the legislation that ultimately halted America's bombing in Cambodia and thus effectively ended the U.S. involvement in war in Southeast Asia. It became known as the Eagleton Amendment. He deemed it the proudest accomplishment of his career. Another feat Eagleton cherished: "I am proud that, when Senator Muskie ran for president in 1972, he directed me to take over our Environmental Subcommittee and we passed the first major Clean Air and Clear Water Acts." He regretted not having been able to participate in the debates over Robert Bork's Supreme Court nomination and the "horrible, disastrous" Iraq War. "That war will go down in American history as one of our greatest blunders," Eagleton prophesied. "I could and should have done more" in the Senate, he lamented. "I had the energy. I had the desire." He meditated on the greatness of the Catholic Church, and ended with, "So go forth in love and peace—be kind to dogs—and vote Democratic."

He never once mentioned those eighteen days in July 1972, for which he has been most remembered.[23]

A Note on Sources

Throughout this book I call upon private memos, notes, and other in-tracampaign communication; unpublished memoirs, remembrances, and recordings; contemporaneous newspaper articles, magazine stories, and television broadcasts; primary and secondary source books; and personal interviews with many of the living key players. It is worth noting that, in some instances, when transcripts, recordings, or contemporaneous newspaper accounts are unavailable, the dialogue in this book comes from the memories of the participants who lived these conversations. The sources are all indicated in the notes that follow. Where there are discrepancies in recollections of the partici-pants and the documentation, I tended to give greater weight to the contemporaneous written record.

I began my research for this book in August 2009, the summer before my senior year at Amherst College, when this project was still a thesis and I received a grant from the school to visit the Thomas F. Eagleton Papers at the University of Missouri, Columbia. While I had done some preliminary reading on the events of July 1972, the trip fueled my curiosity about Senator Eagleton's eighteen-day vice presidential candidacy and fostered my passion for archival research. A wealth of primary material collected there and at other archives throughout the country forms the spine of this work. I include most of the archival collections that I consulted in the abbreviations list at the head of the endnotes.

When Senator McGovern donated the first portion of his per-sonal papers to Princeton University in 1984, he required research-ers to seek his permission to include any quotations in their work. I am grateful to Senator McGovern for granting me permission to do so freely. The McGovern Papers, at both Princeton and Dakota Wesleyan universities, provide an unvarnished look at Senator Mc-Govern's life and campaign, and they are a testament to the openness he has long professed.

Several sources deserve special mention for helping to shape my understandings of Senator McGovern, Senator Eagleton, and their era:

Robert Sam Anson's excellent authorized and uncensored biography of Senator McGovern, *McGovern: A Biography*, which was published amid the 1972 presidential campaign, helped ground me in the life and times of the South Dakotan well before my encounter with the primary sources. Phone conversations with Mr. Anson were also very instructive. Senator McGovern's own memoir, *Grassroots: The Autobiography of George McGovern*, similarly introduced me to several of the characters and many of the events covered in this book, including Senator McGovern himself and the Eagleton affair, offering me Senator McGovern's perspective all the while.

Senator Eagleton lacked biographical treatment when I began research for this project, and his unpublished memoir, housed in his papers at the University of Missouri, Columbia, was crucial to outlining the arc of his life through 1972 and fundamental to re-creating the events of the eighteen days. It was also critical to my ability to provide Senator Eagleton's perspective as his vice presidential candidacy unfolds in the narrative. James N. Giglio's biography of Senator Eagleton, *Call Me Tom: The Life of Thomas F. Eagleton,* did not appear until August 2011, toward the end of my research, but it provided some new information on Eagleton's early life. Professor Giglio has written about the Eagleton affair with a historian's detachment, and I also consulted his December 2009 article in the *Presidential Studies Quarterly,* which was adapted for the chapter on the vice presidential candidacy in *Call Me Tom.* I typically cite Giglio's book and article only where information was previously uncorroborated.

Theodore H. White's *The Making of the President 1972,* Bruce Miroff's *The Liberals' Moment,* and Rick Perlstein's *Nixonland* all offer excellent overviews of the 1972 presidential campaign and the context of the era. White and Miroff also include journalistic and historical treatment, respectively, of the Eagleton affair. As with Giglio, I cite Miroff and White primarily when I had not corroborated information elsewhere or where their accounts were especially helpful.

In the aftermath of the election, several former McGovern aides wrote personal memoirs of their experiences on the campaign: Dick

Dougherty's *Goodbye, Mr. Christian,* Gary Hart's *Right from the Start,* Gordon Weil's *The Long Shot,* and Kristi Witker's *How to Lose Everything in Politics.* Their insights on the characters in my narrative and accounts of certain events helped me tremendously as I constructed this book. Each of the aides' books includes a review of the Eagleton affair, and their remembrances of certain pivotal conversations helped to enhance my narrative. I cite these books throughout the text because they were written immediately after the campaign. Ted Van Dyk published his memoir, *Heroes, Hacks, and Fools,* in 2007, and this book also came in handy.

After Eagleton's withdrawal from the ticket, several publishing houses expressed interest in a firsthand account of his vice presidential candidacy. Though he toyed with the idea, Eagleton ultimately passed on the project—but not until writing a draft, portions of which he later shared with Teddy White. Throughout the notes I refer to this manuscript, mentioned earlier as Eagleton's unpublished memoir, as Eagleton's "Minibiography" because that is how Eagleton thought of the project. "This book is merely one political chronicle of one political practitioner experiencing but one segment of his life," he wrote in his prologue. "It really isn't an autobiography since autobiographies are written by elderly people in anticipation of death and in dread fear that their words may be lost forever. I am not in fear of imminent death, either physical or political, and, quite frankly, after having written this book, I hope that some of my words are lost forever. . . . What is this then? Perhaps it can best be described as a minibiography of a still not very old man (age forty-three) who literally found himself in the midst of a political crisis."

While I had the full cooperation of the top aides in the McGovern campaign, I could not say the same for all of Eagleton's key staffers. Several resisted participation for reasons that I can understand: resentment that the memory of Senator Eagleton has revolved around these eighteen days, desire to move on, preservation of attorney-client privilege, and uncomfortable experiences with past interviews.

Luckily, in preparation for his minibiography, Eagleton summoned the recollections of several of his aides, and the resulting memos from Doug Bennet, Ed Filippine, and Bob Maynard can be found in the Eagleton Papers. Each informed my understanding of the events of Eagleton's vice presidential candidacy from the perspective of the Eagleton camp. Doug Bennet titled his highly detailed memo "Eighteen Days," and it was especially helpful to me. I also found the transcript of a 1976 interview with Bennet, conducted by Richard A. Harrison and housed at the Douglas J. Bennet Jr. Papers at Wesleyan University, to be very useful.

I am grateful to three key Eagleton aides who did not write accounts in 1972, but who helped me significantly nonetheless. Gene Godley, Ruth Herbst, and Mike Kelley each spent hours meeting with me in person, talking with me by telephone, and/or corresponding with me by e-mail; they shared personal, poignant, and often hilarious memories of a man they deeply admired. Like the other Eagleton friends who spoke with me, these three staffers brought Thomas Eagleton to life. I am thankful for their commitment to helping me faithfully portray the perspective of the Eagleton camp, as well as their effort to impart the humanity of a man they treasure.

I first read Timothy Crouse's *The Boys on the Bus* as a high school senior and was transfixed by his accounts of life on the campaign press bus and "Zoo Plane." Crouse's keen analysis of the media environment informed my encounter with the journalism of the era throughout my research. The strength and depth of the political reportage of the time was as vital to my narrative as were the internal McGovern and Eagleton campaign memos. I relied primarily on the coverage of five newspapers and two magazines, and I cite the work of their journalists and others throughout: *Los Angeles Times, Miami Herald, Newsweek, New York Times, St. Louis Post-Dispatch, Time, Washington Post.* The NBC *Nightly News* broadcasts of July 1972 are all available online, and reviewing this footage provided me another layer of understanding, further immersing me in an era I did not live but have sought to capture. They can be accessed through the Vanderbilt Television News Archives (http://tvnews.vanderbilt .edu/) at subscribing institutions, or for free at the NBCUniversal Archives (http://www.nbcuniversalarchives.com/).

When Senator Eagleton returned to St. Louis after retiring from the Senate, he co-taught, with Professor Joel K. Goldstein, a seminar on The Presidency and the Constitution at the St. Louis University School of Law. Professor Goldstein also happens to be a leading expert on the American vice presidency, an interest he developed while working on his senior thesis at Princeton. His first book, *The Modern American Vice Presidency,* offers a phenomenal overview of the office, and Professor Goldstein also graciously sent me a copy of the special issue of the *St. Louis University Law Journal* that he helped coordinate shortly after Senator Eagleton's death in celebration of his life. It proved extraordinarily useful. My conversations with Professor Goldstein similarly helped to contextualize the vice presidency and the vice presidential nominating process.

I also interviewed several leading psychiatrists, a few of whom have worked at Barnes Hospital in St. Louis. These conversations improved my understanding of electroshock—its place in history and ongoing relevance—as well as the various conceptions of depression. The names of these doctors are listed among those of my other interviewees.

Notes

Author Interviewees (2011)

Robert Sam Anson, Ned Barry, Tom Bernstein, Robert S. Boyd, Peter Breggin, John Britton, Charles Conway, David Cooper, Phil DeGozzaldi, Sam DeSimone, Nancy Downs, Dorothy Dubuque, Mark Feldstein, Max Fink, Andrea Gibbs, Gene Godley, Lucianne Goldberg, Joel Goldstein, Gary Hart, Ruth V. Herbst, John Holum, Marc Howard, Clark Hoyt, Brooks Jackson, Marcia Johnston, Michael J. Kelley, Charles Kellner, Jonathan Z. Larsen, Dale Ledbetter, Carl Leubsdorf, Sarah Lisanby, Frank Mankiewicz, George S. McGovern, Bob McNeely, Burton Pines, Matthew Rudorfer, Harold Sackeim, Richard G. Stearns, Steve Tuber, Wilson Utter, Gordon Weil, Richard Weiner, Gregory Wierzynski, Jules Witcover, Kristi Witker, Scott O. Wright, Phil Zeidman.

Abbreviations

AP	Associated Press
DJBP	Douglas J. Bennet Jr. Papers, Special Collections and Archives, Olin Library, Wesleyan University, Middletown, CT
ESMOH	Edmund S. Muskie Oral History Collection, Edward S. Muskie Archives and Special Collections Library, Bates College, Lewiston, ME, accessed online at http://abacus.bates.edu/muskie-archives/EADFindingAids/MOH.html
FFMP	Frank F. Mankiewicz Papers, John F. Kennedy Presidential Library and Museum, Boston
GLWP	Gordon L. Weil Papers, George J. Mitchell Department of Special Collections and Archives, Hawthorne-Longfellow Library, Bowdoin College, Brunswick, ME
GSMDWUP	George S. McGovern Papers, McGovern Library/DWU Archives, Dakota Wesleyan University, Mitchell, SD
GSMPUP	George S. McGovern Papers, Seeley G. Mudd Manuscript Library, Princeton University
HRHP	H. R. Haldeman Papers, Nixon Presidential Library and Museum, Yorba Linda, CA
HSTOH	Harry S. Truman Library and Museum, Oral History Interviews, Independence, MO, accessed online at http://www.trumanlibrary.org/oralhist/oral_his.htm
LAT	*Los Angeles Times*
MH	*Miami Herald*

NEOBT   Nixon Executive Office Building Tapes, accessed via Nixon Presi-
         dential Library and Museum CDs and website, http://nixon
         .archives.gov/forresearchers/find/tapes/index.php, and Nixon
         Tapes.org, http://nixontapes.org/chron4e.html
NPLM   Richard Nixon Papers, Nixon Presidential Library and Museum,
         Yorba Linda, CA
NWHOOT   Nixon White House Oval Office Tapes, accessed via Nixon Presi-
         dential Library and Museum CDs and website
NWHTT   Nixon White House Telephone Tapes, accessed via Nixon Presiden-
         tial Library and Museum website and NixonTapes.org, http://
         nixontapes.org/chron4a.html
NYT   *New York Times*
PMOH   Politics in Missouri Oral History Project, University of Missouri/
         The State Historical Society of Missouri, Columbia, accessed on-
         line at http://shs.umsystem.edu/manuscripts/invent/3929trans
         .html
RSSP   Robert Sargent Shriver Papers, John F. Kennedy Presidential Library
         and Museum, Boston
SES   Senator Eagleton Symposium, ed. R. Taylor Matthews III, special is-
         sue, *St. Louis University Law Journal* 54, no. 1 (2007)
SLPD   *St. Louis Post-Dispatch*
TFEP   Thomas F. Eagleton Papers, Western Historical Manuscript Collec-
         tion—Columbia, University of Missouri/The State Historical
         Society of Missouri, Columbia
THWP   Theodore H. White Papers, John F. Kennedy Presidential Library and
         Museum, Boston
UPI   United Press International
WP   *Washington Post*

The Conundrum

1. Christopher Lydon, "Missouri's Contribution to the Ticket," *NYT,* July 14,
   1972; John Kifner, "The Rise and Fall of Tom Eagleton," *NYT,* August 1, 1972;
   Mary Russell, "Eagleton Adds Witty, Low-Key Style to Slate," *WP,* July 14,
   1972; Robert S. Boyd, "Once the 'Forgotten Man' of Missouri, Eagleton Is
   McGovern's Political Twin," *MH,* July 14, 1972; Ruth V. Herbst, interview
   by the author.
2. Thomas Eagleton and George McGovern as remembered in Thomas Eagleton, "Minibiography," manuscript, chapter 9, pp. 1–5, collection 5736, box
   22, TFEP.
3. Adam Clymer, "Thomas F. Eagleton, 77, a Running Mate for 18 Days, Dies,"
   NYT, March 5, 2007.

The Candidate

1. Robert Sam Anson, *McGovern: A Biography* (New York: Holt, Rinehart and Winston, 1972), 177.
2. Robert Sam Anson, "Just Plain George," *Harper's*, November 1972, 84.
3. George McGovern, *Grassroots: The Autobiography of George McGovern* (New York: Random House, 1977), 4, 6, 13; Christopher Lydon, "Mild-Spoken Nominee with a Strong Will to Fight," *NYT*, July 13, 1972; Anson, *McGovern*, 16.
4. Mildred McGovern Brady quoted in Christopher Lydon, "McGovern's Sisters Recall Boyhood Hopes," *NYT*, October 8, 1972.
5. McGovern, *Grassroots*, 10–13; Anson, *McGovern*, 29, 30, 31, including McGovern quotation, 31.
6. Molly Sinclair, "Wife of Front-Runner Is Tireless, Smooth, Rarely Ruffled," *MH*, July 9, 1972; Anson, *McGovern*, 31–34; McGovern, *Grassroots*, 17, 19, 21–22. See Eleanor McGovern with Mary Finch Hoyt, *Uphill: A Personal Story* (Boston: Houghton Mifflin, 1974), for additional information on Eleanor's background and youth, including the loss of her mother when Eleanor was only eleven.
7. McGovern, *Grassroots*, 19–20, 22–23; Stephen E. Ambrose, *The Wild Blue: The Men and Boys Who Flew the B-24s over Germany 1944–45* (New York: Touchstone, 2002), 42, 43, 57; McGovern to Bob Pennington, letter, 2 August 1943, GSMDWUP, quoted in Ambrose, *Wild Blue*, 65–66.
8. McGovern, *Grassroots*, 23–30; Anson, *McGovern*, 38–39, 42, 45, 281; Ambrose, *Wild Blue*, 21; Laura Hillenbrand, *Unbroken: A World War II Story of Survival, Resilience, and Redemption* (New York: Random House, 2010), 59–60.
9. Anson, *McGovern*, 52–53; McGovern, *Grassroots*, 29–32; McGovern, "From Cave to Cave," 1946 oration, box 5A, "E Miscellaneous Correspondence" folder, GSMDWUP.
10. Anson, "Just Plain George," 79; McGovern quoted in Christopher Lydon, "The Great Coalfield War," *NYT Book Review*, July 9, 1972, 4, 34; Richard W. Leopold, "Viewpoint: George McGovern at NU," *Daily Northwestern*, October 13, 1972; McGovern, *Grassroots*, 38–39, 48–49.
11. Exchange with professor quoted in Anson, "Just Plain George," 79; Anson, *McGovern*, 20; Joseph McGovern to George McGovern, letter, ibid., 49–50; McGovern quoted ibid., 52.
12. Eleanor McGovern quoted in Lydon, "Mild-Spoken Nominee"; Anson, *McGovern*, 66–67, 70–71, including McGovern quotations, 66, 70–71; McGovern, *Grassroots*, 49–51, 53.
13. Anson, *McGovern*, 69, 74–77, 79, 84; McGovern, *Grassroots*, 57–58, 63–70; Spencer Rich, "How Fellow Senators Rate George McGovern," *MH*, July 31, 1972; Saul Friedman, "McGovern's Men," *MH*, July 9, 1972; Kristi Witker, *How to Lose Everything in Politics* (Chicago: Academy Chicago, 1988), 65; Eleanor McGovern, *Uphill*, 89.

14. Anson, *McGovern*, 94–98; McGovern, *Grassroots*, 79–83; Eleanor McGovern, *Uphill*, 102–3.

15. Anson, *McGovern*, 100–105; McGovern, *Grassroots*, 83–84; Eleanor McGovern, *Uphill*, 104–5.

16. McGovern, *Grassroots*, 87–88; Anson, *McGovern*, 112, 116, including McGovern quotation, 116; Eleanor McGovern, *Uphill*, 107.

17. Anson, *McGovern*, 119, 121–22, 125, including Cunningham quotation, 125; McGovern, *Grassroots*, 89–90.

18. Anson, *McGovern*, xi; Sinclair, "Wife of Front-Runner"; Eleanor McGovern, *Uphill*, 109–10.

19. Anson, *McGovern*, 74, 126, including quotation from former aide, 87; "South Dakota," *New Yorker*, August 19, 1972, 21; Rich, "How Fellow Senators Rate McGovern"; John Holum, interview by the author.

20. McGovern quoted in Anson, *McGovern*, 143, 150, 165; "South Dakota," 21; Rich, "How Fellow Senators Rate McGovern."

21. William Greider, "Candidate McGovern: Quite Self-Contained," *WP*, July 14, 1972; Norman Mailer, "St. George and the Godfather," in *Some Honorable Men: Political Conventions, 1960–1972* (Boston: Little, Brown, 1976), 324; Anson, "Just Plain George," 80; Anson, *McGovern*, 282–83.

22. Greider, "Candidate McGovern"; Anson, "Just Plain George," 84.

23. Greider, "Candidate McGovern"; Anson, "Just Plain George," 84; Anson, *McGovern*, 2, 5, 7–9, including Allard Lowenstein quotation, 5; McGovern, *Grassroots*, 109–11.

   For more information on New Politics and its various definitions, see Lewis Chester, Godfrey Hodgson, and Bruce Page, *An American Melodrama: The Presidential Campaign of 1968* (New York: Viking, 1969), 375–401, including Jack Newfield's "campus, ghetto, and suburb" alliance description, 376; Tom Wicker, "In The Nation: The New Politics," *NYT*, March 21, 1968; Theodore H. White, *The Making of the President 1972* (New York: Atheneum, 1973; New York: Harper Perennial Political Classics, 2010), 38–47; Irving Kristol, "The Old Politics, the New Politics, The New, New Politics," *NYT Sunday Magazine*, November 24, 1968, 49ff.; Herbert Mitgang, "The New Politics, the Old Casualties," *NYT*, January 6, 1969; Rick Perlstein, *Nixonland: The Rise of a President and the Fracturing of America* (New York: Scribner, 2008), 507. Citations for *Making of the President 1972* are to the Harper Perennial edition.

24. Anson, *McGovern*, 8–9, including McGovern quotation, 9; McGovern, *Grassroots*, 117.

25. Anson, *McGovern*, 192–97, including McGovern quotation, 197; McGovern, *Grassroots*, 117–18, 120; Friedman, "McGovern's Men"; Eleanor McGovern, *Uphill*, 29, 120–23.

26. McGovern quoted, respectively, in Anson, *McGovern*, 199; "McGovern," *New Yorker*, August 24, 1968, 24. McGovern, *Grassroots*, 121; Eleanor McGovern, *Uphill*, 92, 131.

27. Theodore White quoted in Anson, *McGovern*, 9–10.
28. Anson, *McGovern*, 247; Minority Report of the Rules Committee adopted by the Democratic National Convention on August 27, 1968, quoted in *Cong. Rec.*, 92nd Cong., 1st Sess., September 22, 1971, 32918.
29. White, *Making of the President 1972*, 22–23; McGovern, *Grassroots*, 136–37; Lawrence F. O'Brien, *No Final Victories: A Life in Politics—from John F. Kennedy to Watergate* (New York: Ballantine, 1974), 293–94.
30. McGovern, *Grassroots*, 137; McGovern quoted in Anson, *McGovern*, 248; *Cong. Rec.*, 92nd Cong., 1st Sess., September 22, 1971, 32918.
31. McGovern, *Grassroots*, 141; *Cong. Rec.*, 92nd Cong., 1st Sess., September 22, 1971, 32915, 32921; O'Brien, *No Final Victories*, 294–96; White, *Making of the President 1972*, 24–32.
32. White, *Making of the President 1972*, 28–32; 39, 165–66.
33. For the facts of Chappaquiddick incident, see Perlstein, *Nixonland*, 397–400.
34. Kennedy staffer and McGovern quoted in Anson, *McGovern*, 258–59.
35. Ribicoff quoted in Anson, *McGovern*, 259; McGovern quoted in Anson, *McGovern*, 262, 278–79.

The Campaign

1. Loye Miller Jr., "McGovern Started First, Fell Behind; He's the One They Have to Catch," *MH*, July 9, 1972; Gary Warren Hart, *Right from the Start: A Chronicle of the McGovern Campaign* (New York: Quadrangle/ New York Times Book, 1973), 11–12; Gary Hart, interview by the author.
2. David Remnick, "Gary Hart in Exile," *New Yorker*, April 19, 1993, 41–42; Kurt Andersen, "The Man Who Wears No Label," *Time*, March 12, 1984; Hart, *Right from the Start*, 3, 11–12; Friedman, "McGovern's Men," July 9, 1972; Myra MacPherson, "The Man Behind the Man Out Front," *WP*, April 30, 1972; Anson, *McGovern*, 263; Gary Hart, interview by the author.
3. McGovern quoted in Hart, *Right from the Start*, 13.
4. Dartmouth honorary degree citation quoted in Miller, "McGovern Started First."
5. McGovern quoted ibid.
6. White, *Making of the President 1972*, 25, 42; Friedman, "McGovern's Men"; Anson, *McGovern*, xi, 261; Rick Stearns, interview by the author; Hart, *Right from the Start*, 16.
7. For the best account of the Cedar Point Farm meeting, see Teddy White's notes, "Staff Discussion with Senator George McGovern; Cedar Point Farm, St. Michaels, Maryland," 25 July 1969 [*sic*; actual date of meeting was July 25, 1970, as reported in *Making of the President 1972* and elsewhere], box 38r, "McGovern (1 of 7)" folder, THWP; White, *Making of the President 1972*, 41–44; Anson, *McGovern*, 278–79; Hart, *Right from the Start*, 16–18; Charles Guggenheim to McGovern, memorandum, August 1969, quoted in Anson,

McGovern, 266; "Guidelines to 1972 Campaign," notes, circa 1970, box 691, "1970 notes" folder, GSMPUP; "Priorities," notes, circa 1970, box 691, "1970 notes" folder, GSMPUP; "Memo to File, Re: Senator McGovern's 'Debriefing' Comments Following Return from 12-day Speaking Schedule," October 27, 1970, memorandum, box 691, "1970 notes" folder, GSMPUP; McGovern to Pennington, 30 May 1945, quoted in Ambrose, *Wild Blue,* 256. For more information on the escalating media attention on the plight of the "Middle American" at the turn of the decade, see esp. "The Troubled American: A Special Report on the White Majority," *Newsweek,* October 6, 1969; "Man and Woman of the Year: The Middle Americans," *Time,* January 5, 1970; Peter Schrag, "The Forgotten American," *Harper's,* August, 1969.

8. "Guidelines to 1972 Campaign."
9. "Guidelines to 1972 Campaign"; McGovern notes on interior jacket cover of his notebook, circa April 1970, box 691, "1970 notes" folder, GSMPUP; McGovern notes on tri-folded piece of printer paper, circa 1970, box 691, "1970 notes" folder, GSMPUP.
10. McGovern quoted in Anson, *McGovern,* 267, 287; Christopher Lydon, "McGovern Gives Lesson in Patience," *NYT,* December 16, 1971; McGovern quoted in Christopher Lydon, "McGovern Backers Decry One-Issue Image, but Vietnam Remains as the Key Factor in His Campaign," *NYT,* February 22, 1972; Witker, *How to Lose,* 91.
11. Patrick Anderson, "The Taste of Success," *NYT Sunday Magazine,* May 14, 1972, 14–15; Lydon, "McGovern Gives Lesson in Patience"; Leo Tolstoy, *War and Peace,* as quoted in Hart, *Right from the Start,* 103; Hart quoted in Lydon, "McGovern Gives Lesson in Patience."
12. Edmund Muskie quoted in Perlstein, *Nixonland,* 536–37; Miller, "McGovern Started First."
13. Miller, "McGovern Started First"; Frank Mankiewicz and Tom Braden, "McGovern: Lurking in the Shadows," *WP,* January 19, 1971.
14. McGovern quoted in William Montalbano and Don Bonning, "Teamwork Spelled Victory for McGovern," *MH,* July 13, 1972; John Holum, Marcia Johnston, Frank Mankiewicz, Gordon Weil, and Phil Zeidman, interviews by the author.
15. Mankiewicz quoted in Anson, *McGovern,* 198–99; Holly Mankiewicz quoted in Myra MacPherson, "For the Love of Politics," *WP,* July 27, 1972; Margie Bonnett, "Frank Mankiewicz: A Rebel with Causes—One Lost, One Shattered by an Assassin—Rides to the Rescue of America's Endangered Public Radio Network," *People,* May 24, 1982; "Front and Center for George McGovern," *Time,* May 8, 1972; Hart, *Right from the Start,* 78; Richard Meryman, "The Infighting Was 'Ferocious,'" *Life,* July 21, 1972, 30.
16. Mankiewicz quoted ("used car") in William A. McWhirter, "Inside the Winning Team," *Life,* June 2, 1972, 38–42; Richard Dougherty, *Goodbye, Mr. Christian: A Personal Account of McGovern's Rise and Fall* (Garden City, NY:

Doubleday, 1973), 37; Mankiewicz quoted ("All my fantasies") in MacPherson, "For the Love of Politics."

17. Mankiewicz to McGovern, memorandum, October 25, 1971, box 20, "Mankiewicz, Memos to McGovern" folder, FFMP; Mankiewicz to McGovern, "Re: Some Pending Decisions, and Some Good Advice," memorandum, circa 1971, box 20, "Mankiewicz, Memos to McGovern" folder, FFMP.

18. Hart, *Right from the Start,* 78–80; Dougherty, *Goodbye, Mr. Christian,* 40, 121–23, 141–48; Witker, *How to Lose,* 37, 48, 56–57, 73, 83–84, 100–102; Anson, *McGovern,* 260; White, *Making of the President 1972,* 104; Gary Hart, John Holum, Marcia Johnston, Frank Mankiewicz, Rick Stearns, Gordon Weil, and Kirsti Witker, interviews by the author.

19. Christopher Lydon, "McGovern: Maybe It's Serious after All," *NYT,* April 30, 1972; Anderson, "Taste of Success," 78; "Advice from Harvard," *Time,* May 1, 1972; Patrick H. Caddell to McGovern, memorandum, December 29, 1971, box 38s, "McGovern (7 of 7)" folder, THWP; Miller, "McGovern Started First."

20. Caddell to McGovern, December 29, 1971.

21. Martin Plissner to Distribution List, memorandum, January 3, 1972, box 380, "CBS News: Campaign Reps/Plissner" folder, THWP; Caddell to McGovern, December 29, 1971; R. W. Apple Jr., "Muskie Campaign Still Lacks Spark," *NYT,* November 21, 1971.

22. Hart, *Right from the Start,* 115–16, 121; Miller, "McGovern Started First"; Rick Stearns, interview by author; Hart quoted in Ernest R. May and Janet Fraser, eds., *Campaign '72: The Managers Speak* (Cambridge: Harvard University Press, 1973), 41. Montalbano and Bonning, "Teamwork Spelled Victory for McGovern"; Bill Kovach, "M'Govern Hailed in New Hampshire; Speaks to Workers at Shore Factory that Gave Spark to Primary Campaign," *NYT,* August 11, 1972.

23. Perlstein, *Nixonland,* 623; Timothy Crouse, *The Boys on the Bus* (New York: Ballantine, 1974), 33–39, 103, 321; Garry Wills, "Death of a Salesman," *New York Review of Books,* October 4, 1973; Jeff Gralnick to Ted Van Dyk, Steve Robbins, and Frank Mankiewicz, "Re: Some thoughts on television studio arrangements that advance men should keep in mind when arranging live or taped talk show appearances," memorandum, circa December 1971, box 28, "Jeff Gralnick" folder, FFMP; James David Barber, *The Presidential Character: Predicting Performance in the White House* (Englewood Cliffs, NJ: Prentice Hall, 1972), 1; Kathleen Hall Jamieson and Paul Waldman, *The Press Effect: Politicians, Journalists, and the Stories That Shape the Political World* (New York: Oxford University Press, 2003), 25–26. Barber's book provided academic substantiation to the value of attending to the personal along with the political in campaign reportage. Barber emphasized that a candidate's "individual character, worldview, and political style," as demonstrated through his life, career, and campaign, presage how he would perform as president.

24. Jules Witcover, *The Making of an Ink-Stained Wretch: Half a Century Pounding the Political Beat* (Baltimore: Johns Hopkins University Press, 2005), 148; Perlstein, *Nixonland*, 628–29; Crouse, *Boys on the Bus*, 54–56, 63–66; Jamieson and Waldman, *Press Effect*, 36–37; Hart, *Right from the Start*, 13; Witker, *How to Lose*, 12–14; "The Press: King of the Epithet," *Time*, January 31, 1972; "Publishers: The Eagle and The Chickens," *Time*, February 23, 1968; Muskie letter from Florida quoted in Carl Bernstein and Bob Woodward, *All the President's Men* (1974; rpt., New York: Pocket Books, 2006), 129; David Broder, "Muskie Denounces Publisher," *WP*, February 27, 1972; Bill Kovach, "Muskie Attack on Paper; Many See Senator Hurt," *NYT*, February 29, 1972; William Loeb editorial in Aaron Latham, "Can the Pistol-Packing Publisher Win It for the Cowboy Star?" *New York*, February 2, 1976; Joel K. Goldstein, "Remembering David S. Broder and Edmund Muskie," March 17, 2011, kent.bates.edu/librarynews/node/401, accessed April 28, 2011. For video of Muskie's speech, see "Ed Muskie cries before New Hampshire primary in 1972 (or did he?)" YouTube, http://www.youtube.com/watch?v=LiLL8ZAXGys, accessed May 30, 2011.

25. Bernstein and Woodward, *All the President's Men*, 129; Perlstein, *Nixonland*, 629–31; Seymour M. Hersh, "Teams of Agents; Drive Viewed as Way to Help McGovern Get Nomination; Aid for McGovern Held Aim of Wide Campaign Inquiry by Fraud Unit; Letter to Muskie Cited; Agents Organized; Two Groups Merged," *NYT*, May 3, 1973.

26. Miller, "McGovern Started First"; McGovern staff's perception of Muskie's support—or lack thereof—quoted in Christopher Lydon, "Elated McGovern Looks Ahead," *NYT*, March 9, 1972; Christopher Lydon, "McGovern's Route to the Top," *NYT*, June 11, 1972.

27. Crouse, *Boys on the Bus*, 69; Christopher Lydon, "McGovern Gibes at 'Park Ave. Populism,'" *NYT*, February 26, 1972; Lydon, "Mild-Spoken Nominee"; "Front and Center for George McGovern," *Time*, May 8, 1972.

28. "Front and Center"; the *Nation* quoted in Anson, *McGovern*, 268; McGovern, Harris poll, and Mankiewicz quoted in Anderson, "Taste of Success," 73–74.

29. "The Confrontation of the Two Americas," *Time*, October 2, 1972; McGovern quoted, respectivelty, in Greider, "Candidate McGovern"; Anson, *McGovern*, 286; Hugh Sidey's analysis quoted in "Introducing . . . the McGovern Machine," *Time*, July 24, 1972.

30. Rowland Evans and Robert Novak quoted in Crouse, *Boys on the Bus*, 124; Robert Novak, *The Prince of Darkness: 50 Years Reporting in Washington* (New York: Three Rivers, 2008), 226.

31. Richard Reeves quoted in Crouse, *Boys on the Bus*, 70–71; Richard Reeves, "The City Politic: The Education of George McGovern," *New York*, June 6, 1972, 8; Lydon, "McGovern: Maybe It's Serious after All"; William V. Shannon, "The Legends of George McGovern," *NYT Sunday Magazine*, July 2, 1972, 24.

32. May and Fraser, *Campaign '72*, 289; Anderson, "Taste of Success," 76; Carl Leubsdorf, interview by the author.
33. McGovern quoted in Anderson, "Taste of Success," 13.

The Wrench

1. Warren Weaver Jr., "4 Challenge McGovern's Right to All 271 California Delegates," *NYT*, June 10, 1972; Mankiewicz quoted in Victor S. Navasky, "A Funny Thing Happened on the Way to the Coronation," *NYT Sunday Magazine*, July 23, 1972, 9; McGovern and Humphrey quoted in Christopher Lydon, "Humphrey Resolved to Fight to the Finish Despite Risks of Widening Party Rifts," *NYT*, July 7, 1972; Steven V. Roberts, "Pressures and Fears Unite 'Stop McGovern' Coalition," *NYT*, July 10, 1972; Willie Brown, John Burton, Delores Huerta, John Tunney, and Alan Cranston, "Prepared for the Delegates to the Democratic National Convention," pamphlet, undated, box 38q, "Democratic Nat'l Conv. (1 of 4)" folder, THWP; Humphrey in "Democrats: A Setback for McGovern," *Time*, July 10, 1972; McGovern interview by the author.
2. McGovern, *Grassroots*, 150; "Mandate for Reform, Guideline B-6, p. 44" in "Prepared for the Delegates"; "Mandate for Reform" in *Cong. Rec.*, 92nd Cong., 1st Sess., 22 September 1971, 22916; Editorial, "Feuding Democrats," *NYT*, July 3, 1972.
3. R. W. Apple Jr., "Muskie Refuses to Back M'Govern; Remains In Race," *NYT*, June 10, 1972; McGovern, *Grassroots*, 195; Muskie quoted in Hart, *Right from the Start*, 201.
4. Weaver, "4 Challenge"; R. W. Apple Jr., "3 Obstacles Still in Path of McGovern Nomination," *NYT*, June 25, 1972; Roberts, "Pressures and Fears"; AP, "California Primary Upheld in Challenge to McGovern," *NYT*, June 23, 1972; "Democrats: A Setback for McGovern," *Time*, July 10, 1972; Tom Wicker, "Fair Play in Miami," *NYT*, July 9, 1972; James M. Naughton, "McGovern: The Air Went Out of the Whoopee Cushions," *NYT*, July 9, 1972; McGovern, "Confidential Memorandum on the Eagleton Incident for the Information Only of Key Campaign Aides," handwritten, circa 1973, box 4, "Eagleton" folder, GSMDWUP; McGovern, "My Experience with the Eagleton Matter," short manuscript, 9 March 1976, box 4, "Eagleton" folder, GSMDWUP.
5. Humphrey quoted in Christopher Lydon, "Humphrey Says His Staying in Race Could Help Victor Gain Party Unity," *NYT*, June 23, 1972; Mailer, "St. George and the Godfather," in *Some Honorable Men*, 18; James Reston, "McGovern's Threat," *NYT*, July 9, 1972; Hart, *Right from the Start*, 210. McGovern quoted in, respectively, Richard Meryman, "George McGovern Talks Intimately about Himself," *Life*, July 7, 1972, 31; Mailer, "St. George and the Godfather," 23–24.
6. Thomas W. Ottenad, "Watershed Week for Democrats," *SLPD*, July 9, 1972;

McGovern in Saul Friedman, "McGovern's Willing to Swap Daley Seats for California's 151," *MH*, July 10, 1972.

7. Eagleton, "Minibiography," chapter 1, pp. 1, 5, and chapter 2, p. 1; Fred W. Lindecke, "Eagleton Breaks with Hearnes over McGovern," *SLPD*, July 10, 1972; Edward Filippine to Eagleton, memorandum, August 16, 1972, collection 5736, box 22, TFEP p. 4–9; Fred W. Lindecke, "Hearnes's Holding Action," *SLPD*, July 9, 1972; Gene Godley, interview by the author; William V. Shannon, "Who for No. 2?" *NYT*, July 7, 1972; R. W. Apple Jr., "Options for a Game Anyone Can Play," *NYT*, July 2, 1972; James M. Naughton, "Beyond the Grass Roots a Bitter-Sweet Dilemma," *NYT*, June 25, 1972; Max Frankel, "Impassioned Plea; Dakotan Urges Party to Lead the Nation in Healing Itself," *NYT*, July 14, 1972; Loye Miller Jr., "'Power Brokers' Still Play a Tough Game," *MH*, July 9, 1972.

8. Muskie, as remembered by Eagleton in "Minibiography," chapter 2, pp. 1–2.

9. Janet Chusmir, "'Simple' Tastes Run to High Style," *MH*, July 9, 1972; Meryman, "Infighting Was 'Ferocious,'" 30; AP, "Famous? Dishes Won't Wait," *MH*, July 10, 1972; UPI, "Mrs. McGovern Shows Her 'Dishwater Hands,'" *NYT*, July 10, 1972; Hart, *Right from the Start*, 211–12, 214; Robert S. Boyd, "Candidates Control the Action from Afar," *MH*, July 11, 1972; Eleanor McGovern, *Uphill*, 178–79; Marcia Johnston, interview by the author.

10. Hart, *Right from the Start*, 211–12, 214; Boyd, "Candidates Control the Action"; R. W. Apple Jr., "It Was a Coup with Uncertain Prospects," *NYT*, July 16, 1972. Special thanks to my college art history professor Carol Clark for her help analyzing the architecture of the Miami Beach Convention Hall.

11. Hart, *Right from the Start*, 214–15; Boyd, "Candidates Control the Action"; Stearns quoted in Hunter S. Thompson, *Fear and Loathing on the Campaign Trail '72* (New York: Popular Library, 1973), 298–99; Apple, "3 Obstacles."

12. Loye Miller Jr., "'Ole Larry Will Pull It All Together' Again," *MH*, July 9, 1972; O'Brien, *No Final Victories*, 5–6, 306; Johnston, interview by the author.

13. Miller, "'Ole Larry'"; Robert B. Semple Jr., "How 3 Aides Decided Key Rule Issue," *NYT*, July 10, 1972; O'Brien, *No Final Victories*, 306, 313–16. DNC counsel Joseph A. Califano Jr. and Rules Committee chairman Rep. James G. O'Hara of Michigan advised O'Brien on the decision; Max Frankel, "Party Rulings Enhance M'Govern's Candidacy; Convention Opens Today," *NYT*, July 10, 1972; Navasky, "Funny Thing Happened," 9; Max Frankel, "Fight in Prospect: Front-Runner Is about 50 Votes Short of Floor Control," *NYT*, July 9, 1972; Stearns quoted in Thompson, *Fear and Loathing*, 291. For a great syponsis of the considerations, see "A Guide to Rules Dispute," *NYT*, July 9, 1972. O'Brien had to determine which type of majority should rule because Rule 6-E of the convention guidelines did not stipulate.

14. Hart, *Right from the Start*, 221; Apple, "Coup with Uncertain Prospects"; Thompson, *Fear and Loathing*, 292–95; Warren Weaver Jr., "23 Challenges on Seating Face Convention Tonight," *NYT*, July 10, 1972; White, *Making of the*

President 1972, 172–73; Navasky, "Funny Thing Happened," 36. Reports on the number of women on the original thirty-two-member South Carolina delegation vary, from seven to nine.

15. R. W. Apple Jr., "Convention Notes: Irate Leader of Ohio Bloc Says It's His 'Last Go at This,'" *NYT*, July 12, 1972; Hart, *Right from the Start*, 220–24; Frankel, "Party Rulings Enhance M'Govern's Candidacy"; Thompson, *Fear and Loathing*, 292–94; Warren Weaver Jr., "South Carolina Vote Balks Women's Bid," *NYT*, July 11, 1972; Witker, *How to Lose*, 111, 120–21, 125.

16. Hart, as he remembered his words in Hart, *Right from the Start*, 223.

The Upstart

1. McGovern and Eagleton conversation, as remembered in Eagleton, "Minibiography," chapter 2, pp. 1–2.

2. Ibid., 2.

3. David S. Broder, "Sen. Eagleton: His Stand on Issues, Politics and Duties," *WP*, July 14, 1972; Lindecke, "Eagleton Breaks with Hearnes"; R. W. Apple Jr., "Convention Notes: Inside and Outside," *NYT*, July 11, 1972.

4. Eagleton, "Minibiography," chapter 1, pp. 1–3; James N. Giglio, *Call Me Tom* (Columbia: University of Missouri Press, 2011), 4, 6–7, 10, 18–19; Clark Hoyt, "Eagleton: A Driven Man," *MH*, July 27, 1972; James P. Aylward, interview by James R. Fuchs, June 19, 1968, Second Oral History Interview with Aylward, transcript, HSTOH; Dorothy Dubuque, interview by the author.

5. Eagleton, "Minibiography," chapter 1, p. 4; Hoyt, "Eagleton: A Driven Man"; John Coyne, "Eagleton: He Has Risen from the Ashes of '72. But Where Can He Fly?" *St. Louis*, May 1978, 76; Kottmeyer quoted in Ronald D. Willnow, "The New Politics Is Nothing New to Eagleton," *SLPD*, July 14, 1972; Stephan Darst, "Eagleton's Wake," *Harper's*, December 1972, 76; Boyd, "Once the 'Forgotten Man'"; Thomas F. Eagleton, interview by Will Sarvis, November 3, 1998, transcript, PMOH; "Thomas F. Eagleton Farewell Address" in *SES*, 32.

6. "E. Dwight Salmon, 98, a Professor at Amherst," *NYT*, November 4, 1993; Dwight Salmon quoted in Frank Greve, "Amherst Remembers Eagleton: Quick-Witted, Serious, Lively," *Holyoke* [MA] *Transcript-Telegram*, July 14, 1972; Ned Barry, Phil DeGozzaldi, Andrea Gibbs, and Wilson Utter, interviews by the author.

7. Willnow, "New Politics"; Giglio, *Call Me Tom*, 16–17; Herbst and Dubuque, interviews by the author; Eagleton quoted in Ronald D. Willnow, "Liberal Gets No. 2 Spot," *SLPD*, July 16, 1972; Kifner, "Rise and Fall," 24; Coyne, "Eagleton," 76.

8. Eagleton, "Minibiography," chapter 1, p. 6; Gene Godley, interview by the author; William Buckley, "Tribute to Senator Tom Eagleton," *SES*, 18; Hoyt, "Eagleton: A Driven Man"; Darst, "Eagleton's Wake," 76–78; Coyne, "Eagleton," 76; Giglio, *Call Me Tom*, 17.

9. Eagleton, "Minibiography," chapter 1, p. 6; Eagleton aide quoted in Coyne, "Eagleton," 76.

10. Tom Bartimus, "Tom Was Beau in St. Louis, Mo.," *Springfield* [MO] *Union,* August 18, 1978; Barbara Eagleton with Winzola McLendon, "Mrs. Eagleton's Own Story: A Wife's View of the Year's Most Dramatic Personal Crisis," *Ladies' Home Journal,* October 1972, 154; Patricia Rice, "Politician's Life Style Nothing New to Mrs. Eagleton," *SLPD,* July 16, 1972.

11. Rice, "Politician's Life Style"; Hoyt, "Eagleton: A Driven Man"; Eagleton, "Minibiography," chapter 2, p. 1.

12. Eagleton, "Minibiography," chapter 2, p. 2; Darst, "Eagleton's Wake," 77; Mark Eagleton Sr. as remembered by Mark Eagleton Jr. quoted in Willnow, "New Politics"; Eagleton, interview by Sarvis; Mark Abels, "Eulogy for Senator Thomas F. Eagleton," *SES,* 4; Giglio, *Call Me Tom,* 41; family friend quoted in Kifner, "Rise and Fall"; Coyne, "Eagleton," 76; Willnow, "New Politics."

13. Eagleton, "Minibiography," chapter 2, p. 3; Jonathan Z. Larsen to Time Nation, "Re: Eagleton vs. Curtis: The Ying and Yang of Missouri Politics," memorandum, October 24, 1968, private collection of Jonathan Z. Larsen; Editorial, "Mr. Eagleton on Wiretapping," *SLPD,* December 12, 1957; Eagleton, interview by Sarvis; Patricia Sullivan, "Watergate Committee Chief Counsel Samuel Dash Dies," *WP,* May 30, 2004; Eagleton, "On the Threat to Constitutional Rights by Wire Tapping," presented in Congress before the United States Senate Committee on the Judiciary's Subcommittee on Constitutional Rights, May 22, 1958, collection 0674, folder 219, TFEP; "Stronger Wiretap Ban Urged by Prosecutor," *Washington Star,* May 22, 1958; "Limited Wiretaps by F.B.I. Favored," *NYT,* May 23, 1958; Thomas F. Eagleton FBI File, 1072207-000-62-HQ-104623—Section 1 (771625), in the author's possession.

14. Ed Quick, "Tom Eagleton—An Appreciation," *SES,* 51; U.S. Const. amend. IV; Archibald Cox, "In Memorium: Paul A. Freund," *Harvard Law Review* 106, no. 1 (1992): 10; Louis D. Brandeis in *Casey v. United States,* 276 U.S. 413, 425 (1928); Melvin I. Urofsky, "The Conservatism of Mr. Justice Brandeis," *Modern Age* 23 (1979): 46.

15. Q. Tamm to Clyde A. Tolson, memorandum, "National Association of County and Prosecuting Attorneys," March 6, 1958; Eagleton to Hoover, memorandum, March 10, 1958; A. K. Bowles to Mr. Trotter, memorandum, "National Association of County and Prosecuting Attorneys (NACPA) Thomas Eagleton, Circuit Court, St. Louis, Missouri," March 13, 1958; Hoover to Eagleton, letter, March 4, 1958; memorandum to Mr. Trotter, "Re: NACPA; Thomas Eagleton, Circuit Court, St. Louis, Missouri," undated; Thomas F. Eagleton FBI File, 1072207-000-62-HQ-104623—Section 1 (771625), in the possession of author.

16. James J. Murphy, "Eagleton in Missouri: The Record in Local and State Office," *SES,* 40–41; "Nominees and Issues in Four Top Missouri Contests,"

SLPD, November 4, 1960; Larsen to Time Nation, "Re: Eagleton vs. Curtis"; Willnow, "New Politics."

17. Bob Griesedieck to Eagleton, letter, October 13, 1959, c. 0674, f. 106, TFEP; Eagleton to Griesedieck, letter, October 27, 1959, c. 0674, f. 106, TFEP; Eagleton, "On Youth," joke notes, undated, c. 0674, f. 106, TFEP.

18. Willnow, "New Politics"; Marsh Clark, as remembered in Darst, "Eagleton's Wake," 78; Eagleton, interview by Sarvis; Scott O. Wright, interview by the author; Editorial, "Eagleton on School Busses," *SLPD,* August 2, 1960; Quick, "Tom Eagleton—An Appreciation," 53–54; Joe D. Holt, interview by Will Sarvis, January 3, 1997, transcript, PMOH; Flake McHaney, interview by Will Sarvis, October 27, 1998, transcript, PMOH; Murphy, "Eagleton in Missouri," 41.

19. Quick, "Tom Eagleton—An Appreciation," 53; Giglio, *Call Me Tom,* 49; Eagleton, interview by Sarvis; Hal Hunter Jr., interview by Will Sarvis, October 27, 1998, transcript, PMOH; R. Leon Saalwaechter, interview by Will Sarvis, October 12, 1998, transcript, PMOH; Keith Wilson Jr., interview by Niel M. Johnson, March 8, 1989, transcript, HSTOH; "Eagleton on School Busses"; Herbert A. Trask, "Democrat Gets Landslide Vote; Long, Eagleton also Nominated," *SLPD,* August 3, 1960; "Eagleton Calls Hocker Charge of Vote Fraud 'M'Carthyism,'" *SLPD,* November 4, 1960.

20. Eagleton, "Minibiography," chapter 2, p. 5; Hoyt, "Eagleton: A Driven Man"; Barbara Eagleton elsewhere reported that Tom's weight dropped from 180 to 153 pounds, in "Mrs. Eagleton's Own Story," 155; John Britton, interview by the author.

21. Editorial, "Decision of an Urban Electorate," *SLPD,* November 9, 1960; Herbert A. Trask, "Democrats Win Major Races as State Lines Up with Kennedy," *SLPD,* November 9, 1960; Robert A. Dunlap, "Reardon Easy Winner over Rival in Circuit Attorney Race," *SLPD,* November 9, 1960; Murphy, "Eagleton in Missouri," 41.

22. "Notes on Meeting between Senator Thomas F. Eagleton and Jack Anderson, Columnist," unattributed memorandum, August 1, 1972, pp. 3–4, c. 5736, box 22, "'72 Files" folder, TFEP; Jack Anderson with George Clifford, *The Anderson Papers: From the Files of America's Most Famous Investigative Reporter* (New York: Random House, 1973), 158–59; Giglio, *Call Me Tom,* 55; Scott O. Wright and John Britton, interviews by the author.

23. "Eagleton Is in Hospital," *SLPD,* December 17, 1960; "Eagleton Tells of 1960 Illness," *SLPD,* August 4, 1972; Barbara Eagleton, "Mrs. Eagleton's Own Story," 155.

24. Louis J. Rose, "Missouri Friends Return Eagleton's Loyalty," *SLPD,* July 30, 1972; Robert R. Welborn, interview by Will Sarvis, March 24, 1997, transcript, MPOH; Ronald Reed Jr., interview by Will Sarvis, May 15, 1996, transcript, MPOH, Eagleton, interview by Sarvis; Eagleton, "Minibiography," chapter 3, p. 1; Giglio, *Call Me Tom,* 56–57; Kifner, "Rise and Fall."

25. Rose, "Missouri Friends Return Eagleton's Loyalty"; Giglio, *Call Me Tom*, 56; Kifner, "Rise and Fall"; Eagleton, "Minibiography," chapter 3, p. 2; Willnow, "New Politics"; Wright and Britton, interviews by the author.

26. Willnow, "Liberal Gets No. 2 Spot"; Herbst, interview by the author.

27. Murphy, "Eagleton in Missouri," 43; Thomas F. Eagleton with Robert D. Kingsland, "Capital Punishment: ' . . . and May God Have Mercy upon Your Soul,'" *SLPD*, January 20, 1963; Thomas F. Eagleton with Robert D. Kingsland, "Eagleton Advocates Appointing Legislative Interim Committee to Study Capital Punishment," *SLPD*, January 21, 1963.

28. Eagleton to Godley, Murphy, Kelley, Quick, Atwood, Lewis, Stephan, "Re: Right to Life—Speech in St. Louis on October 21st," memorandum, October 11, 1973, box 22, TFEP; Gene Godley, Mike Kelley, and Ruth Herbst, interviews by the author.

29. Eagleton, "Minibiography," chapter 3, p. 3; Murphy, "Eagleton in Missouri," 44; Hoyt, "Eagleton: A Driven Man."

30. Kevin Eagleton in Giglio, *Call Me Tom*, 60; "Eagleton Has Check-Up," *SLPD*, December 28, 1964.

31. Kifner, "Rise and Fall"; Murphy, "Eagleton in Missouri," 44–45; Willnow, "Liberal Gets No. 2 Spot"; "T. F. Eagleton, Democrat, and GOP's T. B. Curtis Compete for U.S. Senate," *SLPD*, November 3, 1968; Herbst, interview by the author.

32. Larsen to Time Nation, "Re: Eagleton vs. Curtis"; Thomas W. Ottenad, "Eagleton Would Take Tests if 3 Others Do," *SLPD*, July 16, 1972; Kifner, "Rise and Fall"; "Eagleton in Hospital," *SLPD*, September 21, 1966; Giglio, *Call Me Tom*, 60.

33. William Lambert, "Strange Help—Hoffa Campaign of the U.S. Senator from Missouri," *Life*, May 26, 1967, 28; Douglas E. Kneeland, "Long of Missouri Faces Vote Contest," *NYT*, September 12, 1967; Editorial, "The Men Who Were Right," *SLPD*, November 3, 1968; Ronald Reed Jr., interview by Sarvis; Giglio, *Call Me Tom*, 63–64; Eagleton, "Minibiography," chapter 3, pp. 6–9; Laurily Keir Epstein, "Tom Eagleton and Matt Reese: One Aspect of the New Politics," c. 5736, box 12, TFEP, p. 2; Wright, interview by the author.

34. Eagleton quoted in "T. F. Eagleton, Democrat, and GOP's T. B. Curtis," and in Willnow, "Liberal Gets No. 2 Spot"; "Peace Possible if Rivals Want It, Eagleton Says," *SLPD*, November 3, 1968.

35. Hoyt, "Eagleton: A Driven Man"; Gigilio, *Call Me Tom*, 66, 70; Epstein, "Tom Eagleton and Matt Reese," 5–29; Herbst, Kelley, and Burton Pines, interviews by the author; Eagleton, "Minibiography," chapter 3, pp. 8–9; "Long Calls Missouri Defeat 'Victory for Snooper,'" *NYT*, August 8, 1968; Eagleton, interview by Sarvis; James Ed Reeves, interview by Will Sarvis, September 16, 1998, transcript, MPOH.

36. Larsen to Time Nation, "Re: Eagleton vs. Curtis"; "T. F. Eagleton, Democrat, and GOP's T. B. Curtis"; Eagleton quoted in Giglio, *Call Me Tom*, 70–71, 74–75;

Eagleton quoted in John Herbers, "Impact of Wallace Campaign Is Weighed by Senatorial Rivals in Missouri," *NYT,* September 9, 1968; Fred W. Lindecke, "Nixon Seen as GOP's Only State-Wide Hope," *SLPD,* November 3, 1968; Frank Leeming Jr., "Democrats End Campaign at Old-Time Rally," *SLPD,* November 4, 1968; Editorial, "Hearnes, Eagleton, and Danforth," *SLPD,* November 6, 1968.

37. Larsen to Time Nation, "Re: Eagleton vs. Curtis"; Larsen, interview by the author; Fred W. Lindecke, interview by Will Sarvis, June 5, 1996, transcript, MPOH; "Senator Thomas F. Eagleton," *St. Louis Journalism Review,* October 1972, c. 5736, box 12, TFEP, p. 6; Giglio, *Call Me Tom,* 76. As reported by James Giglio, other journalists—including Jack Flach of the *St. Louis Globe-Democrat*—had heard rumors about Eagleton's depression and alcoholism, but they could never follow through or confirm the information.

38. Lindecke quoted in "Senator Thomas F. Eagleton," 6; Thomas W. Ottenad, "Inquiry on Eagleton Leak," *SLPD,* October 10, 1972; Anderson, *Anderson Papers,* 157.

39. Friend quoted in Bartimus, "Tom Was Beau"; Barbara Eagleton in Jean Sharley Taylor, "Mrs. Eagleton Off and Running—Literally," *LAT,* July 27, 1972.

40. Hoyt, "Eagleton: A Driven Man," July 27, 1972.

41. "Long Quits; Eagleton Sworn In," *SLPD,* December 27, 1968; Eagleton, "Minibiography," chapter 4, p. 1.

42. Eagleton quoted in Christopher Lydon, "Missouri's Contribution to the Ticket," *NYT,* July 14, 1972.

43. Mary Russell, "Eagleton Adds Witty, Low-Key Style to Slate"; Eagleton in "Campaign Too Costly, Eagleton Asserts," *SLPD,* November 6, 1968; Stennis quoted in Hoyt, "Eagleton: A Driven Man"; Willnow, "New Politics"; William K. Wyant Jr., "Eagleton's Role in Foreign Policy," *SLPD,* July 18, 1972; Max Frankel, "2 Presidents, 2 Peace Efforts," *NYT,* September 20, 1969; AP, "Democratic Senator's Plan Defines War-Making Power," *NYT,* March 2, 1971; Coyne, "Eagleton," 77; Quick, "Tom Eagleton—An Appreciation," 51.

44. David S. Broder, "Sen. Eagleton: His Stand on Issues, Politics and Duties," *WP,* July 14, 1972; Eagleton quoted in "T. F. Eagleton, Democrat, and GOP's T. B. Curtis"; Max Frankel, "Impassioned Plea: Dakotan Urges Party to Lead the Nation in Healing Itself; McGovern Names Eagleton Running Mate; Calls Nixon 'Fundamental Issue,'" *NYT,* July 14, 1972; Calvin Trillin, "Missouri: The Folks at Home," *New Yorker,* May 16, 1970, 108; Kelley and Godley, interviews by the author.

45. Eagleton quoted in Willnow, "Liberal Gets No. 2 Spot"; Gene Godley, "Proposed Legislative Program," memorandum, August 17, 1972, TFEP; Godley, interview by the author; Hoyt, "Eagleton: A Driven Man"; Eagleton quoted in Lydon, "Missouri's Contribution to the Ticket"; Eagleton quoted in Broder, "Sen. Eagleton"; Leon G. Billings, "Eagleton and the Environment: Prom-

ises Made; Promises Kept," *SES,* 91–96; Leon G. Billings, interview by Don Nicholl, January 27, 2003, transcript, ID 388, ESMOH; Eagleton, interview by Sarvis.

46. Hoyt, "Eagleton: A Driven Man"; Giglio, *Call Me Tom,* 10–11, 103–4, including Eagleton quotation, 104.

47. Willnow, "New Politics"; Britton, Godley, and Herbst, interviews by the author; Rose, "Missouri Friends Return Eagleton's Loyalty"; Hoyt, "Eagleton: A Driven Man"; George Vecsey, *Stan Musial: An American Life* (New York: ESPN, 2011), 292.

48. AP, "Mrs. Eagleton Was Relieved When Her Husband Quit Race," *SLPD,* August 3, 1972; Rice, "Politician's Life Style"; Leigh Jackson, "An Old Alum Tells Her What to Expect at Sidwell Friends," *Reading* [PA] *Eagle,* January 11, 1993; Maxine Cheshire, "Hot Tidbits for Lunch," *WP,* July 13, 1972; Giglio, *Call Me Tom,* 206; Andrea Gibbs, interview by the author.

49. Godley and Herbst, interviews by the author; Giglio, *Call Me Tom,* 204–5; "Thomas F. Eagleton Farewell Address," 31.

50. Rose, "Missouri Friends Return Eagleton's Loyalty."

51. Trillin, "Folks at Home," 108–9.

52. As recalled by Dolores Stover in interview by Don Nicholl, September 20, 2002, transcript, ID 367, ESMOH.

53. Herbst, interview by the author; George C. Wilson, "Eagleton among Select Few to Win War with Pentagon," *WP,* July 14, 1972.

54. Sally Thran, "Eagleton Aids Forming National Campaign Staff," *SLPD,* July 23, 1972; Mike Kelley, interview by the author.

55. Tran, "Eagleton Aids," July 23, 1972; Godley, interview by the author.

The Game

1. Muskie and McGovern quoted in William Montalbano, "Careful Strategy Pays Off," *MH,* July 11, 1972; Jack Rosenthal, "Muskie Supports Panel on Credentials Question," *NYT,* July 11, 1972.

2. Montalbano, "Careful Strategy Pays Off."

3. Hart and Stearns conversation, as remembered in Hart, *Right from the Start,* 226. Weaver, "South Carolina Vote."

4. Hart, *Right from the Start,* 221–24; Apple, "Convention Notes"; Gordon L. Weil, *The Long Shot: George McGovern Runs for President* (New York: Norton, 1973), 142–43; Thompson, *Fear and Loathing,* 307.

5. Mankiewicz quoted in Hart, *Right from the Start,* 227.

6. Hart and Mike Wallace exchange, as remembered in Hart, *Right from the Start,* 226–27.

7. Saul Friedman, "How McGovern Men Beat Party Pros," *MH,* July 12, 1972; Hart, *Right from the Start,* 227; Weil, *Long Shot,* 142; Thompson, *Fear and Loathing,* 309.

8. Schoumacher quoted in Thompson, *Fear and Loathing*, 286. See ibid., 309, for reaction at McGovern headquarters.

9. Montalbano, "Careful Strategy Pays Off"; Max Frankel, "6 Rivals' Tactics Fail as Dakotan Regains His 151 Delegates," *NYT*, July 11, 1972.

10. Eleanor McGovern quoted in Montalbano, "Careful Strategy Pays Off."

11. McGovern quoted ibid.

12. Eagleton, "Minibiography," chapter 2, p. 4; Douglas Bennet to Eagleton, "Re: Eighteen Days—The Eagleton Vice-Presidential Candidacy," memorandum, August 8, 1972, p. 1, found in both c. 5736, box 22, TFEP, and box 37, folder 5, DJBP; Filippine to Eagleton, memorandum, August 16, 1972, pp. 11, 13–15.

13. Conversation as remembered by Eagleton in "Minibiography," chapter 2, pp. 4–5.

14. Filippine to Eagleton, memorandum, August 16, 1972, p. 10.

15. Humphrey quoted in Clark Hoyt, "An Era Died in 2 Minutes, 48 Seconds," *MH*, July 12, 1972; Max Frankel, "Alabamian Wooed; McGovern Supports Jackson's View on Defense Issue; Humphrey and Muskie Yield to McGovern, Who Moves for Unity," *NYT*, July 12, 1972; Christopher Lydon, "Minnesotan to Campaign; Humphrey Defends Campaign Tactics," *NYT*, July 12, 1972.

16. Muskie quoted in Mike Toner, "Sen. Muskie's Swan Song Impassioned," *MH*, July 12, 1972.

17. Filippine to Eagleton, memorandum, August 16, 1972, pp. 9–12.

18. Eagleton, "Minibiography," chapter 2, p. 6; Weil, *Long Shot*, 202–3; Dougherty, *Goodbye, Mr. Christian*, 130–31, 177, 228–31; Witker, *How to Lose*, photo insert; Richard Reeves, "The City Politic: Fear and Trembling on the McGovern Staff," *New York*, July 3, 1972, 6–7; David E. Rosenbaum, "Frederick Dutton, Adviser to the Kennedys and the Saudis, Is Dead at 82," *NYT*, June 27, 2005; R. W. Apple Jr., "Ex-Kennedy Aides Weigh Strategy," *NYT*, August 26, 1968.

19. Conversation as remembered by Eagleton in "Minibiography," chapter 2, p. 6; Filippine to Eagleton, memorandum, 16 August 1972, p. 13.

20. Thomas W. Ottenad, "Kennedy Likely to Get Offer," *SLPD*, July 12, 1972.

21. John Herbers, "McGovern Forces Shape Planks to Suit Candidate," *NYT*, July 13, 1972; Navasky, "Funny Thing Happened," 39, 41, including Salinger quotation, 41; James M. Naughton, "McGovern, Praising 2 Rivals, Turns to Task of Party Unity," *NYT*, July 12, 1972; James Reston, "McGovern Victory: New Tasks; Real Battle Starting on Uniting Party to Win in November," *NYT*, July 12, 1972; Bill Kovach, "Delegates' Mood Shifts; Healing Sets In," *NYT*, July 12, 1972; Ben A. Franklin, "McGovern's Gain Embitters Labor," *NYT*, July 12, 1972; Witker, *How to Lose*, 125; Phil Zeidman, interview by the author.

22. James Reston, "After California," *NYT*, June 7, 1972; James Reston, "A Fumble at the Hour of Triumph," *NYT*, July 14, 1972; James Reston, "Come Home, America!'" *NYT*, July 14, 1972; William Greider, "Sen. McGovern in Credibility Gap," *WP*, July 21, 1972; Tom Wicker, "New Breed and Old," *NYT*, July 13, 1972.

23. Sheila Hixon and Ruth Rose, eds., *The Official Proceedings of the Democratic National Convention, 1972* (Washington, DC: Democratic National Committee, 1972), 349; Phil Zeidman, interview by the author.

24. Lawrence E. Taylor, "Senator McGovern, in Victory, Is Happy but Restrained," *SLPD,* July 13, 1972.

25. McGovern, Mankiewicz, Riefe, and protester quotations from demonstration at the Doral drawn from Robert D. Shaw Jr., "McGovern Takes a 'High Risk,' Confronts Angry War Foes," *MH,* July 13, 1972; Robert Sanford, "McGovern, Protesters Meet," *SLPD,* July 13, 1972; James M. Naughton, "Protesters Find Candidate Firm: McGovern Says He Won't Shift Positions on Any Fundamental Stands," *NYT,* July 13, 1972.

26. AP, "Mrs. McGovern Enthusiastic and Doesn't Try to Hide It," *SLPD,* July 13, 1972.

27. Ribicoff quoted in Taylor, "Senator McGovern, in Victory"; Richard Dudman, "McGovern Is Nominated; Eagleton Is Running-Mate," *SLPD,* July 13, 1972.

28. White, *Making of the President 1972,* 183; Morrison quoted in Taylor, "Senator McGovern, In Victory."

29. Martin quoted in Taylor, "Senator McGovern, in Victory."

30. Eleanor McGovern quoted in William Montalbano, "Victory Caps Long Struggle as Underdog," *MH,* July 13, 1972.

31. Ibid.; Eleanor McGovern quoted in Dudman, "McGovern Is Nominated"; Max Frankel, "A Stunning Sweep: Senator Seeks Unity—Wallace Rules Out Third-Party Race," *NYT,* July 13, 1972; Eleanor McGovern, *Uphill,* 184–86. After the Illinois delegation's vote, McGovern went on to receive a total of 1,715.35 votes. Henry Jackson was the runner-up, with 534.50.

32. Montalbano, "Victory Caps Long Struggle"; Eleanor McGovern, *Uphill,* 186.

33. Taylor, "Senator McGovern, In Victory"; Frankel, "Stunning Sweep"; White, *Making of the President 1972,* 183; Eleanor McGovern, *Uphill,* 185.

34. Eleanor McGovern quoted in AP, "Mrs. McGovern Enthusiastic"; Taylor, "Senator McGovern, In Victory"; Frankel, "Stunning Sweep"; White, *Making of the President 1972,* 183; Witker, *How to Lose,* 131.

35. Mary McGovern quoted in AP, "Mrs. McGovern Enthusiastic."

The Pipedream

1. Mankiewicz and Hart, interviews by the author; Arthur Schlesinger Jr., "On the Presidential Succession," *Political Science Quarterly* 89, no. 3 (1974): 488–89, including quotations of the Constitutional Convention's Committee of Detail's August 6, 1787, draft and the proposals of Gouverneur Morris of Pennsylvania and James Madison of Virginia, respectively.

2. Ibid., 489–90, including Hugh Williamson and Alexander Hamilton quotations, 489; Alexander Hamilton, *Federalist* no. 76 in Isaac Kramnick, ed., *The Federalist Papers* (New York: Penguin, 1987), 392–96, quotation from 395;

Joel K. Goldstein, *The Modern American Vice Presidency: The Transformation of a Political Institution* (Princeton: Princeton University Press, 1982), 5.

3. Goldstein, *Modern American Vice Presidency*, 4; John D. Feerick, "The Vice-Presidency and the Problems of Presidential Succession and Inability," *Fordham Law Review* 32 (1964): 457, 460–62; Woodrow Wilson, *Congressional Government: A Study in American Politics* (Boston: Houghton, Mifflin, 1901), 240–41; U.S. Const. art. II, § 1, cl. 3.

4. Schlesinger, "On the Presidential Succession," 484, 491; Samuel White quoted in John D. Feerick, *From Failing Hands: The Story of Presidential Succession* (New York: Fordham University Press, 1965), 73; James G. O'Hara, testimony before the Vice Presidential Selection Commission of the Democratic National Committee, November 7, 1973 (mimeo.), 10; Goldstein, *Modern American Vice Presidency*, 66.

5. James M. Naughton, "Dakotan Believed to Drop Hope of Kennedy on Ticket," *NYT*, July 6, 1972; Hart quoted in Mary Russell, "McGovern Still Woos Kennedy," *WP*, July 12, 1972; Frank Mankiewicz quoted in Navasky, "Funny Thing Happened," 43.

6. Richard Scammon and Ben J. Wattenberg, *The Real Majority: An Extraordinary Examination of the American Electorate*, quoted in Robert D. Shaw Jr., "Just What Is a Democrat?" *MH*, July 9, 1972; Richard Dougherty, "Some Notes for Consideration with Ted," box 695, GSMPUP.

7. Dougherty, *Goodbye, Mr. Christian*, 11–15, 41, 76, 89–93, 118–19 in particular; Hart, *Right from the Start*, 155; Weil, *Long Shot*, 201–3; Witker, *How to Lose*, 46 and photo insert; Eric Pace, "Richard Dougherty, 65, Dies; Museum Official and Author," *NYT*, January 1, 1987; Christopher Lydon, "Two More about McGovern—the Best and the Worst," book review, *NYT*, October 14, 1973.

8. Dougherty, "Some Notes for Consideration with Ted"; White, *Making of the President 1972*, 197; Anson, *McGovern*, 211.

9. McGovern quoted in Jules Witcover, "Kennedy to Advise on No. 2 Spot, Not Be Forced into It," *LAT*, June 24, 1972; Mankiewicz and McGovern, interviews by the author; Witker, *How to Lose*, 16; Thompson, *Fear and Loathing*, 379; McGovern, *Grassroots*, 193; McGovern quoted in Joe McGinniss, "Second Thoughts of George McGovern," *NYT Sunday Magazine*, May 6, 1973, 97–98; McGovern quoted in Douglas E. Kneeland, "McGovern Said to Narrow Choice for Running Mate," *NYT*, July 12, 1972; Thomas W. Ottenad, "Kennedy Likely to Get Offer," *SLPD*, July 12, 1972.

10. Hart quoted in Haynes Johnson, "Characters Trapped by Circumstances," *WP*, December 3, 1972; Ottenad, "Kennedy Likely to Get Offer"; Weil, *Long Shot*, 159–62; Hart, *Right from the Start*, 204–5; Weil quoted in Anson, *McGovern*, 279; Dougherty, *Goodbye, Mr. Christian*, 151.

11. Dougherty, *Goodbye, Mr. Christian*, 140.

12. Stearns quoted in McWhirter, "Inside the Winning Team," 40; Weil, interview by the author.

13. Fred Dutton to McGovern memorandum, May 30, 1972, "Campaign Assessment and Needs at about This Point," box 694, "Staff/Files 1972" folder, GSMPUP; McWhirter, "Inside the Winning Team," 40.

14. Anonymous staffer's memo, which begins, "You may consider this memo presumptuous," box 692, "Senator's Personal Notes" folder, GSMPUP. By process of elimination—excluding third-person references to other staffers, assessing its content, and double-checking with Gordon Weil, who reviewed the memo on my behalf—I have attributed this anonymous memo to Fred Dutton.

15. Ibid.

16. Dougherty, *Goodbye, Mr. Christian,* 141; Dutton's "You may consider this memo presumptuous" memo.

17. Ted Kennedy quoted in AP, "Ted Kennedy Goes Sailing on Convention's First Day," *SLPD,* July 11, 1972.

18. Ottenad, "Kennedy Likely to Get Offer"; Kneeland, "McGovern Said to Narrow Choice for Running Mate"; Johnson, "Characters Trapped by Circumstances."

19. John Adams and Thomas Jefferson quoted in Goldstein, *Modern American Vice Presidency,* 135; John Adams quoted in Joseph J. Ellis, *Founding Brothers: The Revolutionary Generation* (New York: Vintage, 2002), 166; Theodore Roosevelt quoted in Schlesinger, "On the Presidential Succession," 492, and in Irving G. Williams, *The Rise of the Vice Presidency* (Washington, DC: Public Affairs, 1956), 81; Dwight Eisenhower quoted in Schlesinger, "On the Presidential Succession," 478, 486; Lyndon Johnson quoted ibid., 486, cited from *Time,* November 14, 1969.

20. Schlesinger, "On the Presidential Succession," 479–81, including U.S. Constitution quotation, 479; Marshall quotation ibid., 480, and Williams, *Rise of the Vice Presidency,* 109–10; Goldstein, *Modern American Vice Presidency,* 3, 13, 134–42, 167–75, 320–21; Jane Mayer, *The Dark Side: The Inside Story of How the War on Terror Turned into a War on American Ideals* (New York: Doubleday, 2008).

Mayer details how Vice President Dick Cheney spearheaded the Bush administration's dismantling of the constitutional separation of war powers between the executive and legislative branches. While President George W. Bush was "The Decider," Cheney and his legal counselor, David Addington, were the influencers, compelling Bush to decide as they pleased in most cases. "Cheney almost invariably had the final word with the president," Mayer writes, and Addington edited and even rewrote some of the paperwork that crossed Bush's desk. The following example illustrates the magnitude of their power: "When a White House colleague in conflict with Addington challenged officials at the Office of Management and Budget, asking why they allowed Addington to single-handedly rewrite their budget proposals before they were passed on to the president for his signature, they responded, 'We have to! It's what the vice president wants!'" According to Mayer's analysis, "As Cheney grew into the most influential vice president in American history, Addington, as his surrogate, became one of the most powerful unelected officials in the government—'Cheney's Cheney.'" Quotations, 63, 53.

21. Lyndon Johnson quoted in Schlesinger, "On the Presidential Succession," 479, originally shared by Doris Kearns Goodwin.

22. Dougherty, "Some Notes for Consideration with Ted."

23. Schlesinger, "On the Presidential Succession," 487; Goldstein, *Modern American Vice Presidency*, 14, 59, 87–88. Per Goldstein, Adlai Stevenson's and Barry Goldwater's running mates, John Sparkman of Alabama and William E. Miller of New York, respectively, were the only vice presidential candidates who completed campaigns from 1952 to 1972 never to go on to be seriously considered for a presidential run, or actually run.

24. Weil, interview by the author; Dougherty, *Goodbye, Mr. Christian*, 39, 47, 72, 150; Weil, *Long Shot*, esp. 204; Hart, *Right from the Start*, 37; Witker, *How to Lose*, 6, 100–101, photo insert; Anson, *McGovern*, 279; Richard Reeves, "The City Politic: Fear and Trembling on the McGovern Staff," *New York*, July 3, 1972, 6–7; Weil quoted in McWhirter, "Inside the Winning Team," 42; Steven V. Roberts, "Bad Dream Comes to End for McGovern Workers," *NYT*, August 6, 1972; James M. Naughton, "McGovern System: Broad Responsibility for the Staff," *NYT*, August 18, 1972; Lydon, "Two More about McGovern."

25. Johnson, "Characters Trapped by Circumstances"; Thomas W. Ottenad, "Picking No. 2 Man: Job Began Month Ago," *SLPD*, July 14, 1972; Ted Van Dyk, *Heroes, Hacks, and Fools: Memoirs from the Political Inside* (Seattle: University of Washington Press, 2007), 138.

The fifteen slips of paper containing the McGovern staffers' top choices for vice presidential nominee can be found in the Gordon Weil Papers, box 1, folders 5, 12, 13. All but two of the fourteen slips bear their authors' names. They are: Bill Dougherty, Dick Dougherty, John Douglas, Joe Grandmaison, John Holum, Kirby Jones, Frank Mankiewicz, Yancey Martin, Marian Pearlman, Pierre Salinger, Eli Segal, and Ted Van Dyk. John Douglas's name is on two of the sheets and thus counted only once. My familiarity with the subjects' handwriting leads me to believe that Gary Hart and Gordon Weil were the authors of the two unsigned lists. Further supporting this theory, Hart and Weil were the two staffers responsible for organization, so they did not need to identify their own lists. (Weil confirmed his handwriting.) Holum, Grandmaison, Pearlman, and Weil were the four staffers who did not put Kennedy at the top of their lists. Dougherty, Hart, Mankiewicz, Segal, and Weil were the five who included Eagleton. Interestingly, Eagleton's name found its way onto the lists of the people with four of the highest positions in the McGovern campaign. Woodcock—who was listed six times—was the second-most-mentioned option after Kennedy, followed by Eagleton, Lucey, and Ribicoff, with five mentions each.

26. Kneeland, "McGovern Said to Narrow Choice"; Johnson, "Characters Trapped by Circumstances"; Weil, *Long Shot*, 157, 160; Weil and Mankiewicz, interviews by the author.

27. Bennet to Eagleton, "Re: Eighteen Days," 2; Weil, *Long Shot*, 162.

28. Carl P. Leubsdorf, "Demos Admit Eagleton Illness Knowledge," *Salt Lake Tribune*, November 15, 1972, including David Schoumacher quotation.

29. McGovern quoted in Taylor, "Senator McGovern, in Victory"; Ottenad, "Picking No. 2 Man"; Kennedy in *NBC Nightly News*, July 13, 1972; Weil, *Long Shot*, 159–61; Hart, *Right from the Start*, 239; Weil and McGovern, interviews by the author.

30. Filippine to Eagleton, memorandum, August 16, 1972, p. 16; Bennet to Eagleton, "Re: Eighteen Days," 3; Greg Wierzynski, interview by the author.

The Selection

1. Eagleton, "Minibiography," chapter 3, p. 1; Boyd, "Once the 'Forgotten Man'"; Filippine to Eagleton, "Re: Events of Thursday, July 13, 1972," memorandum, August 3, 1972, c. 5736, box 22, TFEP, p. 1; Filippine to Eagleton, memorandum, August 16, 1972; Godley, Herbst, and Kelley, interviews by the author; Sally Thran, "Eagleton Aids Forming National Campaign Staff," *SLPD*, July 23, 1972; Bennet, "Re: Eighteen Days," 5; Barbara Alexander and Donald G. Alexander, interview by Andrea L'Hommedieu, September 18, 2003, transcript, ID 409, ESMOH.

2. Thran, "Eagleton Aids"; "Wesleyan's Fifteenth President," website, http://www.wesleyan.edu/president/pastpresidents/bennet.html; "Guide to the Douglas Bennet Papers, 1940–2004," website, http://www.wesleyan.edu/libr/schome/FAs/be2009-32.xml; Herbst, Kelley, and Zeidman, interviews by the author; Bennet quoted in James M. Naughton, "Muskie Appears More Relaxed, Even Stoical, after Primary Setbacks," *NYT*, April 23, 1972.

3. Bob Maynard to Eagleton, "Re: My Recollections of Miami, etseq.," memorandum, September 5, 1972, c. 5736, box 22, TFEP, 3; Godley and Carl Leubsdorf, interviews by the author; Bennet, "Re: Eighteen Days," 5.

4. Mike Gravel quoted in Robert Sanford, "Open Selection of No. 2 Man Sought by Eager Aspirants," *SLPD*, July 12, 1972.

5. Endicott Peabody campaign materials described in Sanford, "Open Selection of No. 2."

6. Ottenad, "Picking No. 2 Man"; Kennedy in *NBC Nightly News*, July 13, 1972; Mankiewicz quoted in J. Anthony Lukas, *Common Ground: A Turbulent Decade in the Lives of Three American Families* (New York: Vintage, 1986), 585; Weil, *Long Shot*, 161–62; Hart, *Right from the Start*, 239; Weil, interview by the author.

7. Marquis Childs, "The Democrats' Health," *SLPD*, July 17, 1972; Ottenad, "Picking No. 2 Man"; Weil, *Long Shot*, 161.

8. Frank Mankiewicz, "Walter Cronkite Could Have Been Our Vice President," *WP*, July 25, 2009; Mankiewicz, interview by the author; George McGovern, "Help Wanted," *NYT*, August 29, 2008; Witker, *How to Lose*, 130; Mankiewicz, as remembered by Dougherty in *Goodbye, Mr. Christian*, 153.

9. Weil, interview by the author; Wesley Granberg-Michaelson, *Unexpected Destinations: An Evangelical Pilgrimage to World Christianity* (Grand Rapids, MI: Eerdmans, 2011), 78.

10. Hart, *Right from the Start*, 240; Dougherty, as remembered by Dougherty in *Goodbye, Mr. Christian*, 152; Weil's notes, box 1, folders 12–13, GLWP; Weil, interview by the author; Jack Thomas, "The Loner in Winter: Former Mayor Kevin White Is Being Robbed by Alzheimer's–But Bolstered by a Dear Friend," *Boston Globe*, June 20, 2005; AP, "Nancy Kissinger Faces Surgery," *Nashua* [NH] *Telegraph*, February 7, 1976; "Surgery Sidelines White" *Boston Globe*, October 15, 1970; AP, "White's Condition Is Good," *Lewiston* [ME] *Evening Journal*, October 16, 1970.

11. Hart and Stearns quoted in Johnson, "Characters Trapped by Circumstances"; Weil, *Long Shot*, 162–63; Hart, *Right from the Start*, 239–40; White, *Making of the President 1972*, 195–6; Dougherty, *Goodbye, Mr. Christian*, 152–54, 157; Witker, *How to Lose*, 131–32; Stearns, Weil, and Witcover, interviews by the author.

12. Weil notes, folders 12–13, GLWP; Weil, *Long Shot*, 162–64, 170–71; Dougherty, *Goodbye, Mr. Christian*, 154; Hart, *Right from the Start*, 239–40; Van Dyk, *Heroes, Hacks, and Fools*, 138; Witker, *How to Lose*, 130; Stearns, Weil, and Witcover, interviews by the author.

13. William Chapman, "Choice Gives Ticket Balance," *WP*, July 14, 1972; McGovern, *Grassroots*, 196–97; Ottenad, "Picking No. 2 Man"; Stewart Udall to McGovern, "George, Some Quick Notes," memorandum, box 692, "Senator's Personal Notes" folder, GSMPUP; Hart, *Right from the Start*, 240–41; Weil, *Long Shot*, 165; Van Dyk, *Heroes, Hacks, and Fools*, 138; White, *Making of the President 1972*, 195–96.

14. McGovern quoted in Lukas, *Common Ground*, 587; Chapman, "Choice Gives Ticket Balance"; McGovern, *Grassroots*, 197; Weil, *Long Shot*, 165; Hart, *Right from the Start*, 241; Douglas E. Kneeland, "Marathon Session Sifted Long Roster of Candidates," *NYT*, July 14, 1972; Van Dyk, *Heroes, Hacks, and Fools*, 138; Stearns and McGovern, interviews by the author. Same sources contributed to next two paragraphs.

15. Ribicoff quoted in Chapman, "Choice Gives Ticket Balance"; Nadine Brozan, "Ribicoff Is Eulogized for Many Facets of His Public Service," *NYT*, February 26, 1998.

16. Stearns, interview by the author; White quoted in Lukas, *Common Ground*, 588.

17. McGovern, *Grassroots*, 197; Weil, *Long Shot*, 165–66; Hart, *Right from the Start*, 241–42; Van Dyk, *Heroes, Hacks, and Fools*, 138; Lukas, *Common Ground*, 587–89; Bennet, "Re: Eighteen Days," 4; Weil, interview by the author.

18. Ted Kennedy's view, as presented in Johnson, "Characters Trapped by Circumstances"; McGovern, *Grassroots,* 197; Hart, *Right from the Start,* 242; Weil, *Long Shot,* 167–68.

19. Claude Hooten quoted in Anne Taylor Flemming, "Kennedy: Time of Decision," *NYT Sunday Magazine,* June 24, 1979, 17.

20. Johnson, "Characters Trapped By Circumstances"; McGovern, *Grassroots,* 198; Weil, *Long Shot,* 167–68; Dougherty, *Goodbye, Mr. Christian,* 156; Van Dyk, *Heroes, Hacks, and Fools,* 138; Weil, interview by the author.

21. Bennet to Eagleton, "Re: Eighteen Days," 5; Filippine to Eagleton, "Re: Events of Thursday, July 13, 1972," 2; Eagleton, "Minibiography," chapter 3, p. 2; Thomas W. Ottenad, "Eagleton Gets Job of Healing Party Rifts," *SLPD,* July 14, 1972; Maynard to Eagleton, "Re: My Recollections," 4; Godley, interview by the author.

22. McGovern, *Grassroots,* 196–98; McGovern aide quoted in Chapman, "Choice Gives Ticket Balance"; McGovern and Holum, interviews by the author; McGovern quoted in Weil, *Long Shot,* 168; McGovern quoted in McGinniss, "Second Thoughts of George McGovern," 98; Giglio, *Call Me Tom,* 265; Hart, *Right from the Start,* 242; White, *Making of the President 1972,* 197; Doug Bennet to Mike Kelley, memorandum, November 27, 1972, box 37, folder 7, DJBP; Davis Merritt, "Nelson Picked to Mediate, Cushion, and Witness Eagleton Resignation," *MH,* August 2, 1972; Van Dyk, *Heroes, Hacks, and Fools,* 139. Senator Nelson's wife, Carrie Lee Nelson, told James Giglio that her husband had known before recommending Eagleton for the nomination that he, in Giglio's words, "had suffered from depression."

23. White, *Making of the President 1972,* 197–98; Hart, *Right from the Start,* 242; McGovern, *Grassroots,* 199.

24. McGovern quoted in Ottenad, "Picking No. 2 Man"; McGovern, *Grassroots,* 199; Van Dyk, *Heroes, Hacks, and Fools,* 139; Witker, *How to Lose,* 132–33; McGovern, Mankiewicz, Weil, and Stearns, interviews by the author.

25. Bennet quoted in Eagleton, "Minibiography," chapter 3, p. 2; Van Dyk, *Heroes, Hacks, and Fools,* 139; Bennet to Kelley, memorandum, November 27, 1972.

26. McGovern quoted in Ottenad, "Picking No. 2 Man"; Clark Hoyt, "Demo Conflict Grows over Eagleton Quiz," *MH,* August 4, 1972; Bennet to Eagleton and Kelley, "Re: Eagleton Selection as Vice President," memorandum, October 5, 1972, box 37, folder 7, DJBP.

The moment of the pause is most plausibly when McGovern made his offer to Eagleton, though it is not known for certain since McGovern's end of the conversation was not recorded.

27. Transcription of Bob Hardy recording, "Conversation with George McGovern," July 13, 1972, c. 5736, box 22, TFEP; Godley, interview by the author. Even better, Gene Godley provided me the original recording in its original format, a reel-to-reel tape, which I had converted into an audio CD. Hear-

ing the scene in room 605 at the Ivanhoe for myself afforded me a feeling for the atmosphere, the excitement, that permeated the room. I have tried to replicate the sensation of listening to the recording in these pages. This is the source for the conversation through the conclusion of Bob Hardy's interview with Eagleton, except where otherwise noted.

28. Mankiewicz quoted in Eagleton, "Minibiography," chapter 3, p. 4A. As indicated in note 26, Hardy recorded only Eagleton's side of the conversation; Mankiewicz's comment here comes from other sources, including as presented in Eagleton's "Minibiography," and, as we shall see, the question's wording has been the subject of debate.

29. Charlene Prost, "Tape Backs Eagleton's Report of Talk with Mankiewicz," *MH,* August 4, 1972.

30. Eagleton, "Minibiography," chapter 3, pp. 3–4.

31. Ibid., chapter 3, p. 3; Thomas W. Ottenad, "Only One Question Was Asked about His Past, Eagleton Says," *SLPD,* August 3, 1972; Leubsdorf, interview by the author.

32. Doug Bennet, interview by Richard A. Harrison, June 1976, Washington, DC, transcript, box 37, folder 6, DJBP; Eagleton, "Minibiography," chapter 3, p. 4A; "Conversation with George McGovern"; Hardy recording; Godley, interview by the author; Prost, "Tape Backs Eagleton's Report"; McGovern, interview by the author. In our June 2011 interview, McGovern told me that Eagleton admitted to Eleanor and him that he had decided not to disclose his history of mental illness up front because he feared it would spoil his shot at the nomination, an assessment contrary to the reasoning Eagleton provided at the time.

33. Eagleton, "Minibiography," chapter 3, pp. 3–4; White, *Making of the President 1972,* 199; Filippine to Eagleton, "Re: Events of Thursday, July 13, 1972," 6, 9.

34. Eagleton, Hart, and Mankiewicz quoted in Hoyt, "Demo Conflict Grows"; Eagleton, "Minibiography," chapter 3, pp. 3–4; Maynard to Eagleton, "Re: My Recollections," 5; Mankiewicz, McGovern, and Weil, interviews by the author; Bennet, interview by Harrison, 2–3; Weil, *Long Shot,* 169; Ottenad, "Only One Question Was Asked"; Prost, "Tape Backs Eagleton's Report"; White, *Making of the President 1972,* 199.

35. McGovern, interview by the author.

36. Mankiewicz quoted in *NBC Nightly News,* July 13, 1972.

37. Stearns, interview by the author.

38. Eagleton quoted in Russell, "Eagleton Adds Witty, Low-Key Style to Slate"; Filippine quoted in Maynard to Eagleton, "Re: My Recollections," 6.

39. Filippine to Eagleton, "Re: Events of Thursday, July 13, 1972," 10; Filippine to Eagleton, memorandum, August 16, 1972, p. 7; Maynard to Eagleton, "Re: My Recollections," 6; McGovern, *Grassroots,* 199; Frankel, "Impassioned Plea"; "Text of Address by McGovern Accepting the Democratic Presidential Nomination," *NYT,* July 14, 1972.

40. Jack Perkins in *NBC Nightly News,* July 13, 1972.
41. Filippine to Eagleton, "Re: Events of Thursday, July 13, 1972," 13–14; Filippine to Eagleton, memorandum, August 16, 1972, pp. 17–18.

The Running Mate

1. Marc Howard and Robert Sam Anson, interviews by the author; conversation as remembered by Robert Sam Anson, as presented in Anson, "Party Lines: Why McGovern Had to Dump Eagleton," *New Times,* circa 1976, p. 12, in c. 5736, box 12, TFEP; Dougherty, *Goodbye, Mr. Christian,* 158; Weil, *Long Shot,* 170.
2. Reston, "A Fumble at the Hour of Triumph"; Mankiewicz, interview by the author.
3. Eagleton quoted in Ottenad, "Eagleton Gets Job of Healing Party Rifts" and Curt Matthews, "Eagleton Is Nominated; 39 Others Sought Post," *SLPD,* July 14, 1972; Bennet, "Re: Eighteen Days," 8–9; Maynard to Eagleton, "Re: My Recollections," 6–7; Filippine to Eagleton, "Re: Events of Thursday, July 13, 1972," 14.
4. Eagleton, Muskie, and Humphrey quoted in Ottenad, "Eagleton Gets Job of Healing Party Rifts."
5. Mike Gravel quoted in Matthews, "Eagleton Is Nominated"; David S. Broder, "Euphoria in Unity," *WP,* July 15, 1972; *Newsweek* quoted in Thompson, *Fear and Loathing,* 319.
6. Eagleton quoted in Ottenad, "Eagleton Gets Job of Healing Party Rifts," and in Boyd, "Once the 'Forgotten Man' of Missouri"; Thran, "Eagleton Aids."
7. Fred W. Lindecke, "Eagleton Unites Missouri Delegation," *SLPD,* July 14, 1972; Matthews, "Eagleton Is Nominated"; White, *Making of the President 1972,* 185.
8. Frankel, "Impassioned Plea"; Lindecke, "Eagleton Unites Missouri Delegation"; Matthews, "Eagleton Is Nominated."
9. Barbara Eagleton quoted in Matthews, "Eagleton Is Nominated," and in Robert Sanford, "Mrs. Eagleton—A 'Political Wife,'" *SLPD,* July 14, 1972.
10. Eagleton, "Minibiography," chapter 3, p. 8; Bill Kovach, "The Gathering Ends with Roar of Unity," *NYT,* July 15, 1972.
11. Eagleton quoted in Matthews, "Eagleton Is Nominated"; *NBC Nightly News,* July 13, 1972; Ottenad, "Picking No. 2 Man."
12. Michael J. Howlett and Ted Kennedy quoted in Taylor Pensoneau, "Kennedy Helped to Curb Disunity," *SLPD,* July 14, 1972.
13. White, *Making of the President 1972,* 186. McGovern quoted in "The Campaign: McGovern's First Crisis: The Eagleton Affair," *Time,* August 7, 1972.
14. White, *Making of the President 1972,* 184–86.
15. "Text of Address by McGovern Accepting the Democratic Presidential Nomination."

16. Bennet, "Re: Eighteen Days," 11.

17. White, *Making of the President 1972*, 185; Kovach, "Gathering Ends with Roar of Unity."

18. Bennet, "Re: Eighteen Days," 12–13; Weil, *Long Shot*, 171; Bennet, interview by Harrison, 3–5; Johnson, "Characters Trapped by Circumstances"; White, *Making of the President 1972*, 200; Weil, interview by the author.

19. Mankiewicz quoted in Johnson, "Characters Trapped by Circumstances" (Teddy White reports in *Making of the President 1972* [200] that this conversation took place in the Starlight Roof on the eighteenth floor of the Doral); Weil, interview by the author.

20. J. Brian Atwood to Thomas Eagleton, "Re: Conversation with Scott Lilly," memorandum, September 7, 1972, c. 5736, box 22, TFEP; Mankiewicz, interview by the author.

21. Johnson, "Characters Trapped by Circumstances"; Weil, *Long Shot*, 164–65; Stearns, interview by the author.

22. Informant quoted in "Characters Trapped by Circumstances."

The Investigation

1. Filippine to Eagleton, memorandum, August 16, 1972, p. 20; Wierzynski, interview by the author; Bennet "Re: Eighteen Days," 17; Weil, *Long Shot*, 172–73; *St. Louis Post-Dispatch* in John Kifner, "The Rise and Fall of Tom Eagleton," *NYT*, August 1, 1972; Jonathan Larsen to Time Nation, "Re: Eagleton vs. Curtis."

2. Mankiewicz quoted in Johnson, "Characters Trapped by Circumstances"; Bennet, interview by Harrison, 5; Mankiewicz, interview by the author.

3. Saul Friedman, "McGovern's Men," *MH*, July 9, 1972; AP, "Henry Kimelman, McGovern Aide, Dies at 88," *NYT*, November 13, 2009; "McGovern's Henry the K," *Time*, August 7, 1972; Anson, *McGovern*, 257–59; Johnston, interview by the author.

4. Bennet, interview by Harrison, 5; Bennet, "Re: Eighteen Days," 17; Christopher Lydon, "Eagleton to Woo Labor and Daley," *NYT*, July 16, 1972; Filippine to Eagleton, memorandum, August 16, 1972, pp. 19–20.

5. Eagleton quoted in Lydon, "Eagleton to Woo Labor and Daley"; AP, "Eagleton Home," *NYT*, July 15, 1972.

6. Johnson, "Characters Trapped by Circumstances"; Weil, *Long Shot*, 172; Bennet, interview by Harrison, 5. Bennet, "Re: Eighteen Days," 17; Eagleton aide quoted in Haynes Johnson, "First Hint of the Problem," *WP*, December 4, 1972; Robert S. Boyd, "McGovern Orders Aides to Shut Up on Running Mate," *MH*, July 28, 1972; Hart, *Right from the Start*, 250–51.

7. Bennet, "Re: Eighteen Days," 20, Insert A, 22; Van Dyk, *Heroes, Hacks, and Fools*, 140; conversation as remembered by Hart, in Hart, *Right from the Start*, 251–52, and in Johnson, "First Hint of the Problem"; Holum and Mankiewicz,

interviews by the author. The accounts suggest that this conversation may have been two separate discussions, but it is presented as one here.

8. Bennet, "Re: Eighteen Days," 23; CBS, *Face the Nation,* July 16, 1972, transcript, c. 0674, folder 2823, TFEP; Hart and Mankiewicz quoted in Johnson, "First Hint of the Problem."

9. Clark Hoyt, interview by the author; Clark Hoyt (via AP), "Reporter Recounts How He Ferreted Out the Eagleton Story in 1972," *Pittsburgh Tribune-Review,* March 6, 2007.

10. Hoyt, interview by the author; Hoyt, correspondence with the author; "Hill Announces Clark F. Hoyt '60 as the 2011 Commencement Speaker," March 2, 2011, http://www.thehill.org/RelId/800635/pagenum/3/ISvars/default/Hill_announces_Clark_F__Hoyt_'60_as_the_2011_Commencement_speaker.htm; Clark Hoyt, address at the 160th annual commencement of The Hill School, May 28, 2011, QuickTime Movie, http://www.thehill.org/RelId/872806/pagenum/2/ISvars/default/Hill_celebrates_160th_Commencement_exercises.htm; Heinz-Dietrich Fischer and Erika J. Fischer, *Complete Biographical Encyclopedia of Pulitzer Prize Winners, 1917–2000: Journalists, Writers, and Composers on Their Ways to the Coveted Awards* (Munich: K. G. Saur Verlag GmbH, 2002), 111.

11. David W. Merritt, "Rejected as 'Crackpot,' Caller Triggered Probe," *MH,* July 27, 1972; John S. Knight, "John S. Knight's Notebook: Eagleton Story Is Sad, He Should Withdraw," *MH,* July 30, 1972; Hoyt, interview by the author; Hoyt, correspondence with the author; Hoyt, "Reporter Recounts."

12. Hoyt, interview by the author.

13. Merritt, "Rejected as 'Crackpot.'"

14. Robert Boyd, interview by the author.

15. Mike Kelley, handwritten note on United States Senate memorandum pad regarding conversation with Dick Dudman, October 17, 1972, box 22, TFEP. I recognized the handwriting as Mike Kelley's, and Ruth Herbst corroborated this for me. Mike Kelley graciously decoded his handwriting and helped me faithfully interpret the content of his note.

16. David Cooper, interview by the author; *St. Louis Post-Dispatch* report on Agnew's knowledge summarized in UPI, "'Eagleton Data to Agnew,'" *San Francisco Examiner,* November 7, 1972. With the Eagleton story already in the past, the *Free Press* never published the results of Cooper's investigation.

17. Hoyt, interview by the author.

18. "Eagleton Is in Hospital," *SLPD,* December 17, 1960; "Eagleton Has Check-Up," *SLPD,* December 28, 1964; "Eagleton in Hospital," *SLPD,* September 21, 1966.

19. Hoyt, interview by the author; Hoyt, correspondence with the author.

20. Hoyt and Boyd, interviews by the author; Hoyt, "Reporter Recounts."

21. Hoyt and Boyd, interviews by the author; Hoyt, "Reporter Recounts"; Hoyt, "Eagleton: A Driven Man"; CBS, *Face the Nation,* July 16, 1972, transcript.

22. Hart quoted in Johnson, "First Hint of the Problem"; Weil, *Long Shot,* 173;

Hart, *Right from the Start,* 252; Bennet, handwritten notes on legal pad, box 37, folder 7, DJBP; Johnston, interview by the author.

23. Johnson, "First Hint of the Problem"; Hart, *Right from the Start,* 253; Bennet to Eagleton, "Re: Eighteen Days," 24–25; Memorandum of Call from Susan Garro to Bennet and Kelley, undated, box 37, folder 3, DJBP; "Susan Garro, volunteer who took call re: Eagleton," undated notecard, box 4, "Eagleton" folder, GSMDWUP; Bennet, handwritten notes on legal pad, box 37, folder 7, DJBP; Hoyt and Johnston, interviews by the author.

24. Greg Wierzynski and Burton Pines, interviews by the author.

25. Bob Boyd and Clark Hoyt, "Eagleton Memo," memorandum, July 23, 1972, box 460, "Eagleton Issues" folder, GSMPUP; Hoyt, interview by the author.

26. Curt Matthews, "AFL-CIO Neutral on Presidency," *SLPD,* July 19, 1972; Robert Adams, "Eagleton Would Try to Solve Urban Crisis," *SLPD,* July 19, 1972.

27. Dougherty, *Goodbye, Mr. Christian,* 162; AP, "McGovern Celebrating Birthday at Retreat," *SLPD,* July 19, 1972.

28. Hart's notes in McGovern, *Grassroots,* 202; Bennet, interview by Harrison, 8–9; Hart, *Right from the Start,* 253.

29. Dick Dougherty to McGovern, CC: Pat Donovan, Fred Dutton, Steve Robbins, Chris Turpin, "Re: Press Requirements and the Well-Being of the Candidate," memorandum, July 21, 1972, box 695, "July 1972" folder, GSMPUP.

30. Mankiewicz, interview by the author; Bruce Miroff, *The Liberals' Moment: The McGovern Insurgency and the Identity Crisis of the Democratic Party* (Lawrence: University Press of Kansas, 2007), 94; James N. Giglio, "The Eagleton Affair: Thomas Eagleton, George McGovern, and the 1972 Vice Presidential Nomination," *Presidential Studies Quarterly* 39, no. 4 (2009): 658.

    For another possible wording, see Bennet to Kelley, memorandum, December 12, 1972, box 37, folder 7, DJBP: "McGovern told staff people during the campaign that the doctors had said the diagnosis was paranoid, suicidal, and likely to break under the strains of the presidency."

    Furthermore, in a memo commenting on an early draft of Eagleton's unpublished memoir, Bennet wrote, "You obviously shouldn't publish the records," which further underscores the impression that the diagnosis and/ or language would have been immediately disqualifying. See Bennet to Eagleton, "Re: Book—First Reading," memorandum, September 7, 1972, box 37, folder 7, DJBP.

31. Hart's notes in McGovern, *Grassroots,* 202; Christopher Lydon, "Eagleton Tells of Shock Therapy on Two Occasions," *NYT,* July 26, 1972; Johnson, "First Hint of the Problem," including Hart's recollections; Hart, *Right from the Start,* 253–54.

32. Sam Krupnick to Rose Mary Woods, letter, July 19, 1972, accessed via Nixon Library, http://nixonlibrary.gov/virtuallibrary/documents/dec08/072372 _buchanan.pdf; Richard Nixon and Rose Mary Woods, conversation, July

21, 1972, unknown time between 3:35 p.m. and 3:43 p.m., NWHOOT, no. 750-4, MP3 recording, http://nixon.archives.gov/forresearchers/find/ tapes/tape750/750–004.mp3, finding aid, http://nixon.archives.gov/for researchers/find/tapes/finding_aids/tapesubjectlogs/oval750.pdf; Dorothy Dubuque and Ruth Herbst, interviews and correspondence with the author; Carl Bernstein and Bob Woodward, "Vast GOP Undercover Operations Originated in 1969," *WP*, May 17, 1973; Patrick J. Buchanan, *Right from the Beginning* (Washington, DC: Regnery Gateway, 1990), 297; Buchanan to Charles Colson, memorandum, July 23, 1972, accessed via Nixon Library, http:// nixonlibrary.gov/virtuallibrary/documents/dec08/072372_buchanan.pdf, including Colson's handwritten response.

33. McGovern, *Grassroots,* 203; Mankiewicz, as remembered by Eagleton in "Eagleton's Own Odyssey," *Time,* August 7, 1972; Mankiewicz and Hart, interviews by the author.

34. Edward Shorter, *A History of Psychiatry: From the Era of the Asylum to the Age of Prozac* (New York: Wiley, 1997), 282; Harry Nelson, "Depression Chief Indication for Shock Treatment," *LAT,* July 26, 1972; Phil Zeidman, interview by the author.

35. Shorter, *History of Psychiatry,* 14, 26, 160–61, 221–22; Kitty Dukakis and Larry Tye, *Shock: The Healing Power of Electroconvulsive Therapy* (New York: Avery, 2007), 48, 63, 108; Suzanne Murray, "Depression," manuscript, 1972, c. 5736, box 22, TFEP, p. 12; Edward Shorter and David Healy, *Shock Therapy: A History of Electroconvulsive Treatment in Mental Illness* (New Brunswick, NJ: Rutgers University Press, 2007), 84–85; Stephen R. Shuchter, Nancy Downs, and Sidney Zisook, *Biologically Informed Psychotherapy for Depression* (New York: Guilford, 1996), 13–14, 19, 156–57; David Eagleman, *Incognito: The Secret Lives of the Brain* (New York: Pantheon, 2011), 172.

　　See, in particular, the work of Karl Abraham, Sigmund Freud, and Gerald Klerman for psychoanalytic theories of mental illness and depression, including Abraham, "Notes on the Psychoanalytic Investigation and Treatment of Manic-Depressive Insanity and Allied Conditions" in *Selected Papers of Karl Abraham* (London: Hogarth, 1948); Sigmund Freud, "Mourning and Melancholia" in James Strachey, ed. and trans., *The Standard Edition of the Complete Psychological Works of Sigmund Freud,* vol. 14 (London: Hogarth, 1957); Gerald Klerman et al., *Interpersonal Psychotherapy of Depression* (New York: Basic, 1984).

36. Sarah H. Lisanby, "Electroconvulsive Therapy for Depression," *New England Journal of Medicine* 257 (2007): 1939–45; Harold Sackeim et al., "The Cognitive Effects of Electroconvulsive Therapy in Community Settings," *Neuropsychopharmacology* 32 (2007): 252; Kellner, Sackeim, Rudorfer, and Lisanby, interviews by the author; Angel V. Peterchev et al., "Electroconvulsive Therapy Stimulus Parameters: Rethinking Dosage," *ECT Journal* 26, no. 3 (2010): 159–74; Timothy Spellman et al., "Differential Effects of High

Dose Magnetic Seizure Therapy (MST) and Electroconvulsive Shock (ECS) on Cognitive Function," *Biological Psychiatry* 63, no. 12 (2008): 1163–70; Stefan Rowny et al., "Translational Development Strategy for Magnetic Seizure Therapy," *Experimental Neurology* 1 (2009): 27–35.

37. Shorter, *History of Psychiatry*, 160–61, 222; Shorter and Healy, *Shock Therapy*, 84–85, 99; Dukakis and Tye, *Shock*, 22, 67, 92, 93, 95, 108, 144, 146, 198; "The Most Common Mental Disorder," *Time*, August 7, 1972; Stuart Auerbach, "Shock Treatment Is Widely Used, but Controversial," *WP*, July 26, 1972; "Depression and Electroshock," *Newsweek*, August 7, 1972, 20; Richard C. Hermann et al., "Diagnoses of Patients Treated with ECT; A Comparison of Evidence-Based Standards with Reported Use," *Psychiatric Services* 50, no. 8 (1999): 1059–65; John A. P. Millet and Eric P. Mosse, "On Certain Psychological Aspects of Electroshock Therapy," *Psychosomatic Medicine* 6 (1944): 226–36; Nolan D. C. Lewis, "The Present Status of Shock Therapy of Mental Disorders," *Bulletin of the New York Academy of Medicine*, April 1943, 236; Joel Braslow, *Mental Ills and Bodily Cures* (Berkeley: University of California Press, 1997), 104; "Practice Parameter for Use of Electroconvulsive Therapy with Adolescents," AACP Official Action, *Journal of the American Academy of Child and Adolescent Psychiatry* 43, no. 12 (2004): 1521–39.

38. Dukakis and Tye, *Shock*, 90–91, 100–101, 111–15. Shorter and Healy, *Shock Therapy*, 144, 155–56; Gerald N. Grob, *The Mad among Us: A History of the Care of America's Mentally Ill* (New York: Free Press, 1994), 269; Ken Kesey, *One Flew over the Cuckoo's Nest* (New York: Signet, 1963), 64–65, 164, 242; Eagleton quoted in R. W. Apple Jr., "Eagleton Is Firm Despite Pressure from 2 Party Chiefs," *NYT*, July 31, 1972.

39. Charles Conway, Max Fink, Matthew Rudorfer, Mike Kelley, and Frank Mankiewicz, interviews by the author; Max Fink, e-mail correspondence with the author, August 7, 2011; Candace O'Connor, "Rethinking Psychiatry: 'Troublemakers' in the Department of Psychiatry Later Were Hailed for Having Reshaped the Profession," *Washington University in St. Louis School of Medicine Magazine: Outlook*, February 2011, http://outlook.wustl.edu/2011/feb/psychiatry; Dukakis and Tye, *Shock*, 127; Shuchter, Downs, and Zisook, *Biologically Informed Psychotherapy for Depression*, 17; Eli Robins and Samuel B. Guze, "Establishment of Diagnostic Validity in Psychiatric Illness: Its Application to Schizophrenia," *American Journal of Psychiatry* 126, no. 7 (1970): 107–11; John Arnold Lindon to Frank Mankiewicz, letter, July 27, 1972, "Eagleton" folder, box 17, FFMP.

40. Louis Harris quoted in R. W. Apple Jr., "The Question Raised by Eagleton," *NYT*, July 27, 1972; Dukakis and Tye, *Shock*, 107–9, 115.

41. Dougherty, *Goodbye, Mr. Christian*, 166–70, including McGovern "foremost consultant" quotation, 166; Rowland Evans and Robert Novak, "Is McGovern Really Boss?" *WP*, July 24, 1972, including McGovern "I'm sorry" quotation; Robert Adams, "O'Brien to Head McGovern's Campaign," *SLPD*, July

20, 1972; James M. Naughton, "O'Brien Gets Post in M'Govern Drive," *NYT*, July 21, 1972; Hart, *Right from the Start*, 257; photograph with Joel Weisman, "Daley Challengers Ordered to Court," *WP*, July 21, 1972.

42. White, *Making of the President 1972*, 188–90; Witker, *How to Lose*, 109, 127, 139–40; O'Brien, *No Final Victories*, 318–25; Olga Curtis, "First Woman in Top Demo Job: 'A Little Scared, Pretty Humble,'" *MH*, July 29, 1972.

43. Naughton, "O'Brien Gets Post"; Dougherty, *Goodbye, Mr. Christian*, 166–70; Evans and Novak, "Is McGovern Really Boss?"; Adams, "O'Brien to Head McGovern's Campaign"; Hart, *Right from the Start*, 257.

44. Johnson, "First Hint of the Problem," including McGovern quotation as remembered by Hart; McGovern, *Grassroots*, 203; Hart, *Right from the Start*, 255–56.

45. Mankiewicz's memories, as cited in Johnson, "First Hint of the Problem"; Mankiewicz, interview by the author.

46. Hart quoted in Johnson, "First Hint of the Problem"; Hart, *Right from the Start*, 256; Hart, interview by the author; Weil, *Long Shot*, 174.

47. Hart in Johnson, "First Hint of the Problem"; McGovern, *Grassroots*, 203; Boyd, "McGovern Orders Aides to Shut Up."

48. McGovern quoted in Hart, *Right from the Start*, 256.

49. Boyd and Hoyt, interviews by the author.

50. Hoyt, interview by the author.

51. Boyd and Hoyt, "Eagleton Memo," memorandum, July 23, 1972, box 460, "Eagleton Issues" folder, GSMPUP; Boyd and Hoyt, "Eagleton Memo," memorandum, July 23, 1972, c. 5736, box 22, TFEP.

52. Boyd and Hoyt, interviews by the author; Merritt, "Rejected as 'Crackpot.'"

53. Evans and Novak, "Is McGovern Really Boss?"; Adams, "O'Brien to Head McGovern's Campaign"; Naughton, "O'Brien Gets Post"; McGovern quoted in Tim O'Brien, "McGovern 'Furious' at Staff," *WP*, July 24, 1972; Dougherty, *Goodbye, Mr. Christian*, 166–70, including McGovern quotation, 169–70; Hart, *Right from the Start*, 257.

54. William Greider, "Vacation Ordeal," *WP*, July 29, 1972; Hart, *Right from the Start*, 257.

55. Hoyt, interview by the author; Merritt, "Rejected as 'Crackpot.'"

The Disclosure

1. Eagleton quoted in Douglas E. Kneeland, "M'Govern to Seek Johnson Support Despite War View," *NYT*, July 24, 1972; Weil, *Long Shot*, 174; Boyd and Hoyt, "Eagleton Memo," TFEP and GSMPUP; Haynes Johnson, "Disclosure Failed to Allay the Doubts," *WP*, December 5, 1972; Mankiewicz, interview by the author.

2. Mankiewicz, as recalled by Hoyt in interview with the author; Boyd, interview by the author; Merritt, "Rejected as 'Crackpot.'"

3. Mankiewicz quoted in Johnson, "Disclosure Failed to Allay the Doubts";
    Bennet to Eagleton, "Re: Eighteen Days," 27; Bennet to Jim Murphy, "Re:
    Issues," memorandum, July 20, 1972, box 34, folder 6, DJBP; Bennet to Eagle-
    ton, memorandum, July 24, 1972, box 37, folder 7, DJBP; Bennet, "Agenda
    for Meeting with McGovern," typewritten outline notes, circa July 24, 1972,
    box 37, folder 7, DJBP.

    Bennet's reference to Murphy's "return" in his memo implies that Mur-
    phy was not in Washington on July 20—that is, that he was already either
    in St. Louis or in Minnesota.

4. Hoyt, interview by the author; Merritt, "Rejected as 'Crackpot.'"
5. Conversation as reported by Dougherty in *Goodbye, Mr. Christian*, 172.
6. Bennet to Eagleton, "Re: Eighteen Days," 30.
7. Hoyt, interview by the author; Merritt, "Rejected as 'Crackpot.'"
8. Conversation as reported in Eagleton, "Minibiography," chapter 5, pp. 3–4;
    Dougherty, *Goodbye, Mr. Christian*, 173; McGovern, *Grassroots*, 204; Bennet,
    interview by Harrison, 10; McGovern's notes on meeting with Eagleton in
    cabin 22, July 25, 1972, box 692, "Senator's Personal Notes" folder, GSMPUP;
    "Eagleton's Own Odyssey."
9. Dougherty, *Goodbye, Mr. Christian*, 173–74.
10. Conversation as re-created in Dougherty's notes in McGovern, *Grassroots*,
    205–6, and in Dougherty, *Goodbye, Mr. Christian*, 176.
11. Bruce Miroff, *Liberals' Moment*, 92, including Mankiewicz quotation; George
    McGovern, *Terry: My Daughter's Life-and-Death Struggle with Alcoholism* (New
    York: Villard, 1996), 81–100, esp. 96–97 for influence of Terry's condition
    on the Eagleton decision; Bennet, interviewed by Harrison, 10; Eleanor
    McGovern, *Uphill*, 79–80, 82–83, 120–23; Carl P. Leubsdorf, "McGovern Still
    Mourns '72 Loss," *Lawrence* [KS] *Journal-World*, July 13, 2007.

    As McGovern outlined in *Terry*, following his daughter's arrest for
    marijuana possession amid her father's 1968 Senate campaign, she had
    taken a turn for the worse; Terry slumped into a depression, ratcheted up
    her alcohol consumption, and experimented with LSD. After the New Year,
    she was hospitalized for six months and underwent intensive treatment that
    entailed a combination of medication and psychoanalysis. At age nineteen,
    she escaped from the Charlottesville, Virginia, hospital, and tried to take
    her life, swigging down vodka and an overdose of pills, which turned out
    to be placebos supplied by a friend. After her release from the hospital,
    Terry continued treatment.
12. In box 445 of the McGovern Papers at Princeton, "Personal—Mc" folder,
    there is an envelope containing several medical bills. They include bills
    from the University of Virginia for Terry's hospitalization, from January 6
    to July 25, 1969, listing treatment with Doriden (glutethimide) tablets, milk
    of magnesia, cascara fluid extract, among others, as well as for a clinical lab
    procedure on March 19, which followed a fee for an emergency room visit on

March 16, 1969. Blue Cross Blue Shield Federal Employee supplement benefits claims for Terry dated March 25, 1970, for "emotional, nervous disorder"; supplement benefits claims dated June 30, 1970, for both Terry McGovern and Eleanor F. McGovern for "nervousness, depression"; and a bill to George S. McGovern from the University of Virginia Clinic, Private Division, in Charlottesville, Virginia, for thirty-one "one hour Psychotherapy session[s] with Dr. Vamik D. Volkan, M.D., Associate Professor of Psychiatry, University of Virginia School of Medicine" between July 1971 and September 15, 1971; McGovern to Vamik D. Volkan, October 26, 1997, box 15, folder 16, Vamik D. Volkan Papers, Historical Collections and Services, Claude Moore Health Sciences Library, University of Virginia.

13. McGovern, *Terry*, 87–88; McGovern, *Grassroots*, 16. In GMPPUP, box 445, "Personal—McG" folder, see esp. George McGovern to Larry McGovern, letter, August 6, 1971; George McGovern to Lynn Carroll, letter, August 6, 1971; Larry McGovern to George McGovern, letter, September 26, 1971; Larry to George, letter, October 12, 1971; Larry to George, letter, October 26, 1971; George to Larry, letter, December 6, 1971; Larry to George, letter, December 7, 1971; Larry to George, letter, December 17, 1971.

14. Anson, *McGovern*, 125; Joe McGinniss, "Second Thoughts of George McGovern," *NYT Sunday Magazine*, May 6, 1973, 32.

15. Ted Van Dyk, *Heroes, Hacks, and Fools*, 144–45; AP, "Judge Releases McGovern Birth Certificate," *Morning Record* (Meriden-Wallingford, CT), August 9, 1973; UPI, "McGovern Surrounded by Dispute over Birth Record," *Dispatch* (Lexington, NC), August 10, 1973; George Lardner Jr., "Goldberg a Veteran at Recording Gossip," *WP*, February 4, 1998; Mark Feldstein and Lucianne Goldberg, interviews by the author; Bob Woodward and Carl Bernstein, "Leak Involving McGovern Proposed," *WP*, August 2, 1973; Joseph Kraft, "Fratricidal White House Led to Leak of 'Horrors,'" *Pittsburgh Post-Gazette*, August 4, 1973.

On the night of Eagleton's withdrawal from the ticket, Nixon and Haldeman discussed whether they should soon break word of McGovern's illegitimate child. "It's probably too late to use the letter from Fort Wayne, is it?" the president asked Haldeman in a phone conversation. "I don't think we ought to," he replied. "I don't think we oughtta, I don't think we want to use it at all." Nixon agreed. "You just never know how that sort of thing is going to react," Nixon said. Haldeman and the president ultimately decided to table the information until needed—keep it "in the bank," as Nixon phrased it. (See H. R. Haldeman and Richard Nixon, telephone conversation, July 31, 1972, unknown time between 10:16 p.m. and 10:25 p.m., NWHTT no. 28-21, MP3 recording, http://nixontapeaudio.org/chron4/rmn_e028_21 .mp3; "Nixon Presidential Materials Staff, Tape Subject Log," July 31, 1972, http://whitehousetapes.net/028.)

I also unearthed a memo in Gordon Weil's personal papers outlining a litany of rumors about McGovern and his staffers, probably created to prepare the campaign to defend against smears. Several of the rumors relate to McGovern's history of philandering over the years, from youth through the campaign. (See GLWP, box 1, folders 12 and 13.)

Lucianne Goldberg, who was hired by CREEP to pose as a reporter on the McGovern press bus and feed the Nixon campaign updates, told me in an interview that she had "nothing to do" with this sort of leak.

16. Bennet, interview by Harrison, 10; Eagleton as remembered in Eagleton, "Minibiography," chapter 5, pp. 4–5; McGovern, *Grassroots*, 205–6; Dougherty, *Goodbye, Mr. Christian*, 178–79; Kelley and Mankiewicz, interviews by the author.

17. Boyd and Hoyt, interviews by the author; Hoyt, "Reporter Recounts."

18. Eagleton, "Minibiography," chapter 5, pp. 4–5; Mankiewicz quoted in Johnson, "Disclosure Failed to Allay the Doubts"; Bennet, interview by Harrison, 11; McGovern, *Grassroots*, 206; Kelley and Mankiewicz, interviews by the author.

19. Mankiewicz's words, as remembered by Hoyt in interview by the author; Dougherty's end of the exchange as recalled in *Goodbye, Mr. Christian*, 181.

20. Crouse, *Boys on the Bus*, 339–40; Dougherty, *Goodbye, Mr. Christian*, 161; William Greider, "Vacation Ordeal," *WP*, July 29, 1974.

21. Bennet to Eagleton, "Re: Eighteen Days," 33; William Greider, "Eagleton Reveals Illness," *WP*, July 26, 1972; Crouse, *Boys on the Bus*, 344–45; Bennet, interview by Harrison, 11; Boyd, Hoyt, Brooks Jackson, Leubsdorf, Mankiewicz, McNeely, and Witker, interviews by the author.

22. Boyd, Hoyt, and Mankiewicz, interviews by the author; Bennet, interview by Harrison, 11; Mankiewicz as remembered by Hart in Johnson, "Disclosure Failed to Allay the Doubts."

23. Telephone conversation between Hart and Mankiewicz as remembered by Hart in Johnson, "Disclosure Failed to Allay the Doubts," and in Hart, *Right from the Start*, 258. The last quotation, attributed to Mankiewicz, merges language from both accounts; Mankiewicz, interview by the author.

24. Robert McNeely, interview by the author.

25. Christopher Lydon, "Eagleton Tells of Shock Therapy on Two Occasions," *NYT*, July 26, 1972; Greider, "Eagleton Reveals Illness."

26. Press conference re-created primarily from Eagleton and McGovern quotations and descriptions in Lydon, "Eagleton Tells of Shock Therapy"; Greider, "Eagleton Reveals Illness"; Robert S. Boyd and Clark Hoyt, "Eagleton Reveals Past Mental Care; McGovern Rejects His Offer to Quit," *MH*, July 26, 1972; UPI, "Excerpts from Eagleton News Parley," *NYT*, July 26, 1972; Hoyt, "Reporter Recounts."

27. Crouse, *Boys on the Bus*, 345; Dougherty, *Goodbye, Mr. Christian*, 188.

28. McGovern quoted in Eagleton, "Minibiography," chapter 5, p. 7; McGovern, *Grassroots*, 207.

29. Eagleton quoted in Hoyt, "Eagleton: Driven Man"; Boyd and Hoyt, interviews by the author.

30. Eagleton quoted in Boyd and Hoyt, "Eagleton Reveals Past Mental Care"; Boyd and Hoyt, interviews by the author.
31. Hoyt, interview by the author; Hoyt, "Reporter Recounts"; Eagleton quoted in Boyd and Hoyt, "Eagleton Reveals Past Mental Care."
32. Eagleton quoted in Merritt, "Rejected as 'Crackpot.'"
33. Eagleton quoted in Boyd and Hoyt, "Eagleton Reveals Past Mental Care"; Hoyt, "Eagleton: A Driven Man"; Eagleton as remembered by Hoyt in interview by the author; Hoyt, "Reporter Recounts."
34. Hoyt, interview by the author; Hoyt, "Reporter Recounts."
35. Godley, Kelley, and McNeely, interviews by the author.

The Aftershock

1. Dougherty, *Goodbye, Mr. Christian*, 190; Crouse, *Boys on the Bus*, 346–47; McGovern quoted in Ottenad, "Eagleton Would Take Tests," and Thomas W. Ottenad, "Decision on Eagleton Reported Imminent," *SLPD*, July 30, 1972.
2. Leubsdorf, interview by the author; Leubsdorf quoted in Crouse, *Boys on the Bus*, 346.
3. Leubsdorf, interview by the author; McGovern quoted in Carl P. Leubsdorf (AP), "McGovern First Learned Details of Eagleton's Illness on Tuesday," *Evening News* (Sault Ste. Marie, MI), July 26, 1972; McGovern and Mankiewicz quoted in Carl P. Leubsdorf (AP), "McGovern Adopts 'Wait-See' Attitude in Eagleton's Psychiatric Care, Shock Treatment Revelations," *Robesonian* (Lumberton, NC), July 26, 1972; McGovern quoted in Crouse, *Boys on the Bus*, 347; Mankiewicz quoted in Ottenad, "Eagleton Would Take Tests"; Mankiewicz quoted in Greider, "Eagleton Reveals Illness"; Mankiewicz quoted in Lydon, "Eagleton Tells of Shock Therapy."
4. Anthony Summers, *The Arrogance of Power: The Secret World of Richard Nixon* (New York: Penguin, 2000), 311–12; J. Y. Smith, "H. R. Haldeman Dies," *WP*, November 13, 1993; H. R. Haldeman, interview by Dale E. Treleven, June 18, 1991, transcript, California State Archives State Government Early History Program, University of California, Los Angeles; Earl Mazo and Stephen Hess, *Nixon: A Political Portrait* (New York: Popular Library, 1968), 276; Crouse, *Boys on the Bus*, 228; White, *Making of the President 1972*, 220–23; Bernstein and Woodward, *All the President's Men*, 128, 131, 161–62, 177–79; Stanley I. Kutler, *Wars of Watergate: The Last Crisis of Richard Nixon* (New York: Norton, 1992), 192.

    Though he was widely believed to have been an Eagle Scout, Haldeman admitted otherwise in his oral history interview with Treleven toward the end of his life. Haldeman said he was a Life Scout, just a few merit badges short of becoming an Eagle.
5. H. R. Haldeman and Clark MacGregor, telephone conversation, July 25,

1972, unknown time between 5:45 P.M. and 5:54 P.M., NWHTT, no. 27-62, MP3 recording, http://nixontapeaudio.org/chron4/rmn_e027_62.mp3.

6. H. R. Haldeman and Bob Dole, telephone conversation, July 25, 1972, unknown time between 5:55 P.M. and 5:57 P.M., NWHTT, no. 27-63, MP3 recording, http://nixontapeaudio.org/chron4/rmn_e027_63.mp3.

7. H. R. Haldeman and Spiro Agnew, telephone conversation, July 25, 1972, unknown time between 6:24 P.M. and 6:34 P.M., NWHTT, no. 27-64, MP3 recording, http://nixontapeaudio.org/chron4/rmn_e027_64.mp3.

8. Haldeman handwritten note no. 34, July 25, 1972, box 46, "H Notes July–Aug.–Sept. 1972 [July 22, 1972, to August 16, 1972]" folder, HRHP. This document can be viewed online at http://nixon.archives.gov/virtuallibrary/documents/jun09/072572_Haldeman.pdf.

In interviews with the author, Ruth Herbst and Mike Kelley said they could not verify whether Eagleton had ever been treated at Johns Hopkins, but they found the idea inconceivable that he could have been.

9. Haynes Johnson, "1,000 Per Cent to Zero," *WP*, December 6, 1972; Bennet, interview by Harrison, 11; Godley, Jackson, Kelley, and McNeely, interviews by the author.

10. Vanderbilt Television News Archive website, programs broadcast in July 1972, http://tvnews.vanderbilt.edu/siteindex/1972-7/; Robert Abernethy and Eagleton quoted in Johnson, "1,000 Per Cent to Zero"; Eagleton, "Mini-biography," chapter 6, p. 3; Bennet, interview by Harrison, 11; Godley and Kelley, interviews by the author.

11. Barbara Eagleton quoted in Taylor, "Mrs. Eagleton Off and Running."

12. Secretary call slip notes for McGovern, "From [Bill] Gruver in L.A. reporting on Eagleton's press conf," July 26, 1972, box 460, "Eagleton Issues" folder, GSMPUP.

13. Eagleton quoted in Loye Miller Jr., "'I'll Quit if I Hurt Nominee': Eagleton Hits Campaign Trail," *MH*, July 27, 1972; Loye Miller Jr., "Eagleton Seems Cool in Face of Pressure to Quit Campaign," *MH*, July 28, 1972; Godley and Kelley, interviews by the author; Eagleton quoted in Ottenad, "Eagleton Would Take Tests"; Eagleton, "Minibiograpy," chapter 6, p. 3; Eagleton quoted in Christopher Lydon, "Eagleton Hints He'll Quit Race if Polls Are Negative," *NYT*, July 27, 1972.

14. Eagleton quoted in Ottenad, "Eagleton Would Take Tests"; Miller, "'I'll Quit If I Hurt Nominee.'"

15. Lydon, "Eagleton Tells of Shock Therapy"; Eagleton quoted in Lydon, "Eagleton Hints He'll Quit Race"; Miller, "'I'll Quit If I Hurt Nominee'"; Eagleton quoted in Ottenad, "Eagleton Would Take Tests."

16. Secretary call slip notes to McGovern, "From [Bill] Gruver in L.A. reporting on Eagleton's press conf"; Eagleton quoted in Lydon, "Eagleton Hints He'll Quit Race."

17. H. R. Haldeman and Richard Nixon, conversation, July 26, 1972, unknown

time between 9:02 A.M. and 11:05 A.M., NEOBT, no. 350-34, MP3 recording, http://nixontapeaudio.org/chron4/rmn_e350_034.mp3; Stanley I. Kutler, *Abuse of Power: The New Nixon Tapes* (New York: Touchstone, 1998), 106–7; H. R. Haldeman, *The Haldeman Diaries: Inside the Nixon White House* (New York: Putnam, 1994), 486; Richard Nixon, *The Memoirs of Richard Nixon* (New York: Grosset and Dunlap, 1978), 663–65.

18. AP, "National Committee Would Fill Vacancy on Democratic Ticket," *MH,* July 26, 1972; Robert Adams, "Looking into Procedure for Replacing Nominee," *SLPD,* July 28, 1972; Davis Merritt, "Sub for Eagleton: Not Only Who? But How?" *MH,* July 30, 1972; Ottenad, "Eagleton Would Take Tests."

19. Dougherty quoted in Robert S. Boyd, "Telegrams Run 2–1 against Eagleton," *MH,* July 27, 1972; Dougherty, *Goodbye, Mr. Christian,* 189.

20. Dougherty, *Goodbye, Mr. Christian,* 190; Leubsdorf, "McGovern Adopts 'Wait-See' Attitude"; Leubsdorf, interview by the author.

21. McGovern and Dougherty conversation, as reported in Dougherty, *Goodbye, Mr. Christian,* 190–91.

22. Dougherty, *Goodbye, Mr. Christian,* 191.

23. McGovern and Dougherty conversation, as reported in Dougherty, *Goodbye, Mr. Christian,* 190–91; Weil, *Long Shot,* 178. McGovern's handwritten version of the "1,000 percent" statement can be found in box 460, "Eagleton Issues" folder, GSMPUP; Leubsdorf, interview by the author.

24. Dougherty, *Goodbye, Mr. Christian,* 193; Leubsdorf, interview by the author.

25. Johnson, "1,000 Per Cent to Zero"; McGovern statement and Dougherty comment quoted in Douglas E. Kneeland, "M'Govern Urged by Some Backers to Drop Eagleton," *NYT,* July 27, 1972; Crouse, *Boys on the Bus,* 347; Hart quoted in James M. Naughton, "Nixon Disclosure on Health Asked," *NYT,* July 27, 1972; Johnston, interview by the author.

26. Hart quoted in Vera Glaser, "Eagleton to Stay? It's Up to Him, McGovern Aide Says," *MH,* July 27, 1972.

27. Hart quoted ibid.; Naughton, "Nixon Disclosure on Health Asked"; Ziegler quoted in UPI, "Don't Comment on Eagleton, Nixon Tells Staff, Spokesmen," *MH,* July 27, 1972; MacGregor quoted in Lou Cannon, "Nixon Asks for Silence on Eagleton," *WP,* July 27, 1972; Nixon quoted in "Transcript of President's News Conference on Foreign and Domestic Matters," *NYT,* July 28, 1972; Robert B. Semple Jr., "Nixon Terms '72 Election Clearest Choice of Century," *NYT,* July 28, 1972; William Vance, "Nixon: My Campaign Will Stick to Issues," *MH,* July 28, 1972; Johnson, "1,000 Per Cent to Zero"; Kneeland, "M'Govern Urged by Some Backers."

28. MacGregor quoted in Lou Cannon, "Nixon Asks for Silence"; Nixon quotations from the president's conversation with Haldeman, Colson, and other White House aides, July 26 1972, unknown time between 3:10 P.M. and 4:49 P.M., NEOBT, no. 350-46, MP3 recording, http://nixontapeaudio.org/chron4/

rmn_e350_046.mp3; Nixon and Woods, conversation, July 21, 1972, unknown time between 3:35 P.M. and 3:43 P.M., NWHOOT, no. 750-4.

29. UPI, "Candidates' Stability Not a New Question," *MH,* July 26, 1972; Naughton, "Nixon Disclosure on Health Asked"; Paul Clancy, "Did Doctor Switch Story on Nixon's 'Delicate' Problem?" *MH,* July 27, 1972; Jack Anderson, "Questions about Nixon's Psychotherapist Visits," *MH,* July 29, 1972; William M. Blair, "Psychiatric Aid to Nixon Denied," *NYT,* November 14, 1968; Erica Goode, "Arnold Hutschnecker, 102, Therapist to Nixon," *NYT,* January 3, 2001; Louis S. Auchincloss, "Delicate Medical Ethics," *NYT,* November 23, 1968; Nassir Ghaemi, *A First-Rate Madness: Uncovering the Links between Leadership and Mental Illness* (New York: Penguin, 2011), Kindle edition.

30. Arnold Hutschnecker, Julie Nixon Eisenhower, anonymous, Len Garment, and Mark Felt quoted in Summers, *Arrogance of Power,* 91–92, 97; Mark Felt quoted in Bernstein and Woodward, *All the President's Men,* 344.

31. Hutschnecker quoted in Summers, *Arrogance of Power,* 92.

32. Hutschnecker quoted ibid., 98.

33. Jack Dreyfus quoted in Adam Clymer, "Book Offers Peek into Nixon's Mind," *NYT,* August 27, 2000; Summers, *Arrogance of Power,* 317–18, 449.

34. Boyd, "Telegrams Run 2–1 against Eagleton"; Crouse, *Boys on the Bus,* 345–46.

35. Hart, *Right from the Start,* 259; David Brinkley on *NBC Nightly News,* July 26, 1972; Howard Metzenbaum quoted on *NBC Nightly News,* July 27, 1972.

36. "A Newsweek Poll on Eagleton," *Newsweek,* August 7, 1972.

37. McGovern, *Grassroots,* 188–90; Editorial, "Senator Eagleton's Disclosures," *WP,* July 27, 1972; Editorial, "The Eagleton Affair (Cont'd)," *WP,* July 29, 1972; Editorial, "Eagleton as Running Mate," *LAT,* July 27, 1972; Editorial, "Sympathy for Sen. Eagleton Must Not Shade the Issue," *MH,* July 27, 1972.

38. Editorial, "Mr. Eagleton's Medical Record," *SLPD,* July 27, 1972; Editorial, "The Acid Test," *SLPD,* July 28, 1972.

39. William Styron, *Darkness Visible: A Memoir of Madness* (New York: Vintage, 1992), 47.

40. Boyce Rensberger, "Electroshock Now Used Mainly for Treatment of Depression," *NYT,* July 26, 1972; Francis Braceland and American Psychiatric Association quoted in Boyce Rensberger, "Psychiatrists Explain Medical Facts in Depression Controversy," *NYT,* July 29, 1972; Stuart Auerbach, "Shock Treatment Is Widely Used, but Controversial," *WP,* July 26, 1972; Harry Nelson, "Depression Chief Indication for Shock Treatment," *LAT,* July 26, 1972; Philip Meyer, "Illness Won't Impair Eagleton, Experts Say," *MH,* July 26, 1972; Paul Wagman and Robert L. Joiner, "Doctors, Others Here React Favorably," *SLPD,* July 26, 1972; Curt Matthews, "Missourians in Congress Stand by Eagleton," *SLPD,* July 26, 1972; Christine Bertelson, "Shock Therapy Called Common and Speedy," *SLPD,* July 27, 1972; Donald C. Drace, "Many Kinds of Jobs Would Be Closed to Eagleton," *MH,* July 28, 1972; AP, "Depression Curable, Psychiatrists Say," *MH,* July 29, 1972; Edward

Edelson, "Depression: All Around but Little Known," *MH*, July 30, 1972;
UPI, "Medical Group: It's Not an Issue," *MH*, July 31, 1972; Connie Rosenbaum, "Barnes Panel Ordered Eagleton Data Moved," *SLPD*, July 30, 1972.

41. Senator Eagleton's FBI files, Case ID 161–HQ-1052683, in possession of the
author. Information about Senator Eagleton's mental health history surfaces
only in the context of a 1993 to 1995 background check to approve Eagleton's
appointment by President Clinton to the President's Foreign Intelligence
Advisory Board. Twenty pages of the files were missing. Phillip J. O'Connor,
"J. Edgar Hoover Took Notice of Tom Eagleton VP Race," *SLPD*, December
28, 2008.

42. My description of bipolar II disorder is based on an array of research, including my conversations with leading ECT practitioners, critics, and psychologists: Peter Breggin, M.D.; Charles Conway, M.D.; Nancy Downs, M.D.; Max
Fink, M.D.; Sarah Lisanby, M.D.; Charles Kellner, M.D.; Matthew Rudorfer,
M.D.; Harold Sackeim, M.D.; Steve Tuber, Ph.D.; Richard Weiner, M.D.

In particular, see Eagleton's FBI files; Eagleton to Mark Feldstein, letter,
October 19, 2005, private collection of Mark Feldstein; American Psychiatric
Association, *Diagnostic and Statistical Manual of Mental Disorders DSM-IV-TR
Fourth Edition* (Arlington, VA: American Psychiatric Publishers, 2000), sec-
tion on mood disorders beginning at 345; Association for Academic Psychia-
try, "Major Depression," http://www.brown.edu/Courses/BI_278/Other/
Clerkship/Didactics/Readings/major%20depression.pdf; Association for
Academic Psychiatry, "Bipolar Disorder," http://www.brown.edu/Courses/
BI_278/Other/Clerkship/Didactics/Readings/Bipolar%20Disorder.pdf;
Ghaemi, *First-Rate Madness*; Linda Austin, interview by Pam Morris, tran-
script, "Bipolar Disorder: Signs and Symptoms," http://www.muschealth
.com/multimedia/Podcasts/transcription.aspx?podid=30; Franco Bennazzi,
"Bipolar II Disorder: Epidemiology, Diagnosis, and Management," *Central
Nervous System Drugs* 21, no. 9 (2007): 727–40.

On psychoanalytic theories of depression, see Dukakis and Tye, *Shock*,
9, 22, 109–10; Shuchter, Downs, and Zisook, *Biologically Informed Psychotherapy*, 5, 7, 9, 13–14, 19, 36; 156–57; Eagleman, *Incognito*, 172, 206; David Brooks,
The Social Animal: The Hidden Sources of Love, Character, and Achievement
(New York: Random House, 2011), Kindle edition; Abraham, "Psychoanalytic Investigation and Treatment of Manic-Depressive Insanity"; Freud,
"Mourning and Melancholia"; Klerman et al., *Interpersonal Psychotherapy
of Depression*; Allan N. Schore, "A Century after Freud's Project: Is a Rap-
prochement between Psychoanalysis and Neurobiology at Hand?" *Journal
of the American Psychoanalytic Association* 45 (1997): 190–91, 195–200, including quotations from Sigmund Freud, "The Claims of Pscyho-Analysis to
Scientific Interest"; Allan N. Schore, "Relational Trauma and the Develop-
ing of the Right Brain: An Interface of Psychoanalytic Self Psychology and
Neuroscience," *Annals of the New York Academy of Sciences* 1159 (2009): 807–40;

Allan N. Schore, "The Right Brain Implicit Self: A Central Mechanism of the Psychotherapy Change Process" in Jean Petrucelli, ed., *Knowing, Not-Knowing and Sort-of-Knowing: Psychoanalysis and the Experience of Uncertainty* (London: Karnac, 2010), 177–97.

On ECT Basics: Dukakis and Tye, *Shock*, 12–13, 15, 17, 19, 31, 130–31, 167–69, 197–98; Lisanby, "Electroconvulsive Therapy for Depression"; Sackeim et al., "Cognitive Effects of Electroconvulsive Therapy"; Max Fink and Michael Alan Taylor, "Electroconvulsive Therapy: Evidence and Challenges," *Journal of the American Medical Association* 298, no. 3 (2007): 330–32; Peterchev et al., "Electroconvulsive Therapy Stimulus Parameters"; Spellman et al., "Differential Effects"; Rowny et al., "Translational Development Strategy"; Jan-Otto Ottosson, "Electroconvulsive Therapy of Endogenous Depression: An Analysis of the Influence of Various Factors on the Efficacy of the Therapy," *Journal of Mental Science* 108 (1962): 694–703; Milton J. Foust, interviewed by Linda Austin for "What's On Your Mind" podcast program of the Medical University of South Carolina, "ECT and Depression," transcript, http://www.muschealth.com/multimedia/Podcasts/transcription .aspx?podid=3, accessed July 22, 2011; Hermann et al., "Diagnoses of Patients Treated with ECT"; Joan Prudic, Mark Olfson, and Harold A. Sackeim, "Electro-Convulsive Therapy Practices in the Community," *Psychological Medicine* 31, no. 5 (2001): 929–34; Richard M. Glass, "Electroconvulsive Therapy: Time to Bring It Out of the Shadows," *Journal of the American Medical Association* 285, no. 10 (2001): 1346–48; Philip G. Janiack et al., "Efficacy of ECT: A Meta-Analysis," *American Journal of Psychiatry* 142 (1985): 297–302; Harold A. Sackeim et al., "Continuation Pharmacotherapy in the Prevention of Relapse Following Electroconvulsive Therapy: A Randomized Control Trial," *Journal of the American Medical Association* 285, no. 10 (2001): 1299–1307; James W. Thompson and Jack D. Blaine, "Use of ECT in the United States in 1975 and 1980," *American Journal of Psychiatry* 144 (1987): 557–62; Ronald C. Kessler et al., "Prevalence and Treatment of Mental Disorders, 1990 to 2003," *New England Journal of Medicine* 352 (2005): 2515–23; Mitchell S. Nobler et al., "Decreased Regional Brain Metabolism after ECT," *American Journal of Psychiatry* 158 (2001): 305–8; American Psychiatric Association, "APA Urges Reclassification of Electroconvulsive Therapy (ECT) by FDA in order to Maintain Availability," APA press release, December 23, 2009; Duff Wilson, "F.D.A. Is Studying the Risk of Electroshock Devices," *NYT*, January 24, 2011; Duff Wilson, "F.D.A. Panel Is Split on Electroshock Risks," *NYT*, January 29, 2011; Richard D. Abrams, "Comment on Electroconvulsive Therapy Device," http://www.regulations.gov/#!documentDetail;D=FDA -2009-N-0392-1189; Jane E. Brody, "Shock Therapy Loses Some of Its Shock Value," *NYT*, September 19, 2006.

On the "classical (monamine) neurotransmitter theory," see: Kellner et al., *Handbook of ECT*, 2nd ed. manuscript, provided by Charles Kellner to the author; G. R. Heninger et al., "The Revised Monoamine Theory of Depression: A Modulatory Role for Monoamines, Based on New Findings from Monoamine Depletion Experiments in Humans," *Pharmacopsychiatry* 29, no. 1 (1996): 2–11; Laura J. Fochtmann, "Animal Studies of Electroconvulsive Therapy: Foundations for Future Research," *Psychopharmacology Bulletin* 30, no. 3 (1994): 321–444; Per-Arne Fall et al., "ECT in Parkinson's Disease-Dopamine Transporter Visualised by [123I]-beta-CIT SPECT," *Journal of Neural Transmission* 107, nos. 8–9 (2000): 997–1008; Dennis Popeo and Charles H. Kellner, "ECT for Parkinson's Disease," *Medical Hypotheses* 73, no. 4 (1999): 468–69; Shitij Kapur and J. John Mann, "Role of Dopaminergic System in Depression," *Biological Psychiatry* 32, no. 1 (1992): 1–17; Lakshmi N. Yatham et al., "Effect of Electroconvulsive Therapy on Brain 5-HT(2) Receptors in Major Depression," *British Journal of Psychiatry* 196, no. 6 (2010): 474–79; Matthew V. Rudorfer et al., "Disparate Biochemical Actions of Electroconvulsive Therapy and Antidepressant Drugs," *Convulsive Therapy* 4, no. 2 (1988): 133–40; Thomas N. Ferraro et al., "Repeated Electroconvulsive Shock Selectively Alters gamma-Aminobutyric Acid Levels in the Rat Brain: Effect of Electrode Placement," *Convulsive Therapy* 6, no. 3 (1990): 199–208; Ertugrul Esel et al., "The Effects of Electroconvulsive Therapy on GABAergic Function in Major Depressive Patients," *Journal of ECT* 24, no. 3 (2008): 224–28.

On the neuroendocrine theory of depression, see: Kellner et al., *Handbook of ECT* manuscript; C. M. Swartz, "Neuroendocrine Effects of Electroconvulsive Therapy (ECT)," *Psychopharmacology Bulletin* 33, no. 2 (1997): 265–71; R. Kamil and Russell T. Joffe, "Neuroendocrine Testing in Electroconvulsive Therapy," *Psychiatric Clinics of North America* 14, no. 4 (1991): 961–70; Max Fink and Charles B. Nemeroff, "A Neuroendocrine View of ECT," *Convulsive Therapy* 5, no. 3 (1989): 296–304; Bernard J. Carroll, "Informed Use of the Dexamethasone Suppression Test," *Journal of Clinical Psychiatry* 47, no. 1 (1986): 10–12; Luc N. Bourgon and Charles H. Kellner, "Relapse of Depression after ECT: A Review," *Journal of ECT* 16, no. 1 (2000): 19–31; Dukakis and Tye, *Shock*, 201.

On the anticonvulsant theory, see: Kellner et al., *Handbook of ECT* manuscript; David A. Griesemer et al., "Electroconvulsive Therapy for Treatment of Intractable Seizures. Initial Findings in Two Children," *Neurology* 49, no. 5 (1997): 1389–92; Harold Sackeim, "The Anticonvulsant Hypothesis of the Mechanisms of Action of ECT: Current Status," *Journal of ECT* 15, no. 1 (1999): 5–26; Dukakis and Tye, *Shock*, 195, 200.

On the antipsychiatry and anti-ECT movements, as well as the history of psychotropic drugs, see Max Fink, "Impact of the Anti-Psychiatry Movement on the Revival of ECT in the U.S.," manuscript prepared for *Psychiatric Clinics of North America*, special number on electroconvulsive therapy, May 4, 1991, provided by Fink to the author; Peter R. Breggin, "The FDA Should

Test the Safety of ECT Machines," *International Journal of Risk and Safety in Medicine* 22 (2010): 89–92; Peter R. Breggin, "Electroshock Therapy and Brain Damage: The Acute Organic Brain Syndrome as Treatment," *Brain and Behavioral Sciences* 7 (1984): 24–25; Peter R. Breggin, *Electroshock: Its Brain-Disabling Effects* (New York: Springer, 1979); Peter R. Breggin, "Neuropathology and Cognitive Dysfunction from ECT," *Psychopharmacology Bulletin* 22, no. 2 (1986): 476–79; John Read and Richard Bentall, "The Effectiveness of Electroconvulsive Therapy: A Literature Review," *Epidemiologia e Psichiatria Sociale* 19, no. 4 (2010): 334; Marcia Angell, "The Epidemic of Mental Illness: Why?" *New York Review of Books*, June 23, 2011; Marcia Angell, "The Illusions of Psychiatry," *New York Review of Books*, July 14, 2011; John Oldham, Daniel Carlat, Richard Friedman, and Andrew Nierenberg, "'Illusions of Psychiatry': An Exchange," *New York Review of Books*, August 18, 2011; Daniel Carlat, *Unhinged: The Trouble with Psychiatry—A Doctor's Revelations about a Profession in Crisis* (New York: Free Press, 2010), 194; Irving Kirsch, *The Emperor's New Drugs: Exploding the Antidepressant Myth* (New York: Basic, 2011), 20; Peter D. Kramer, "In Defense of Antidepressants," *NYT*, July 10, 2011.

A memoir on ECT-induced memory loss: Jonathan Cott, *On the Sea of Memory: A Journey from Forgetting to Remembering* (New York: Random House, 2005).

43. Jonathan R. T. Davidson, Kathryn M. Connor, and Marvin Swartz, "Mental Illness in U.S. Presidents between 1776 and 1974," *Journal of Nervous and Mental Disease* 194, no. 1 (2006): 47–51; Robert S. Robins and Jerrold M. Post, "Choosing a Healthy President," *Political Psychology* 16, no. 4 (1995): 841–60; Robert E. Gilbert, "Psychological Illness in Presidents," *Political Psychology* 27, no. 1 (2006): 55–75; Ghaemi, *First-Rate Madness*.

44. Eagleton quoted in Miller, "'I'll Quit if I Hurt Nominee.'"

45. Loye Miller Jr. "Eagleton: This Campaign the Test; I Think That I Can Cut the Mustard," *MH*, July 29, 1972.

46. Gene Godley, interview by the author.

47. Miller, "Eagleton: This Campaign the Test"; Eagleton, "Minibiography," chapter 7, p. 2; David Weyl, "Eagleton: McGovern's Missing Man," undated, c. 5736, box 12, TFEP.

48. Eagleton, "Minibiography," chapter 7, p. 3.

49. Bennet, "Re: Eighteen Days," Addenda; Doug Bennet to Mike Kelley, memorandum, July 26, 1972, box 37, folder 7, DJBP; Bennet to Mankiewicz, memorandum of call, July 26, 1972, box 8, "July 1972: 7/21–7/26" folder, FFMP.

The Muckraker

1. Jack Anderson quoted in Christopher Lydon, "Assails Radio Report by Jack Anderson—Vows to Remain on Ticket," *NYT*, July 28, 1972, and in Herald

Wire Services, "I'm Staying on the Ticket, Sen. Eagleton Declares," *MH*, July 28, 1972; Susan Sheehan, "The Anderson Strategy: 'We Hit You—Pow! Then You Issue a Denial, and—Bam!—We Really Let You Have It,'" *NYT Sunday Magazine*, August 13, 1972, 10.

2. Kelley and Eagleton quoted in Eagleton, "Minibiography," chapter 7, p. 4; Bennet, interview by Harrison, 11–12.

3. Bennet, "Re: Eighteen Days," 38–39; conversation between Bennet and Hart, as remembered by Hart in Johnson, "1,000 Per Cent to Zero"; Bennet, interview by Harrison, 12; Hart, *Right from the Start*, 260–61; Greider, "Vacation Ordeal."

4. Eagleton quoted in Christopher Lydon, "Eagleton Asserts on Coast He Will Stay in the Race," *NYT*, July 29, 1972.

5. Bennet, interview by Harrison, 12; Bennet to Godley and Kelley, memorandum, July 28, 1972, box 37, folder 3, DJBP.

6. Miller, "Eagleton Seems Cool"; Thomas W. Ottenad, "Eagleton Denies Driving Allegations," *SLPD*, July 27, 1972; Herald Wire Services, "I'm Staying on the Ticket"; Thomas W. Ottenad, "Eagleton Fights Back, Gets Support of Union," *SLPD*, July 28, 1972; *ABC Evening News*, July 28, 1972, "1972 VP Drama," http://www.youtube.com/watch?v=PgMnyoh5lv8.

7. Ottenad, "Eagleton Denies Driving Allegations"; Herald Wire Services, "I'm Staying on the Ticket"; Ottenad, "Eagleton Fights Back."

8. Ottenad, "Eagleton Denies Driving Allegations"; Herald Wire Services, "I'm Staying on the Ticket."

9. Ottenad, "Eagleton Fights Back"; "Missouri Leaders Reject Drunk Driving Charges," *SLPD*, July 28, 1972; Ottenad, "Eagleton Denies Driving Allegations"; Herald Wire Services, "I'm Staying on the Ticket."

10. Eagleton quoted in Herald Wire Services, "I'm Staying on the Ticket"; Eagleton and crowd reaction quoted in Lydon, "Assails Radio Report by Jack Anderson"; Herald Wire Services, "I'm Staying on the Ticket"; crowd reaction quoted in Ottenad, "Eagleton Fights Back"; Bennet, interview by Harrison, 12; Miller, "Eagleton: This Campaign the Test."

11. Barbara Eagleton quoted in AP, "Backs Mate," photo caption, *Youngstown* [OH] *Vindicator*, July 28, 1972; Barbara Eagleton quoted in UPI, "'Right On,' Mrs. Eagleton Says," *MH*, July 28, 1972.

12. McGovern quoted in Eagleton, "Minibiography," chapter 7, p. 5; Anderson quoted in Lydon, "Assails Radio Report by Jack Anderson," and in Herald Wire Services, "I'm Staying on the Ticket"; Brit Hume, *Inside Story: Tales of Washington Scandals by the Young Reporter Who Helped Jack Anderson Dig Them Out* (Garden City, NY: Doubleday, 1974), 265.

13. Greider, "Vacation Ordeal."

14. Jeremy Larner, *The Candidate*, DVD, directed by Michael Ritchie (1972; Burbank, CA: Warner Home Video, 1997).

15. Greider, "Vacation Ordeal"; McGovern quoted in James M. Naughton, "The McGovern Image," *NYT*, July 31, 1972.

16. William Greider, "The McGovern Course," *WP*, August 1, 1972.

17. Hart, *Right from the Start*, 258; Weil, *Long Shot*, 177–78.

18. McGovern quoted in Dougherty, *Goodbye, Mr. Christian*, 193; Dougherty quoted in Miller, "Eagleton Seems Cool."

19. McGovern quoted in Bennet, "Re: Eighteen Days," 40; Bennet to Eagleton Staff, memorandum, July 28, 1972, box 37, folder 3, DJBP; Miller, "Eagleton Seems Cool"; Hart and Mankiewicz quoted in *NBC Nightly News*, July 27, 1972.

20. Anonymous memorandum of call, July 28, 1972, box 17, "Eagleton, Thomas F." folder, FFMP; Paul D. Hinkle, Edward J. Goodin Jr., and Kevin J. Cross-land to McGovern, letter, July 26, 1972, box 17, "Eagleton, Thomas F." folder, FFMP; Susan Garro to Mankiewicz, memorandum of call regarding Rick Greg, with Pat Broun's commentary at the top, July 28, 1972, box 17, "Eagleton, Thomas F." folder, FFMP.

21. Mankiewicz quoted in Johnson, "1,000 Per Cent to Zero."

22. Karl Menninger quoted in McGovern, *Grassroots*, 210, and in Bob Schieffer, *This Just In: What I Couldn't Tell You on TV* (New York: Putnam, 2003), 186; McGovern, *Terry*, 82; Boyd and Hoyt to Mankiewicz, memorandum, July 23, 1972.

23. Hart quoted in Johnson, "1,000 Per Cent to Zero"; McGovern, *Grassroots*, 210–11; McGovern, *Terry*, 97.

24. Miller, "Eagleton: This Campaign the Test."

The Tablehopping

1. Mike Kelley and Gene Godley, interviews by the author; Editorial, "Candidate Eagleton," *NYT*, July 28, 1972; Eagleton, "Minibiography," chapter 8, p. 1; Gene Godley, "Washington, Hawaii, and Return Trip," memorandum #10, box 37, folder 3; DJBP. Godley, correspondence with the author and notes in Godley's private collection.

2. Joseph Alioto quoted in Eagleton, "Minibiography," chapter 8, p. 2; memorandum of call regarding Bennet's message for Hart, July 28, 1972, box 17, "Eagleton, Thomas F." folder, FFMP.

3. Eagleton and William Smith quoted in Lydon, "Eagleton Asserts on Coast He Will Stay"; Ottenad, "Eagleton Fights Back"; Eunice and Sargent Shriver to Eagleton, telegram, July 27, 1972, c. 5736, box 22, TFEP; Eagleton quoted in Miller, "Eagleton: This Campaign the Test;" AP, "Pickets Ask Eagleton to Abandon Race," *NYT*, July 29, 1972.

4. Eagleton, interview by Eleanor Hoover, Donald Neff, and Karsten Prager, "Eagleton's Own Odyssey."

5. McGovern quoted in Greider, "Vacation Ordeal"; local businessman quoted in "Western Parade Lures M'Govern," *NYT*, July 29, 1972.

6. McGovern quoted in Robert S. Boyd and Loye Miller Jr., "First Task the Nominees Face Is Getting on Same Wavelength," *MH*, July 31, 1972.

7. Greider, "McGovern Course"; Thomas W. Ottenad, "Decision on Eagleton Reported Imminent," *SLPD*, July 30, 1972; McGovern quoted in Douglas E. Kneeland, "M'Govern Defers Eagleton Move Pending Parley," *NYT*, July 30, 1972, and in Robert S. Boyd, "McGovern Slates Showdown on VP," *MH*, July 30, 1972; Mankiewicz quoted in Johnson, "1,000 Per Cent to Zero"; Douglas E. Kneeland, "Behind Eagleton's Withdrawal: A Tale of Confusion and Division," *NYT*, August 2, 1972.

8. Greider, "Vacation Ordeal"; McGovern quoted in Dougherty, *Goodbye, Mr. Christian,* 197; Witcover, *Making of an Ink-Stained Wretch,* 161–62; Witcover, interview by the author.

9. Witcover quoted in Crouse, *Boys on the Bus,* 107–10, 348–49; Witcover, interview by the author; Witcover, *Making of an Ink-Stained Wretch,* 162; Greider, "McGovern Course."

10. Douglas E. Kneeland, "Two Meet Monday; Dakotan Says 'to Great Extent' His Running Mate Must Decide," *NYT*, July 29, 1972; Crouse, *Boys on the Bus,* 350; Greider, "McGovern Course."

11. Crouse, *Boys on the Bus,* 350; McGovern quoted in Greider, "McGovern Course"; Dougherty, *Goodbye, Mr. Christian,* 198.

12. McGovern quoted in Kneeland, "Two Meet Monday"; "McGovern Restudies Decision on Eagleton," *SLPD*, July 29, 1972; Ottenad, "Decision on Eagleton Reported Imminent."

13. Steve McGovern quoted in "McGovern Restudies Decision on Eagleton"; Mankiewicz quoted in Kneeland, "Two Meet Monday."

14. Jules Witcover, "McGovern Wants Eagleton off Ticket," *LAT*, July 29, 1972; Crouse, *Boys on the Bus,* 351; Greider, "McGovern Course"; Dougherty, *Goodbye, Mr. Christian,* 198–99; Witcover, interview by the author; Witcover, *Making of an Ink-Stained Wretch,* 162.

15. Steven V. Roberts, "I've Read the Headlines," *NYT*, July 30, 1972; Greider, "McGovern Course"; Naughton, "The McGovern Image"; Robert S. Boyd, "'McGovern Kindness Stalled Decision,'" *MH*, August 3, 1972.

16. Bennet, "Re: Eighteen Days," 43; Hart, *Right from the Start,* 261; Bennet, interview by Harrison, 13; Hart quoted in Kneeland, "Behind Eagleton's Withdrawal."

The Sunday Shows

1. Bennet to Eagleton, "Subject: What to say to McGovern," memorandum, July 29, 1972, c. 5736, box 22, TFEP; Bennet, "Re: Eighteen Days," 46.

2. Ledbetter and Kelley, interviews by the author; Godley, "Washington, Hawaii and Return Trip"; Bennet, "Re: Eighteen Days," 46; McGovern, *Grassroots,* 211; McGovern quoted in Boyd, "McGovern Slates Showdown"; Eagleton quoted in McGovern, *Grassroots,* 211; Eagleton, "Minibiography," chapter 8, p. 6.

3. Eagleton quoted in Robert Adams, "Eagleton Comes up Smiling," *SLPD*, August 1, 1972.

4. Eagleton as remembered by Ledbetter in interview by the author.

5. Barbara Eagleton as remembered by Ledbetter in interview by the author; UPI, "'Right On,' Mrs. Eagleton Says."

6. Eagleton quoted in Christopher Lydon, "Eagleton Says McGovern Remains Firm in Support," *NYT*, July 30, 1972; anonymous McGovern aide quoted in Douglas E. Kneeland, "Candidates' Staffs Wage Below-Surface Struggle," *NYT*, July 31, 1972; Bennet, "Re: Eighteen Days," 43; Kneeland, "Behind Eagleton's Withdrawal," August 2, 1972; Boyd, "McGovern Slates Showdown on VP."

7. Bennet, "Re: Eighteen Days," 43; Jerry Williams interviewing Jack Anderson, "Anderson on WBZ Radio," transcript, July 28, 1972, c. 5736, box 22, TFEP; Brit Hume, "Jack Anderson and the Eagleton Case," *Washington Monthly*, July–August 1974, 12; Anderson and True Davis quoted in James M. Naughton, "Data on Eagleton Reported Lacking," *NYT*, July 29, 1972.

8. James Laffoon quoted in Maxine Cheshire, "Anderson on Eagleton: A Charge That Didn't Stand Up," *WP*, July 29, 1972; Hume, *Inside Story*, 260–67, 271–72; "Anderson's Source Discloses Identity," *NYT*, July 30, 1972; Hedley Burrell, "Source Revealed," *WP*, July 30, 1972; Brooks Jackson, interview by the author.

9. Anderson and Hume conversation as recalled by Hume in Hume, "Jack Anderson and the Eagleton Case," 7–8, and in Hume, *Inside Story*, 259–60 (see 259–81 for Hume's account of the entire episode); Anderson with Clifford, *Anderson Papers* (see 135–62 for Anderson's account of the entire episode); "Notes on Meeting between Senator Thomas F. Eagleton and Jack Anderson, Columnist," August 1, 1972, c. 5736, box 22, TFEP; Mark Feldstein, *Poisoning the Press: Richard Nixon, Jack Anderson, and the Rise of Washington's Scandal Culture* (New York: Farrar, Straus and Giroux, 2010), 302–3; Feldstein, interview by the author.

10. Anderson quoted in Hume, "Jack Anderson and the Eagleton Case," 10, 19; Anderson quoted in Robert Adams, "Anderson Source: True Davis," *SLPD*, July 30, 1972; Hume, *Inside Story*, 261–66, 281; Bennet, "Re: Eighteen Days," addenda; Mike Kiernan's original script for Anderson's radio broadcast quoted in Feldstein, *Poisoning the Press*, 302–3; Feldstein, interview by the author.

11. Hume, "Jack Anderson and the Eagleton Case," 15–16; "Notes on Meeting between Senator Thomas F. Eagleton and Jack Anderson, Columnist."

12. Bennet, interview by Harrison, 4; Dubuque, Herbst, and Kelley, interviews by the author; Giglio, *Call Me Tom*, 19; Myron Cope, "Harry Has His Own Ways," *Sports Illustrated*, October 7, 1968.

13. Hume, "Jack Anderson and the Eagleton Case," 19; Hume, *Inside Story*, 281.

14. McGovern quoted in Greider, "McGovern Course"; McGovern quoted in

Boyd, "McGovern Slates Showdown on VP"; McGovern quoted in Kneeland, "M'Govern Defers Eagleton Move."

15. McGovern quoted in Boyd, "McGovern Slates Showdown on VP"; Clark Hoyt, "Eagleton: 'I Intend to Stay On,'" *MH*, July 31, 1972; Herald Wire Services, "2 Demo Leaders Urge Eagleton to Withdraw," *MH*, July 31, 1972; Henry Kimelman quoted in James M. Naughton, "If Not 'Tom Who'— Who?" *NYT*, July 30, 1972; Davis Merritt, "Sub for Eagleton: Not Only Who? But How?" *MH*, July 30, 1972; Robert Adams, "Looking into Procedure for Replacing Nominee," *SLPD*, July 28, 1972.

16. Hart quoted in Ottenad, "Decision on Eagleton Reported Imminent"; Hart quoted in Johnson "1,000 Per Cent to Zero."

17. Hart quoted in Bennet "Re: Eighteen Days," 51; Hart, *Right from the Start*, 262; Bennet to Eagleton, "Memo for TFE," memorandum, July 29, 1972, 5 p.m. box 37, folder 3, DJBP; Bennet to Eagleton, memorandum, quoted in Bennet, "Re: Eighteen Days," 47.

18. Bennet to Eagleton, "Memo for TFE," July 29, 1972; Bennet to Eagleton memorandum quoted in Bennet, "Re: Eighteen Days," 47; Connie Rosenbaum, "Barnes Panel Ordered Eagleton Data Moved," *SLPD*, July 30, 1972.

19. John Arnold Lindon to Frank Mankiewicz, letter, July 27, 1972, box 17, "Eagleton" folder, FFMP; Kelley, interview by the author.

20. Bennet to Eagleton, July 29, 1972, memorandum quoted in Bennet, "Re: Eighteen Days," 47; Philip Meyer, "Faith in Ticket Is Hurt, Poll Shows," *MH*, July 30, 1972; Weil, *Long Shot*, 181.

The editors of *Newsweek* and *Time* magazines decided to publish the results of the polls they had commissioned early—on Saturday, two days ahead of their newsstand release. *Newsweek* chief Osborn Elliot cited "widespread interest in the subject and the importance of the issue" as reasons for advanced disclosure. Half of the 5.2 percent who said they planned to switch votes in *Time*'s poll were for McGovern, and the other half of those people were originally undecided.

Newsweek's poll, conducted by Gallup, found that 59 percent of voters did not believe Senator Eagleton's implied medical record made him unfit to serve as vice president, while 28 percent considered it disqualifying. Similarly, *Time*'s survey showed 54 percent of voters did not deem him unfit, while 18.5 percent did. A quarter of all adults and a third of all independents in *Time*'s poll said recent news surrounding Senator Eagleton's mental health made them "less favorable" toward the McGovern-Eagleton ticket than before.

The surveys were conducted on Thursday evening.

"A Newsweek Poll on Eagleton," *Newsweek*, August 7, 1972; "A Time Poll: How the Voters Feel about Eagleton," *Time*, August 7, 1972; Kneeland, "M'Govern Defers Eagleton Move"; Lydon, "Eagleton Says McGovern Remains Firm"; Ottenad, "Decision on Eagleton Reported Imminent."

21. Eagleton, "Airport Speech to Roaring Middle America at Columbia Airport," notes, July 29, 1972, box 37, folder 3, DJBP.

22. Eagleton quoted in Jerry V. Venters, "Eagleton Insists He Is Staying as Nominee," *SLPD,* July 30, 1972; Loye Miller Jr., "Eagleton, Turning Defensive, Says He's an Asset to Ticket," *MH,* July 30, 1972.

23. McGovern quoted in Boyd, "McGovern Slates Showdown on VP."

24. Venters, "Eagleton Insists He Is Staying"; Darst, "Eagleton's Wake," 79; Eagleton quoted on *NBC Nightly News,* July 30, 1972; McGovern in R. W. Apple Jr., "Eagleton Is Firm Despite Pressure from 2 Party Chiefs," *NYT,* July 31, 1972; McGovern quoted in Kneeland, "Candidates' Staffs Wage Below-Surface Struggle"; McGovern quoted in Herald Wire Services, "2 Demo Leaders Urge Eagleton."

25. McGovern and Witcover in combination of material from interview with Witcover by the author and Witcover, *Making of an Ink-Stained Wretch,* 163.

26. Bennet, "Re: Eighteen Days," 48–49; Jim Murphy, e-mail correspondence with the the author, July 28, 2011.

27. Bennet, "Re: Eighteen Days," 48–50, including Eagleton quotation; Kelley, interview by the author.

28. Bennet, "Re: Eighteen Days," 48–50; "Briefing for Face the Nation," staff document, circa July 30, 1972, c. 5736, box 22, TFEP.

29. *Face the Nation* excerpts on *NBC Nightly News,* July 30, 1972.

30. Russell, "Eagleton Adds Witty, Low-Key Style to Slate."

31. Anderson, Eagleton, Herman, and Serafin quoted in "Face the Nation as broadcast over the CBS Television Network and the CBS Radio Network," transcript, July 30, 1972, c. 5736, box 22, TFEP; Mike Kelley, interview by the author.

32. Bob Snyder of CBS News to Eagleton staff, undated, c. 5736, box 22, TFEP; "Reaction on Eagleton by Telegram," *SLPD,* July 31, 1972, including John Woodward quotations.

33. "Reaction on Eagleton by Telegram"; Warren Weaver Jr. and William K. Wyant Jr., "Messages of Support Pour into Senator Eagleton's Office," *SLPD,* August 1, 1972.

34. White, *Making of the President 1972,* 205; Apple, "Eagleton Is Firm"; Schieffer, *This Just In,* 187; Jean Westwood in Laurence Stern, "Party Heads Ask Eagleton to Withdraw," *WP,* July 31, 1972; Eagleton, "Minibiography," chapter 9, p. 3; McGovern as remembered by Mankiewicz quoted in Johnson, "1,000 Per Cent to Zero"; McGovern, *Grassroots,* 212; Dougherty, *Goodbye, Mr. Christian,* 200; Weil, *Long Shot,* 179; Bennet, interview by Harrison, 14; Bennet, "Re: Eighteen Days," 52–53; McGovern, interview by the author.

When I asked McGovern about Westwood's and Paterson's comments, he said, "I had nothing to do with what they said on *Meet the Press,* absolutely nothing." Then McGovern explained that if Westwood did run her remarks by him, "It was one of the thousands of things that were run by me. But if she did, I don't remember that conversation. I think [Westwood and Paterson] were speaking for themselves that day, that's my memory of it. They certainly didn't come to me and say, 'What do you want us to say?' They just went ahead and said what they wanted."

The Precedent

1. Mazo and Hess, *Nixon,* 91–110, including Eisenhower quotation on 91 and Nixon quotation on 92; Richard M. Nixon, *Six Crises* (New York: Touchstone, 1990), 74, 81–86; Perlstein, *Nixonland,* 36–37; Herald Washington Bureau, "Nixon Offered to Quit After 'Checkers' Speech in '52," *MH,* July 26, 1972.
2. Mazo and Hess, *Nixon,* 101.
3. Ibid., 99–100, 102–3; Nixon, *Six Crises,* 87–92.
4. Mazo and Hess, *Nixon,* 105, 108, 112, including Eisenhower quotation on 108; Nixon, *Six Crises,* 92–93, 108.
5. Nixon quoted in Mazo and Hess, *Nixon,* 109–10; Nixon, *Six Crises,* 99–100; Herald Washington Bureau, "Nixon Offered to Quit."
6. Mazo and Hess, *Nixon,* 110–11, 115–16, including Hillings quotation on 116; Nixon, *Six Crises,* 101, 110; Perlstein, *Nixonland,* 38; Herald Washington Bureau, "Nixon Offered to Quit."
7. Perlstein, *Nixonland,* 39.
8. Nixon quoted in Mazo and Hess, *Nixon,* 118–19; Nixon, *Six Crises,* 113–17.
9. Mazo and Hess, *Nixon,* 121, including Eisenhower quotations; Herald Washington Bureau, "Nixon Offered to Quit"; Perlstein, *Nixonland,* 36–41, including Nixon quotation on 40.
10. Eisenhower quoted in Mazo and Hess, *Nixon,* 123, and in Nixon, *Six Crises,* 123–24.

The Decision

1. Eagleton, "Minibiography," chapter 9, p. 1; Bennet, "Re: Eighteen Days," 53, 56; Bennet, interview by Harrison, 15.
2. Van Dyk quoted in Bennet, "Re: Eighteen Days," 53.
3. Bennet, "Re: Eighteen Days," 53, 56; Eagleton, "Minibiography," chapter 9, p. 1; Bennet, interview by Harrison, 15; Weil, *Long Shot,* 180.
4. McGovern quoted in Eagleton, "Minibiography," chapter 9, p. 1.
5. Bennet, "Re: Eighteen Days," 54–55, including Stephan quotation on 55.
6. Mankiewicz and Hart quoted in Johnson, "1,000 Per Cent to Zero."
7. Eagleton, "Minibiography," chapter 9, p. 2; Bennet, "Eighteen Days," 56; McGovern, *Grassroots,* 212–13; Hart and Mankiewicz, interviews by the author.
8. Eagleton, "Minibiography," chapter 9, p. 3.
9. McGovern and Eagleton conversation as remembered by Eagleton in "Minibiography," chapter 9, pp. 2–4 and insert; Bennet, "Eighteen Days," 56.

10. Bennet and Eagleton exchange as remembered by Eagleton in "Minibiography," chapter 9, p. 5.

11. Bennet, "Re: Eighteen Days," 56; AP, "Mrs. Eagleton Was Relieved When Her Husband Quit Race"; Barbara Eagleton with McLendon, "Mrs. Eagleton's Own Story," 153.

12. McGovern, *Grassroots,* 213–14; Arthur Schlesinger Jr. to George McGovern, letter, July 29, 1972, box 460, "Eagleton Issues" folder, GSMPUP; Herald Wire Services, "2 Demo Leaders Urge Eagleton."

Dick Wade was quoted in the *Miami Herald* as saying, "The nature of the illness as exposed in the press is not at the center of the controversy [but rather] his not having told McGovern [before the nomination]."

As reported by Robert Dallek in his 2003 biography of JFK, *An Unfinished Life,* the back pain associated with Addison's disease challenged Kennedy's ability and focus, both before and during his presidency. A mixture of medications enabled him to function, and painkillers and amphetamines kept Kennedy off crutches during his 1960 campaign. Medical records show that on August 23, 1961, for example, Kennedy simultaneously endured an "*E. coli*" urinary tract infection and "acute diarrhea." And doctors were concurrently treating him with penicillin, cortisone, Bentyle, Lomotil, Transentine, paregoric, testosterone, Ritalin, and injections of codeine sulfate and procaine. In *A First-Rate Madness,* Nassir Ghaemi further explores how Kennedy's drug treatments, particularly with anabolic steroids like methyltestosterone and Halotesin, influenced the president's temperament. Ghaemi writes that during the early period of Kennedy's presidency, during which time the Bay of Pigs crisis occurred, JFK "suffered . . . from the wayward psychiatric effects of anabolic steroid abuse." See Dallek, *An Unfinished Life: John F. Kennedy, 1917–1963* (New York: Black Bay, 2004), 414–15, 487–88; Ghaemi, *First-Rate Madness.*

13. Schlesinger's August 6 journal entry in Arthur M. Schlesinger Jr., *Journals: 1952–2000,* a collection edited by Andrew Schlesinger and Stephen Schlesinger (New York: Penguin, 2007), 357.

14. Ken Schlossberg to McGovern, letter, July 31, 1972, box 460, "Eagleton Issues" folder, GSMPUP.

15. Eagleton quoted on *NBC Nightly News,* July 31, 1972; Eagleton, "Minibiography," chapter 10, p. 1; Eagleton quoted in Weaver and Wyant, "Messages of Support"; Eagleton quoted in William Chapman and Washington Post Staff Writers, "Both Cite Need Now for Unity," *WP,* August 1, 1972; Eagleton quoted in Clark Hoyt and William Vance, "Missourian Argues His Case, Says 'My Conscience Is Clear,'" *MH,* August 1, 1972.

16. Eagleton to Ted Kennedy, letter, July 31, 1972, box 212, "Senators, Thomas F. Eagleton" folder, RSSP.

17. Ann R. "Randee" Krakauer, typed notes, undated, c. 5736, box 22, TFEP; Herbst and Kelley, interviews by the author.

18. Eagleton, "Minibiography," chapter 10, p. 1; Chapman and Washington Post Staff Writers, "Both Cite Need Now for Unity."

19. Eagleton, "Minibiography," chapter 10, p. 1; Chapman and Washington Post Staff Writers, "Both Cite Need Now for Unity"; Davis Merritt, "Nelson Picked to Mediate, Cushion, and Witness Eagleton Resignation," *MH,* August 2, 1972; McGovern, *Grassroots,* 214; Adams, "Eagleton Comes up Smiling"; Dougherty quoted in Boyd, "'McGovern Kindness Stalled Decision'"; Dougherty, *Goodbye, Mr. Christian,* 200.

20. Eagleton quoted in Hoyt and Vance, "Missourian Argues His Case"; Clark Hoyt, "Eagleton: Find a Better Way to Pick Running Mate," *MH,* August 4, 1972; Weil, *Long Shot,* 180; McGovern, *Grassroots,* 215; Bennet, "Re: Eighteen Days," 58–59; Giglio, *Call Me Tom,* 127.

21. As presented in McGovern, *Grassroots,* 215; McGovern, "Confidential Memorandum on the Eagleton Incident"; McGovern, "Confidential Note on the Eagleton Affair," typed note, February 10, 1973, Eagleton folder, GSMD-WUP; Eagleton, "Minibiography," chapter 10, p. 2; Eagleton remembered McGovern speaking with the Mayo doctor first, after he was unable to connect with Shobe on the first attempt.

22. Anson, "Party Lines," 13; Anson, interview by the author.

23. Eagleton and McGovern as quoted in Eagleton, "Minibiography," chapter 10, p. 4; Hoyt, "Demo Conflict Grows"; McGovern, "Confidential Memorandum on the Eagleton Incident"; McGovern, "Confidential Note on the Eagleton Affair."

24. Eagleton, "Minibiography," chapter 10, p. 4; Eagleton as quoted in McGovern, *Grassroots,* 215; "Confidential Memo"; Hart, *Right from the Start,* 264; Dougherty, *Goodbye, Mr. Christian,* 200; Anson, "Party Lines," 13. An original draft of Eagleton's statement and its edits can be found in box 37, folder 3, DJBP.

25. McGovern, *Grassroots,* 215; Bennet, "Re: Eighteen Days, 58–59; Eagleton comments as presented by Eagleton in "Minibiography," chapter 10, insert.

26. Eagleton quoted in Douglas E. Kneeland, "Eagleton Tells McGovern It Was 'the Only Decision,'" *NYT,* August 1, 1972.

27. Architect of the Capitol website, "Kennedy Caucus Room," http://www.aoc.gov/cc/cobs/rsob_caucus_rm.cfm, accessed November 24, 2011; Lawrence E. Taylor, "Eagleton Quits Race Reluctantly," *SLPD,* August 1, 1972; Hoyt and Vance, "Missourian Argues His Case"; Kneeland, "Eagleton Tells McGovern"; Eagleton, "Minibiography," chapter 10, p. 5.

28. McGovern and Eagleton quoted in in Radio-TV Monitoring Service, CBS *Campaign '72* special report, "McGovern-Eagleton Press Conference," transcript, July 31, 1972, c. 5736, box 22, TFEP; Kneeland, "Eagleton Tells McGovern"; Hart, *Right from the Start,* 264; Hoyt and Vance, "Missourian Argues His Case"; Taylor, "Eagleton Quits Race Reluctantly."

29. Hoyt and Vance, "Missourian Argues His Case"; Paul Wagman, "Eagleton Glad It's Over, Priest Says," *SLPD,* August 3, 1972.

30. Eagleton and McGovern quoted in Radio-TV Monitoring Service, "McGovern-Eagleton Press Conference"; "McGovern, Eagleton Statements and News Parley," *NYT,* August 1, 1972; McGovern quoted in Kneeland, "Eagleton Tells McGovern."

31. Eagleton, "Minibiography," chapter 10, p. 5.

32. Barbara Eagleton quoted in AP, "Mrs. Eagleton Was Relieved."

33. Jerome F. Wilkerson quoted in Wagman, "Eagleton Glad It's Over"; Bennet, "Re: Eighteen Days," 59; Kelley quoted in Adams, "Eagleton Comes up Smiling"; Barbara Eagleton with McLendon, "Mrs. Eagleton's Own Story," 154; Godley and Kelley, interviews by the author.

34. Wagman, "Eagleton Glad It's Over"; Clark Hoyt, "Eagleton's 'Vice President'—But the Honor Is Fleeting," *MH,* August 2, 1972.

35. Hoyt, "Eagleton's 'Vice President.'"

36. McGovern and Eagleton quoted in Hoyt, "Eagleton's 'Vice President.'"

37. Eagleton quoted in Clark Hoyt, "'Charlie, How about that Campaign,'" *MH,* August 3, 1972; Eagleton quoted in Lawrence E. Taylor, "Campaigners in House Seek Eagleton's Help," *SLPD,* August 2, 1972; Eagleton quoted in Adams, "Eagleton Comes up Smiling"; Taylor, "Eagleton Quits Race Reluctantly"; Eagleton quoted in Post-Dispatch Wire Service, "Eagleton Tells of 1960 Illness," *SLPD,* August 8, 1972; Joe McGinniss, "'I'll Tell You Who's Bitter: My Aunt Hazel,'" *Life,* August 18, 1972, 31; Brody, "Shock Therapy Loses Some of Its Shock Value"; Dick Cavett, "Smiling Through," NYT Opinionator blog, June 27, 2008, http://opinionator.blogs.nytimes.com/2008/06/27/smiling-through/; Dick Cavett, interview by Deborah Serani, "On the Couch . . . with Dick Cavett: An American Icon Shares Wit and Wisdom about Living with Depression," *Psychology Today,* April 21, 2011, http://www.psychology today.com/blog/two-takes-depression/201104/the-couch-dick-cavett; Dick Cavett, "Goodbye, Darkness: A TV Host's Odyssey from Terrifying Depression to Renewed Peace of Mind," *People,* August 3, 1992; Dick Cavett, *Talk Show: Confrontations, Pointed Commentary, and Off-Screen Secrets* (New York: Times Books, 2010), Kindle edition.

38. Mansfield quoted in Robert Adams, "Mansfield Acclaims Eagleton for Courage and Wit under Fire," *SLPD,* August 3, 1972.

39. Henry Kimelman to McGovern, letter, August 1, 1972, box 460, "Eagleton Issues" folder, GSMPUP.

40. Philip Stern to McGovern, letter, August 26, 1972, box 446, "Personal-S 1972," GSMPUP.

41. Nixon to Terry Eagleton, August 2, 1972, President's Personal File, 1969–1974, box 8, "Eagleton, Terry (Thomas F. Eagleton)" folder, NPLM; Nixon to Terry Eagleton, August 2, 1972, in Nixon, *Memoirs of Richard Nixon,* 666–67.

42. Bennet to Mr. and Mrs. Daniel Field, letter, August 9, 1972, box 72, folder 1, DJBP; Bennet to Eliot Glassheim, letter, August 5, 1972, box 72, folder 1, DJBP; Bennet to Diana Walsh Pursglove, letter, August 7, 1972, box 72, folder 1, DJBP.

43. Bennet to Professor Carl E. Schorske, letter, August 30, 1972, box 72, folder 1, DJBP.

The Aftermath

1. McGovern quoted in Fred W. Lindecke, "Eagleton Not Issue, McGovern Says Here," *SLPD*, October 8, 1972, and in James N. Naughton, "Eagleton Joins McGovern in Campaign to Confront the Credibility Issue," *NYT*, October 8, 1972; AP, "Eagleton Joins McGovern Tour," *SLPD*, October 7, 1972; Lawrence E. Taylor, "Eagleton Appearing at McGovern Request," *SLPD*, October 6, 1972; Dougherty, *Goodbye, Mr. Christian*, 236; Hart, *Right from the Start*, 301–2; James M. Naughton, "The Eagleton Impact: McGovern May Have Failed to Gauge Lasting Damage of a Switch in Ticket," *NYT*, October 7, 1972; Karen Van Meter, "'It Was a Mind-Blowing Scene,'" *SLPD*, October 8, 1972.
2. McGovern quoted in Lindecke, "Eagleton Not Issue"; Naughton, "Eagleton Joins McGovern."
3. Taylor, "Eagleton Appearing at McGovern Request"; Miles Rubin quoted in Naughton, "Eagleton Impact"; Filippine to Eagleton, "Re: Dinner with McGovern, Mankiewicz, TFE, Barbara & Kelley," memorandum, October 10, 1972, pp. 1–2, box 22, TFEP.
4. Filippine to Eagleton, "Re: Dinner with McGovern, Mankiewicz, TFE, Barbara & Kelley," 3–4; Barbara Eagleton quoted in McGovern, *Grassroots*, 216, and in Coyne, "Eagleton," 78.
5. Haynes Johnson, "Public Sees McGovern Image Slipping," *WP*, October 2, 1972.
6. Jerome P. Curry, "Eagleton's Resignation Stirred Fears of Many," *SLPD*, October 10, 1972; Matthew J. Troy quoted in "Troy Would Not Vote for Eagleton as Candidate," *NYT*, July 31, 1972; Troy to Eagleton, letter, October 18, 1972, c. 0674, f.2815, TFEP.
7. Eagleton quoted in Lindecke, "Eagleton Not Issue," and in Naughton, "Eagleton Joins McGovern"; "Transcript of Eagleton Speech, Eagleton-McGovern Joint Appearance, Truman Day Dinner, St. Louis, October 7, 1972," c. 5736, box 22, TFEP; Bennet to Eagleton, "Re: McGovern Rally," memorandum, October 6, 1972, box 37, folder 7, DJBP.
8. Eagleton quoted in Lindecke, "Eagleton Not Issue," and in Naughton, "Eagleton Joins McGovern."
9. Haynes Johnson, "It's More a Referendum on Men than Issues," *WP*, November 7, 1972; Anthony Lewis, "A Wing and a Prayer," *NYT*, October 7, 1972; Jack Rosenthal, "Poll Finds Issues not at Issue in '72: No More than 27% Agree on No. 1 Campaign Topic," *NYT*, October 8, 1972; McGovern and Santos Hernandez quoted in Haynes Johnson, "Turned-Off Public Picks Continuity over Change," *WP*, October 1, 1972; Haynes Johnson, "Public Sees McGovern Image Slipping," *WP*, October 2, 1972; Peter H. Dailey in May

and Fraser, *Campaign '72*, 197; John Herbers, "Issues Fade—Party's Getting Rough," *NYT*, October 8, 1972, box 37, folder 7, DJBP.

10. Stanley Kelley Jr., *Interpreting Elections* (Princeton: Princeton University Press, 1983), 108, 117; Frederick T. Steeper and Robert M. Teeter, "Comment on 'A Majority Party in Disarray,'" *American Political Science Review* 70, no. 3 (1978): 806; Tom Wicker, "McGovern with Tears," *NYT Sunday Magazine*, November 5, 1972, 103; Herbers, "Issues Fade"; Johnson, "Turned-Off Public Picks Continuity;" Rosenthal, "Poll Finds Issues Not at Issue." Unlike the other surveys, the Harris Poll found the economy, not the war, to be the most-mentioned issue, cited by 48 percent of voters as a major concern.

11. Kelley, *Interpreting Elections*, 99–100, 111–15, 117, 122–25; Jeanne Kirkpatrick, "The Revolt of the Masses" *Commentary* 55 (1972): 58; Wattenberg quoted in May and Fraser, *Campaign '72*, 233; Samuel Popkin, John W. Gorman, Charles Phillips, and Jeffrey A. Smith, "What Have You Done for Me Lately? Toward an Investment Theory of Voting," *American Political Science Review* 70, no. 3 (1976): 779–805; Arthur H. Miller and Warren E. Miller, "Ideology in the 1972 Election: Myth or Reality—A Rejoinder," *American Political Science Review* 70, no. 3 (1976): 832–49, esp. 836; Arthur H. Miller and Warren E. Miller, "Issues, Candidates, and Partisan Division in the 1972 American Presidential Election," *British Journal of Political Science* 5, no. 4 (1975): 393–434; Philip Meyer, "Demo Bid Impaired by Eagleton Affair?" *MH*, August 2, 1972; Hart, *Right from the Start*, 264; Julian E. Zelizer, "Beyond the Presidential Synthesis: Reordering Political Time" in *A Companion to Post-1945 America*, Blackwell Companions to American History (Malden, MA: Blackwell, 2002), 347; Meg Jacobs and Julian E. Zelizer, "The Democratic Experiment: New Directions in American Political History" in *The Democratic Experiment: New Directions in American Political History* (Princeton: Princeton University Press, 2003), 3–4; Alan Brinkley, "The Problem of American Conservatism," *American Historical Review* 99, no. 2 (1994): 414, 416; Thomas J. Sugrue, *The Origins of the Urban Crisis: Race and Inequality in Postwar Detroit*, Princeton Studies in American Politics (Princeton: Princeton University Press, 1996), 5; Thomas J. Sugrue, "Crabgrass-Roots Politics: Race, Rights, and the Reaction against Liberalism in the Urban North, 1940–64," *Journal of American History* 82, no. 2 (1995): 578; Matthew D. Lassiter, *The Silent Majority: Suburban Politics in the Sunbelt South*, Politics and Society in Twentieth-Century America (Princeton: Princeton University Press, 2006), 312; Lisa McGirr, *Suburban Warriors: The Origins of the New American Right*, Politics and Society in Twentieth-Century America (Princeton: Princeton University Press, 2001); Thomas J. Sugrue, "All Politics Is Local: The Persistence of Localism in Twentieth Century America," in *The Democratic Experiment*, 301–26.

As Popkin et al. argue (799), if issues were the decisive factor, why, then, did voters elect Jim Abourezk in South Dakota, and Dick Clark, Joe Biden, and Walter Mondale—examples of candidates with nearly identical stances on the issues as McGovern—in states that McGovern lost? Popkin and colleagues believe that, without the Eagleton affair, McGovern would have lost by 55 percent to 45 percent, setting him up for a viable candidacy in 1976.

12. Kelley, *Interpreting Elections*, 106–7, 116–7; Wicker, "McGovern in Tears," 103. Additionally, see the previous note for more political science articles that discuss the role of personality in dictating the outcome of the 1972 presidential election.

13. Kelley, *Interpreting Elections*, 116–7; Lewis, "Wing and a Prayer"; Linda Charlton, "'Smear' Campaign Charged by GOP: A Complaint Is Filed with Fair Practices Group," *NYT*, October 8, 1972; Dana L. Spitzer, "Keys McGovern Victory to Mistrust of Nixon," *SLPD*, October 8, 1972; May and Fraser, *Campaign '72*, 231–32; John Herbers, "Issues Fade" (emphasis in original).

14. May and Fraser, *Campaign '72*, 294.

Epilogue

1. AP, "Eagleton Says He Was a Scapegoat in Campaign," *NYT*, November 16, 1972; McGovern quoted in AP, "McGovern Calls Eagleton Affair 'Saddest Part,'" *NYT*, December 13, 1972; McGovern quoted in Joe McGinniss, "Second Thoughts of George McGovern," *NYT Sunday Magazine*, May 6, 1973, 88, 98; McGovern quoted in "M'Govern Denies Magazine Report: Says Article in Times Has 'Fabricated Quotations,'" *NYT*, May 6, 1973.

2. McGovern, "Confidential Memorandum on the Eagleton Incident;" McGovern, interview by the author.

3. Hart, *Right from the Start*, 265; Weil, *Long Shot*, 185; Dougherty, *Goodbye, Mr. Christian*, 204.

4. Eagleton quoted in Haynes Johnson and David Broder, "Eagleton Discounts His Role in Debacle," *WP*, November 15, 1972; "Democrats: Look Back in Anger," *Time*, November 27, 1972; McGovern, *Grassroots*, 190, 216.

5. Eagleton quoted in Andrew C. Miller "Drama, Toil Marked Career," *Kansas City Star*, October 12, 1986. For a sample of obituaries, see Adam Clymer, "Thomas F. Eagleton, 77, a Running Mate for 18 Days, Dies," *NYT*, March 5, 2007; David Goldstein, "'Moral Passion' Pushed Eagleton to National Ticket, Albeit Briefly," *Kansas City Star*, March 5, 2007; McClatchy-Tribune, "Former Sen. Thomas F. Eagleton Dies at 77," *Baltimore Sun*, March 5, 2007.

6. Eagleton to McGovern, letter, December 12, 1980, box 5A, "E Miscellaneous Correspondence" folder, GSMDWUP.

7. Eagleton to McGovern, letter, June 15, 1984, box 5A, "E Miscellaneous Correspondence" folder, GSMDWUP (emphasis in original).

8. McGovern quoted in Miller "Drama, Toil Marked Career"; Eagleton and McGovern quoted in Andrew C. Miller, "Electroshock Issue Stunned Nation," *Kansas City Star*, October 12, 1986.

9. McGovern quoted in Clymer, "Thomas F. Eagleton, 77"; McGovern quoted in Leubsdorf, "McGovern Still Mourns"; McGovern, interview by the author.

10. McGovern, interview by the author. In 2009 George McGovern the historian published a book on the sixteenth president, *Abraham Lincoln* (New York: Times Books, 2009).

11. McGovern, "Why I May Run for President in 1992," handwritten notes, box 4, "1990–1992 Candidacy Announcement Drafts" folder, GSMDWUP.

12. McGovern quoted in "Campaign Notes; Hart and McGovern Exchange Bouquets," *NYT*, January 9, 1984; Hart quoted in E. J. Dionne Jr., "Garry [*sic*] Hart the Elusive Front-Runner," *NYT Sunday Magazine*, May 3, 1987, accessed online at http://www.nytimes.com/1987/05/03/magazine/garry -hart-the-elusive-front-runner.html; Kurt Andersen, "The Man Who Wears No Label: With His Hybrid Ideology, Gary Hart Resists Classification," *Time*, March 12, 1984; "The Ghost of Gary Past," *Time*, December 28, 1987; Jim McGee, Tom Fiedler, and James Savage, "The Gary Hart Story: How It Happened," *MH*, May 10, 1987; Hart quoted in *NYT* editorial in "Kicking the Press Around" *International Herald Tribune*, July 17, 1987; David S. Broder, "The Press after the Stakeout," *WP*, May 12, 1987; A. M. Rosenthal, "On My Mind; Tears of Mrs. Hart," *NYT*, May 10, 1987; see box 5A, "Hart, Gary" folder, GSMDWUP, for George McGovern's underlinings and notes on the Broder and Rosenthal articles.

13. For more information on the *Las Vegas Sun*'s Pulitzer Prize–winning work, see the newspaper's website: "Construction Deaths," *Las Vegas Sun*, http:// www.lasvegassun.com/news/topics/construction-deaths.

14. Hoyt, interview by the author.

15. Boyd, interview by the author.

16. AP, "Ramsey Clark Asserts He Saw F.B.I. Report on Eagleton Health," *NYT*, November 7, 1972; UPI, "'Eagleton Data to Agnew'"; Carl Bernstein and Bob Woodward, "Vast GOP Undercover Operations Originated in 1969," *WP*, May 17, 1973; O'Connor, "J. Edgar Hoover Took Notice"; Mark "Deep Throat" Felt quoted in Bernstein and Woodward, *All the President's Men*, 136, 341; Bob Woodward, e-mail correspondence with the author, January 4, 2012.

17. Frank Mankiewicz, interview by the author; Fred Malek and Stephanie Fenjiro, e-mail correspondence with the author, November 28, 2011.

18. Kelley and Hoyt, interviews by the author.

19. McGovern, "Why I May Run."

20. Eagleton to Jack Lewis, "In Re: 'They Ran, Too, Didn't They?' or 'They Ran, Too' or whatever—biographical sketches of *defeated* Vice-presidential candidates," memorandum, May 7, 1984, c. 5736, box 12, TFEP (emphasis in original); John Danforth quoted in Ira Molotsky and Warren Weaver Jr., "Eagleton's Farewell," *NYT*, October 19, 1986.

21. Eagleton quoted in "Parting Thoughts: An Interview with Tom Eagleton," *Amherst*, Summer 1986, https://www.amherst.edu/aboutamherst/magazine/issues/2006_fallwinter/tom_eagleton; Mike Kelley, interview by the author.

22. Eagleton quoted in Walter Mondale, "The Center Has Held: Tom Eagleton," in *SES*, 35. See also 135 *Cong. Rec.* 5686 (1989).

23. "Thomas F. Eagleton Farewell Address"; John M. Finney, "Senate Panel Votes 24–0 to Bar Cambodian Raids," *NYT*, May 16, 1973.

Acknowledgments

Thomas Eagleton always made a point of saying how lucky he was, and I, too, have felt extraordinarily lucky.

This book began at Amherst College, the alma mater that I share with Thomas Eagleton. We both majored in history and benefited from the painstaking and inspirational instruction of the school's faculty.

I launched my study of Thomas Eagleton and George McGovern under the direction of professors Hilary Moss and John Servos, whose early insights and continued advice have been crucial to this book. As my principal adviser, Professor Moss fervently and patiently coached me as a researcher, writer, and thinker. Professor Marni Sandweiss taught my first course in the history department, and she ignited and nurtured my passion for archival research. I am grateful to Professor Sandweiss for her incredible generosity and for introducing me to Professor Joel Goldstein of the St. Louis University School of Law, an expert on the vice presidency. Professor Joseph J. Ellis of Mount Holyoke, a master of popular history, helped me envision approaches to telling this story. Professor Mitzi Goheen of the Amherst anthropology and black studies departments also defined my college experience.

Additional thanks to the following Amherst College faculty and staff: professors Robert Bezucha, Carol Clark, Catherine Epstein, Susan Niditch, Stanley Rabinowitz, Lisa Raskin, Paul Rockwell, and Martha Saxton; deans Gregory Call, Ben Lieber, and Tom Parker; Maryanne Alos, Rhea Cabin, Daria D'Arienzo, Denise Gagnon, Susan Kimball, and Suzanne Spencer.

History teacher Nancy Banks of the Fieldston School supervised my first academic exploration into the press and the presidency.

A team of archivists and librarians across the country provided excellent guidance and facilitated my research of primary source material: Richard Lindemann of Bowdoin College; Laurie Langland of

Dakota Wesleyan University; Karen Abramson, Michael Desmond, and Sharon Kelly of the John F. Kennedy Presidential Library and Museum; David Travis of the University of Maryland; Dan Linke and Ben Primer of Princeton; Craig Ellefson and Ryan Pettigrew of the Richard Nixon Presidential Library and Museum; Susan Yowell of the University of Virginia; Jennifer Hadley, Rebecca McCallum, and Suzy Taraba of Wesleyan University; Mary Beth Brown, Susan Hart, Laura Jolley, Tom Miller, Bill Stolz, and Nathan Troup of the Western Historical Manuscript Collection at the University of Missouri, Columbia. Thank you also to the staff of the periodicals reading room of the main branch of the New York Public Library for assistance with microfilm. Kim Waldman of AP/Wide World Images and Rosemary Morrow of Redux Pictures ably and patiently assisted me in tracking down photographs. Gene Godley and Ruth Herbst provided additional images, and thank you to Raymond Herbst for scanning and sending me his mother's pictures.

Phillip O'Connor, the staff reporter for the *St. Louis Post-Dispatch* who first examined Eagleton's FBI files, graciously shared the documents with me and then generously tracked down additional pages when it appeared some were missing from the first batch.

■

Ileene Smith, my editor at Yale University Press, took a risk on this first-time author, and poured her heart into editing and championing the book. It is infinitely stronger because of her tough and thoughtful edit. I am grateful to her for giving me this opportunity, as well as for all that she has taught me through this process. At Yale University Press, John Palmer fielded my innumerable questions and expertly answered all of them. Dan Heaton copyedited my manuscript with keen attention. His enthusiasm for the subject matter and vast knowledge of all things politics and baseball made it a better book. Thanks also to Brill Frucht and Jen Doerr for their help in bringing the book through its final stages, and to proofreader Nancy Hulnick and indexer Fred Kameny for their careful and diligent work.

Kathy Robbins, my agent, provided valued advice at every step.

At the Robbins Office, thank you as well to Mike Gillespie, David Halpern, Micah Hauser, and Ian King.

Bloomberg Television afforded me extraordinary flexibility as I completed this project, and I am thankful to the following: Margaret Brennan, Dan Doctoroff, Ben Geldon, Betty Liu, David Rhodes, Janice Slusarz, and Mark White.

I called on Jenny Alperen, Jacob Glass, Donald Lehr, Matt Lerner, and Naomi Oberman-Breindel for assistance at various points, and they all pulled through. Thank you to Diane Silverman for taking my author photo. Amherst classmates Ariadne DeSimone and Laurel Swerdlow kindly connected me with their parents—two great interviewees.

Fellow history major and friend Michael Neff provided important guidance throughout. Further thanks to the following friends as well: Rob Abbey, Jack Baer, Jack Conway, Alex Gonzalez, Jordan Gruskay, Spencer Haught, Tierney Healey, Tom McDonnell, Alex Miller, J. T. Milone, Luke O'Brien, Evan Peters, Nate Sobel, Matt Stolper, and Sam Swenson.

Thank you to my grandparents, Grace and I. Leo Glasser and Vera and Klaus Mayer, for their interest, insights, and loving enthusiasm.

Last—and most important—thank you to my mother, father, brother Nate, and sister Juliana. This book would not have been possible without their tireless support, boundless patience, and exceptional good humor.

It was my mother who first mentioned Thomas Eagleton to me upon seeing his obituary in the *New York Times,* March 2007. Reflecting on the significance of those fateful eighteen days of July 1972, she discerned the intersection of three of my interests: journalism, politics, and Amherst. It is a testament to her understanding of me that the story continues to grip me five years later.

Joshua M. Glasser
Bronx, New York

Index